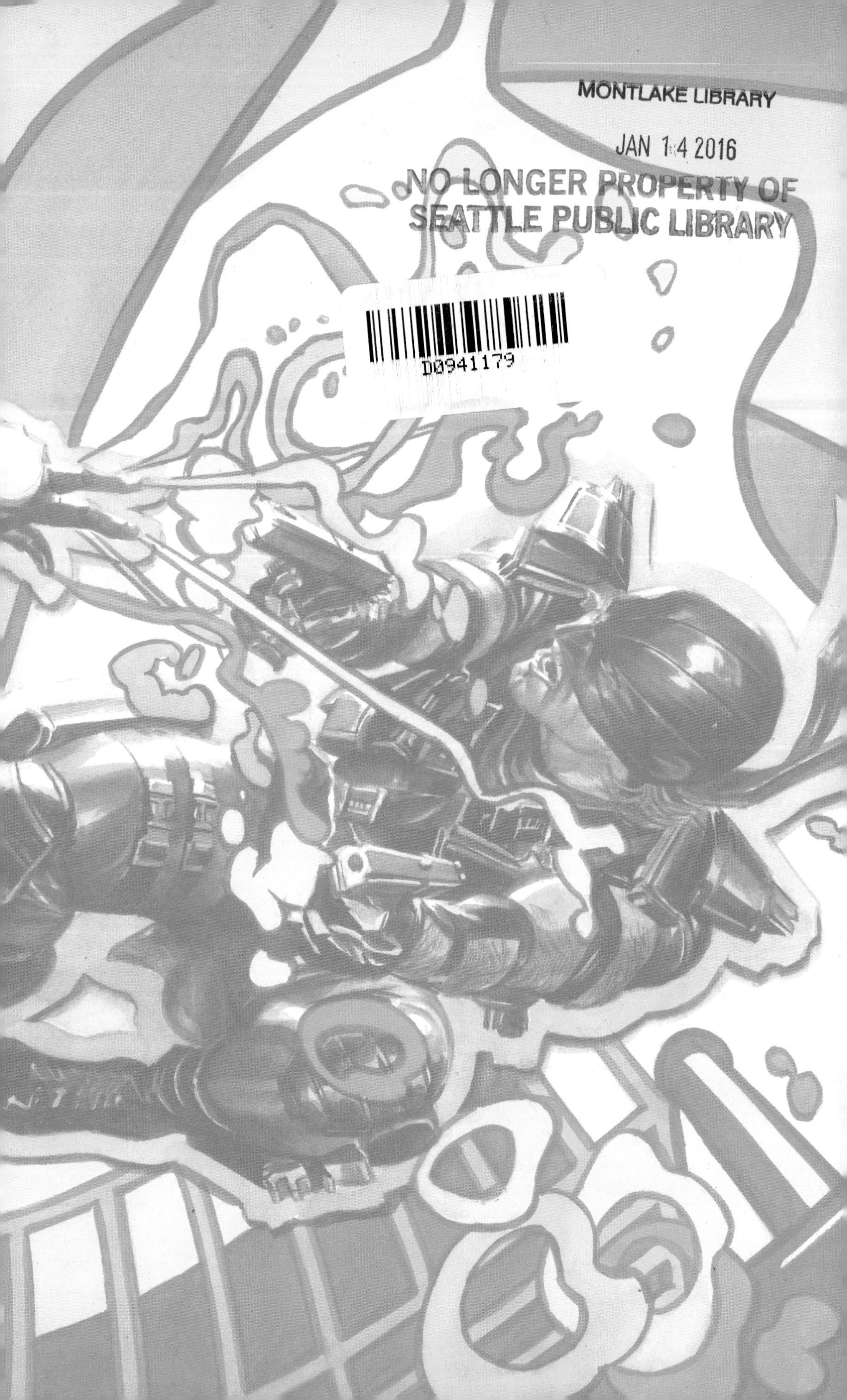

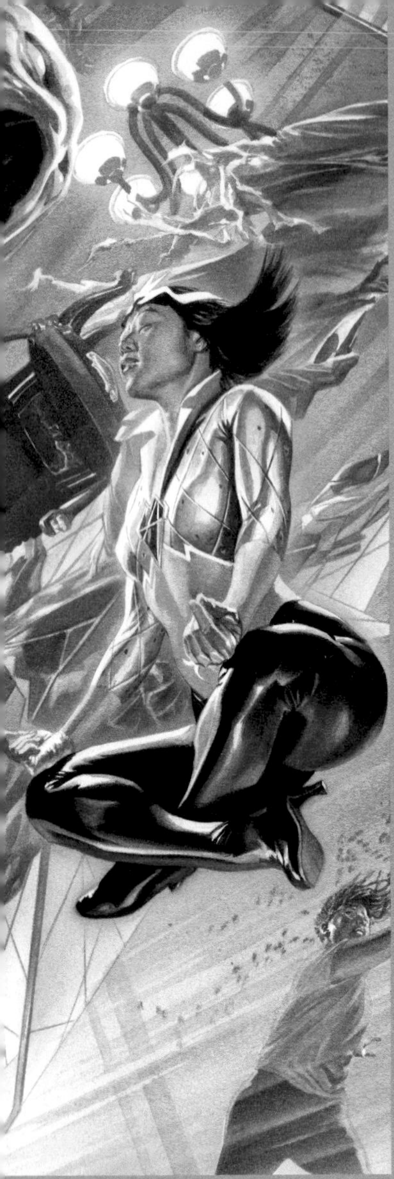
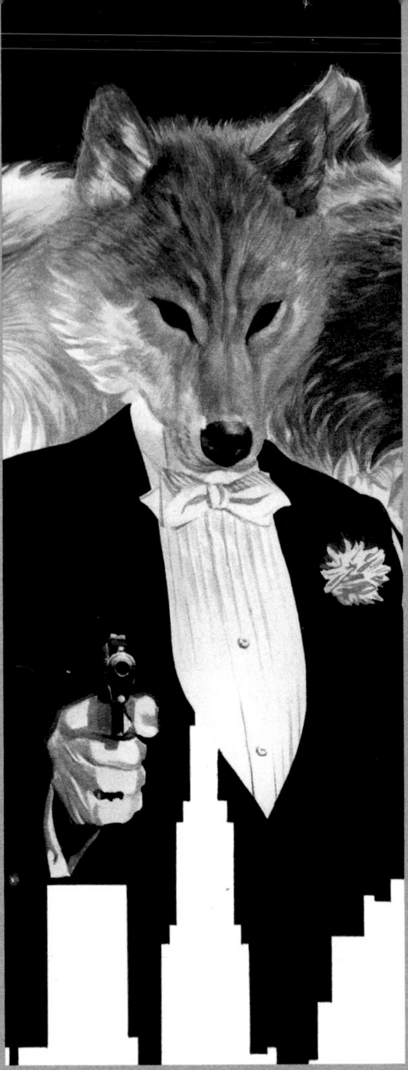
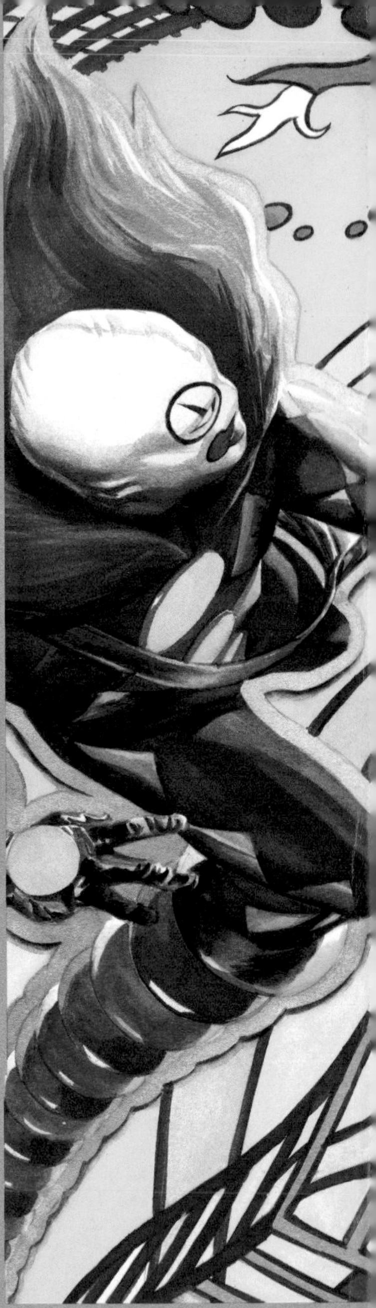

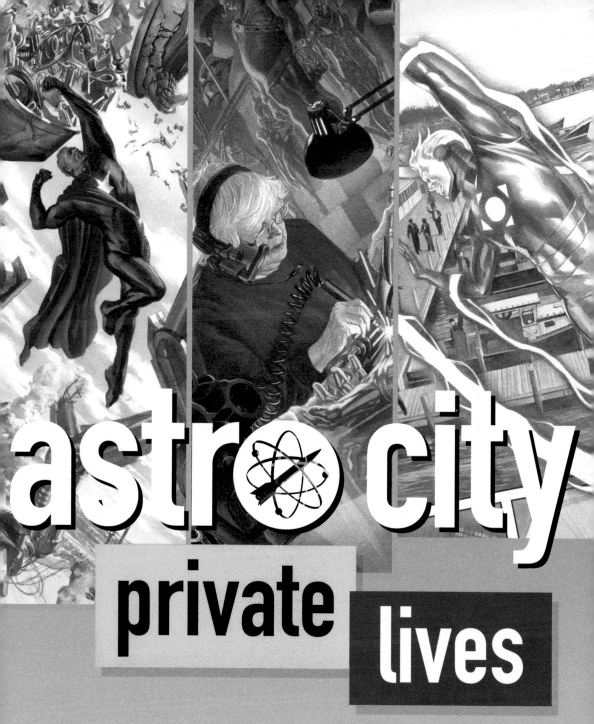

astro city

private lives

kurt busiek
writer

brent eric anderson
artist

alex ross
cover art

graham nolan
artist,
"the deep dark woods"

**alex sinclair &
wendy broome**
colors

**comicraft's john roshell
& jimmy betancourt**
lettering & design

astro city created by **busiek, anderson & ross**

VERTIGO

RICHARD STARKINGS
Art Director

VERTIGO

Kristy Quinn — Editor
Jessica Chen — Assistant Editor
Robbin Brosterman — Design Director – Books

Shelly Bond — Executive Editor – Vertigo
Hank Kanalz — Senior VP – Vertigo & Integrated Publishing

Diane Nelson — President
Dan DiDio and Jim Lee — Co-Publishers
Geoff Johns — Chief Creative Officer
Amit Desai — Senior VP – Marketing & Franchise Management
Amy Genkins — Senior VP – Business & Legal Affairs
Nairi Gardiner — Senior VP – Finance
Jeff Boison — VP – Publishing Planning
Mark Chiarello — VP – Art Direction & Design
John Cunningham — VP – Marketing
Terri Cunningham — VP – Editorial Administration
Larry Ganem — VP – Talent Relations & Services
Alison Gill — Senior VP – Manufacturing & Operations
Jay Kogan — VP – Business & Legal Affairs, Publishing
Jack Mahan — VP – Business Affairs, Talent
Nick Napolitano — VP – Manufacturing Administration
Sue Pohja — VP – Book Sales
Fred Ruiz — VP – Manufacturing Operations
Courtney Simmons — Senior VP – Publicity
Bob Wayne — Senior VP – Sales

Special thanks to: Ellie Collins, Robbie Geiss, Sandy Oh & Dottie Thomas

Certified Chain of Custody
20% Certified Forest Content,
80% Certified Sourcing
www.sfiprogram.org
SFI-01042
APPLIES TO TEXT STOCK ONLY

Library of Congress Cataloging-in-Publication Data

Busiek, Kurt, author.
Astro City : Private Lives / Kurt Busiek, writer ; Brent Anderson, artist.
pages cm
Summary: "When you're the Silver Adept, one of Astro City's newest and most powerful mystic heroes, your life is full of magic, battle, demons, apocalypses and more. When you're the Adept's personal assistant, though, life gets really weird. A look at the woman behind the hero. Collects ASTRO CITY #11–16"— Provided by publisher.
ISBN 978-1-4012-5459-9 (hardback)
1. Graphic novels. I. Anderson, Brent Eric, illustrator. II. Title.

PN6728.A79B79 2015
741.5'973--dc23
2014046034

ASTRO CITY: Private Lives, published by DC Comics, 1700 Broadway, New York, NY 10019.

Cover, sketches and compilation Copyright © 2015 Juke Box Productions.

DC Comics, 1700 Broadway, New York, NY 10019
A Warner Bros. Entertainment Company.

Printed on recyclable paper.
Printed by RR Donnelley, Salem, VA, USA. 2/6/2015. First printing
ISBN: 978-1-4012-5459-9

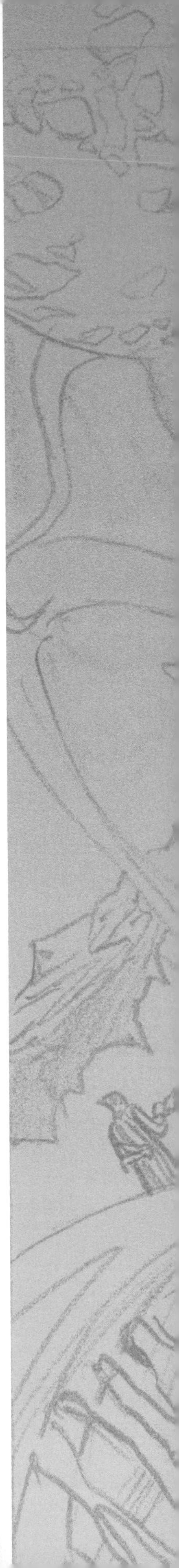

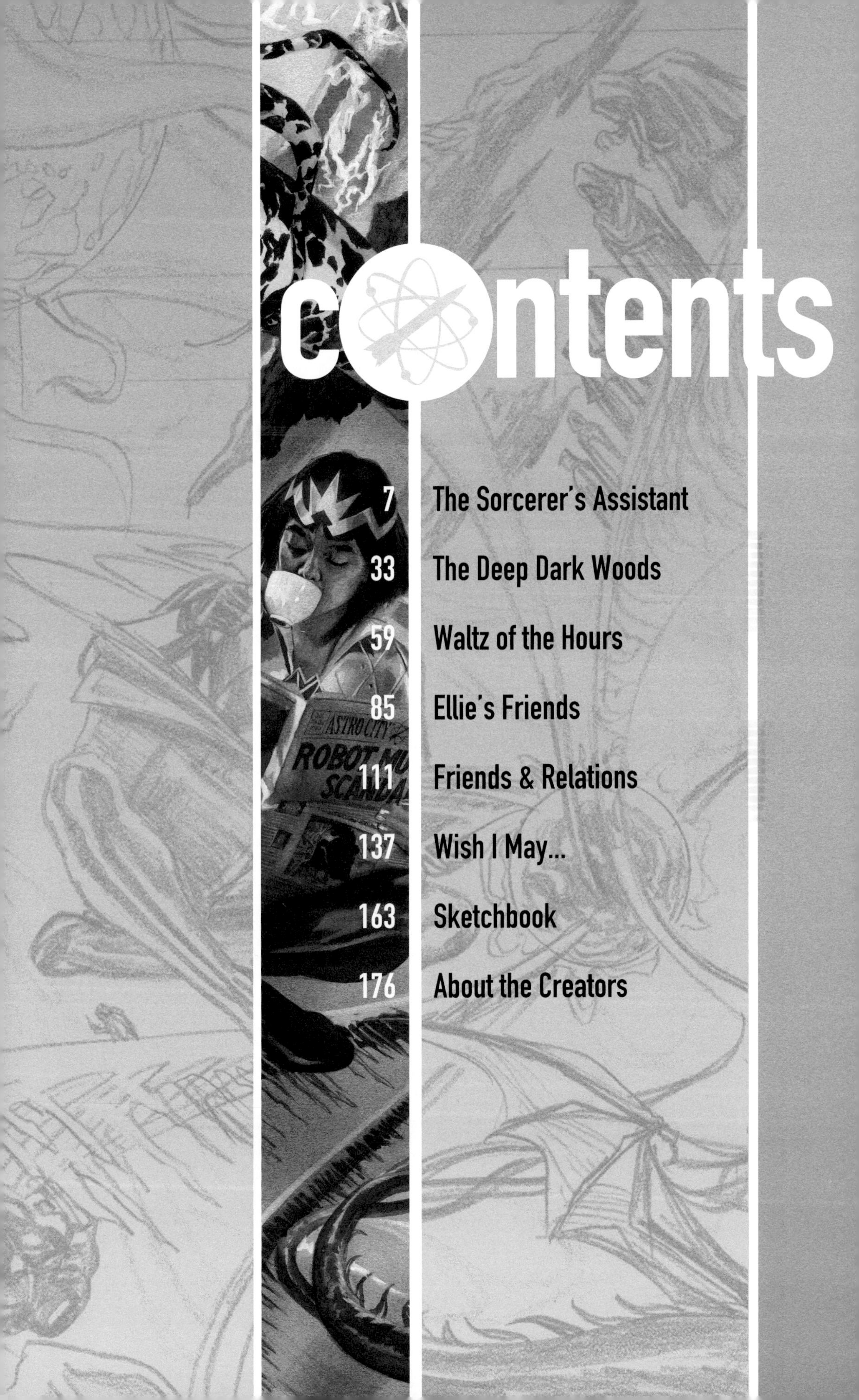
ASTRO CITY

contents

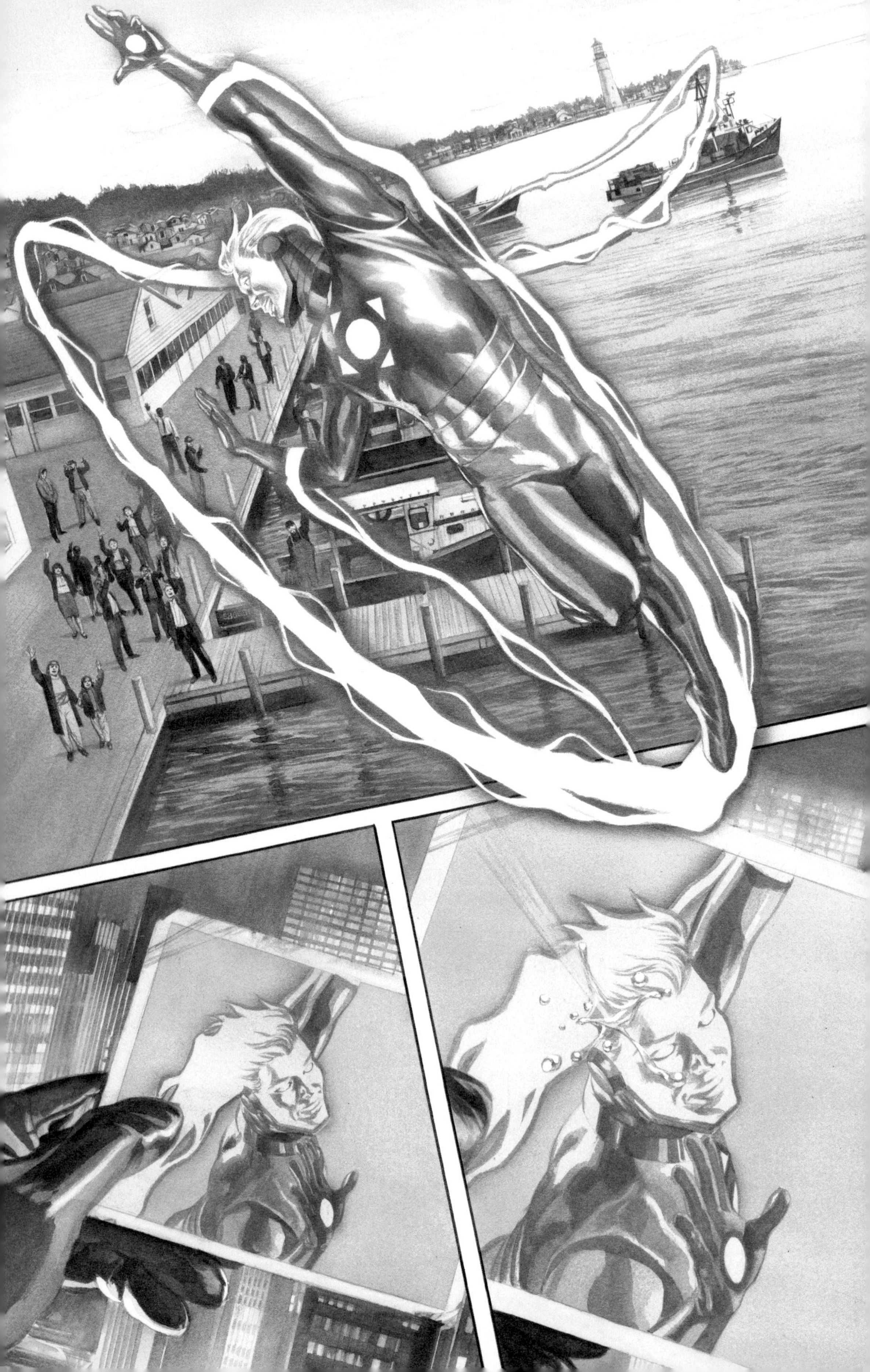

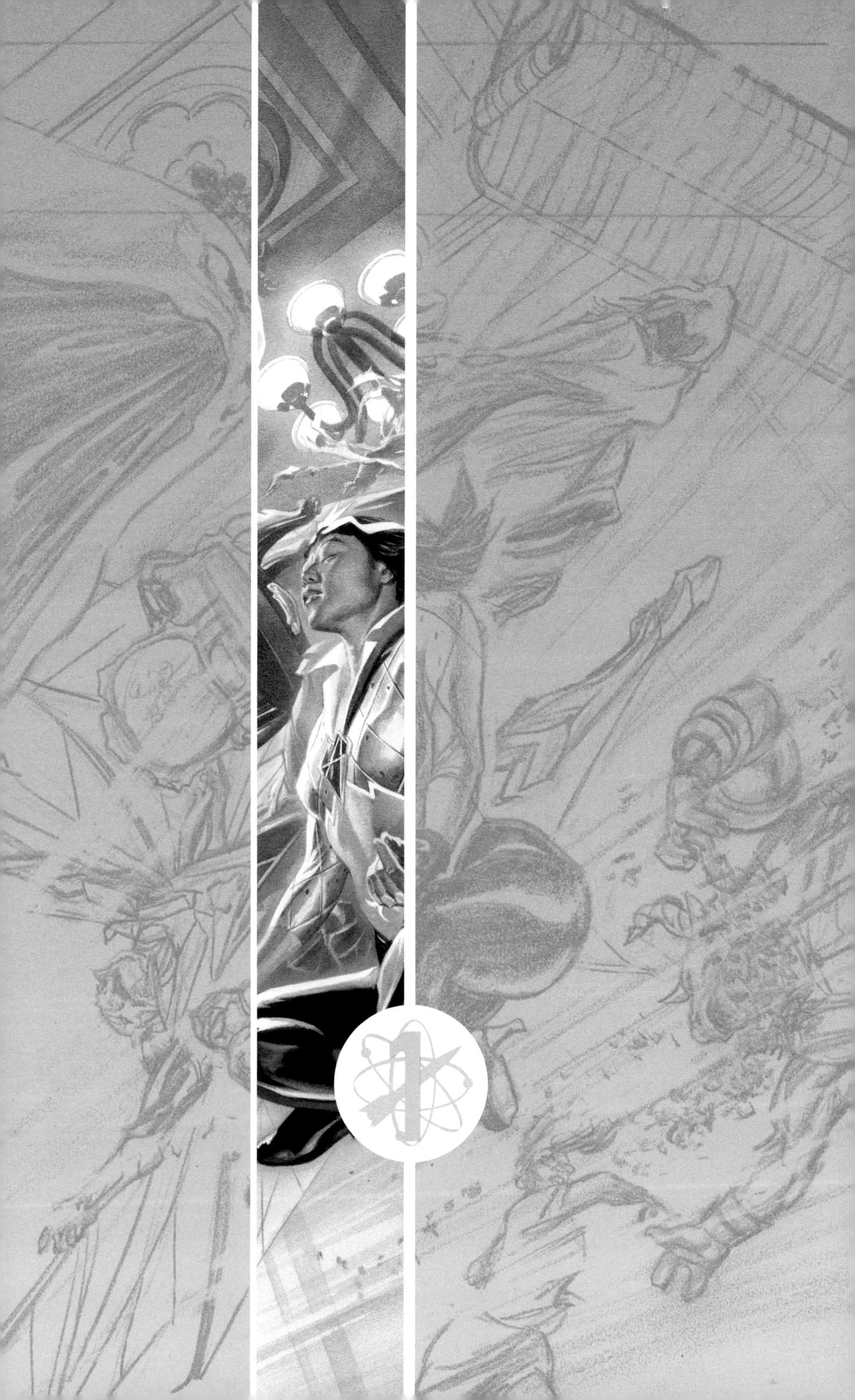

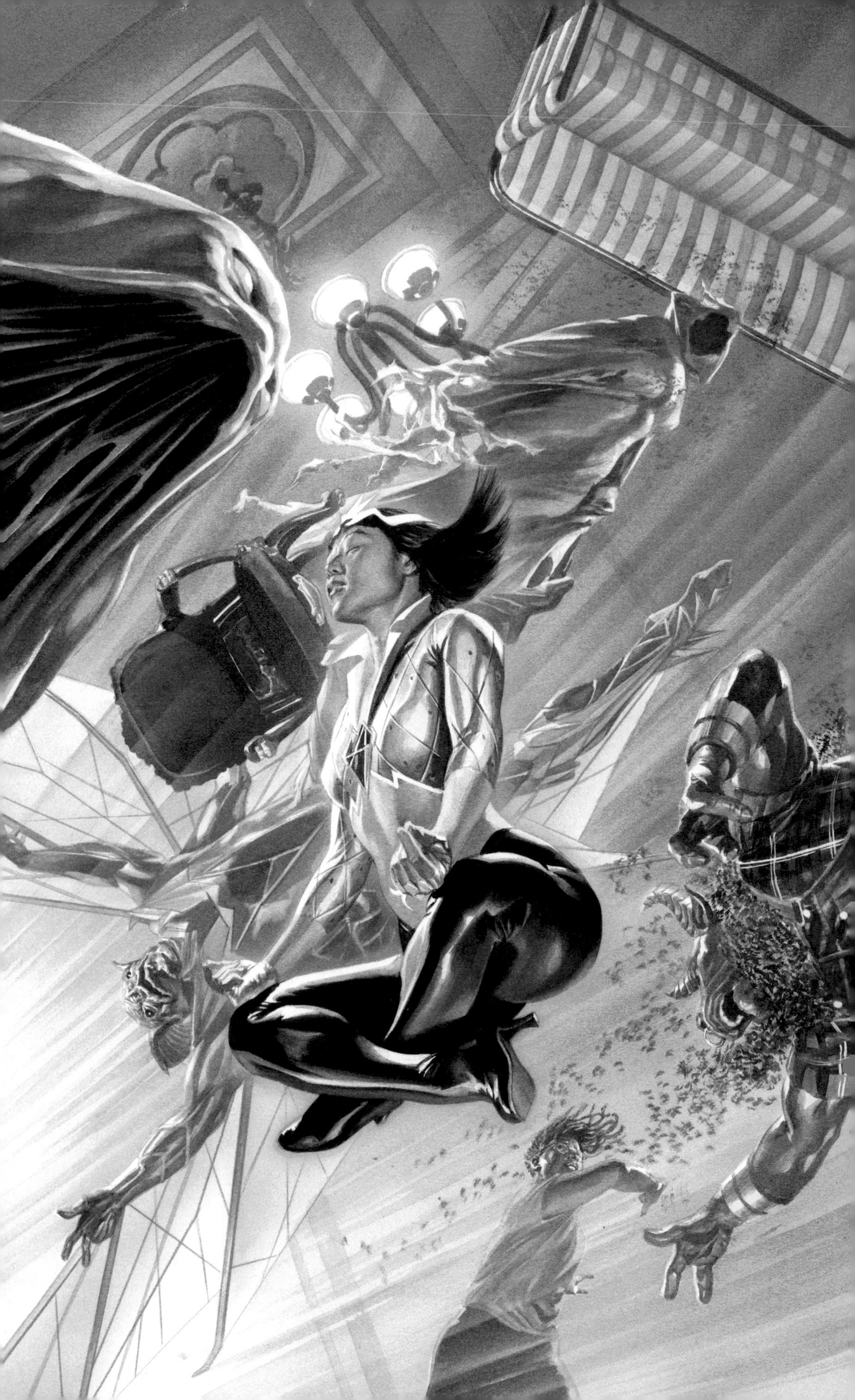

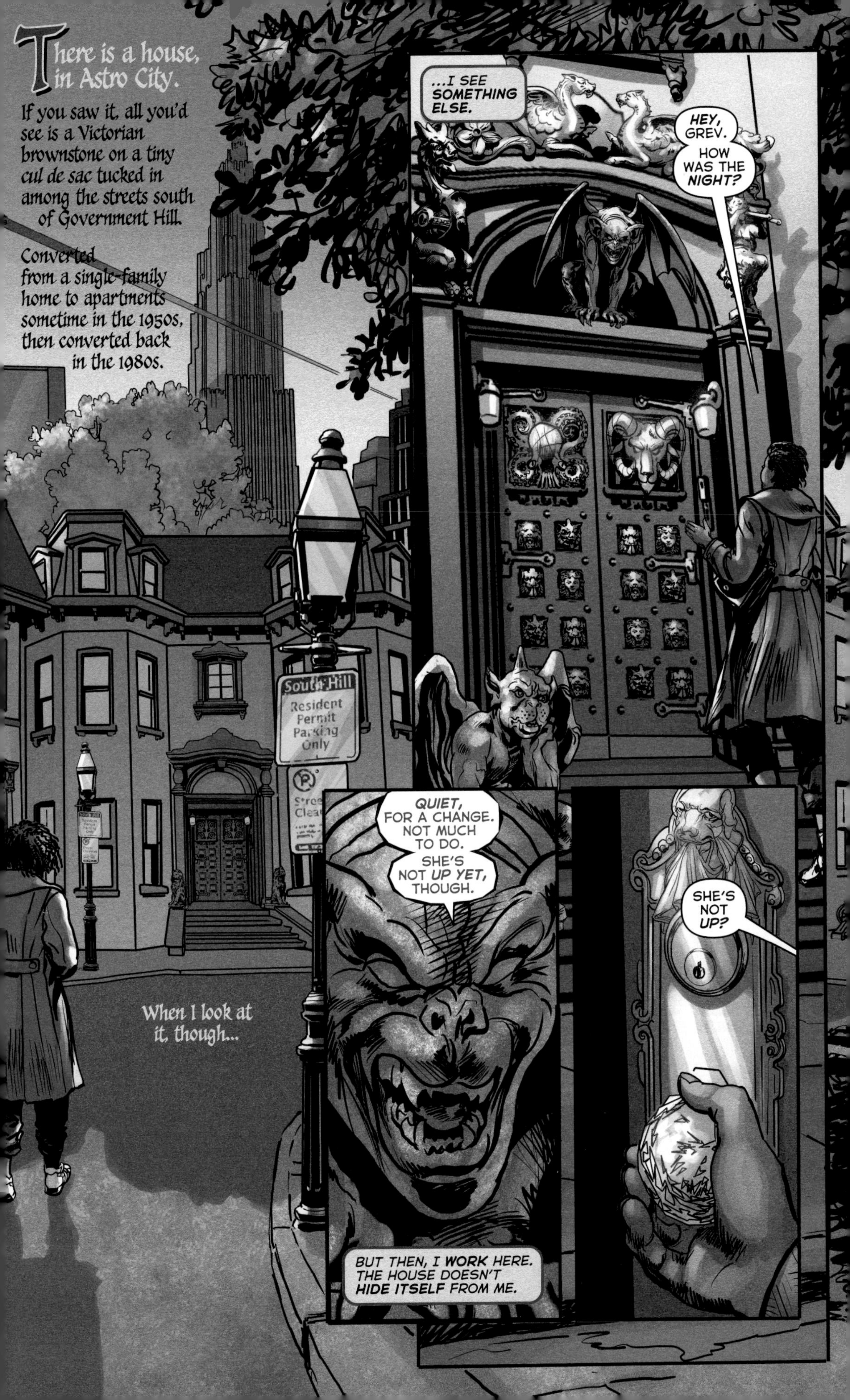
There is a house, in Astro City.
If you saw it, all you'd see is a Victorian brownstone on a tiny cul de sac tucked in among the streets south of Government Hill.
Converted from a single-family home to apartments sometime in the 1950s, then converted back in the 1980s.
When I look at it, though...
...I SEE SOMETHING ELSE.
HEY, GREV.
HOW WAS THE NIGHT?
QUIET, FOR A CHANGE. NOT MUCH TO DO.
SHE'S NOT UP YET, THOUGH.
SHE'S NOT UP?
BUT THEN, I WORK HERE. THE HOUSE DOESN'T HIDE ITSELF FROM ME.
South Hill
Resident Permit Parking Only

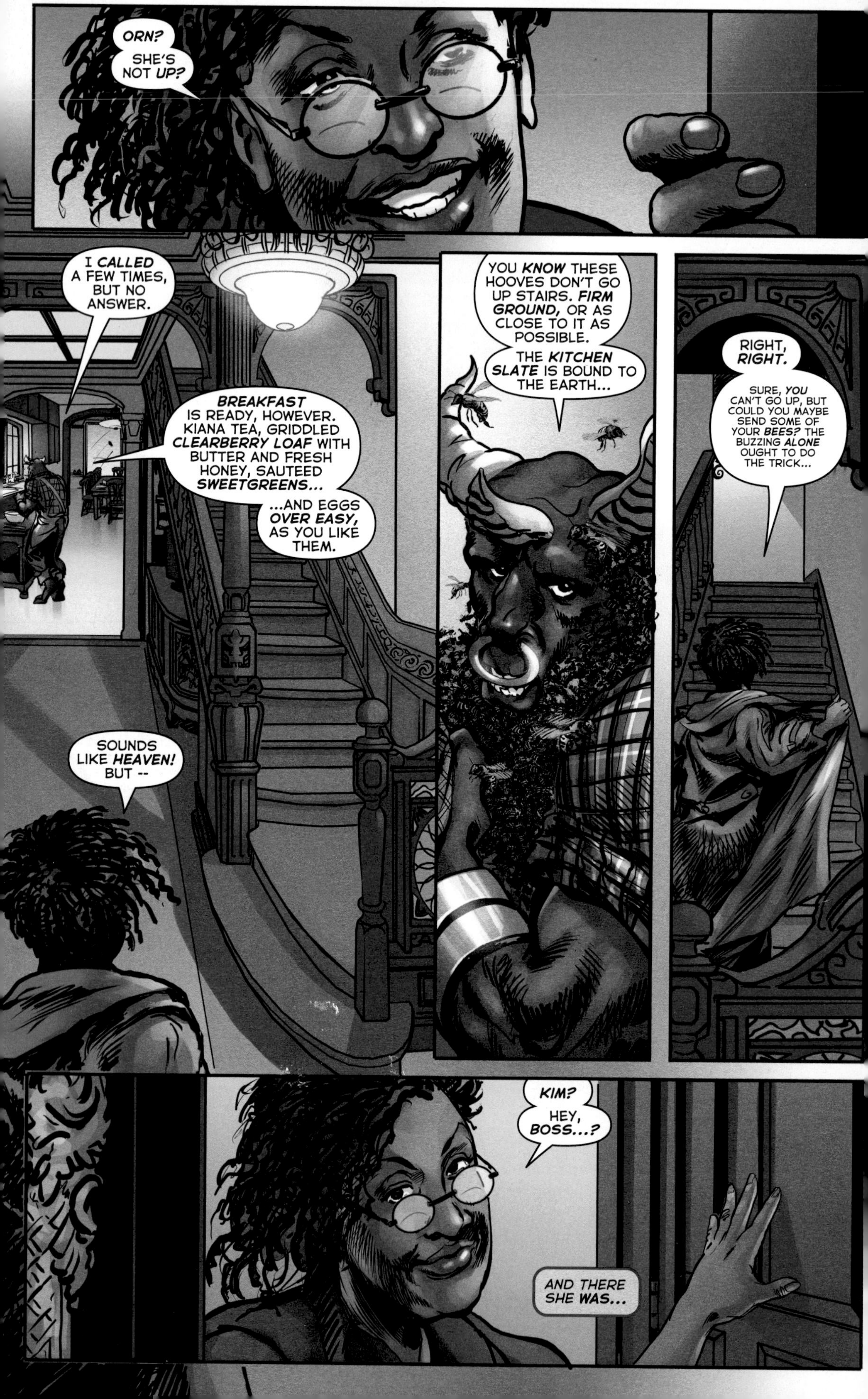
ORN?
SHE'S NOT UP?
I CALLED A FEW TIMES, BUT NO ANSWER.
BREAKFAST IS READY, HOWEVER. KIANA TEA, GRIDDLED CLEARBERRY LOAF WITH BUTTER AND FRESH HONEY, SAUTEED SWEETGREENS...
...AND EGGS OVER EASY, AS YOU LIKE THEM.
SOUNDS LIKE HEAVEN! BUT --
YOU KNOW THESE HOOVES DON'T GO UP STAIRS. FIRM GROUND, OR AS CLOSE TO IT AS POSSIBLE.
THE KITCHEN SLATE IS BOUND TO THE EARTH...
RIGHT, RIGHT.
SURE, YOU CAN'T GO UP, BUT COULD YOU MAYBE SEND SOME OF YOUR BEES? THE BUZZING ALONE OUGHT TO DO THE TRICK...
KIM?
HEY, BOSS...?
AND THERE SHE WAS...

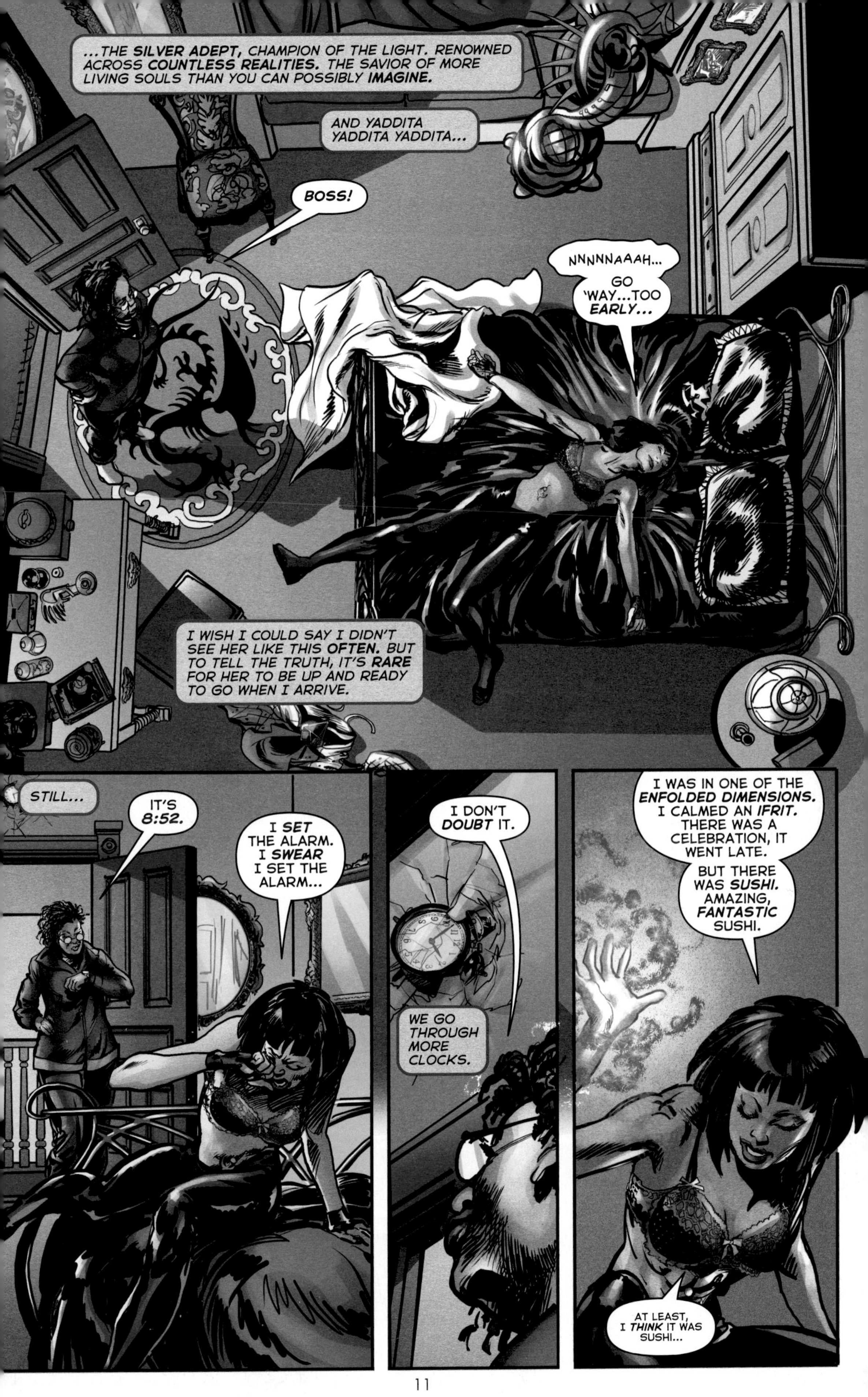
...THE SILVER ADEPT, CHAMPION OF THE LIGHT. RENOWNED ACROSS COUNTLESS REALITIES. THE SAVIOR OF MORE LIVING SOULS THAN YOU CAN POSSIBLY IMAGINE.
AND YADDITA YADDITA YADDITA...
BOSS!
NNNNNAAAH... GO 'WAY...TOO EARLY...
I WISH I COULD SAY I DIDN'T SEE HER LIKE THIS OFTEN. BUT TO TELL THE TRUTH, IT'S RARE FOR HER TO BE UP AND READY TO GO WHEN I ARRIVE.
STILL...
IT'S 8:52.
I SET THE ALARM. I SWEAR I SET THE ALARM...
I DON'T DOUBT IT.
WE GO THROUGH MORE CLOCKS.
I WAS IN ONE OF THE ENFOLDED DIMENSIONS. I CALMED AN IFRIT. THERE WAS A CELEBRATION, IT WENT LATE.
BUT THERE WAS SUSHI. AMAZING, FANTASTIC SUSHI.
AT LEAST, I THINK IT WAS SUSHI...

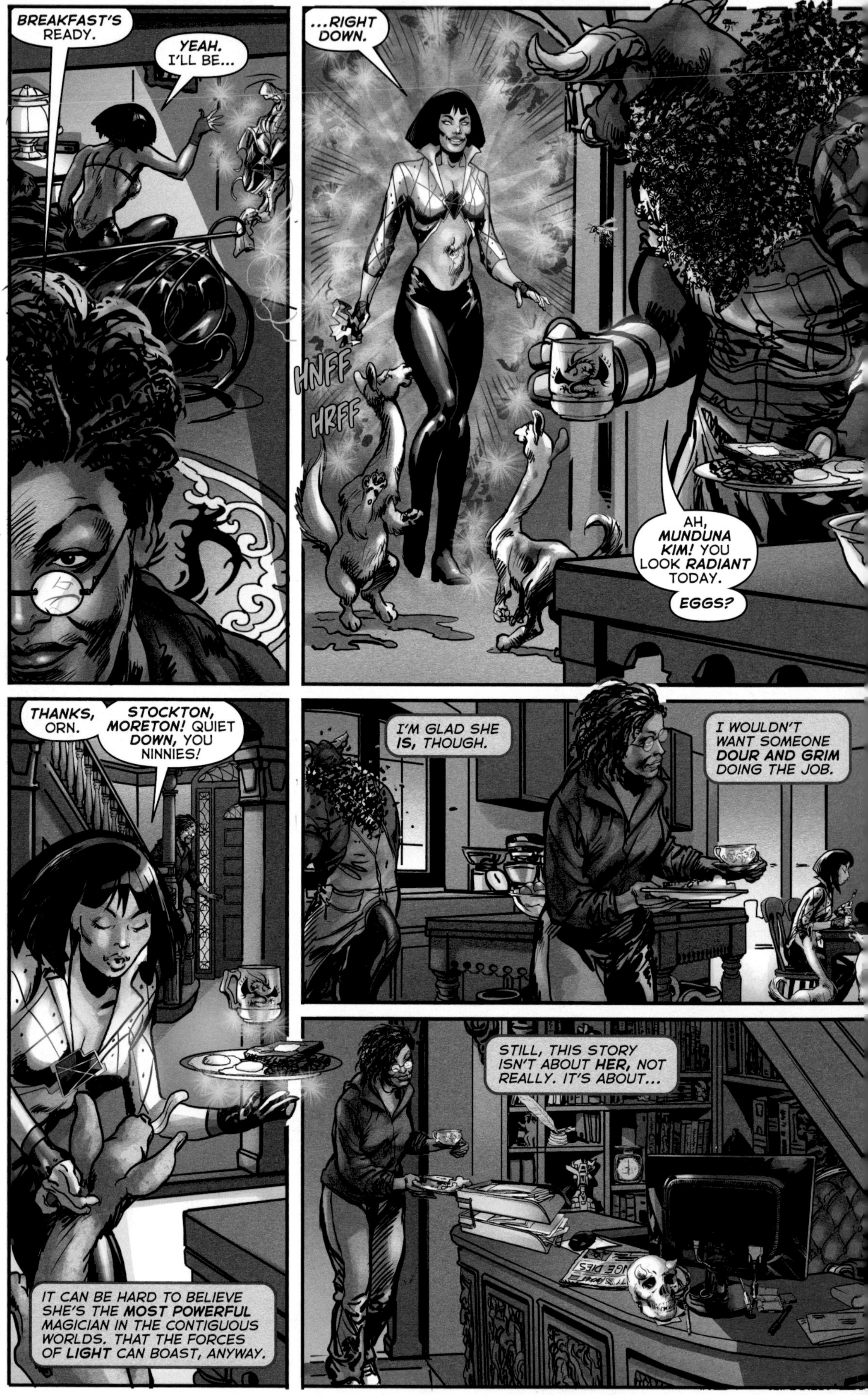
BREAKFAST'S READY.
YEAH. I'LL BE...
...RIGHT DOWN.
HNFF
HRFF
AH, MUNDUNA KIM! YOU LOOK RADIANT TODAY.
EGGS?
THANKS, ORN.
STOCKTON, MORETON! QUIET DOWN, YOU NINNIES!
IT CAN BE HARD TO BELIEVE SHE'S THE MOST POWERFUL MAGICIAN IN THE CONTIGUOUS WORLDS. THAT THE FORCES OF LIGHT CAN BOAST, ANYWAY.
I'M GLAD SHE IS, THOUGH.
I WOULDN'T WANT SOMEONE DOUR AND GRIM DOING THE JOB.
STILL, THIS STORY ISN'T ABOUT HER, NOT REALLY. IT'S ABOUT...

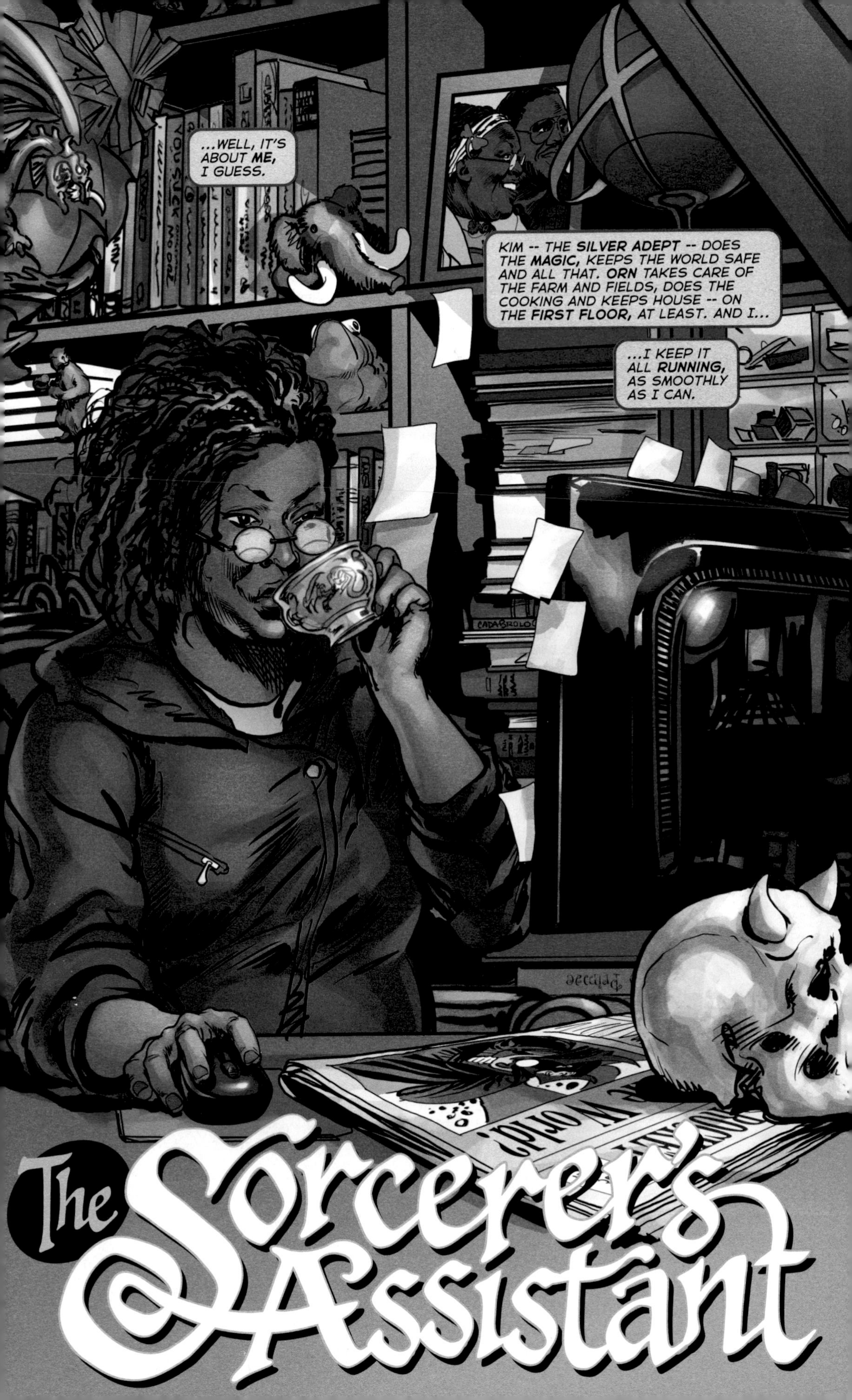
...WELL, IT'S ABOUT ME, I GUESS.
KIM -- THE SILVER ADEPT -- DOES THE MAGIC, KEEPS THE WORLD SAFE AND ALL THAT. ORN TAKES CARE OF THE FARM AND FIELDS, DOES THE COOKING AND KEEPS HOUSE -- ON THE FIRST FLOOR, AT LEAST. AND I...
...I KEEP IT ALL RUNNING, AS SMOOTHLY AS I CAN.
The Sorcerer's Assistant

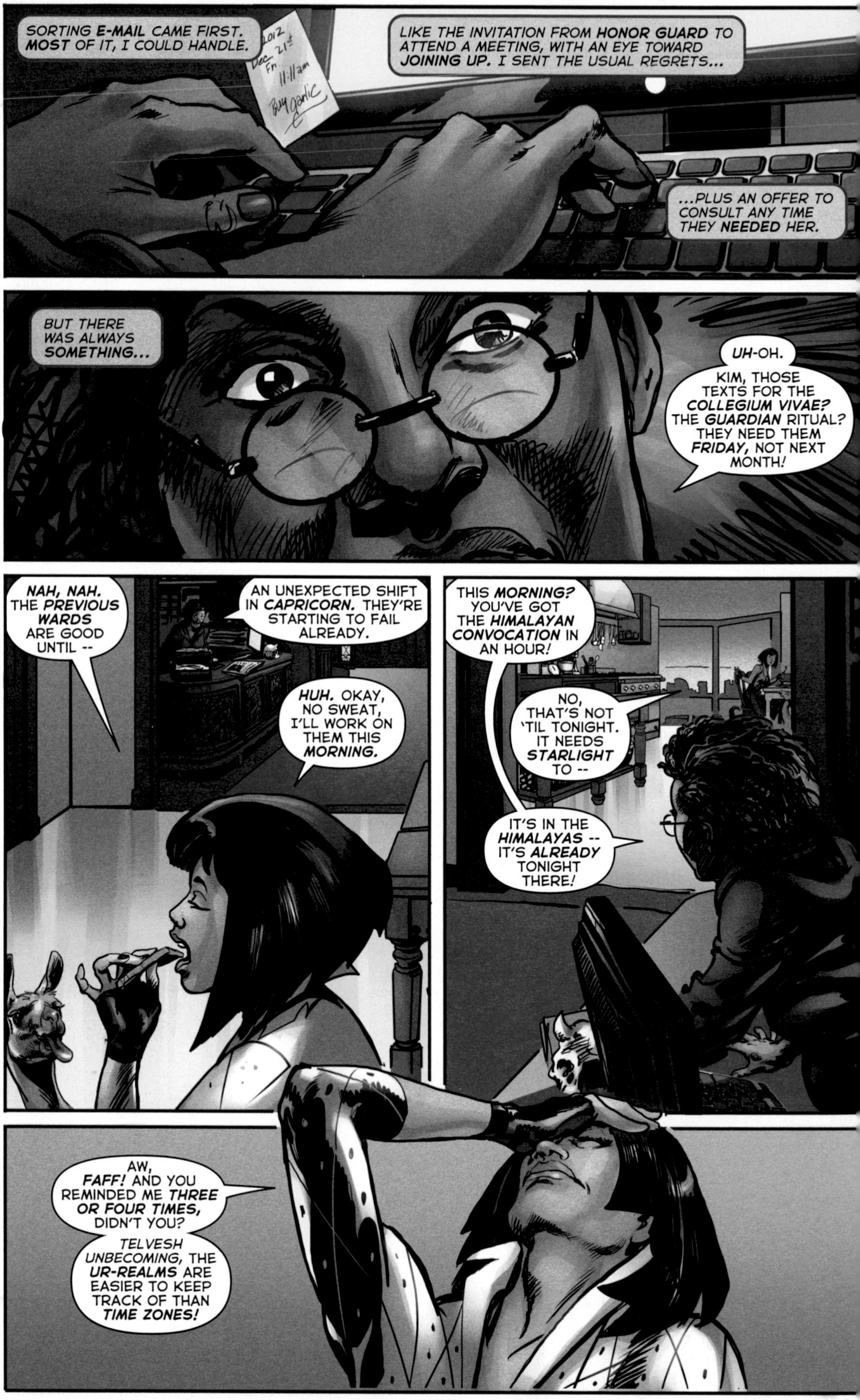
SORTING E-MAIL CAME FIRST. MOST OF IT, I COULD HANDLE.
2012 Dec. 21st Fri. 11:11am Buy garlic
LIKE THE INVITATION FROM HONOR GUARD TO ATTEND A MEETING, WITH AN EYE TOWARD JOINING UP. I SENT THE USUAL REGRETS...
...PLUS AN OFFER TO CONSULT ANY TIME THEY NEEDED HER.
BUT THERE WAS ALWAYS SOMETHING...
UH-OH.
KIM, THOSE TEXTS FOR THE COLLEGIUM VIVAE? THE GUARDIAN RITUAL? THEY NEED THEM FRIDAY, NOT NEXT MONTH!
NAH, NAH. THE PREVIOUS WARDS ARE GOOD UNTIL --
AN UNEXPECTED SHIFT IN CAPRICORN. THEY'RE STARTING TO FAIL ALREADY.
HUH. OKAY, NO SWEAT, I'LL WORK ON THEM THIS MORNING.
THIS MORNING? YOU'VE GOT THE HIMALAYAN CONVOCATION IN AN HOUR!
NO, THAT'S NOT 'TIL TONIGHT. IT NEEDS STARLIGHT TO --
IT'S IN THE HIMALAYAS -- IT'S ALREADY TONIGHT THERE!
AW, FAFF! AND YOU REMINDED ME THREE OR FOUR TIMES, DIDN'T YOU?
TELVESH UNBECOMING, THE UR-REALMS ARE EASIER TO KEEP TRACK OF THAN TIME ZONES!

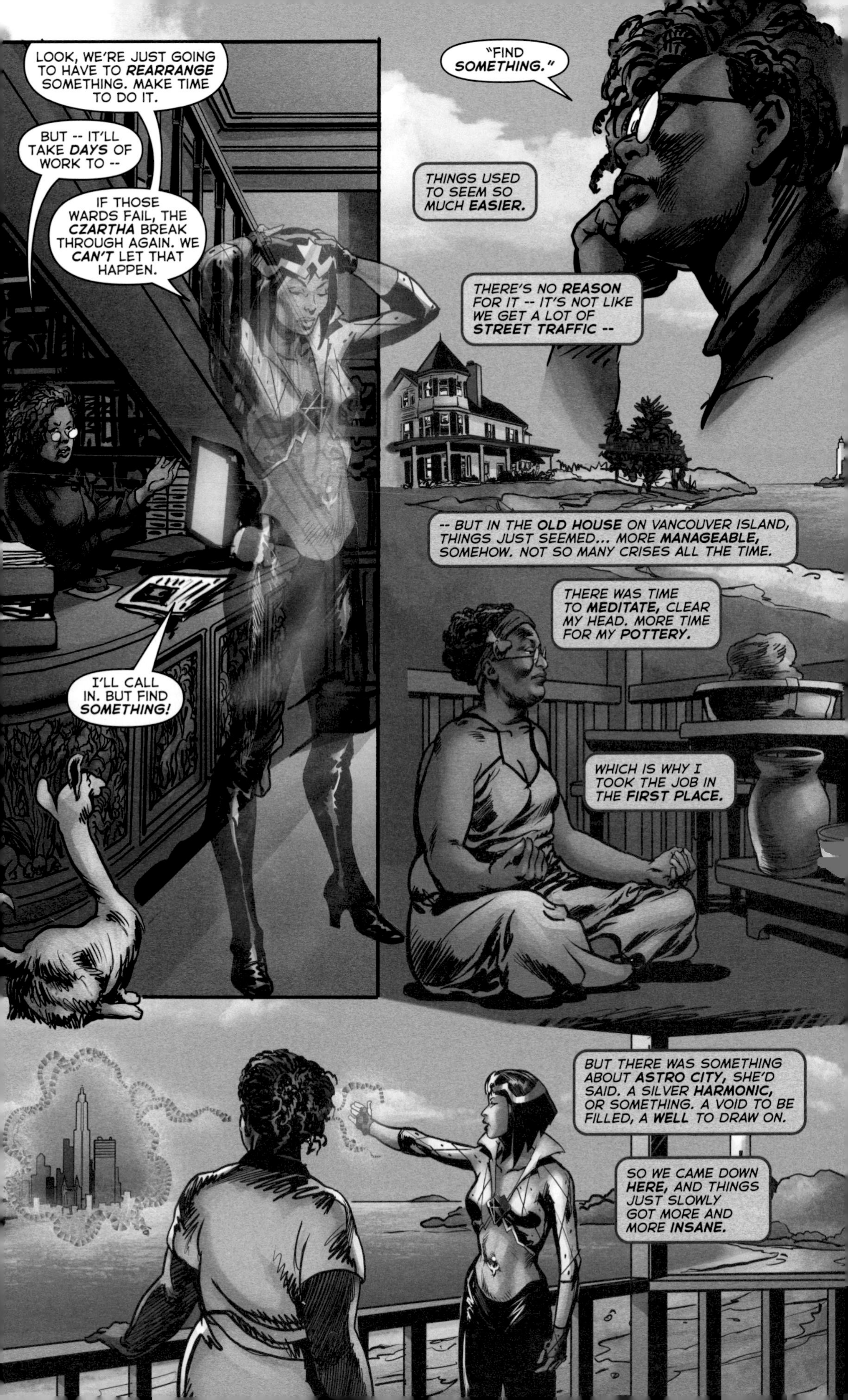

LOOK, WE'RE JUST GOING TO HAVE TO REARRANGE SOMETHING. MAKE TIME TO DO IT.
BUT -- IT'LL TAKE DAYS OF WORK TO --
IF THOSE WARDS FAIL, THE CZARTHA BREAK THROUGH AGAIN. WE CAN'T LET THAT HAPPEN.
I'LL CALL IN. BUT FIND SOMETHING!
"FIND SOMETHING."
THINGS USED TO SEEM SO MUCH EASIER.
THERE'S NO REASON FOR IT -- IT'S NOT LIKE WE GET A LOT OF STREET TRAFFIC --
-- BUT IN THE OLD HOUSE ON VANCOUVER ISLAND, THINGS JUST SEEMED... MORE MANAGEABLE, SOMEHOW. NOT SO MANY CRISES ALL THE TIME.
THERE WAS TIME TO MEDITATE, CLEAR MY HEAD. MORE TIME FOR MY POTTERY.
WHICH IS WHY I TOOK THE JOB IN THE FIRST PLACE.
BUT THERE WAS SOMETHING ABOUT ASTRO CITY, SHE'D SAID. A SILVER HARMONIC, OR SOMETHING. A VOID TO BE FILLED, A WELL TO DRAW ON.
SO WE CAME DOWN HERE, AND THINGS JUST SLOWLY GOT MORE AND MORE INSANE.

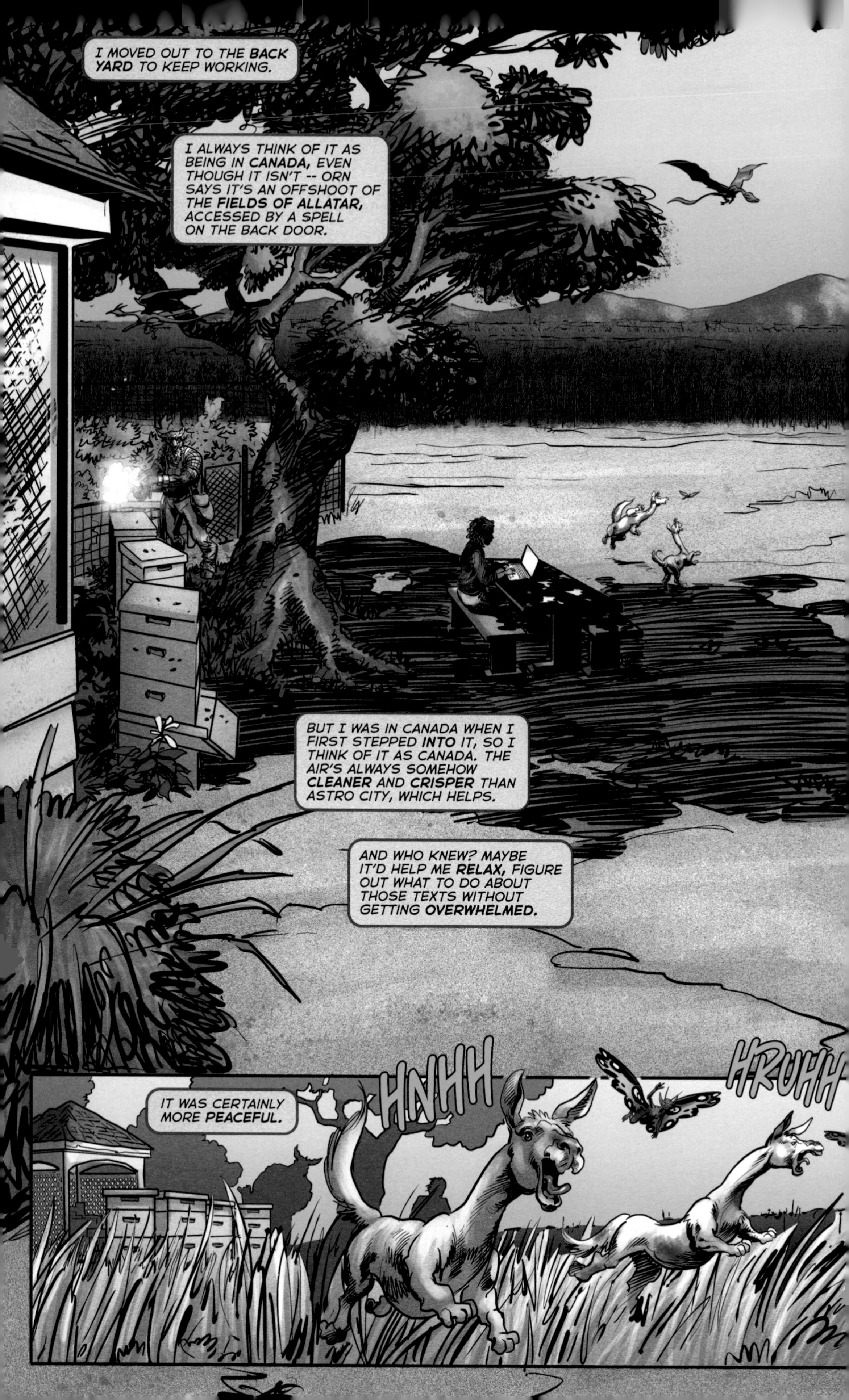

I MOVED OUT TO THE BACK YARD TO KEEP WORKING.
I ALWAYS THINK OF IT AS BEING IN CANADA, EVEN THOUGH IT ISN'T -- ORN SAYS IT'S AN OFFSHOOT OF THE FIELDS OF ALLATAR, ACCESSED BY A SPELL ON THE BACK DOOR.
BUT I WAS IN CANADA WHEN I FIRST STEPPED INTO IT, SO I THINK OF IT AS CANADA. THE AIR'S ALWAYS SOMEHOW CLEANER AND CRISPER THAN ASTRO CITY, WHICH HELPS.
AND WHO KNEW? MAYBE IT'D HELP ME RELAX, FIGURE OUT WHAT TO DO ABOUT THOSE TEXTS WITHOUT GETTING OVERWHELMED.
IT WAS CERTAINLY MORE PEACEFUL.
HNHH
HRUHH

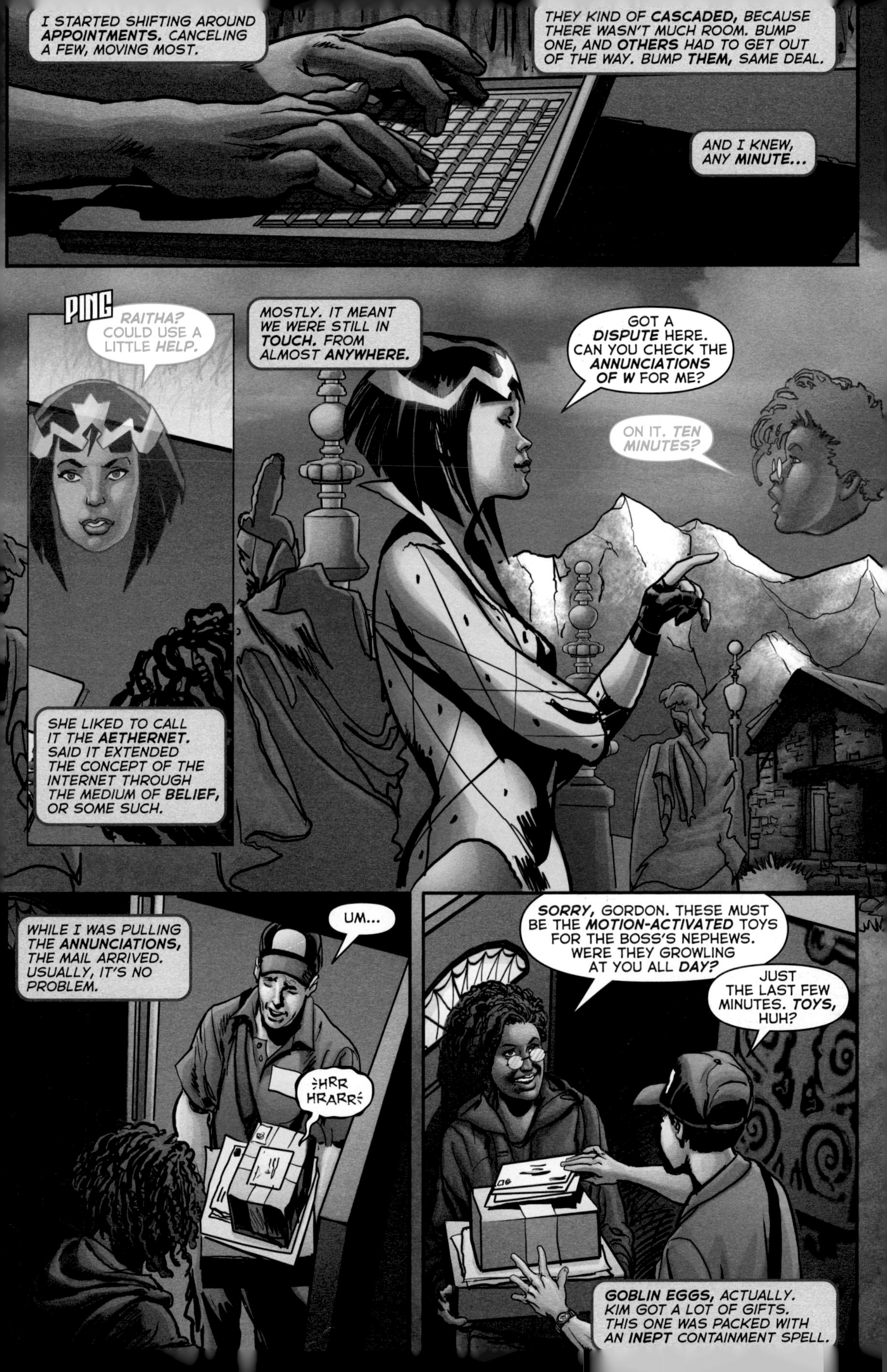
I STARTED SHIFTING AROUND APPOINTMENTS. CANCELING A FEW, MOVING MOST.
THEY KIND OF CASCADED, BECAUSE THERE WASN'T MUCH ROOM. BUMP ONE, AND OTHERS HAD TO GET OUT OF THE WAY. BUMP THEM, SAME DEAL.
AND I KNEW, ANY MINUTE...
PING
RAITHA? COULD USE A LITTLE HELP.
MOSTLY. IT MEANT WE WERE STILL IN TOUCH. FROM ALMOST ANYWHERE.
GOT A DISPUTE HERE. CAN YOU CHECK THE ANNUNCIATIONS OF W FOR ME?
ON IT. TEN MINUTES?
SHE LIKED TO CALL IT THE AETHERNET. SAID IT EXTENDED THE CONCEPT OF THE INTERNET THROUGH THE MEDIUM OF BELIEF, OR SOME SUCH.
WHILE I WAS PULLING THE ANNUNCIATIONS, THE MAIL ARRIVED. USUALLY, IT'S NO PROBLEM.
UM...
HRR HRARR
SORRY, GORDON. THESE MUST BE THE MOTION-ACTIVATED TOYS FOR THE BOSS'S NEPHEWS. WERE THEY GROWLING AT YOU ALL DAY?
JUST THE LAST FEW MINUTES. TOYS, HUH?
GOBLIN EGGS, ACTUALLY. KIM GOT A LOT OF GIFTS. THIS ONE WAS PACKED WITH AN INEPT CONTAINMENT SPELL.

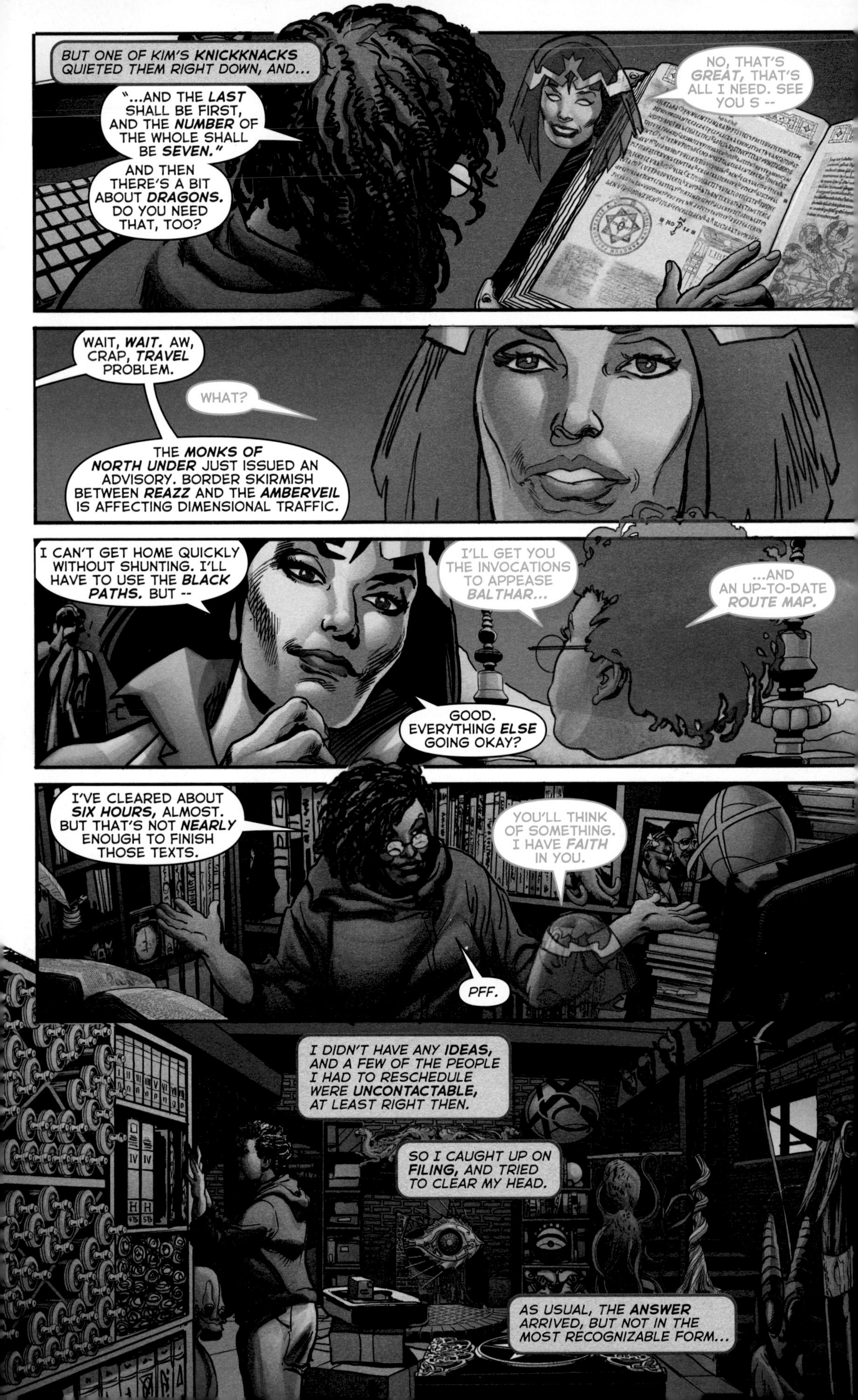
BUT ONE OF KIM'S KNICKKNACKS QUIETED THEM RIGHT DOWN, AND...
"...AND THE LAST SHALL BE FIRST, AND THE NUMBER OF THE WHOLE SHALL BE SEVEN."
AND THEN THERE'S A BIT ABOUT DRAGONS. DO YOU NEED THAT, TOO?
NO, THAT'S GREAT, THAT'S ALL I NEED. SEE YOU S --
WAIT, WAIT. AW, CRAP, TRAVEL PROBLEM.
WHAT?
THE MONKS OF NORTH UNDER JUST ISSUED AN ADVISORY. BORDER SKIRMISH BETWEEN REAZZ AND THE AMBERVEIL IS AFFECTING DIMENSIONAL TRAFFIC.
I CAN'T GET HOME QUICKLY WITHOUT SHUNTING. I'LL HAVE TO USE THE BLACK PATHS. BUT --
I'LL GET YOU THE INVOCATIONS TO APPEASE BALTHAR...
...AND AN UP-TO-DATE ROUTE MAP.
GOOD. EVERYTHING ELSE GOING OKAY?
I'VE CLEARED ABOUT SIX HOURS, ALMOST. BUT THAT'S NOT NEARLY ENOUGH TO FINISH THOSE TEXTS.
YOU'LL THINK OF SOMETHING. I HAVE FAITH IN YOU.
PFF.
I DIDN'T HAVE ANY IDEAS, AND A FEW OF THE PEOPLE I HAD TO RESCHEDULE WERE UNCONTACTABLE, AT LEAST RIGHT THEN.
SO I CAUGHT UP ON FILING, AND TRIED TO CLEAR MY HEAD.
AS USUAL, THE ANSWER ARRIVED, BUT NOT IN THE MOST RECOGNIZABLE FORM...

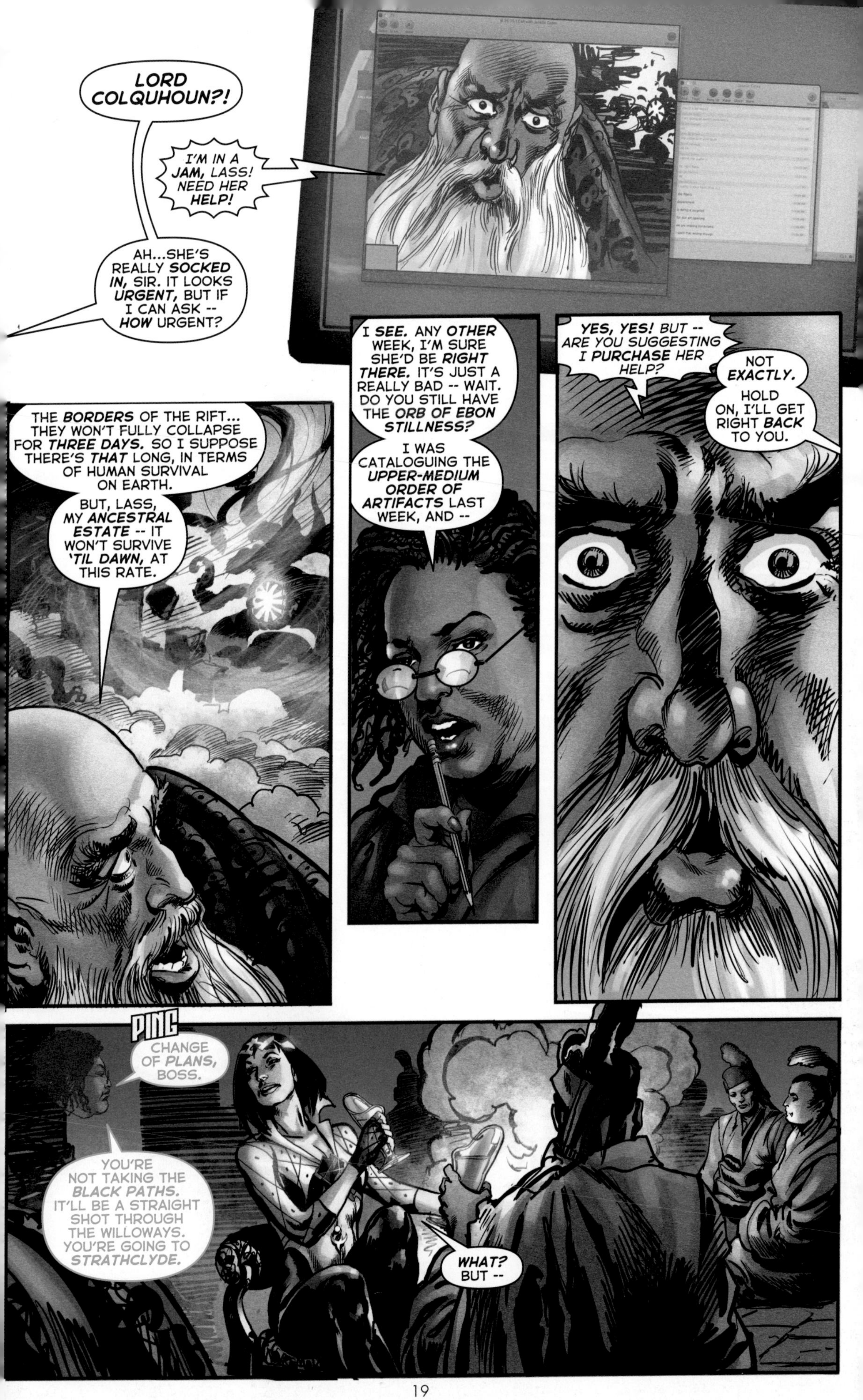
LORD COLQUHOUN?!
I'M IN A JAM, LASS! NEED HER HELP!
AH...SHE'S REALLY SOCKED IN, SIR. IT LOOKS URGENT, BUT IF I CAN ASK -- HOW URGENT?
THE BORDERS OF THE RIFT... THEY WON'T FULLY COLLAPSE FOR THREE DAYS. SO I SUPPOSE THERE'S THAT LONG, IN TERMS OF HUMAN SURVIVAL ON EARTH.
BUT, LASS, MY ANCESTRAL ESTATE -- IT WON'T SURVIVE 'TIL DAWN, AT THIS RATE.
I SEE. ANY OTHER WEEK, I'M SURE SHE'D BE RIGHT THERE. IT'S JUST A REALLY BAD -- WAIT. DO YOU STILL HAVE THE ORB OF EBON STILLNESS?
I WAS CATALOGUING THE UPPER-MEDIUM ORDER OF ARTIFACTS LAST WEEK, AND --
YES, YES! BUT -- ARE YOU SUGGESTING I PURCHASE HER HELP?
NOT EXACTLY.
HOLD ON, I'LL GET RIGHT BACK TO YOU.
PING
CHANGE OF PLANS, BOSS.
YOU'RE NOT TAKING THE BLACK PATHS. IT'LL BE A STRAIGHT SHOT THROUGH THE WILLOWAYS. YOU'RE GOING TO STRATHCLYDE.
WHAT? BUT --

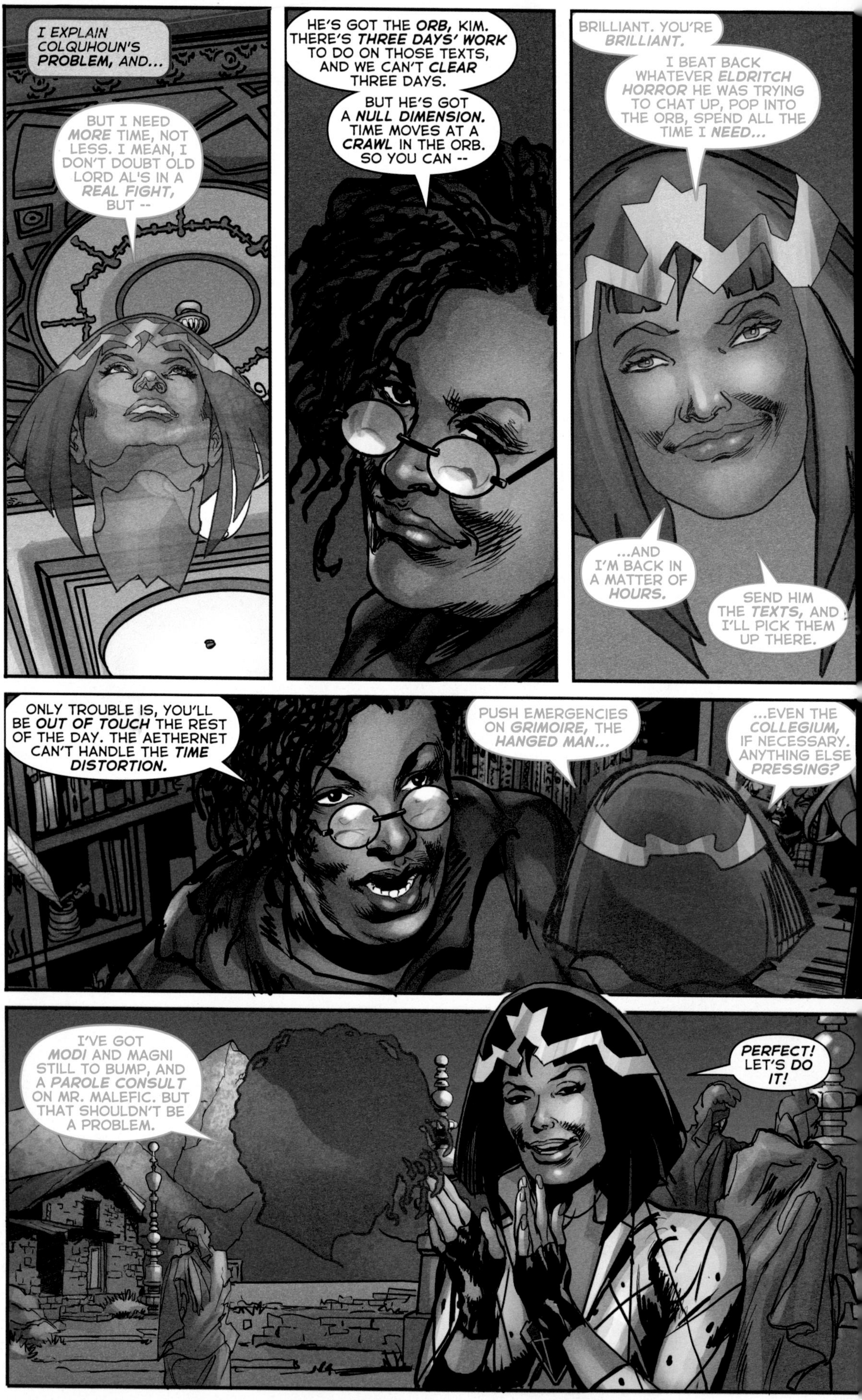
I EXPLAIN COLQUHOUN'S PROBLEM, AND...
BUT I NEED MORE TIME, NOT LESS. I MEAN, I DON'T DOUBT OLD LORD AL'S IN A REAL FIGHT, BUT --
HE'S GOT THE ORB, KIM. THERE'S THREE DAYS' WORK TO DO ON THOSE TEXTS, AND WE CAN'T CLEAR THREE DAYS.
BUT HE'S GOT A NULL DIMENSION. TIME MOVES AT A CRAWL IN THE ORB. SO YOU CAN --
BRILLIANT. YOU'RE BRILLIANT.
I BEAT BACK WHATEVER ELDRITCH HORROR HE WAS TRYING TO CHAT UP, POP INTO THE ORB, SPEND ALL THE TIME I NEED...
...AND I'M BACK IN A MATTER OF HOURS.
SEND HIM THE TEXTS, AND I'LL PICK THEM UP THERE.
ONLY TROUBLE IS, YOU'LL BE OUT OF TOUCH THE REST OF THE DAY. THE AETHERNET CAN'T HANDLE THE TIME DISTORTION.
PUSH EMERGENCIES ON GRIMOIRE, THE HANGED MAN...
...EVEN THE COLLEGIUM, IF NECESSARY. ANYTHING ELSE PRESSING?
I'VE GOT MODI AND MAGNI STILL TO BUMP, AND A PAROLE CONSULT ON MR. MALEFIC. BUT THAT SHOULDN'T BE A PROBLEM.
PERFECT! LET'S DO IT!

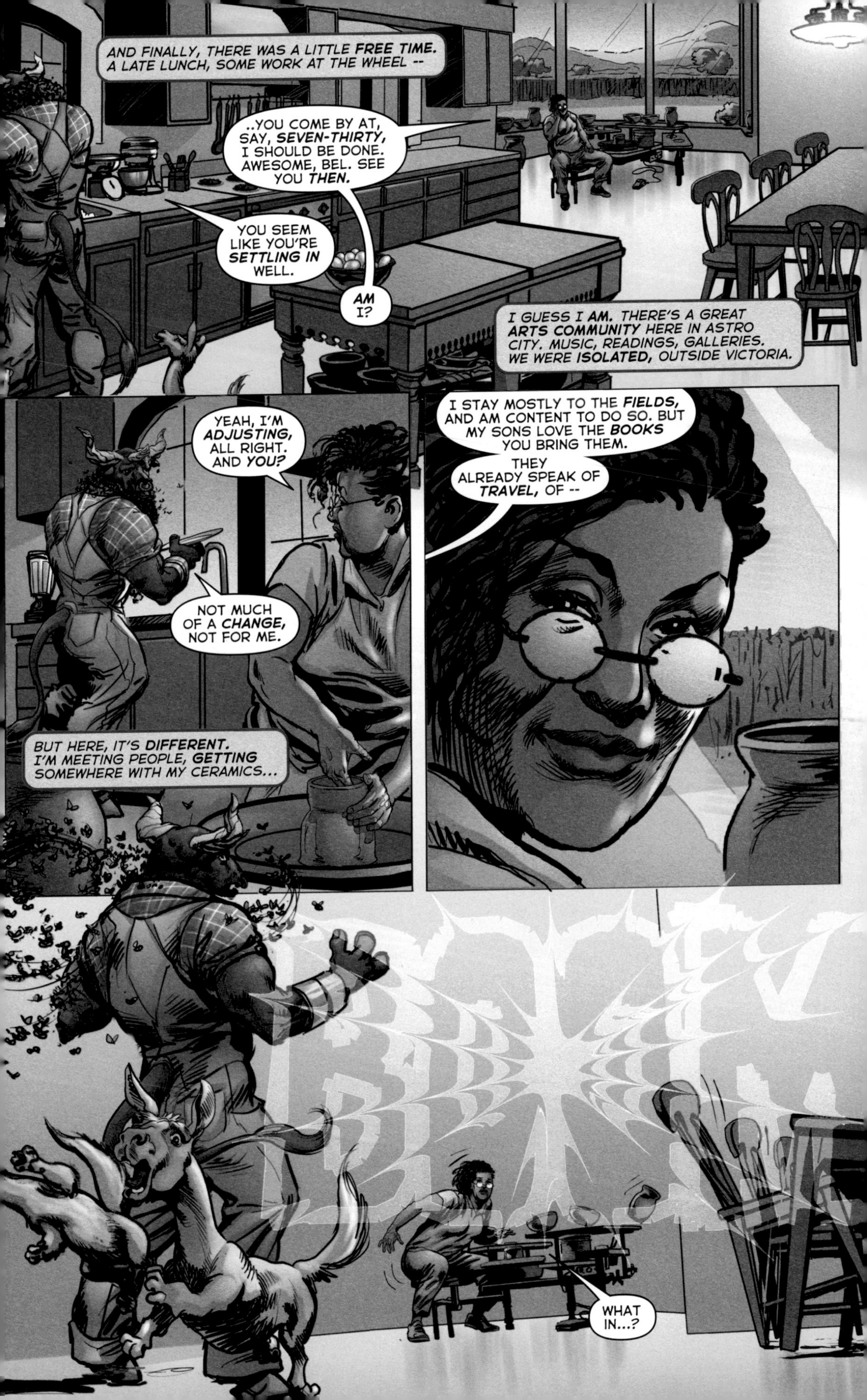
AND FINALLY, THERE WAS A LITTLE FREE TIME. A LATE LUNCH, SOME WORK AT THE WHEEL --
..YOU COME BY AT, SAY, SEVEN-THIRTY, I SHOULD BE DONE. AWESOME, BEL. SEE YOU THEN.
YOU SEEM LIKE YOU'RE SETTLING IN WELL.
AM I?
I GUESS I AM. THERE'S A GREAT ARTS COMMUNITY HERE IN ASTRO CITY. MUSIC, READINGS, GALLERIES. WE WERE ISOLATED, OUTSIDE VICTORIA.
YEAH, I'M ADJUSTING, ALL RIGHT. AND YOU?
NOT MUCH OF A CHANGE, NOT FOR ME.
BUT HERE, IT'S DIFFERENT. I'M MEETING PEOPLE, GETTING SOMEWHERE WITH MY CERAMICS...
I STAY MOSTLY TO THE FIELDS, AND AM CONTENT TO DO SO. BUT MY SONS LOVE THE BOOKS YOU BRING THEM.
THEY ALREADY SPEAK OF TRAVEL, OF --
WHAT IN...?

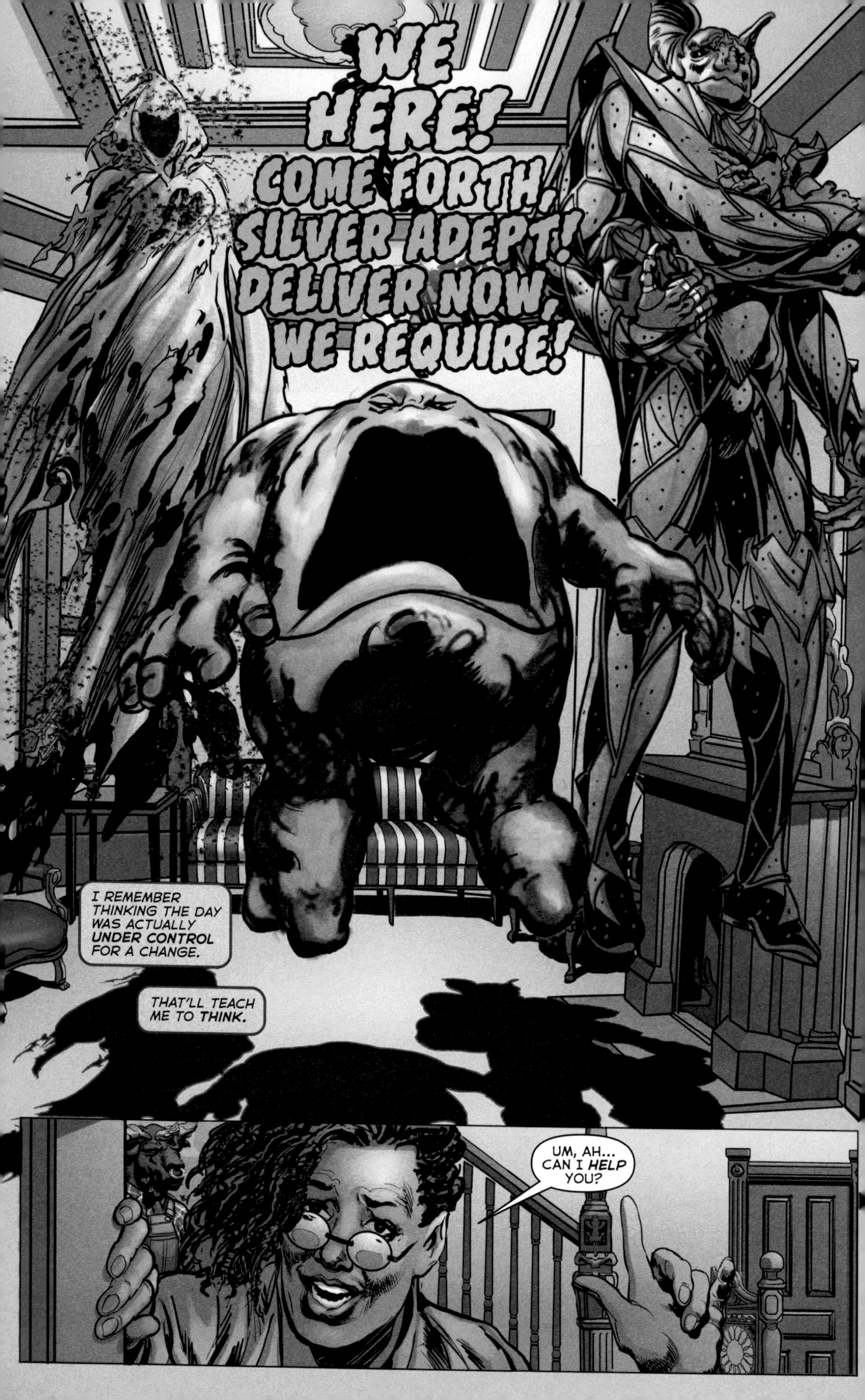
WE HERE! COME FORTH, SILVER ADEPT! DELIVER NOW, WE REQUIRE!
I REMEMBER THINKING THE DAY WAS ACTUALLY UNDER CONTROL FOR A CHANGE.
THAT'LL TEACH ME TO THINK.
UM, AH... CAN I HELP YOU?

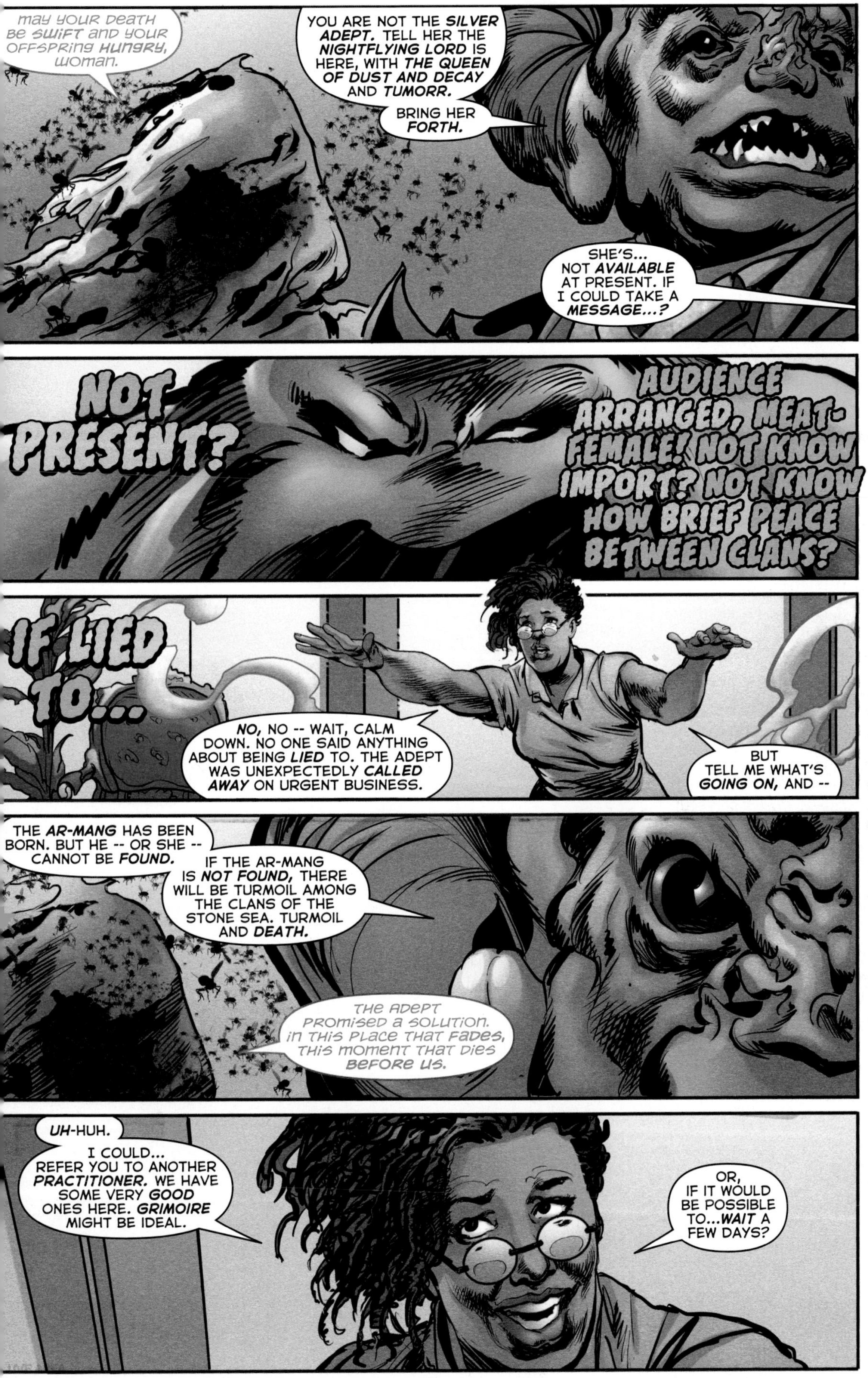

MAY YOUR DEATH BE SWIFT AND YOUR OFFSPRING HUNGRY, WOMAN.
YOU ARE NOT THE SILVER ADEPT. TELL HER THE NIGHTFLYING LORD IS HERE, WITH THE QUEEN OF DUST AND DECAY AND TUMORR.
BRING HER FORTH.
SHE'S... NOT AVAILABLE AT PRESENT. IF I COULD TAKE A MESSAGE...?
NOT PRESENT?
AUDIENCE ARRANGED, MEAT-FEMALE! NOT KNOW IMPORT? NOT KNOW HOW BRIEF PEACE BETWEEN CLANS?
IF LIED TO...
NO, NO -- WAIT, CALM DOWN. NO ONE SAID ANYTHING ABOUT BEING LIED TO. THE ADEPT WAS UNEXPECTEDLY CALLED AWAY ON URGENT BUSINESS.
BUT TELL ME WHAT'S GOING ON, AND --
THE AR-MANG HAS BEEN BORN. BUT HE -- OR SHE -- CANNOT BE FOUND.
IF THE AR-MANG IS NOT FOUND, THERE WILL BE TURMOIL AMONG THE CLANS OF THE STONE SEA. TURMOIL AND DEATH.
THE ADEPT PROMISED A SOLUTION. IN THIS PLACE THAT FADES, THIS MOMENT THAT DIES BEFORE US.
UH-HUH.
I COULD... REFER YOU TO ANOTHER PRACTITIONER. WE HAVE SOME VERY GOOD ONES HERE. GRIMOIRE MIGHT BE IDEAL.
OR, IF IT WOULD BE POSSIBLE TO...WAIT A FEW DAYS?

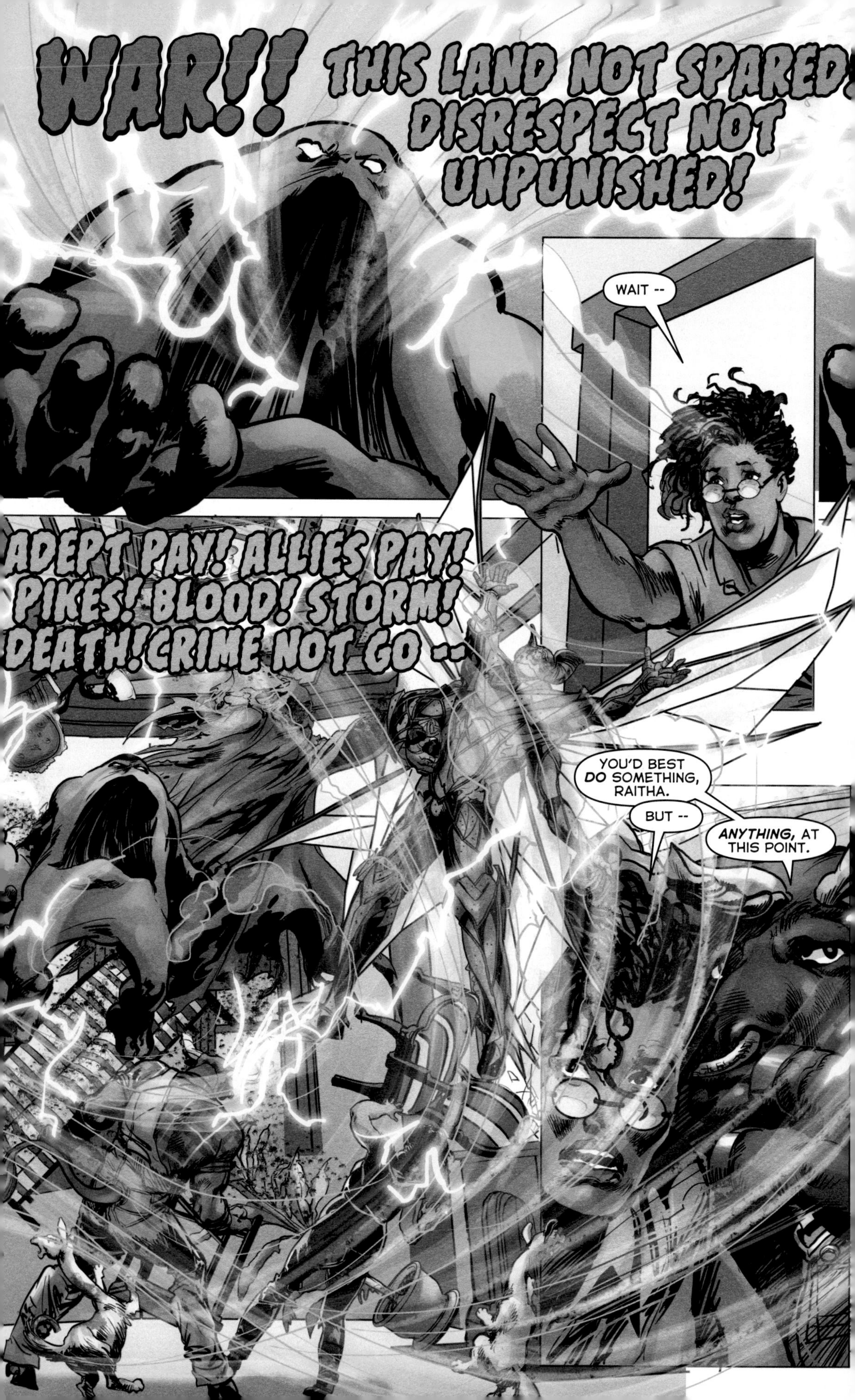
WAR!! THIS LAND NOT SPARED! DISRESPECT NOT UNPUNISHED!
WAIT --
ADEPT PAY! ALLIES PAY! PIKES! BLOOD! STORM! DEATH! CRIME NOT GO --
YOU'D BEST DO SOMETHING, RAITHA.
BUT --
ANYTHING, AT THIS POINT.

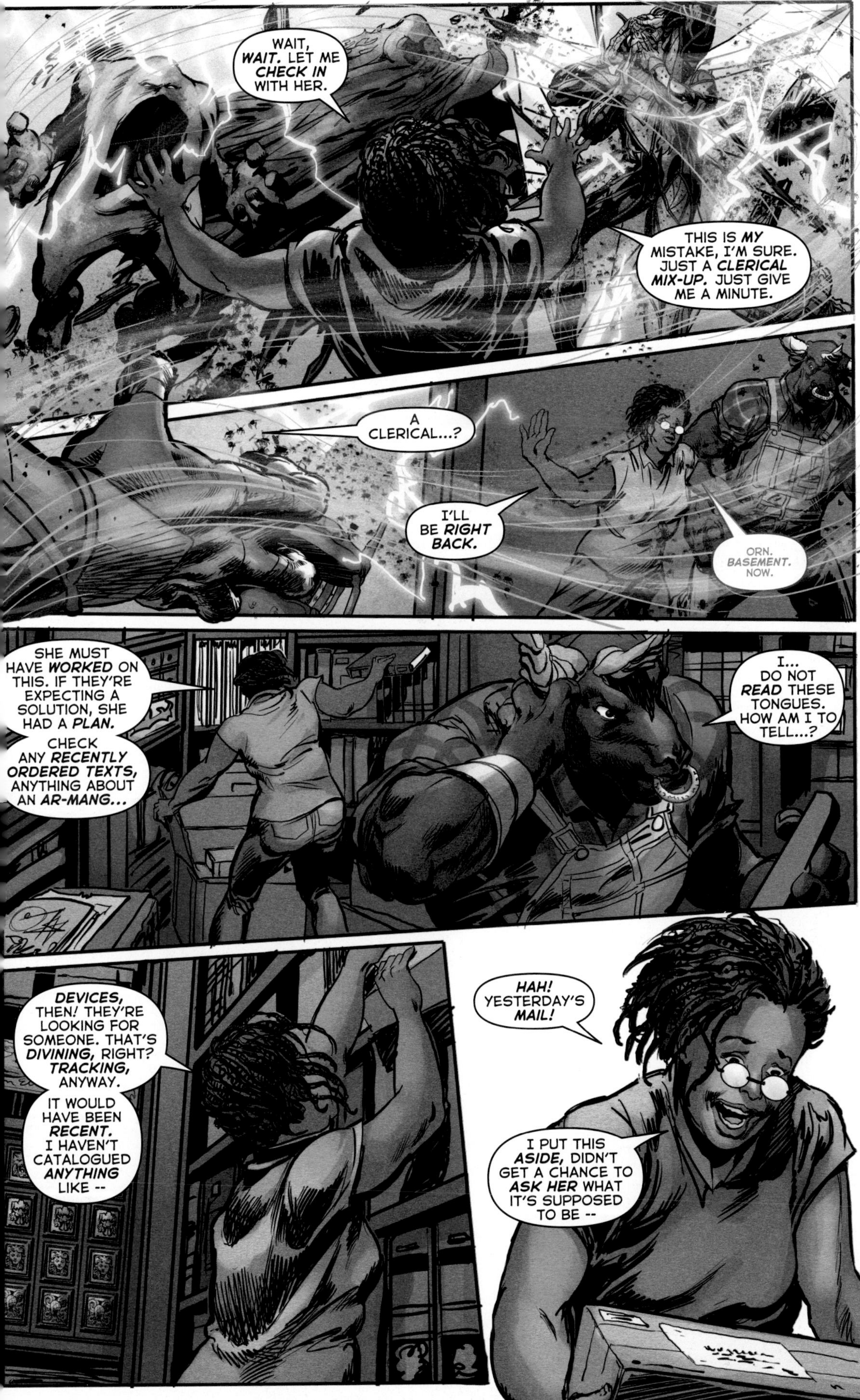
WAIT, *WAIT.* LET ME *CHECK IN* WITH HER.
THIS IS *MY* MISTAKE, I'M SURE. JUST A *CLERICAL MIX-UP.* JUST GIVE ME A MINUTE.
A CLERICAL...?
I'LL BE *RIGHT BACK.*
ORN. *BASEMENT.* NOW.
SHE MUST HAVE *WORKED* ON THIS. IF THEY'RE EXPECTING A SOLUTION, SHE HAD A *PLAN.*
CHECK ANY *RECENTLY ORDERED TEXTS,* ANYTHING ABOUT AN *AR-MANG...*
I... DO NOT *READ* THESE TONGUES. HOW AM I TO TELL...?
DEVICES, THEN! THEY'RE LOOKING FOR SOMEONE. THAT'S *DIVINING,* RIGHT? *TRACKING,* ANYWAY.
IT WOULD HAVE BEEN *RECENT.* I HAVEN'T CATALOGUED *ANYTHING* LIKE --
HAH! YESTERDAY'S *MAIL!*
I PUT THIS *ASIDE,* DIDN'T GET A CHANCE TO *ASK HER* WHAT IT'S SUPPOSED TO BE --

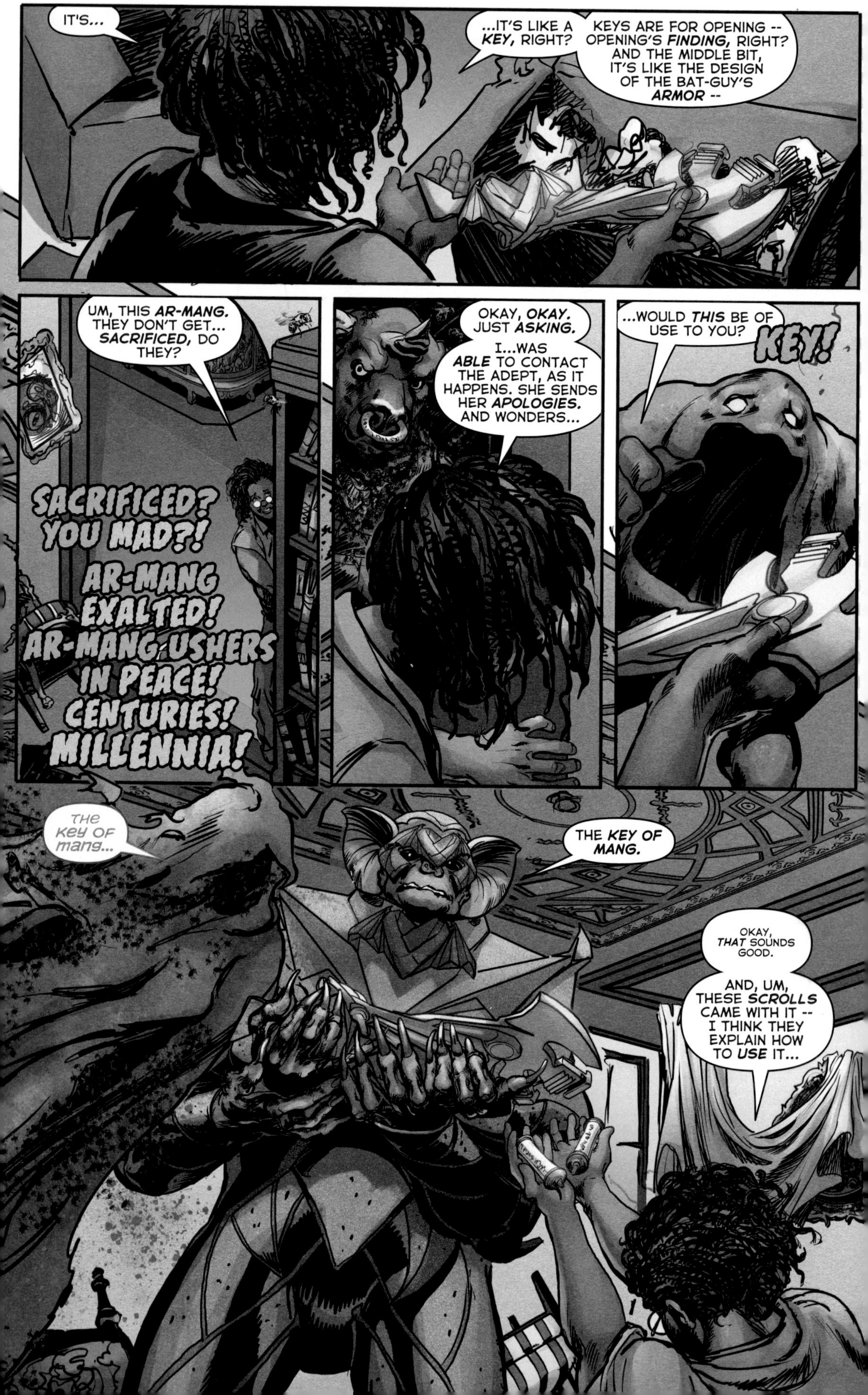
IT'S...
...IT'S LIKE A KEY, RIGHT?
KEYS ARE FOR OPENING -- OPENING'S FINDING, RIGHT? AND THE MIDDLE BIT, IT'S LIKE THE DESIGN OF THE BAT-GUY'S ARMOR --
UM, THIS AR-MANG. THEY DON'T GET... SACRIFICED, DO THEY?
SACRIFICED? YOU MAD?! AR-MANG EXALTED! AR-MANG USHERS IN PEACE! CENTURIES! MILLENNIA!
OKAY, OKAY. JUST ASKING.
I...WAS ABLE TO CONTACT THE ADEPT, AS IT HAPPENS. SHE SENDS HER APOLOGIES. AND WONDERS...
...WOULD THIS BE OF USE TO YOU?
KEY!
The key of mang...
THE KEY OF MANG.
OKAY, THAT SOUNDS GOOD.
AND, UM, THESE SCROLLS CAME WITH IT -- I THINK THEY EXPLAIN HOW TO USE IT...

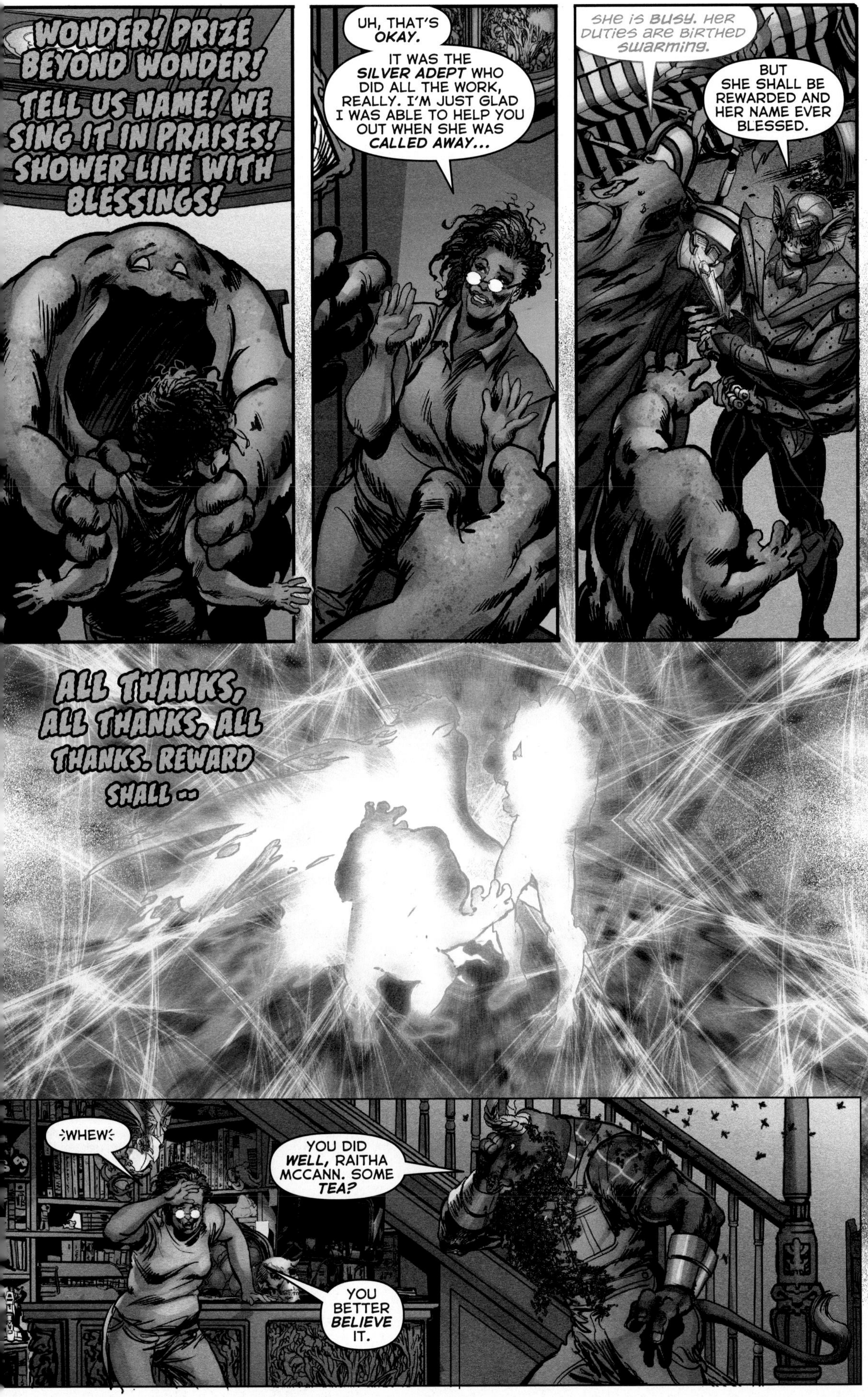
WONDER! PRIZE BEYOND WONDER! TELL US NAME! WE SING IT IN PRAISES! SHOWER LINE WITH BLESSINGS!
UH, THAT'S OKAY.
IT WAS THE SILVER ADEPT WHO DID ALL THE WORK, REALLY. I'M JUST GLAD I WAS ABLE TO HELP YOU OUT WHEN SHE WAS CALLED AWAY...
SHE IS BUSY. HER DUTIES ARE BIRTHED SWARMING.
BUT SHE SHALL BE REWARDED AND HER NAME EVER BLESSED.
ALL THANKS, ALL THANKS, ALL THANKS. REWARD SHALL --
WHEW
YOU DID WELL, RAITHA MCCANN. SOME TEA?
YOU BETTER BELIEVE IT.

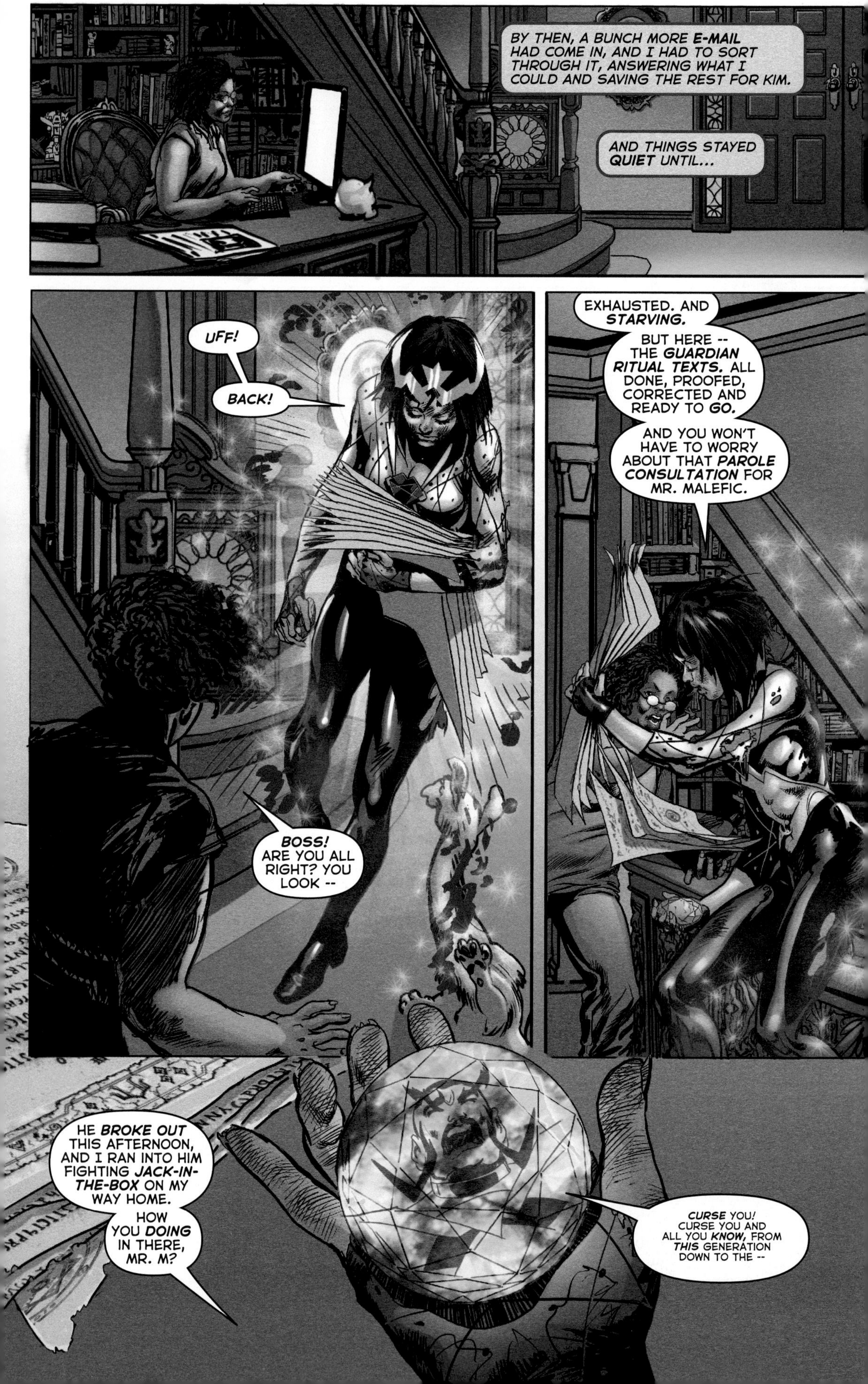
BY THEN, A BUNCH MORE E-MAIL HAD COME IN, AND I HAD TO SORT THROUGH IT, ANSWERING WHAT I COULD AND SAVING THE REST FOR KIM.
AND THINGS STAYED QUIET UNTIL...
UFF!
BACK!
BOSS! ARE YOU ALL RIGHT? YOU LOOK --
EXHAUSTED. AND STARVING.
BUT HERE -- THE GUARDIAN RITUAL TEXTS. ALL DONE, PROOFED, CORRECTED AND READY TO GO.
AND YOU WON'T HAVE TO WORRY ABOUT THAT PAROLE CONSULTATION FOR MR. MALEFIC.
HE BROKE OUT THIS AFTERNOON, AND I RAN INTO HIM FIGHTING JACK-IN-THE-BOX ON MY WAY HOME.
HOW YOU DOING IN THERE, MR. M?
CURSE YOU! CURSE YOU AND ALL YOU KNOW, FROM THIS GENERATION DOWN TO THE --

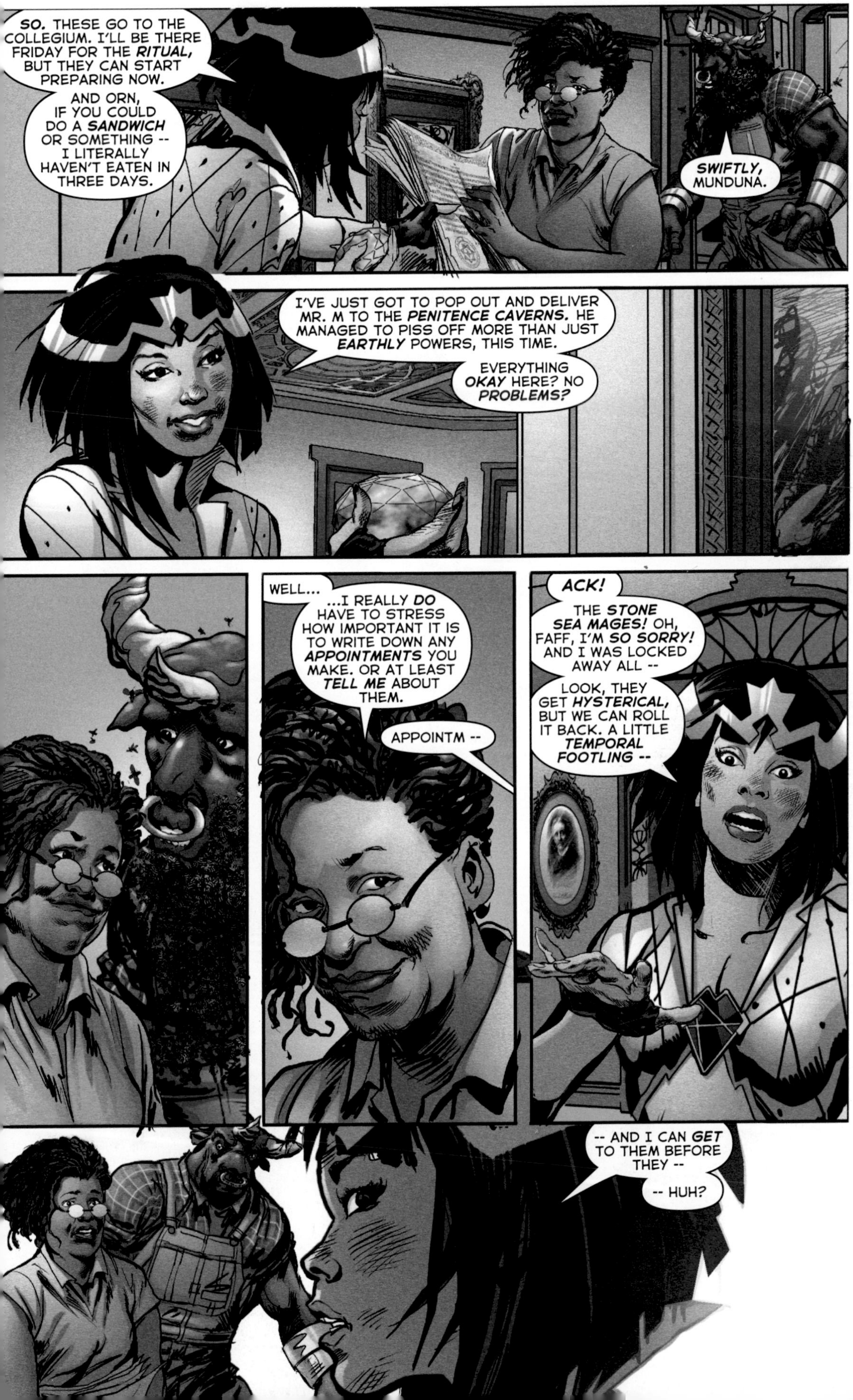
SO. THESE GO TO THE COLLEGIUM. I'LL BE THERE FRIDAY FOR THE RITUAL, BUT THEY CAN START PREPARING NOW.
AND ORN, IF YOU COULD DO A SANDWICH OR SOMETHING -- I LITERALLY HAVEN'T EATEN IN THREE DAYS.
SWIFTLY, MUNDUNA.
I'VE JUST GOT TO POP OUT AND DELIVER MR. M TO THE PENITENCE CAVERNS. HE MANAGED TO PISS OFF MORE THAN JUST EARTHLY POWERS, THIS TIME.
EVERYTHING OKAY HERE? NO PROBLEMS?
WELL...
...I REALLY DO HAVE TO STRESS HOW IMPORTANT IT IS TO WRITE DOWN ANY APPOINTMENTS YOU MAKE. OR AT LEAST TELL ME ABOUT THEM.
APPOINTM --
ACK!
THE STONE SEA MAGES! OH, FAFF, I'M SO SORRY! AND I WAS LOCKED AWAY ALL --
LOOK, THEY GET HYSTERICAL, BUT WE CAN ROLL IT BACK. A LITTLE TEMPORAL FOOTLING --
-- AND I CAN GET TO THEM BEFORE THEY --
-- HUH?

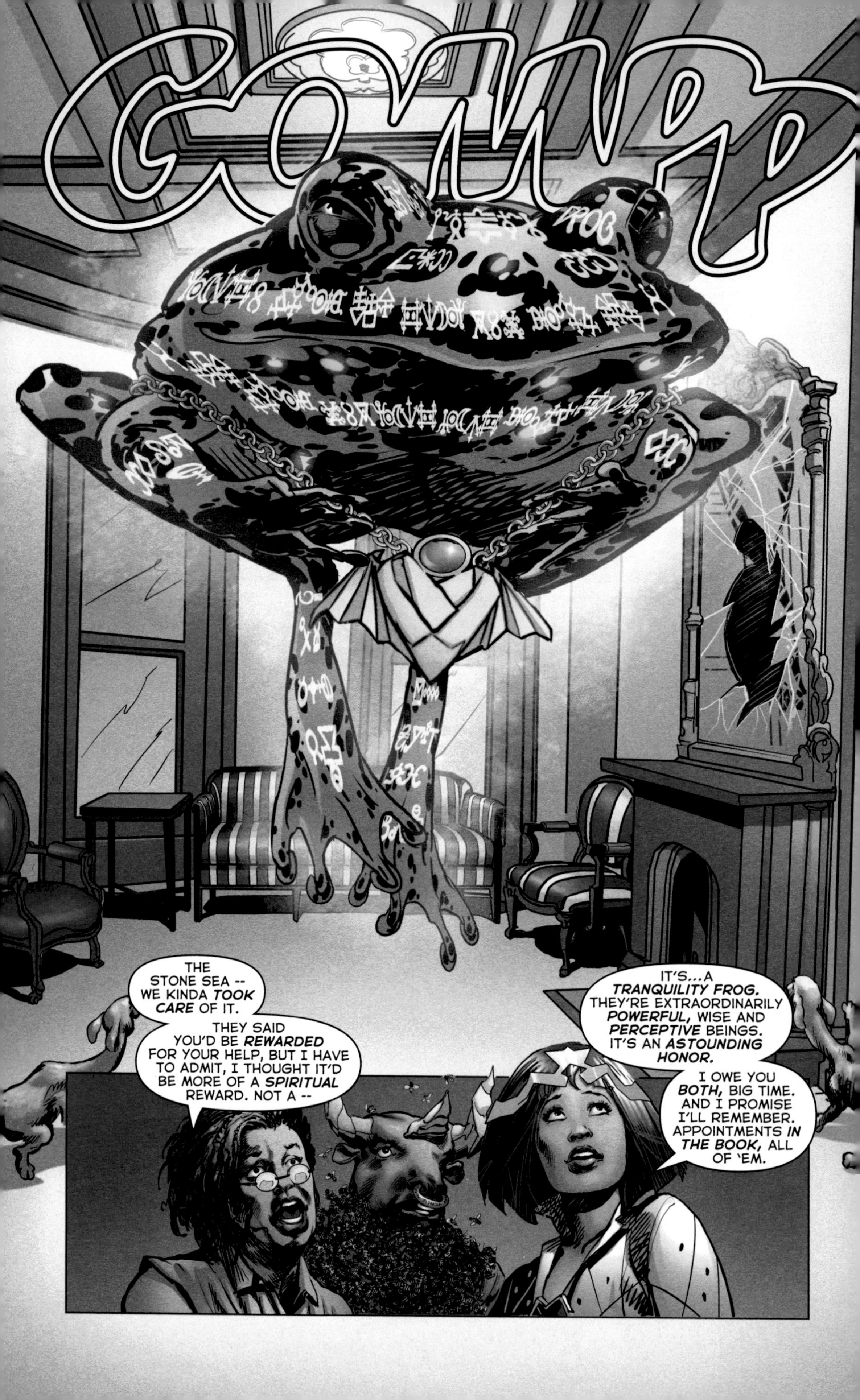
GOMP
THE STONE SEA -- WE KINDA TOOK CARE OF IT.
THEY SAID YOU'D BE REWARDED FOR YOUR HELP, BUT I HAVE TO ADMIT, I THOUGHT IT'D BE MORE OF A SPIRITUAL REWARD. NOT A --
IT'S...A TRANQUILITY FROG. THEY'RE EXTRAORDINARILY POWERFUL, WISE AND PERCEPTIVE BEINGS. IT'S AN ASTOUNDING HONOR.
I OWE YOU BOTH, BIG TIME. AND I PROMISE I'LL REMEMBER. APPOINTMENTS IN THE BOOK, ALL OF 'EM.

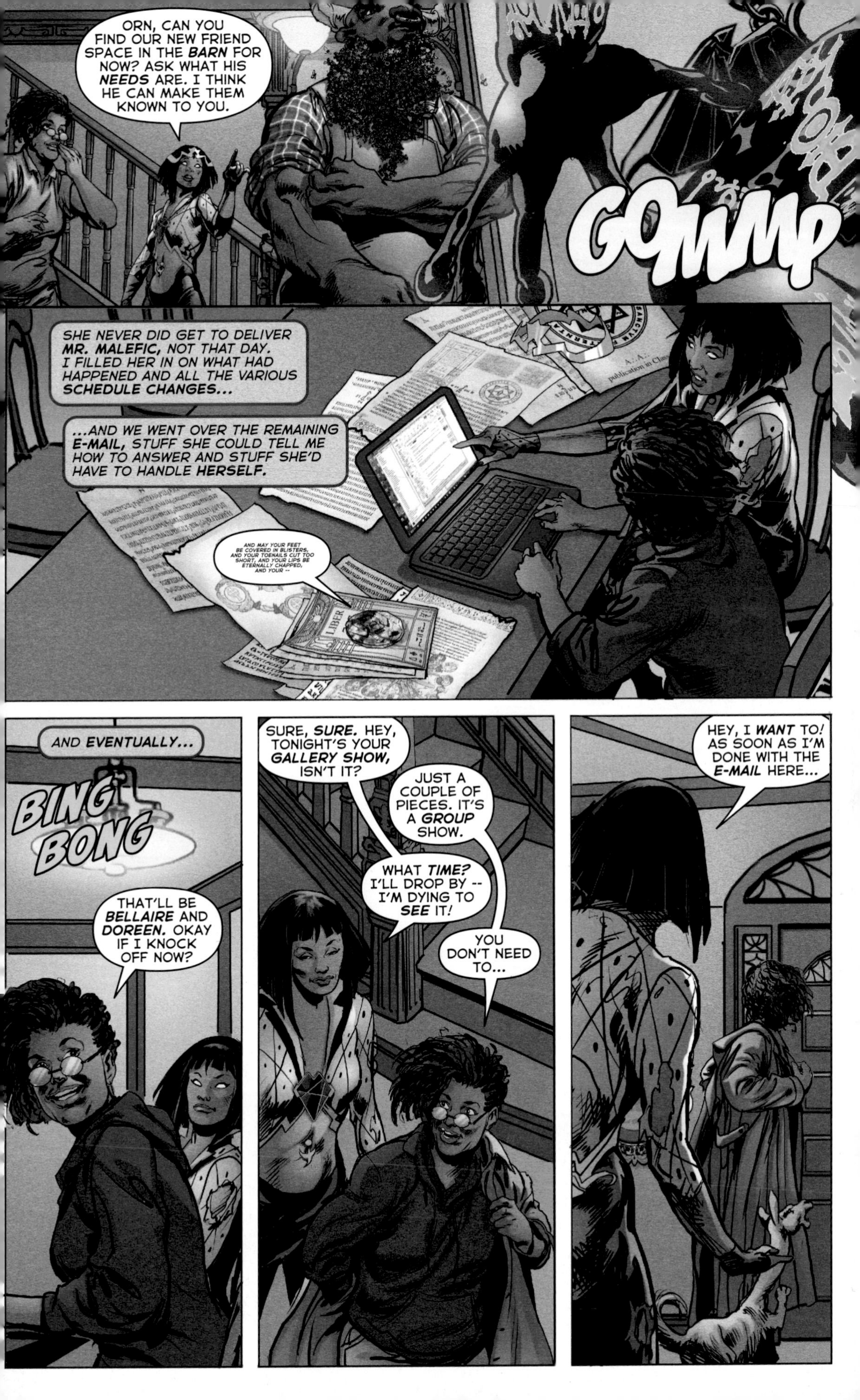
ORN, CAN YOU FIND OUR NEW FRIEND SPACE IN THE BARN FOR NOW? ASK WHAT HIS NEEDS ARE. I THINK HE CAN MAKE THEM KNOWN TO YOU.
GOMMP
SHE NEVER DID GET TO DELIVER MR. MALEFIC, NOT THAT DAY. I FILLED HER IN ON WHAT HAD HAPPENED AND ALL THE VARIOUS SCHEDULE CHANGES...
...AND WE WENT OVER THE REMAINING E-MAIL, STUFF SHE COULD TELL ME HOW TO ANSWER AND STUFF SHE'D HAVE TO HANDLE HERSELF.
AND MAY YOUR FEET BE COVERED IN BLISTERS, AND YOUR TOENAILS CUT TOO SHORT, AND YOUR LIPS BE ETERNALLY CHAPPED, AND YOUR --
LIBER
AND EVENTUALLY...
BING BONG
THAT'LL BE BELLAIRE AND DOREEN. OKAY IF I KNOCK OFF NOW?
SURE, SURE. HEY, TONIGHT'S YOUR GALLERY SHOW, ISN'T IT?
JUST A COUPLE OF PIECES. IT'S A GROUP SHOW.
WHAT TIME? I'LL DROP BY -- I'M DYING TO SEE IT!
YOU DON'T NEED TO...
HEY, I WANT TO! AS SOON AS I'M DONE WITH THE E-MAIL HERE...

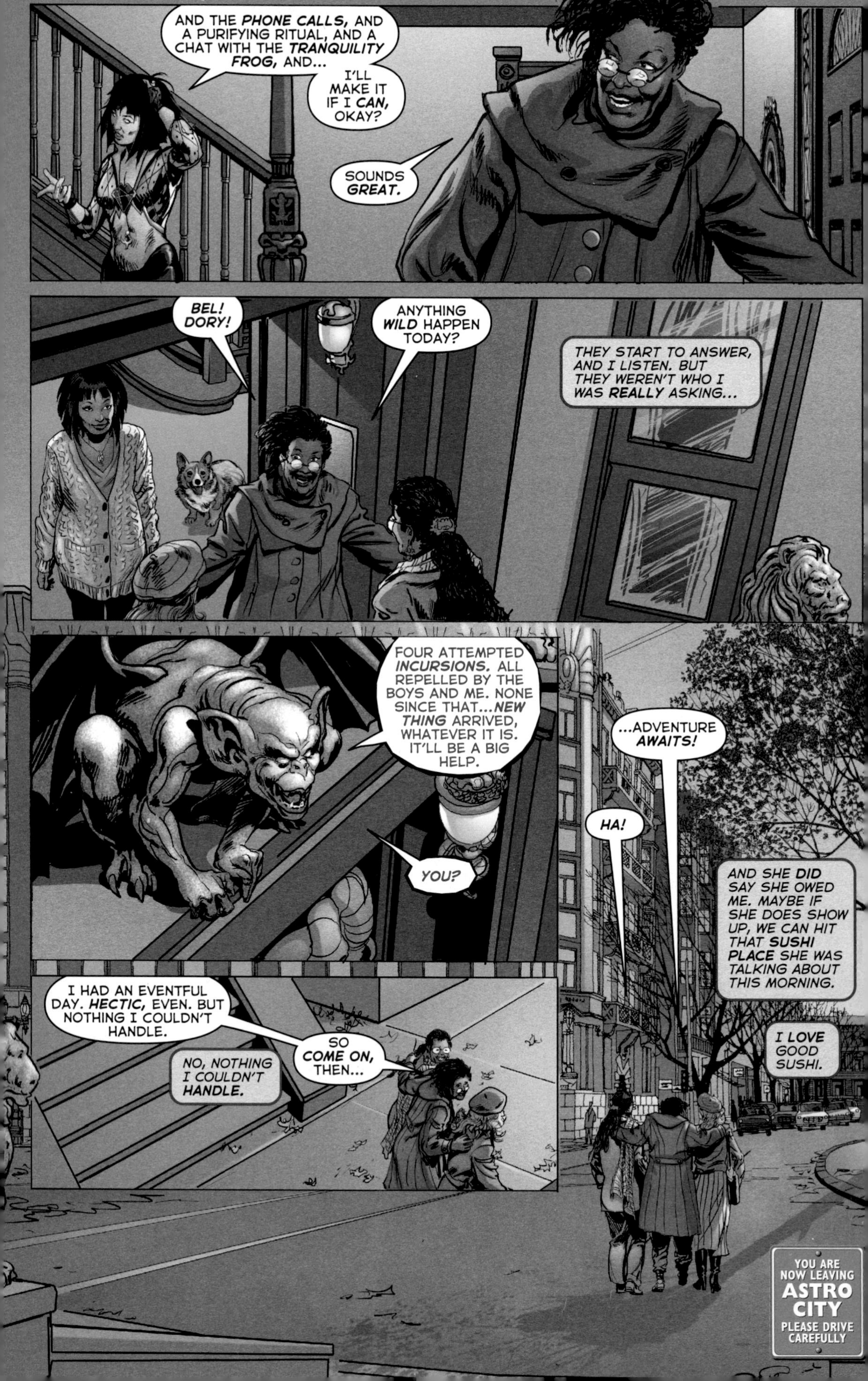
AND THE PHONE CALLS, AND A PURIFYING RITUAL, AND A CHAT WITH THE TRANQUILITY FROG, AND...
I'LL MAKE IT IF I CAN, OKAY?
SOUNDS GREAT.
BEL! DORY!
ANYTHING WILD HAPPEN TODAY?
THEY START TO ANSWER, AND I LISTEN. BUT THEY WEREN'T WHO I WAS REALLY ASKING...
FOUR ATTEMPTED INCURSIONS. ALL REPELLED BY THE BOYS AND ME. NONE SINCE THAT...NEW THING ARRIVED, WHATEVER IT IS. IT'LL BE A BIG HELP.
YOU?
I HAD AN EVENTFUL DAY. HECTIC, EVEN. BUT NOTHING I COULDN'T HANDLE.
NO, NOTHING I COULDN'T HANDLE.
SO COME ON, THEN...
...ADVENTURE AWAITS!
HA!
AND SHE DID SAY SHE OWED ME. MAYBE IF SHE DOES SHOW UP, WE CAN HIT THAT SUSHI PLACE SHE WAS TALKING ABOUT THIS MORNING.
I LOVE GOOD SUSHI.
YOU ARE NOW LEAVING ASTRO CITY PLEASE DRIVE CAREFULLY

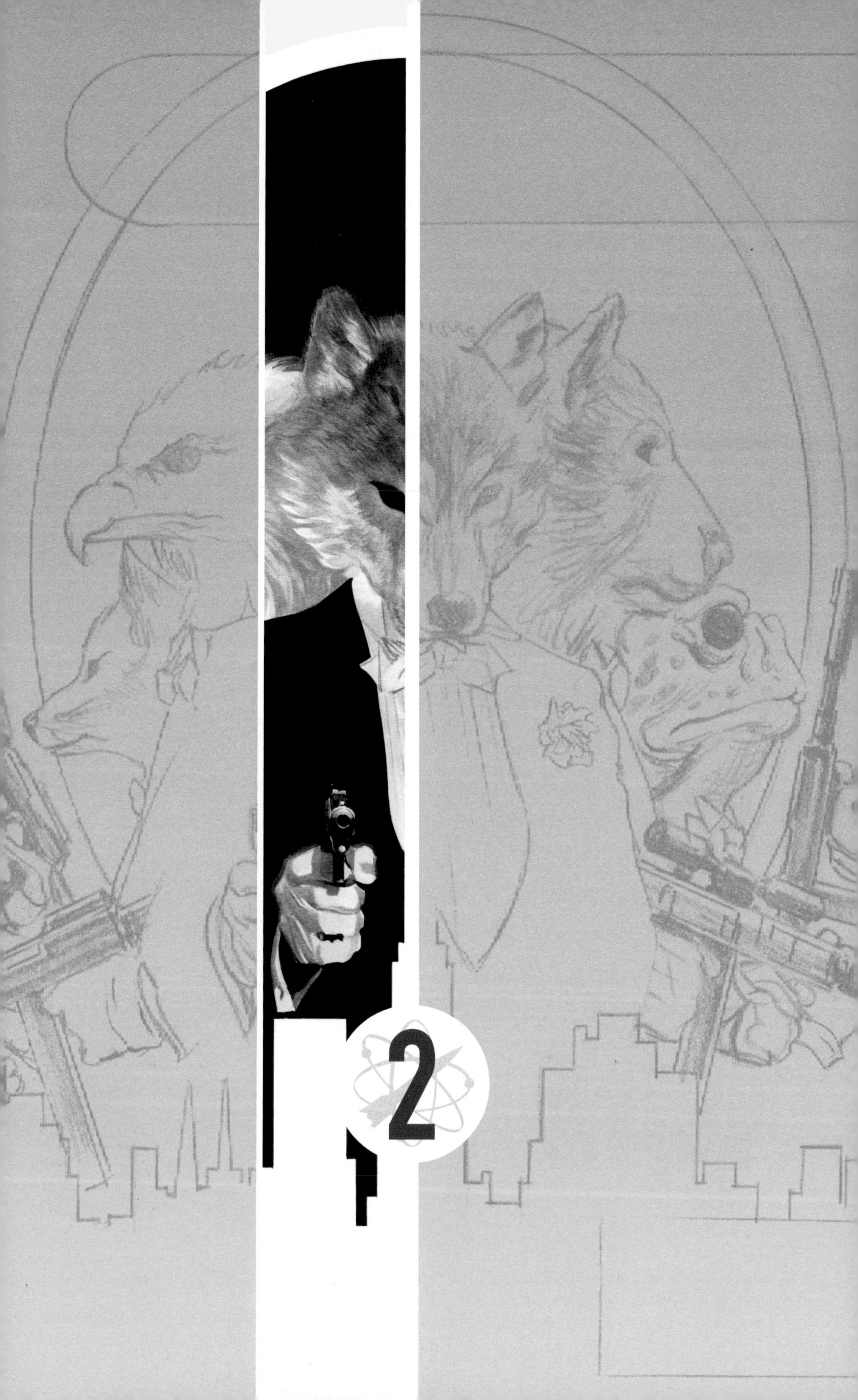
2

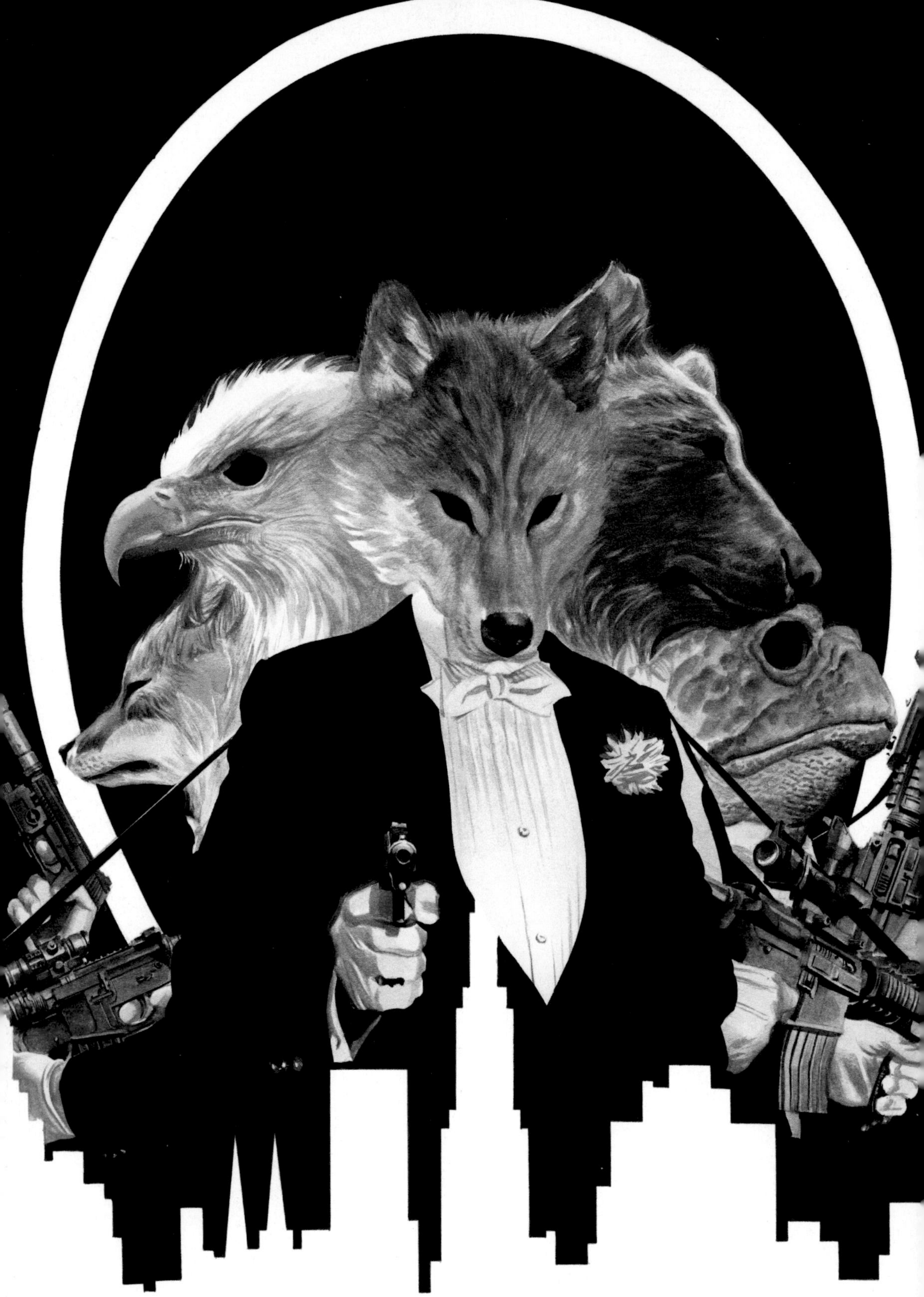

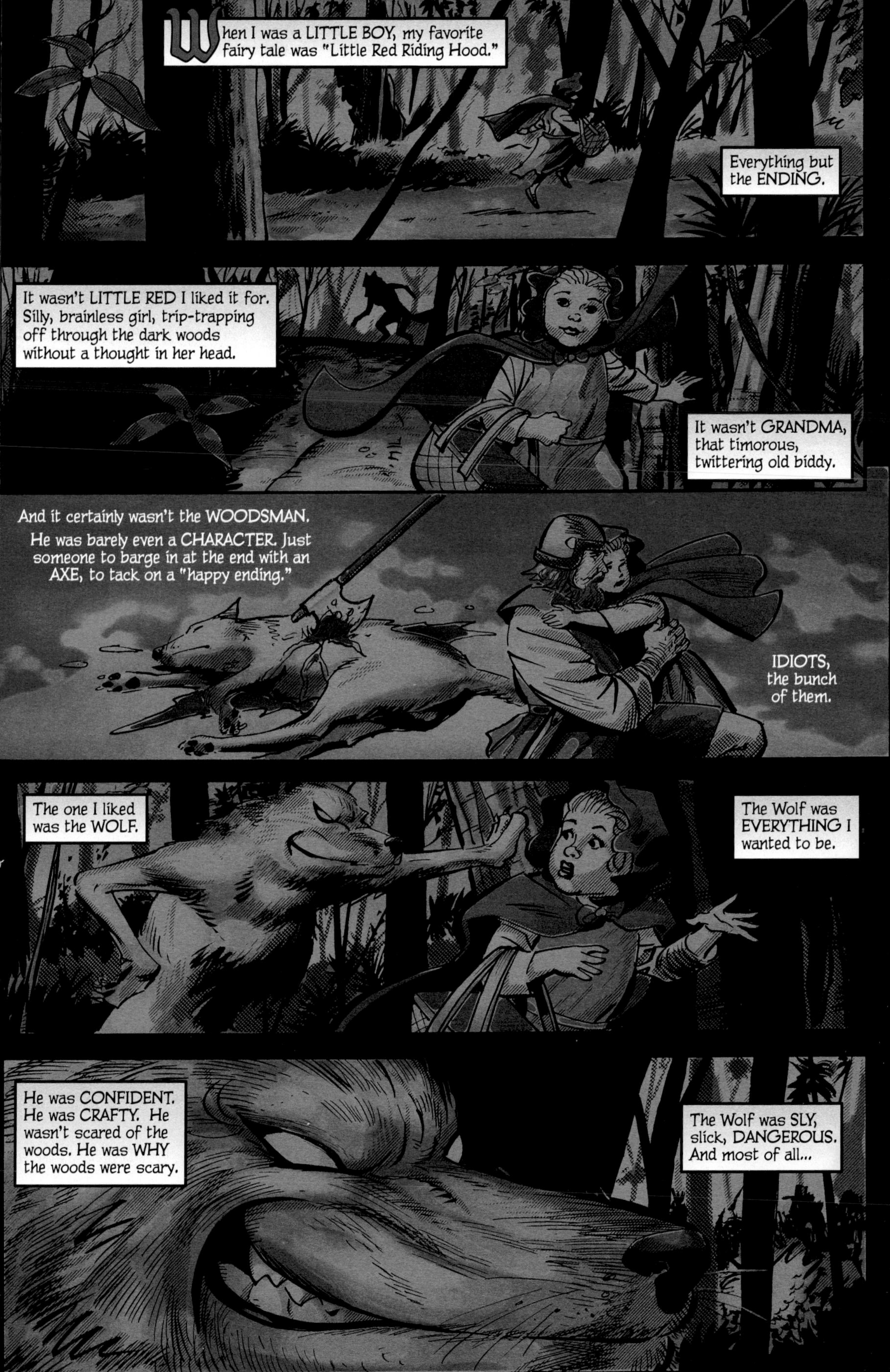
When I was a LITTLE BOY, my favorite fairy tale was "Little Red Riding Hood."
Everything but the ENDING.
It wasn't LITTLE RED I liked it for. Silly, brainless girl, trip-trapping off through the dark woods without a thought in her head.
It wasn't GRANDMA, that timorous, twittering old biddy.
And it certainly wasn't the WOODSMAN.
He was barely even a CHARACTER. Just someone to barge in at the end with an AXE, to tack on a "happy ending."
IDIOTS, the bunch of them.
The one I liked was the WOLF.
The Wolf was EVERYTHING I wanted to be.
He was CONFIDENT. He was CRAFTY. He wasn't scared of the woods. He was WHY the woods were scary.
The Wolf was SLY, slick, DANGEROUS. And most of all...

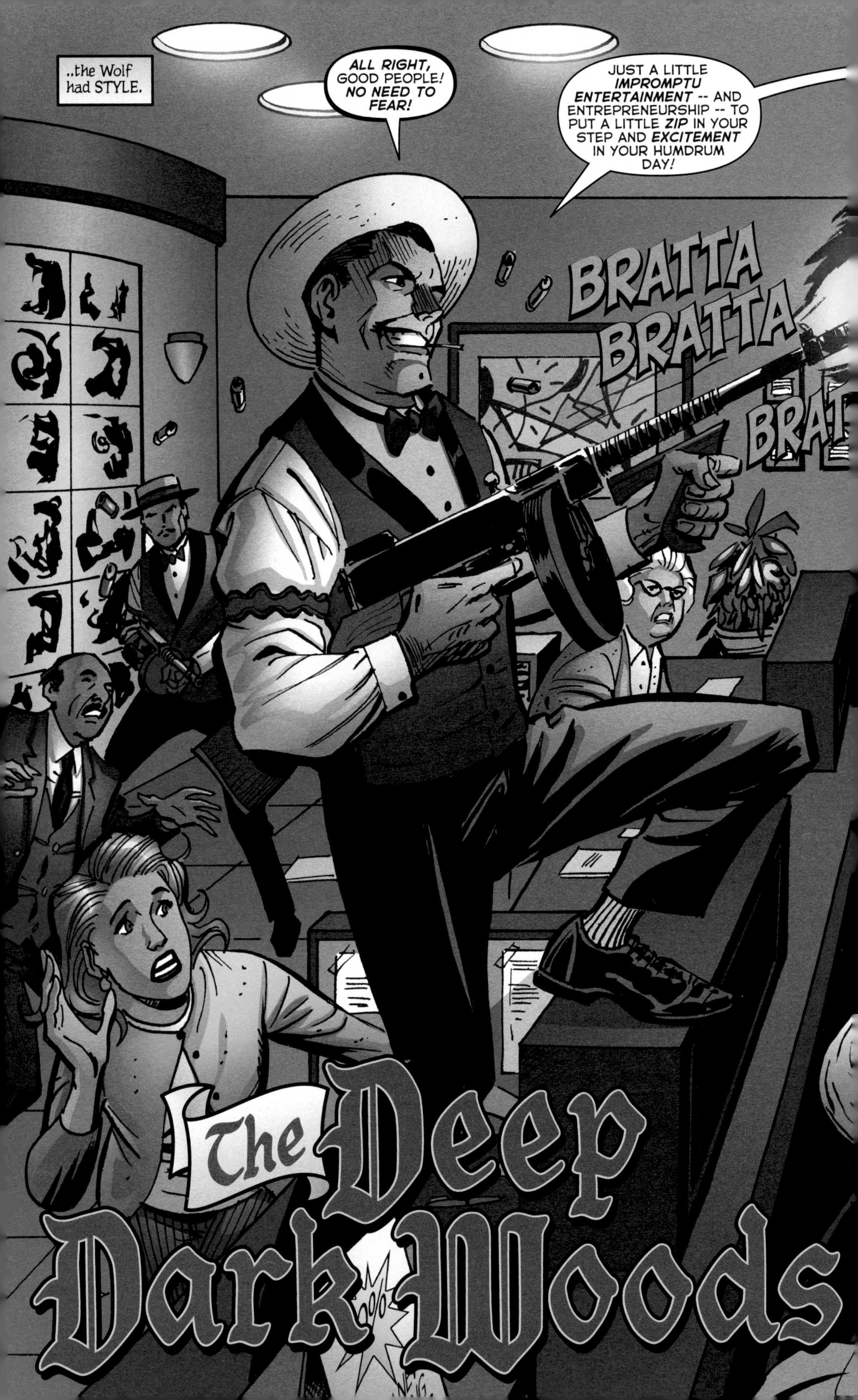
..the Wolf had STYLE.
ALL RIGHT, GOOD PEOPLE! NO NEED TO FEAR!
JUST A LITTLE IMPROMPTU ENTERTAINMENT -- AND ENTREPRENEURSHIP -- TO PUT A LITTLE ZIP IN YOUR STEP AND EXCITEMENT IN YOUR HUMDRUM DAY!
BRATTA
BRATTA
BRAT
The Deep Dark Woods

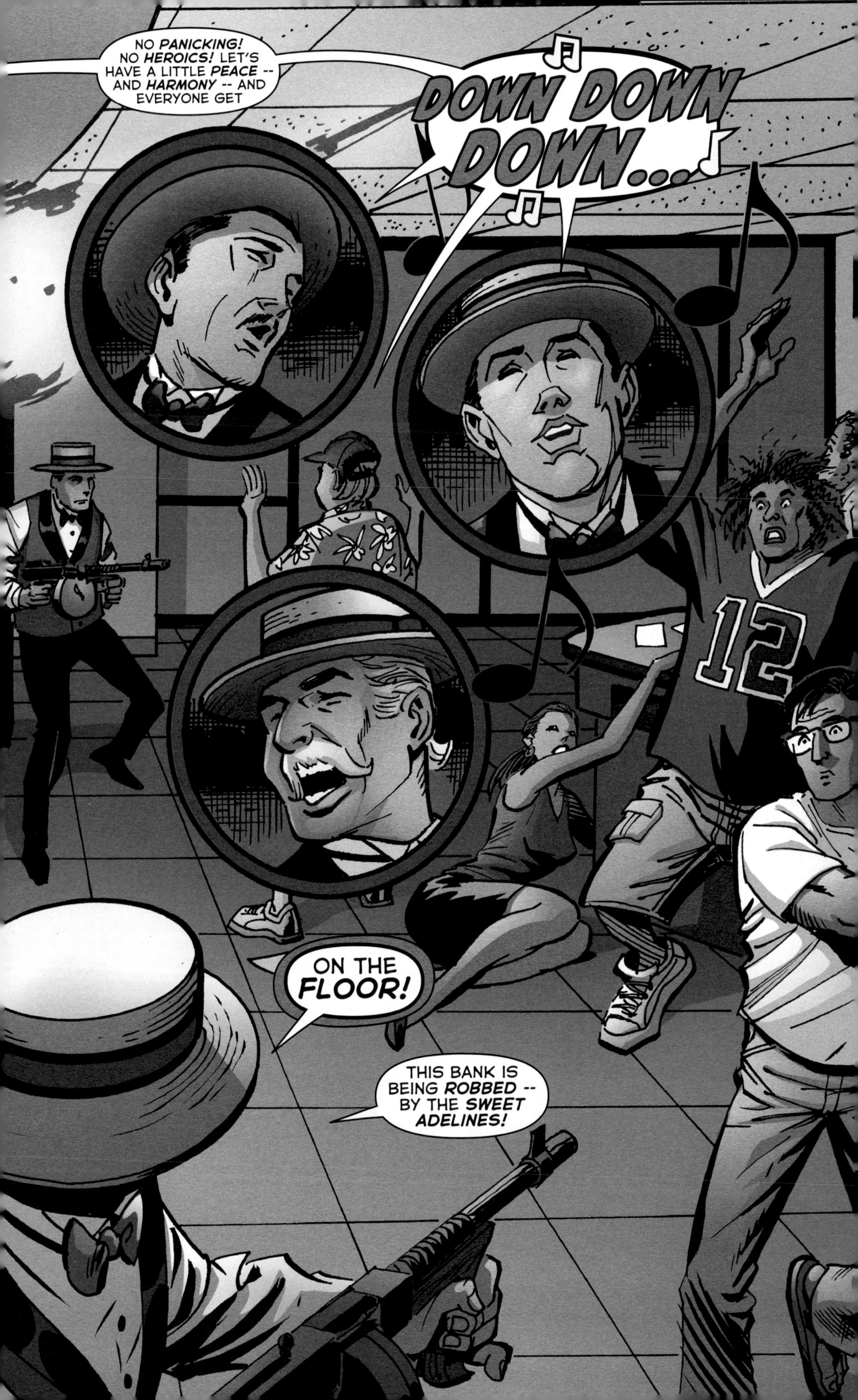
NO PANICKING! NO HEROICS! LET'S HAVE A LITTLE PEACE -- AND HARMONY -- AND EVERYONE GET
DOWN DOWN DOWN...
ON THE FLOOR!
THIS BANK IS BEING ROBBED -- BY THE SWEET ADELINES!
12

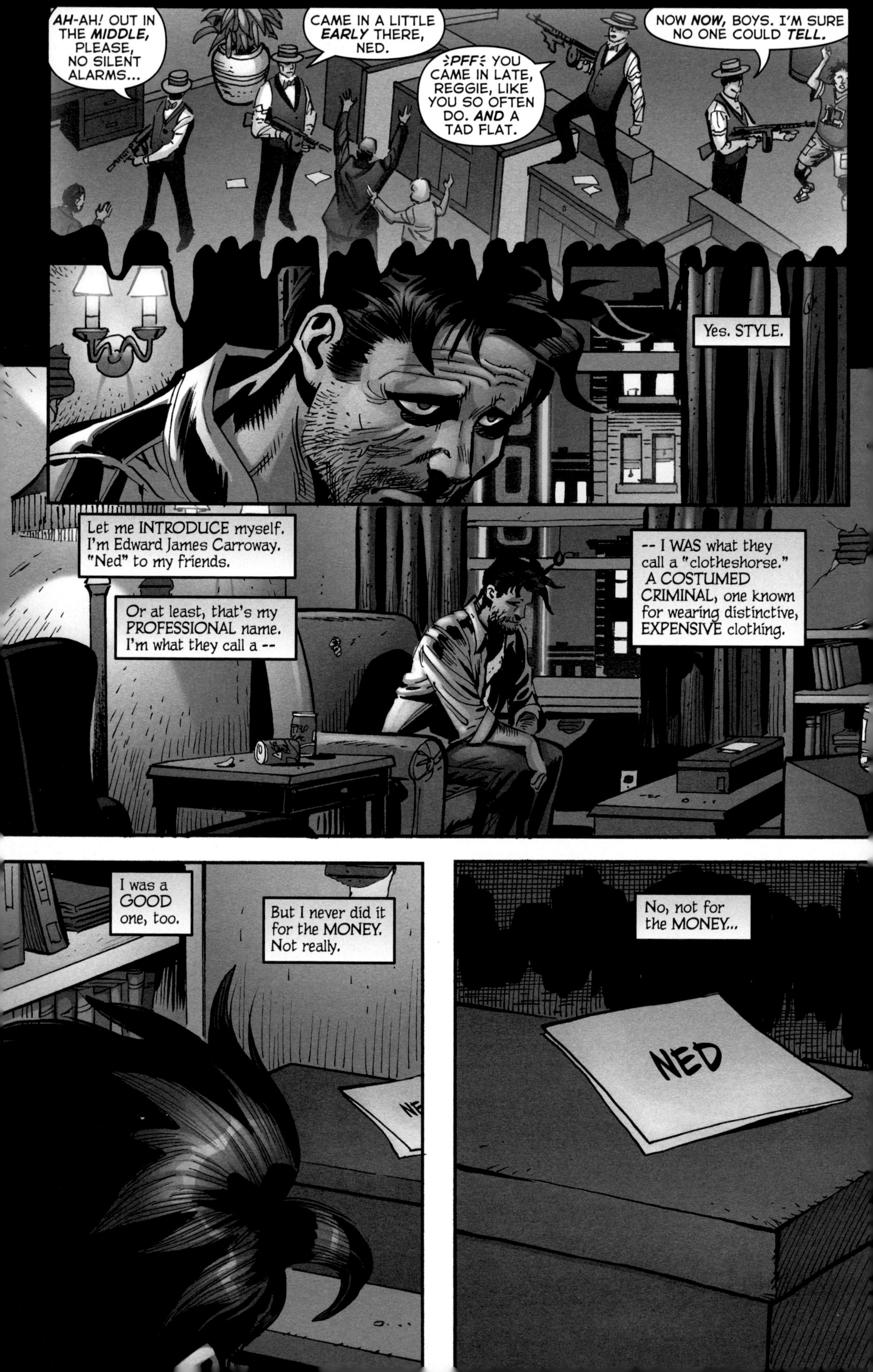
AH-AH! OUT IN THE MIDDLE, PLEASE, NO SILENT ALARMS...
CAME IN A LITTLE EARLY THERE, NED.
PFF YOU CAME IN LATE, REGGIE, LIKE YOU SO OFTEN DO. AND A TAD FLAT.
NOW NOW, BOYS. I'M SURE NO ONE COULD TELL.
Yes. STYLE.
Let me INTRODUCE myself. I'm Edward James Carroway. "Ned" to my friends.
Or at least, that's my PROFESSIONAL name. I'm what they call a --
-- I WAS what they call a "clotheshorse." A COSTUMED CRIMINAL, one known for wearing distinctive, EXPENSIVE clothing.
I was a GOOD one, too.
But I never did it for the MONEY. Not really.
No, not for the MONEY...
NED

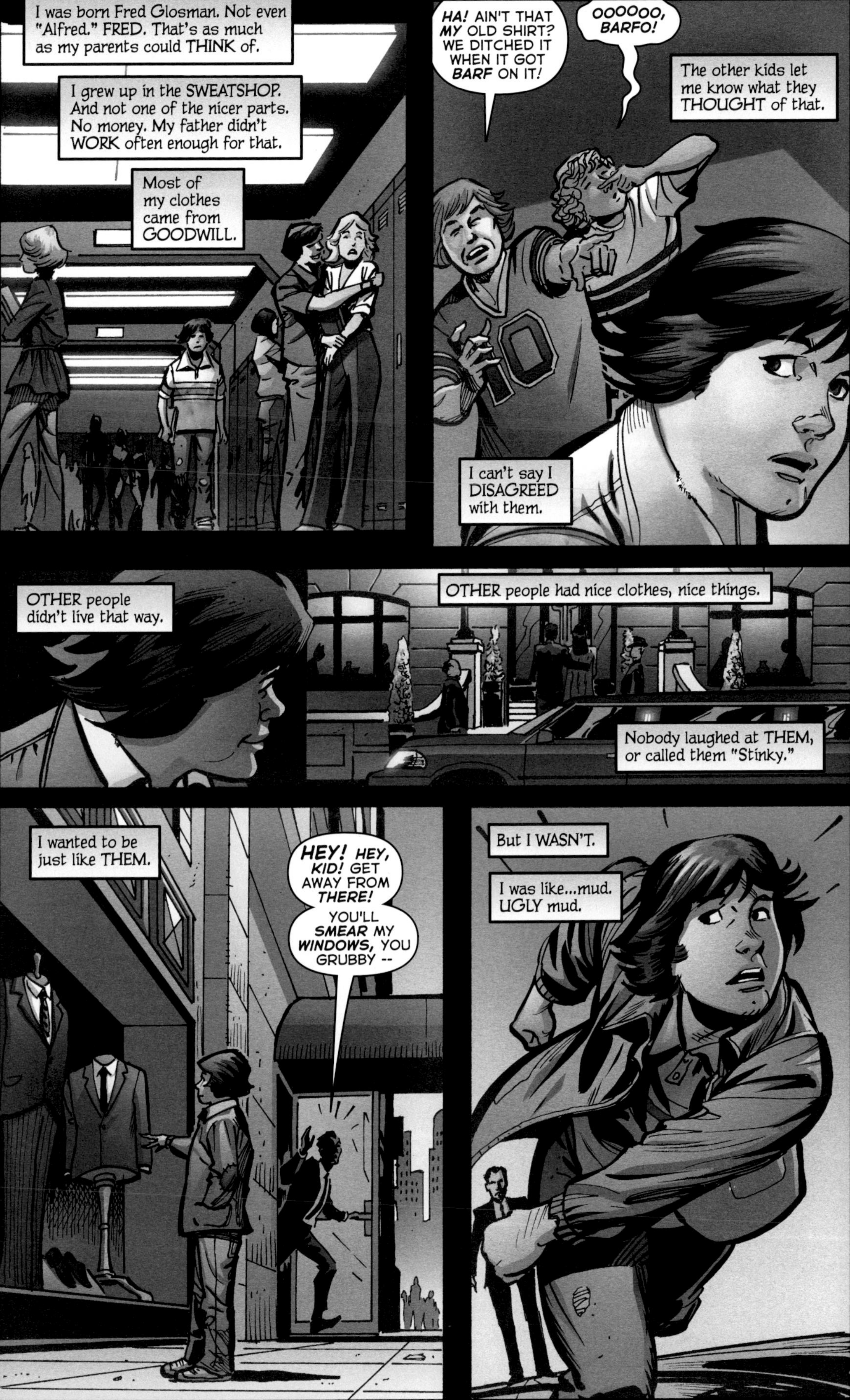

I was born Fred Glosman. Not even "Alfred." FRED. That's as much as my parents could THINK of.
I grew up in the SWEATSHOP. And not one of the nicer parts. No money. My father didn't WORK often enough for that.
Most of my clothes came from GOODWILL.
HA! AIN'T THAT MY OLD SHIRT? WE DITCHED IT WHEN IT GOT BARF ON IT!
OOOOOO, BARFO!
The other kids let me know what they THOUGHT of that.
I can't say I DISAGREED with them.
OTHER people didn't live that way.
OTHER people had nice clothes, nice things.
Nobody laughed at THEM, or called them "Stinky."
I wanted to be just like THEM.
HEY! HEY, KID! GET AWAY FROM THERE!
YOU'LL SMEAR MY WINDOWS, YOU GRUBBY --
But I WASN'T.
I was like...mud. UGLY mud.

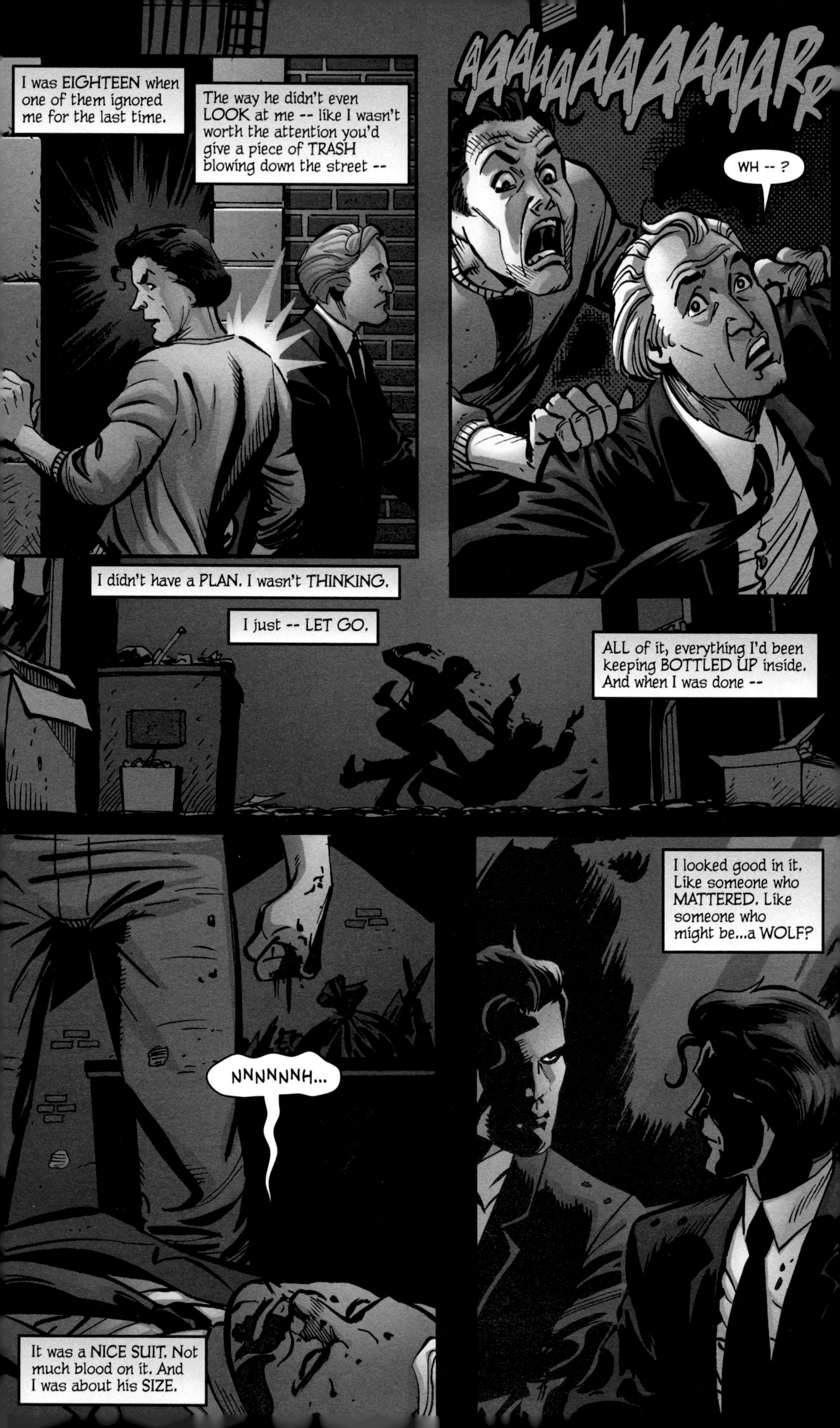
I was EIGHTEEN when one of them ignored me for the last time.
The way he didn't even LOOK at me -- like I wasn't worth the attention you'd give a piece of TRASH blowing down the street --
AAAAAAAAAAAARR
WH -- ?
I didn't have a PLAN. I wasn't THINKING.
I just -- LET GO.
ALL of it, everything I'd been keeping BOTTLED UP inside. And when I was done --
NNNNNNH...
It was a NICE SUIT. Not much blood on it. And I was about his SIZE.
I looked good in it. Like someone who MATTERED. Like someone who might be...a WOLF?

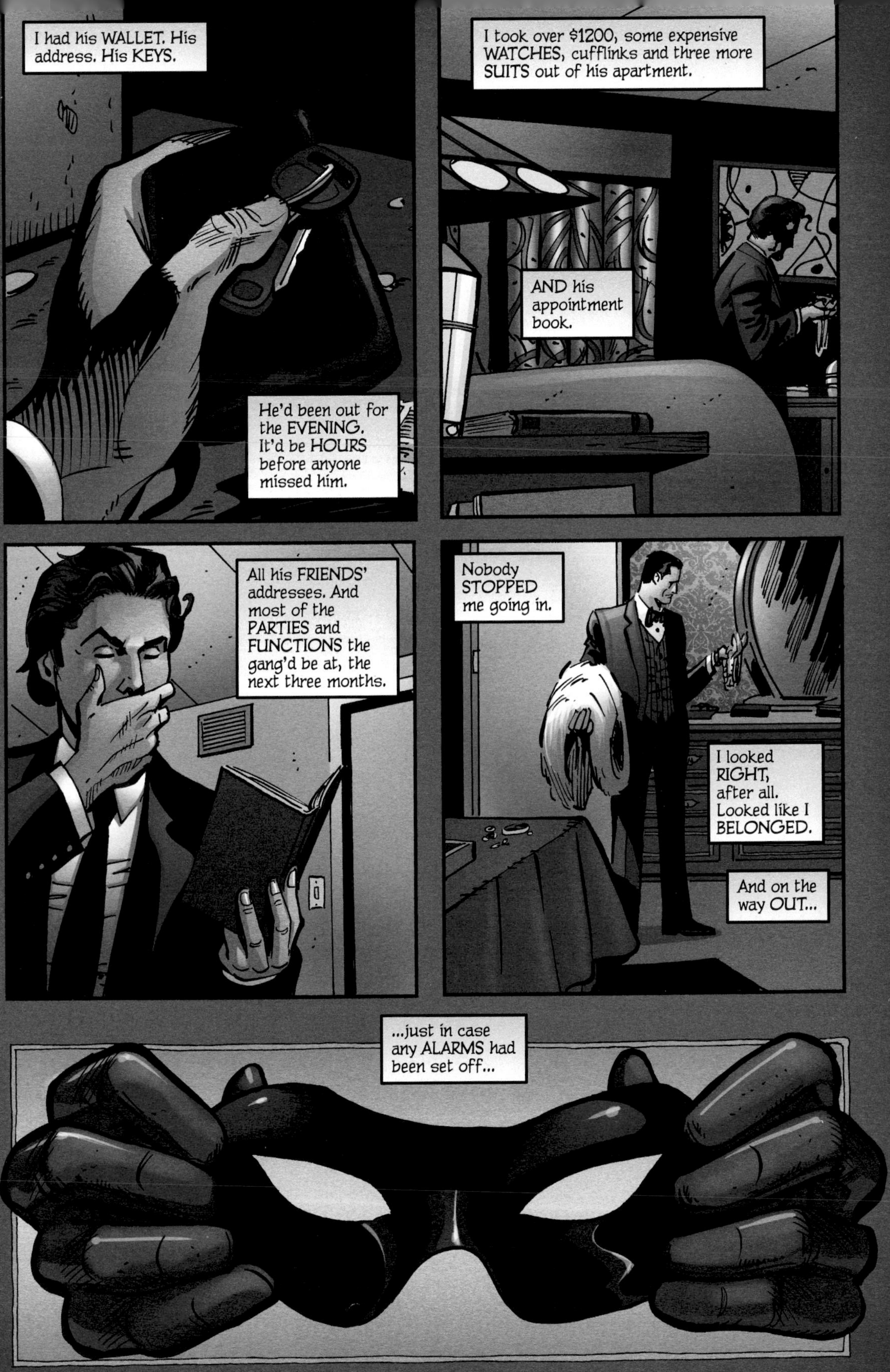
I had his WALLET. His address. His KEYS.
He'd been out for the EVENING. It'd be HOURS before anyone missed him.
I took over $1200, some expensive WATCHES, cufflinks and three more SUITS out of his apartment.
AND his appointment book.
All his FRIENDS' addresses. And most of the PARTIES and FUNCTIONS the gang'd be at, the next three months.
Nobody STOPPED me going in.
I looked RIGHT, after all. Looked like I BELONGED.
And on the way OUT...
...just in case any ALARMS had been set off...

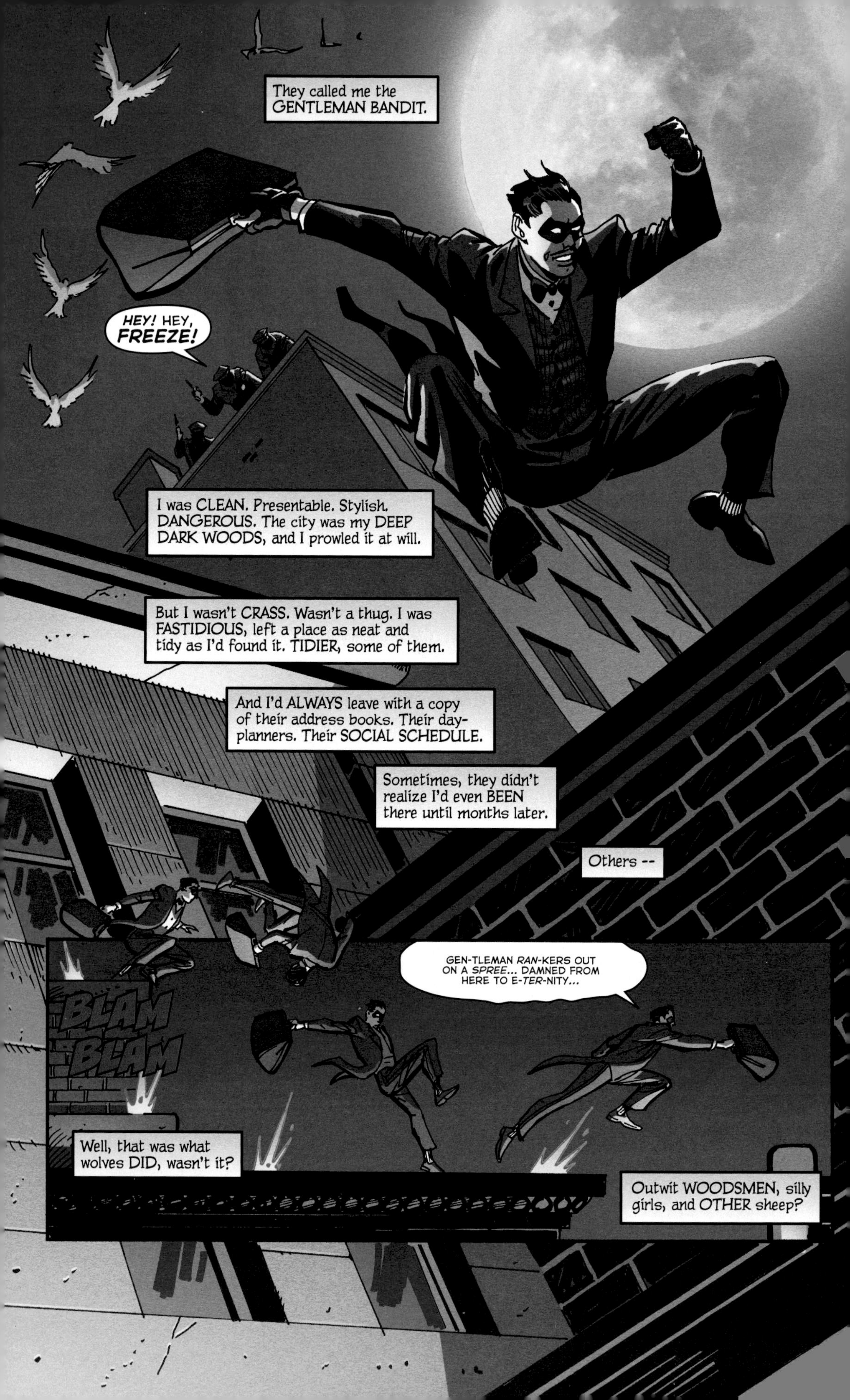
They called me the GENTLEMAN BANDIT.
HEY! HEY, FREEZE!
I was CLEAN. Presentable. Stylish. DANGEROUS. The city was my DEEP DARK WOODS, and I prowled it at will.
But I wasn't CRASS. Wasn't a thug. I was FASTIDIOUS, left a place as neat and tidy as I'd found it. TIDIER, some of them.
And I'd ALWAYS leave with a copy of their address books. Their day-planners. Their SOCIAL SCHEDULE.
Sometimes, they didn't realize I'd even BEEN there until months later.
Others --
GEN-TLEMAN RAN-KERS OUT ON A SPREE... DAMNED FROM HERE TO E-TER-NITY...
BLAM
BLAM
Well, that was what wolves DID, wasn't it?
Outwit WOODSMEN, silly girls, and OTHER sheep?

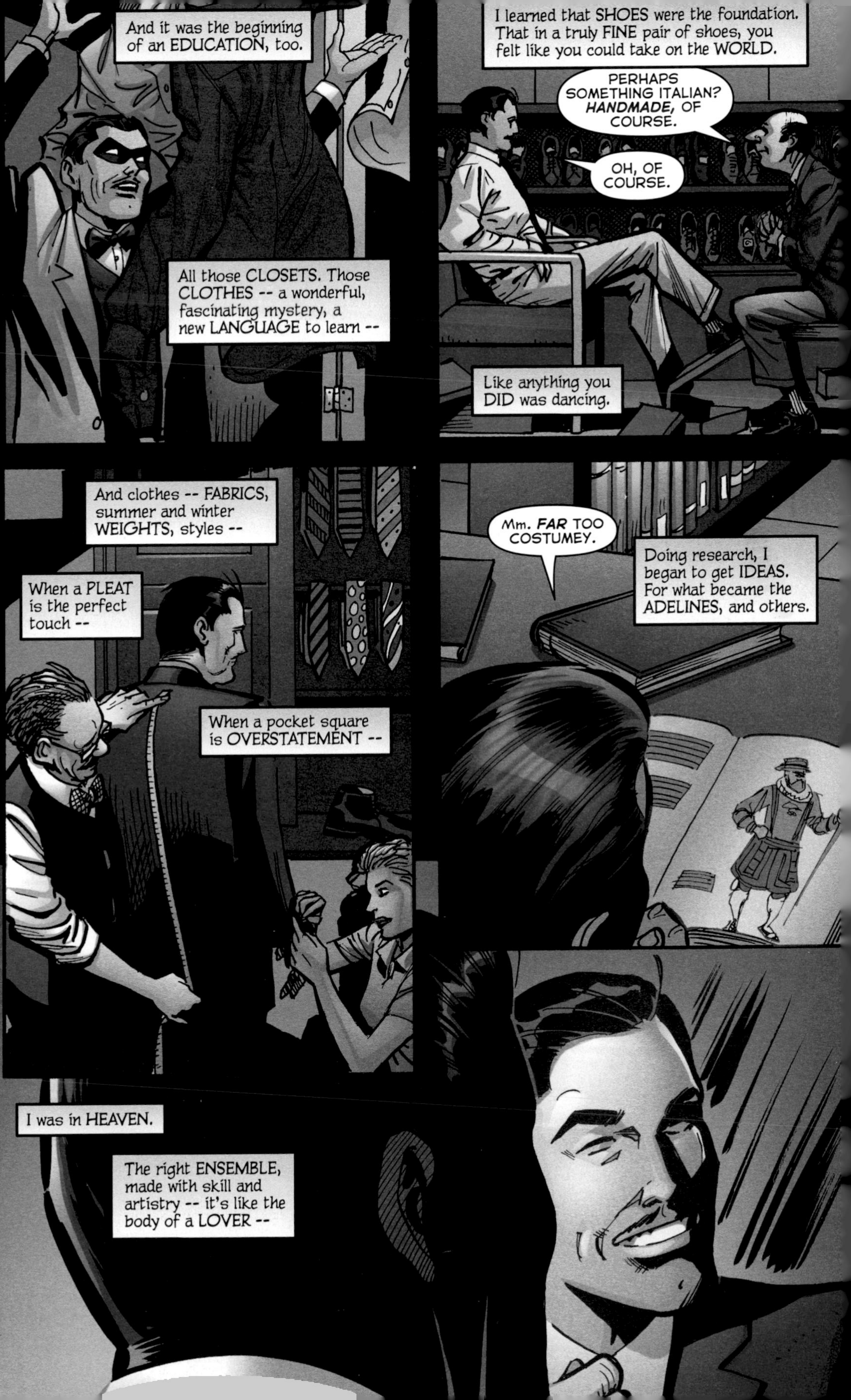
And it was the beginning of an EDUCATION, too.
All those CLOSETS. Those CLOTHES -- a wonderful, fascinating mystery, a new LANGUAGE to learn --
I learned that SHOES were the foundation. That in a truly FINE pair of shoes, you felt like you could take on the WORLD.
PERHAPS SOMETHING ITALIAN? HANDMADE, OF COURSE.
OH, OF COURSE.
Like anything you DID was dancing.
And clothes -- FABRICS, summer and winter WEIGHTS, styles --
When a PLEAT is the perfect touch --
When a pocket square is OVERSTATEMENT --
Mm. FAR TOO COSTUMEY.
Doing research, I began to get IDEAS. For what became the ADELINES, and others.
I was in HEAVEN.
The right ENSEMBLE, made with skill and artistry -- it's like the body of a LOVER --

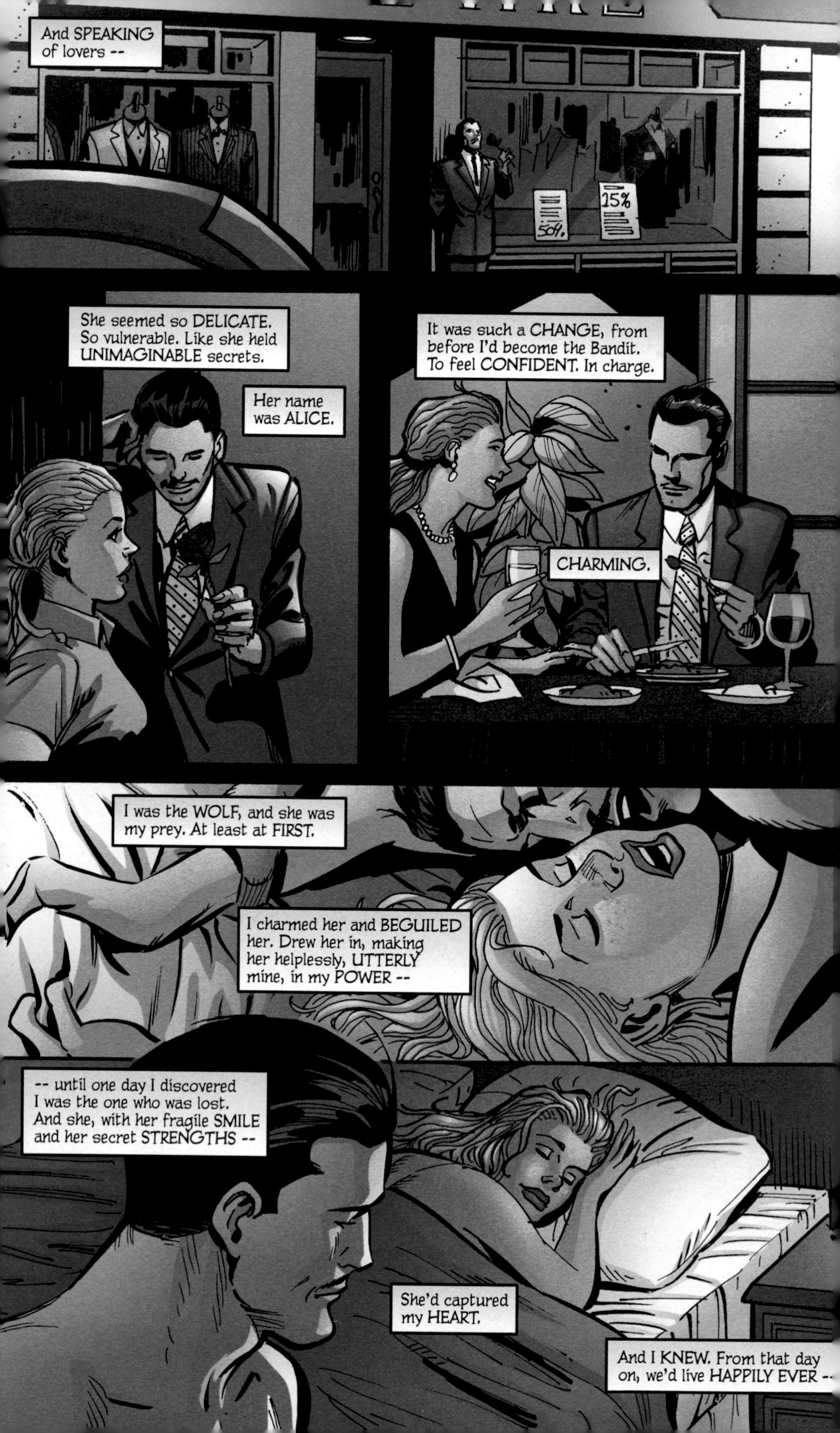
And SPEAKING of lovers --
15%
50%
She seemed so DELICATE. So vulnerable. Like she held UNIMAGINABLE secrets.
Her name was ALICE.
It was such a CHANGE, from before I'd become the Bandit. To feel CONFIDENT. In charge.
CHARMING.
I was the WOLF, and she was my prey. At least at FIRST.
I charmed her and BEGUILED her. Drew her in, making her helplessly, UTTERLY mine, in my POWER --
-- until one day I discovered I was the one who was lost. And she, with her fragile SMILE and her secret STRENGTHS --
She'd captured my HEART.
And I KNEW. From that day on, we'd live HAPPILY EVER --

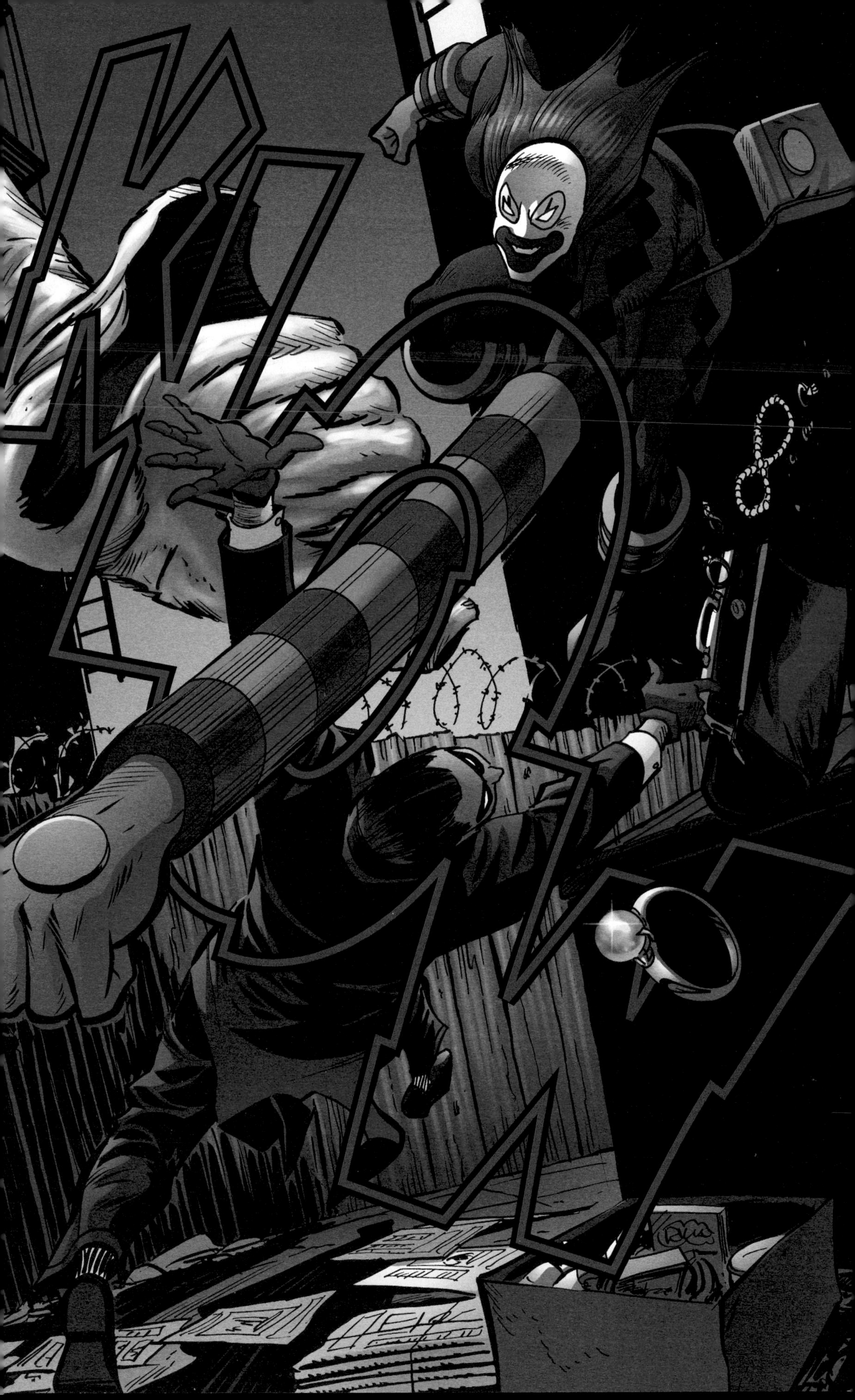

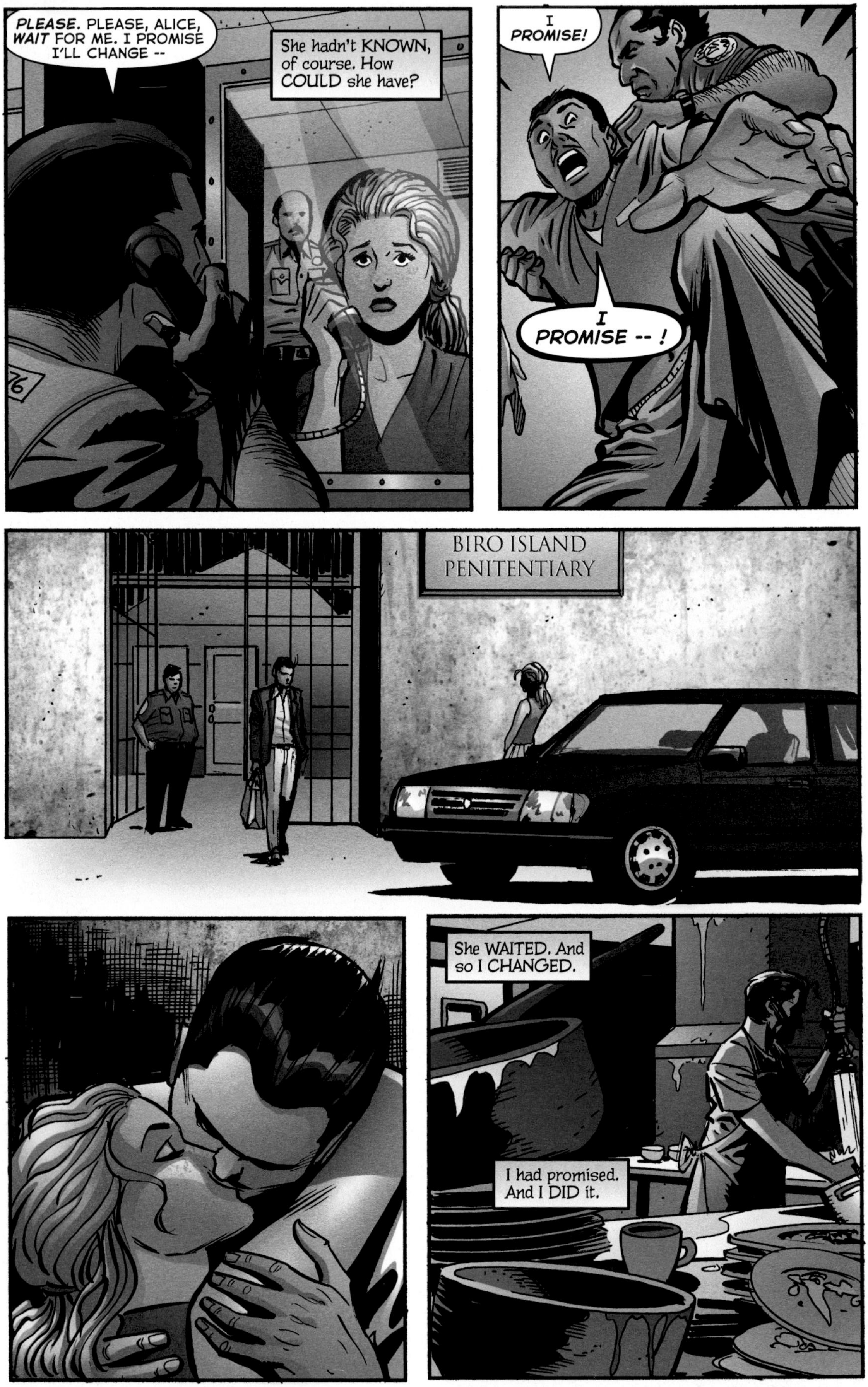
PLEASE. PLEASE, ALICE, WAIT FOR ME. I PROMISE I'LL CHANGE --
She hadn't KNOWN, of course. How COULD she have?
I PROMISE!
I PROMISE -- !
BIRO ISLAND PENITENTIARY
She WAITED. And so I CHANGED.
I had promised. And I DID it.

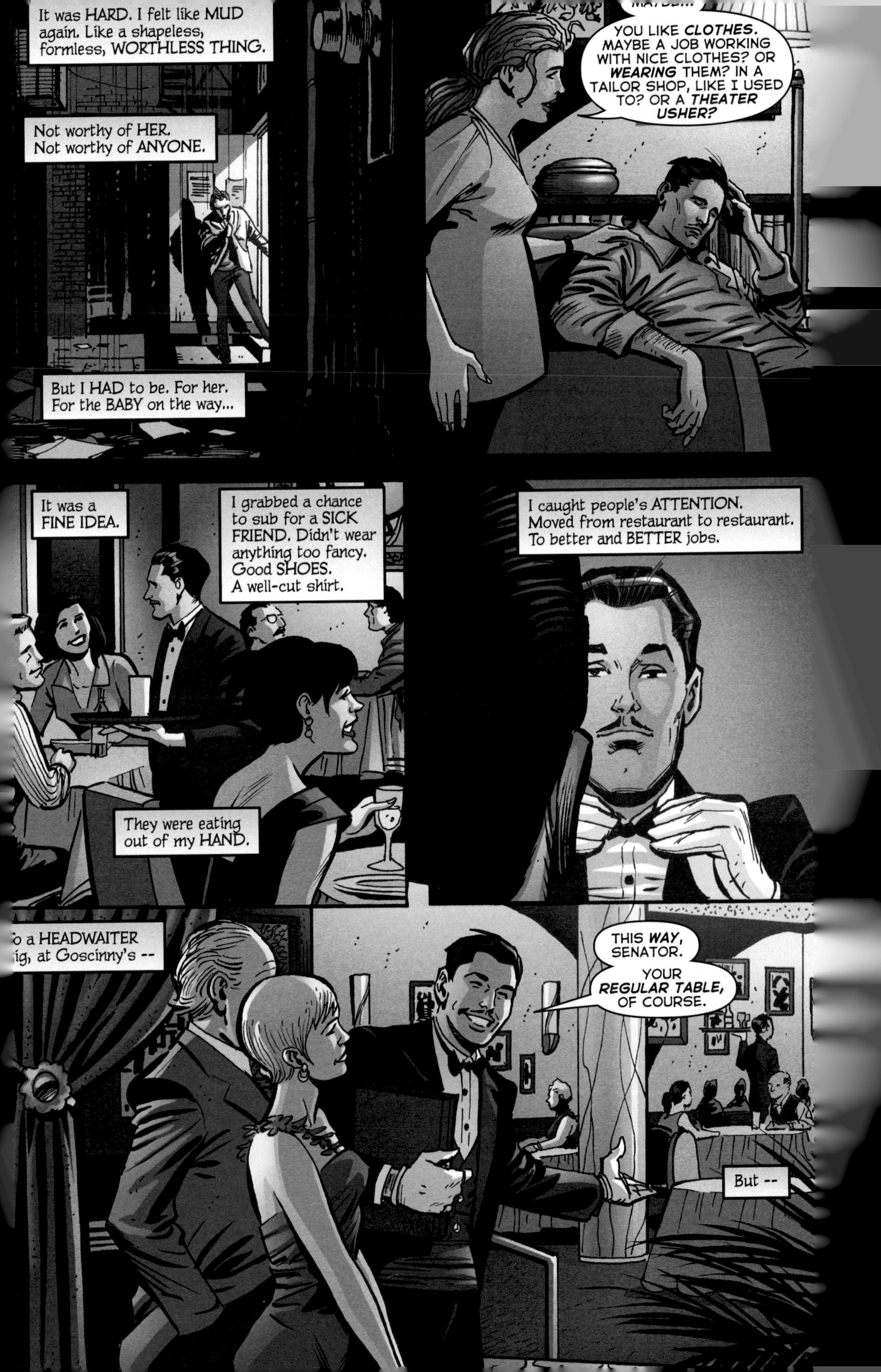
It was HARD. I felt like MUD again. Like a shapeless, formless, WORTHLESS THING.
Not worthy of HER. Not worthy of ANYONE.
But I HAD to be. For her. For the BABY on the way...
YOU LIKE CLOTHES. MAYBE A JOB WORKING WITH NICE CLOTHES? OR WEARING THEM? IN A TAILOR SHOP, LIKE I USED TO? OR A THEATER USHER?
It was a FINE IDEA.
I grabbed a chance to sub for a SICK FRIEND. Didn't wear anything too fancy. Good SHOES. A well-cut shirt.
They were eating out of my HAND.
I caught people's ATTENTION. Moved from restaurant to restaurant. To better and BETTER jobs.
o a HEADWAITER ig, at Goscinny's --
THIS WAY, SENATOR.
YOUR REGULAR TABLE, OF COURSE.
But --

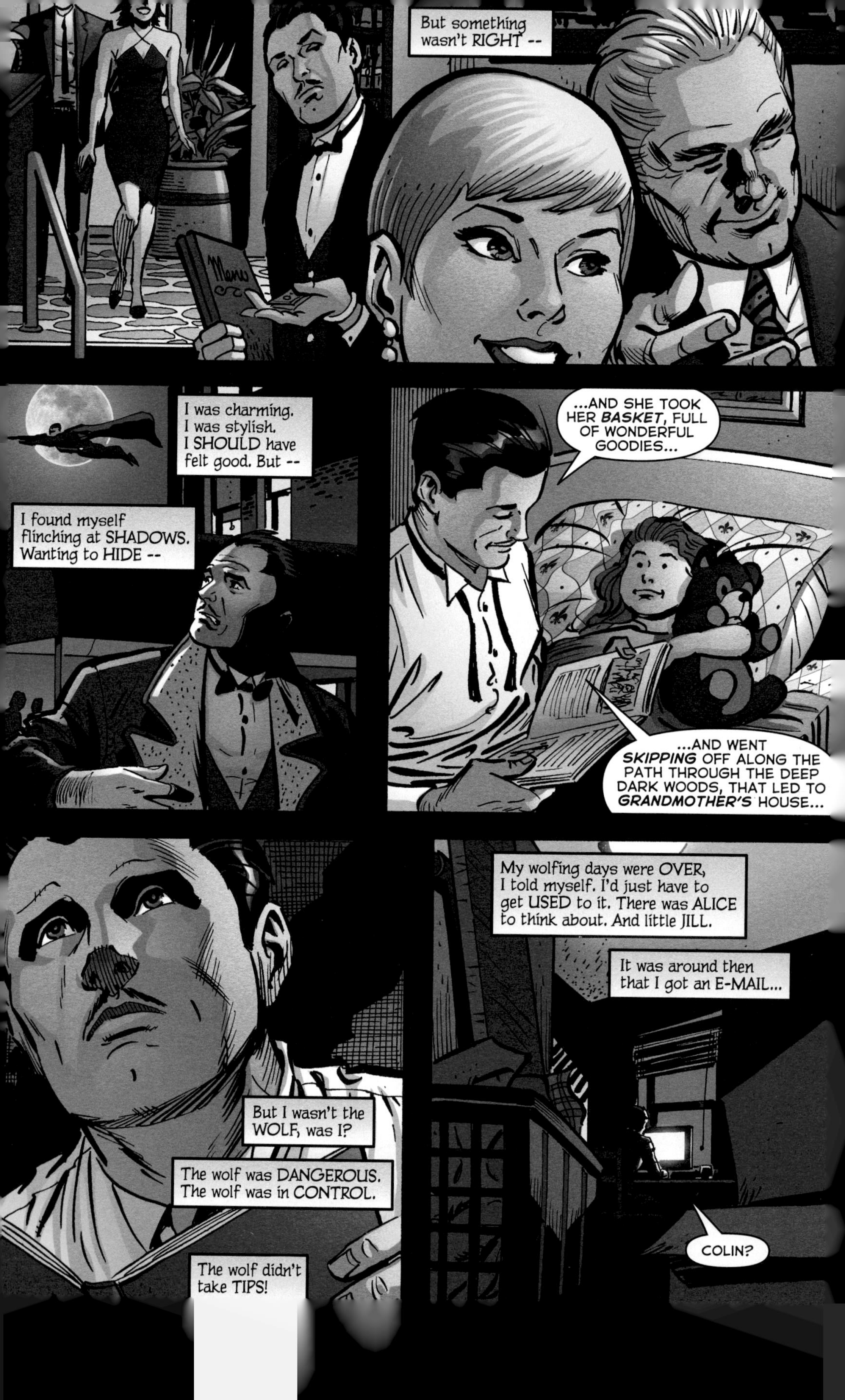
Menu
But something wasn't RIGHT --
I was charming. I was stylish. I SHOULD have felt good. But --
I found myself flinching at SHADOWS. Wanting to HIDE --
...AND SHE TOOK HER *BASKET*, FULL OF WONDERFUL GOODIES...
...AND WENT *SKIPPING* OFF ALONG THE PATH THROUGH THE DEEP DARK WOODS, THAT LED TO *GRANDMOTHER'S* HOUSE...
But I wasn't the WOLF, was I?
The wolf was DANGEROUS. The wolf was in CONTROL.
The wolf didn't take TIPS!
My wolfing days were OVER, I told myself. I'd just have to get USED to it. There was ALICE to think about. And little JILL.
It was around then that I got an E-MAIL...
COLIN?

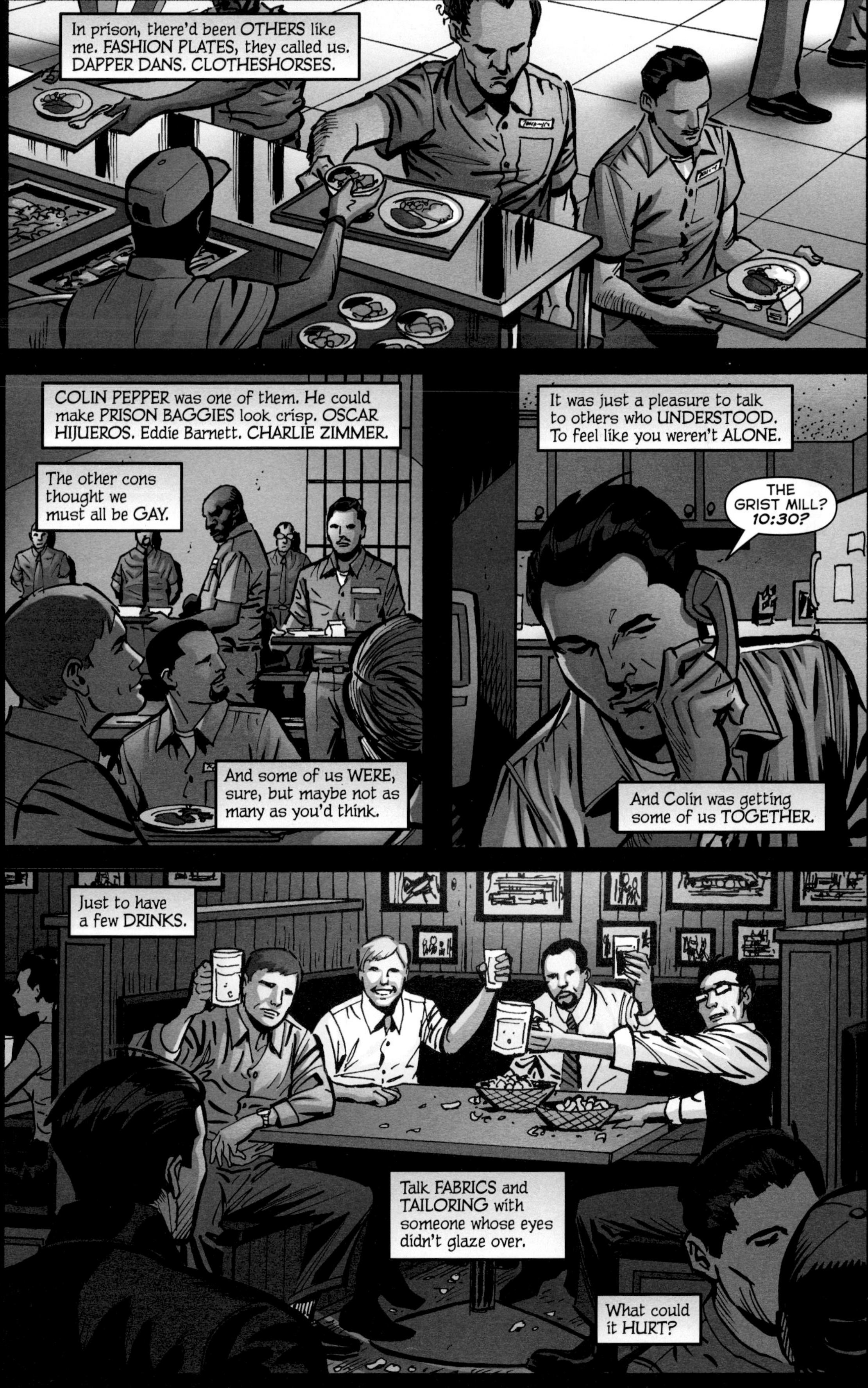
In prison, there'd been OTHERS like me. FASHION PLATES, they called us. DAPPER DANS. CLOTHESHORSES.
COLIN PEPPER was one of them. He could make PRISON BAGGIES look crisp. OSCAR HIJUEROS. Eddie Barnett. CHARLIE ZIMMER.
The other cons thought we must all be GAY.
And some of us WERE, sure, but maybe not as many as you'd think.
It was just a pleasure to talk to others who UNDERSTOOD. To feel like you weren't ALONE.
THE GRIST MILL? 10:30?
And Colin was getting some of us TOGETHER.
Just to have a few DRINKS.
Talk FABRICS and TAILORING with someone whose eyes didn't glaze over.
What could it HURT?

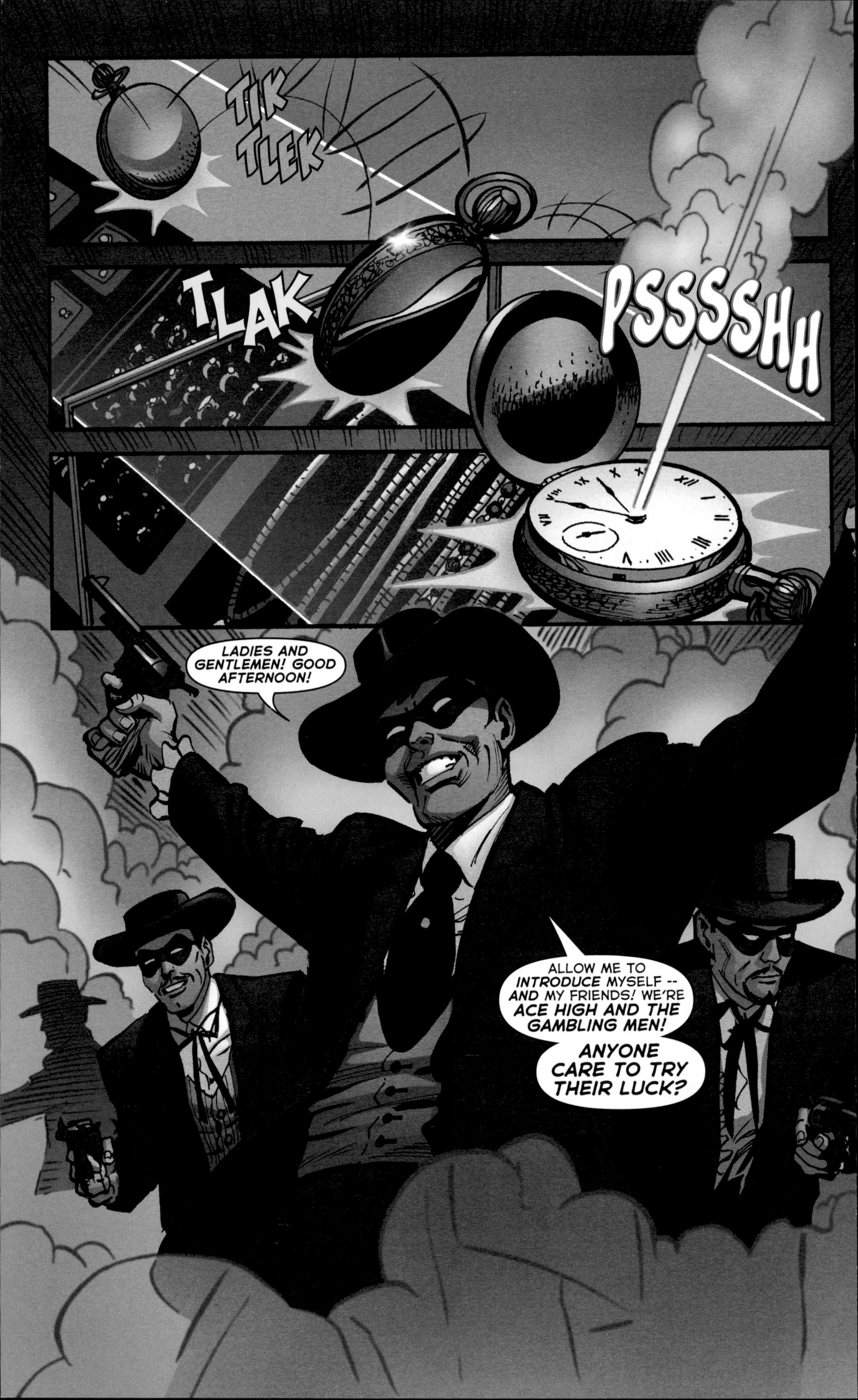
TIK
TLEK
TLAK
PSSSSHH
LADIES AND GENTLEMEN! GOOD AFTERNOON!
ALLOW ME TO INTRODUCE MYSELF -- AND MY FRIENDS! WE'RE ACE HIGH AND THE GAMBLING MEN!
ANYONE CARE TO TRY THEIR LUCK?

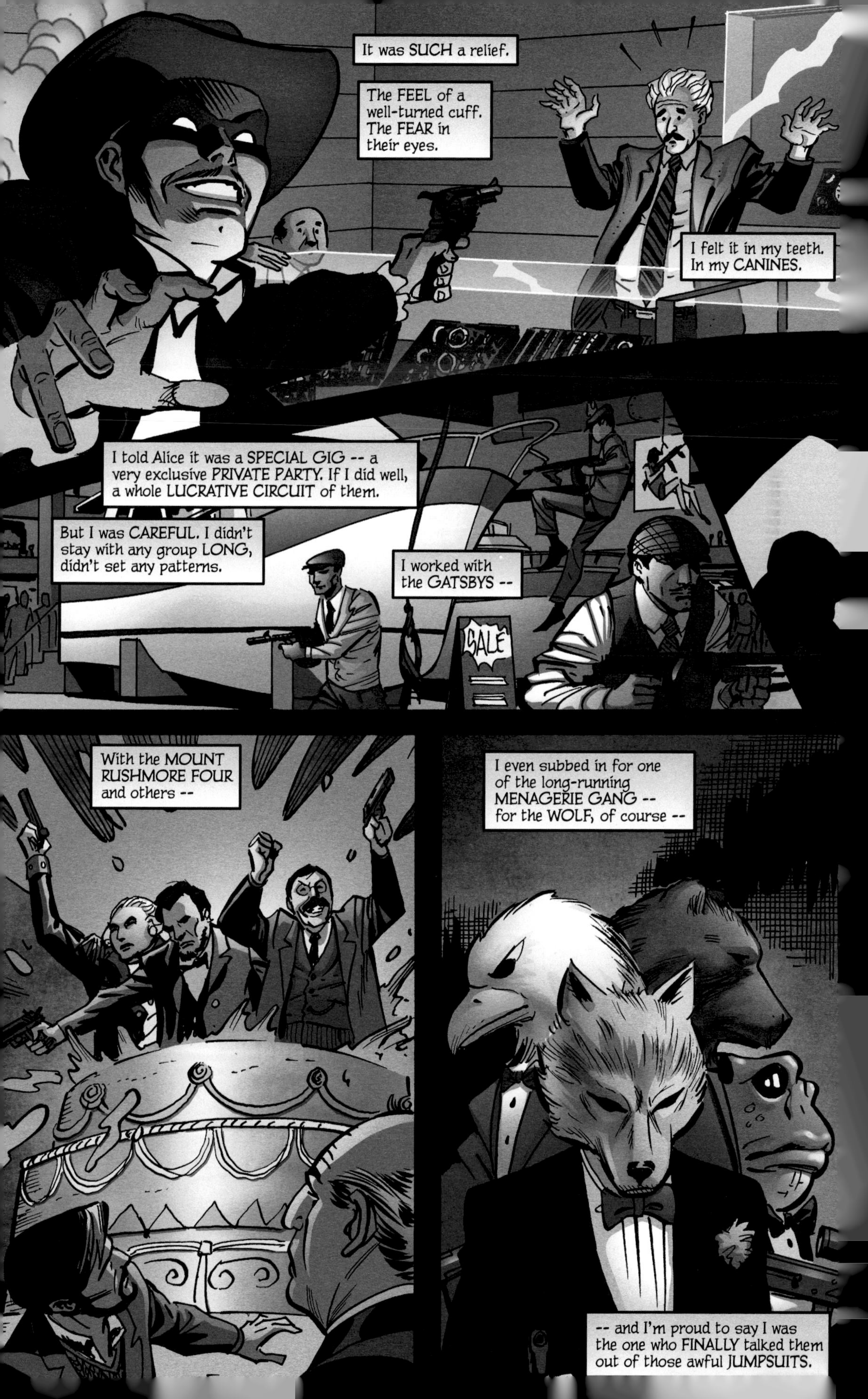
It was SUCH a relief.
The FEEL of a well-turned cuff. The FEAR in their eyes.
I felt it in my teeth. In my CANINES.
I told Alice it was a SPECIAL GIG -- a very exclusive PRIVATE PARTY. If I did well, a whole LUCRATIVE CIRCUIT of them.
But I was CAREFUL. I didn't stay with any group LONG, didn't set any patterns.
I worked with the GATSBYS --
SALE
With the MOUNT RUSHMORE FOUR and others --
I even subbed in for one of the long-running MENAGERIE GANG -- for the WOLF, of course --
-- and I'm proud to say I was the one who FINALLY talked them out of those awful JUMPSUITS.

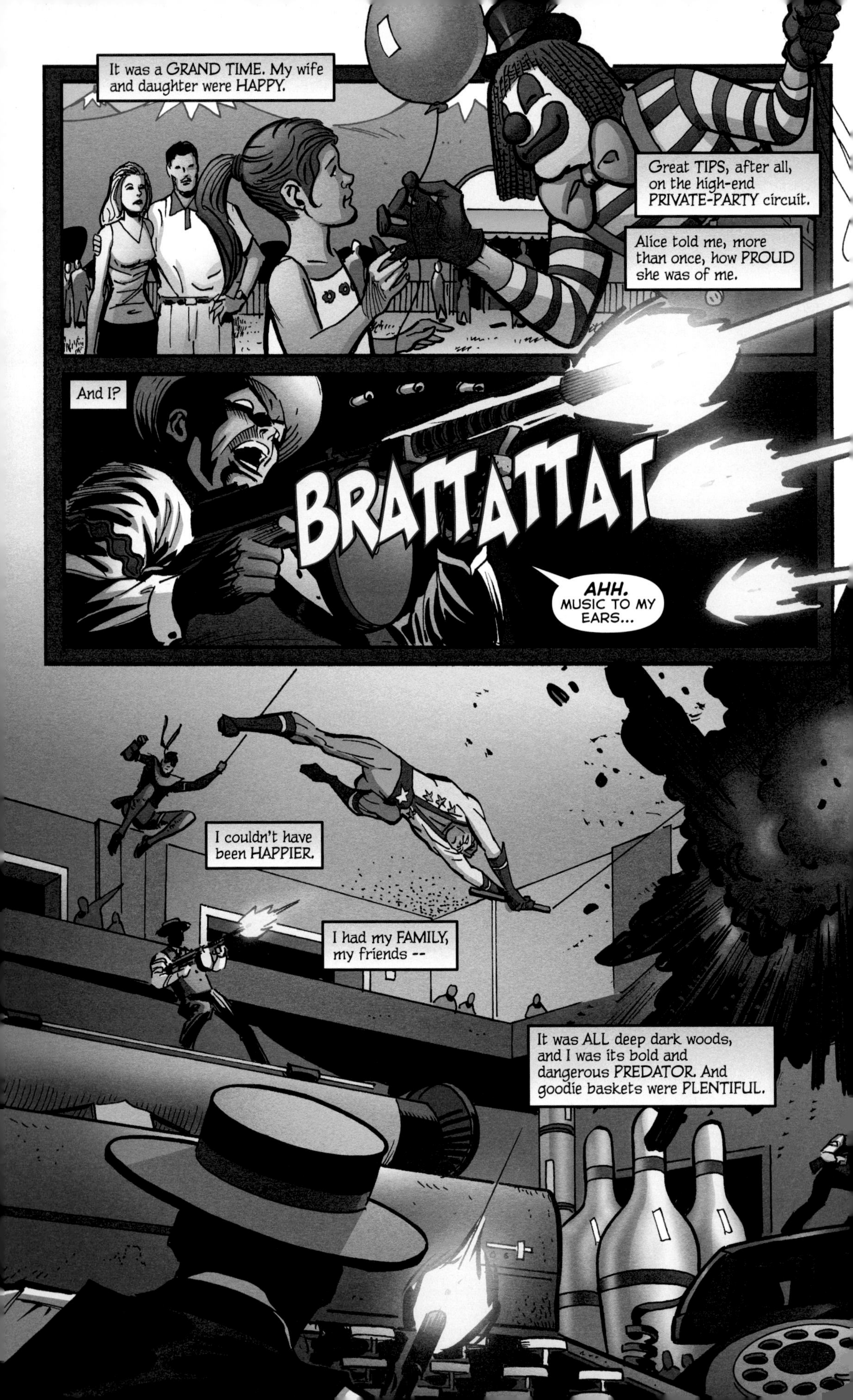
It was a GRAND TIME. My wife and daughter were HAPPY.
Great TIPS, after all, on the high-end PRIVATE-PARTY circuit.
Alice told me, more than once, how PROUD she was of me.
And I?
BRATTATTAT
AHH. MUSIC TO MY EARS...
I couldn't have been HAPPIER.
I had my FAMILY, my friends --
It was ALL deep dark woods, and I was its bold and dangerous PREDATOR. And goodie baskets were PLENTIFUL.

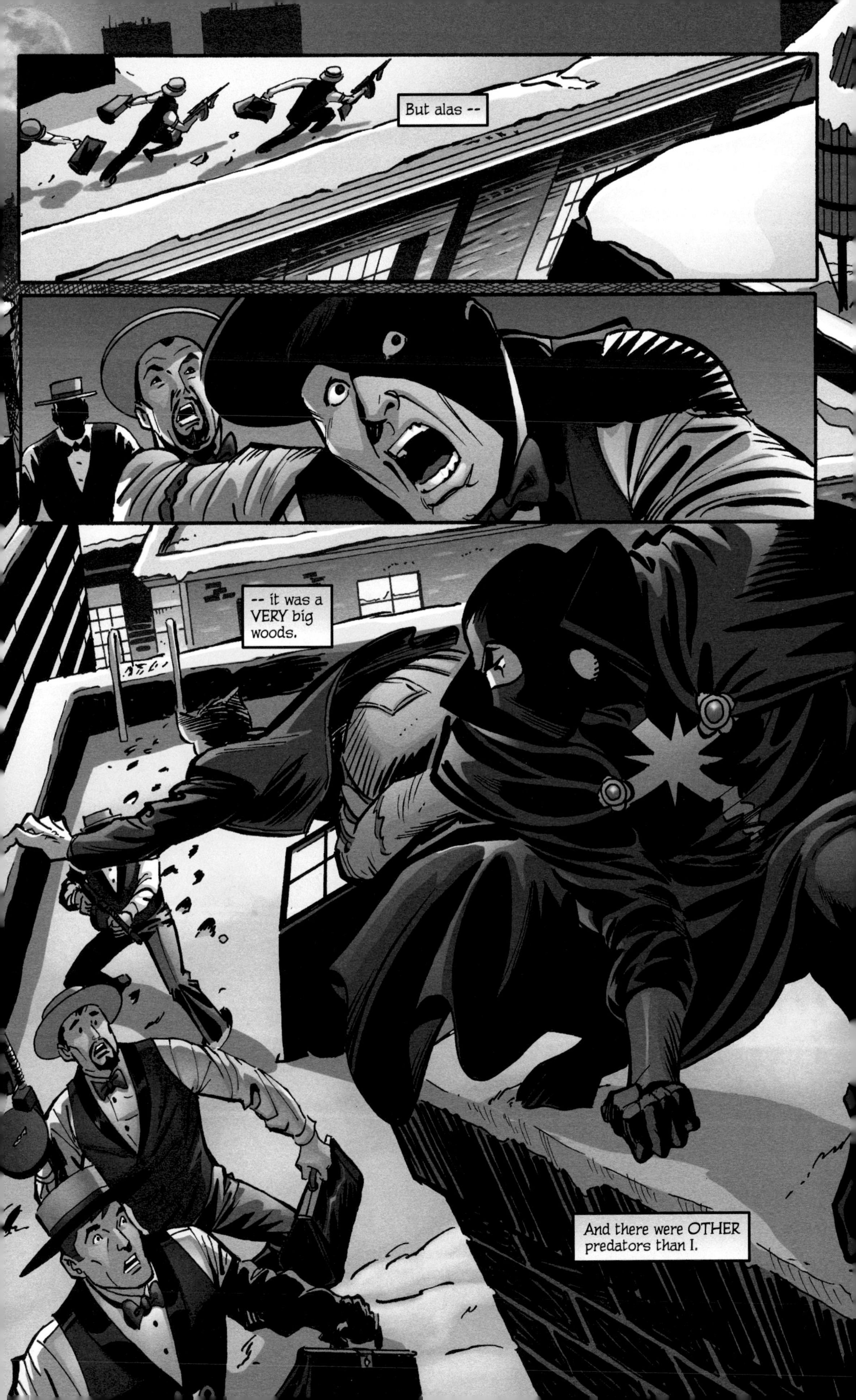
But alas --
-- it was a VERY big woods.
And there were OTHER predators than I.

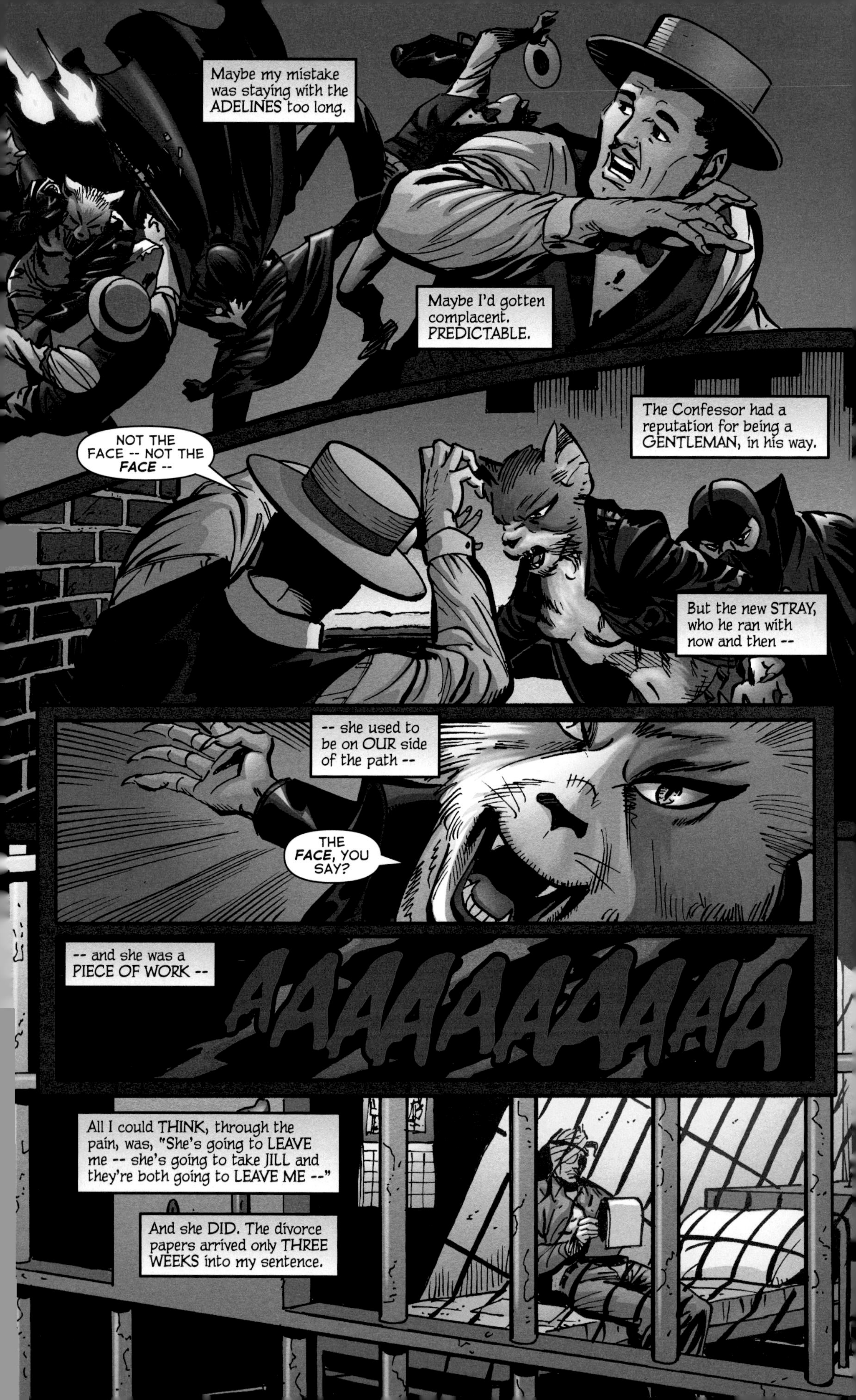
Maybe my mistake was staying with the ADELINES too long.
Maybe I'd gotten complacent. PREDICTABLE.
The Confessor had a reputation for being a GENTLEMAN, in his way.
NOT THE FACE -- NOT THE FACE --
But the new STRAY, who he ran with now and then --
-- she used to be on OUR side of the path --
THE FACE, YOU SAY?
-- and she was a PIECE OF WORK --
AAAAAAAAAAA
All I could THINK, through the pain, was, "She's going to LEAVE me -- she's going to take JILL and they're both going to LEAVE ME --"
And she DID. The divorce papers arrived only THREE WEEKS into my sentence.

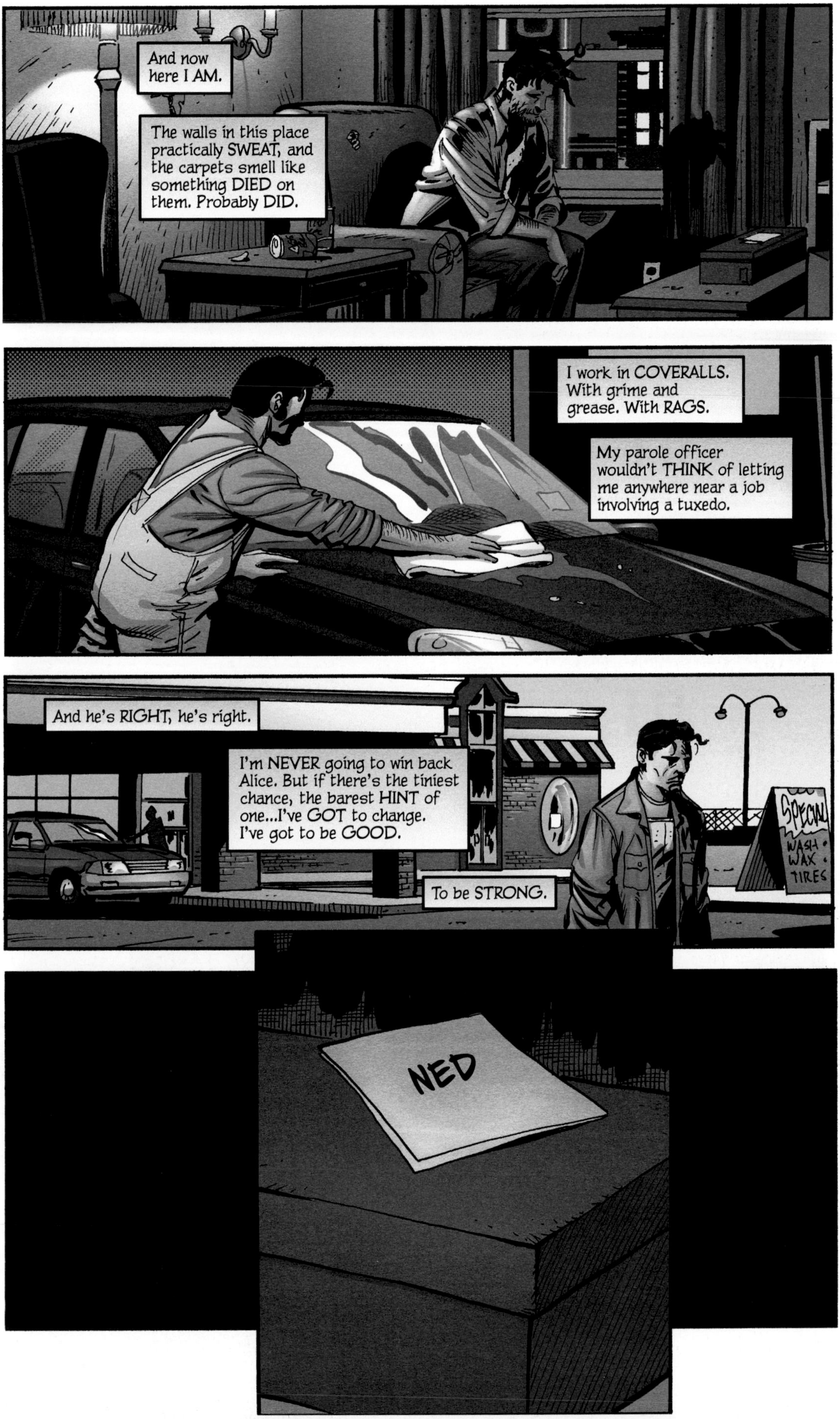
And now here I AM.
The walls in this place practically SWEAT, and the carpets smell like something DIED on them. Probably DID.
I work in COVERALLS. With grime and grease. With RAGS.
My parole officer wouldn't THINK of letting me anywhere near a job involving a tuxedo.
And he's RIGHT, he's right.
I'm NEVER going to win back Alice. But if there's the tiniest chance, the barest HINT of one...I've GOT to change. I've got to be GOOD.
To be STRONG.
SPECIAL
WASH
WAX
TIRES
NED

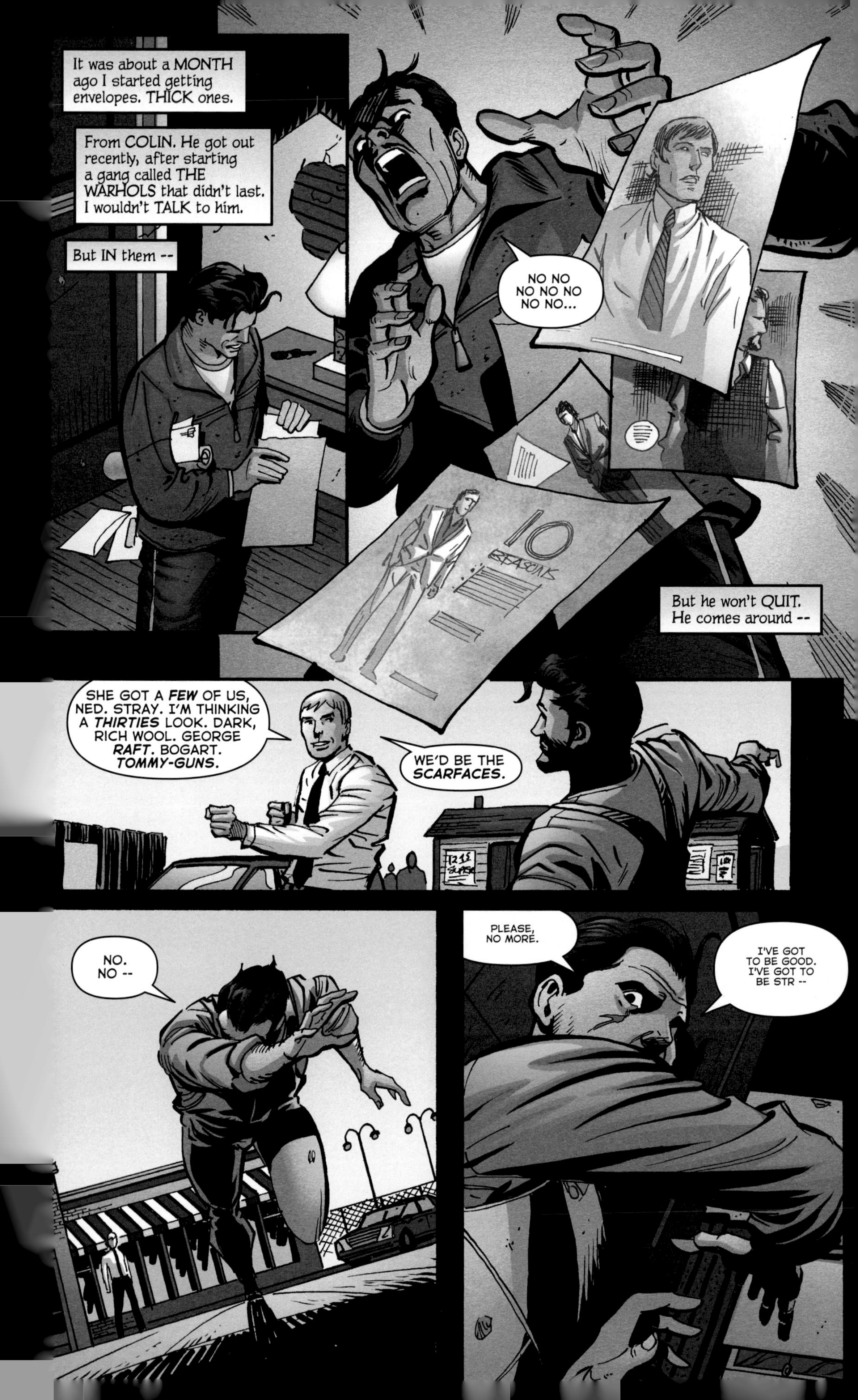
It was about a MONTH ago I started getting envelopes. THICK ones.
From COLIN. He got out recently, after starting a gang called THE WARHOLS that didn't last. I wouldn't TALK to him.
But IN them --
NO NO NO NO NO NO NO...
10 REASONS
But he won't QUIT. He comes around --
SHE GOT A FEW OF US, NED. STRAY. I'M THINKING A THIRTIES LOOK. DARK, RICH WOOL. GEORGE RAFT. BOGART. TOMMY-GUNS.
WE'D BE THE SCARFACES.
NO. NO --
PLEASE, NO MORE.
I'VE GOT TO BE GOOD. I'VE GOT TO BE STR --

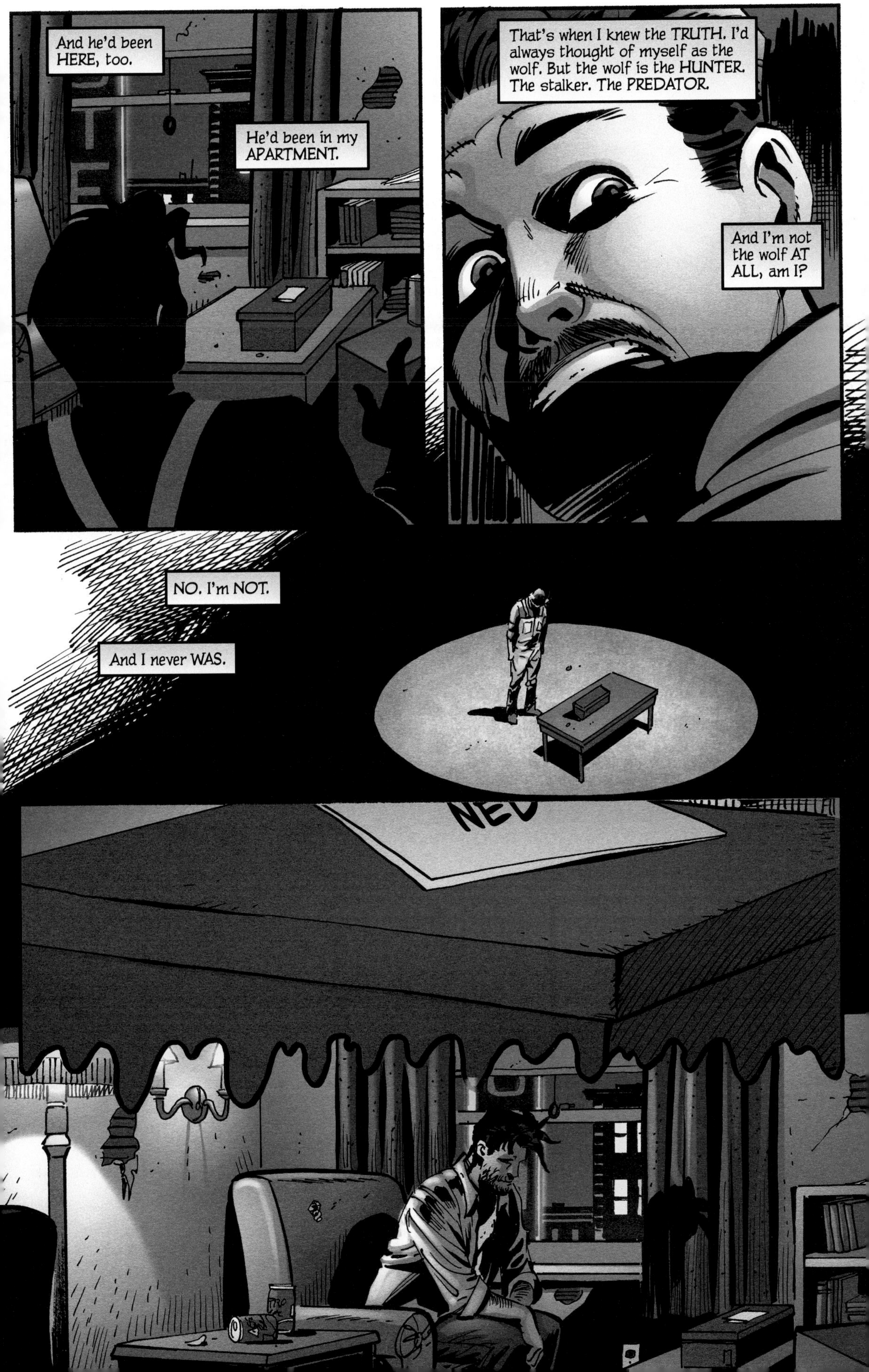
And he'd been HERE, too.
He'd been in my APARTMENT.
That's when I knew the TRUTH. I'd always thought of myself as the wolf. But the wolf is the HUNTER. The stalker. The PREDATOR.
And I'm not the wolf AT ALL, am I?
NO. I'm NOT.
And I never WAS.

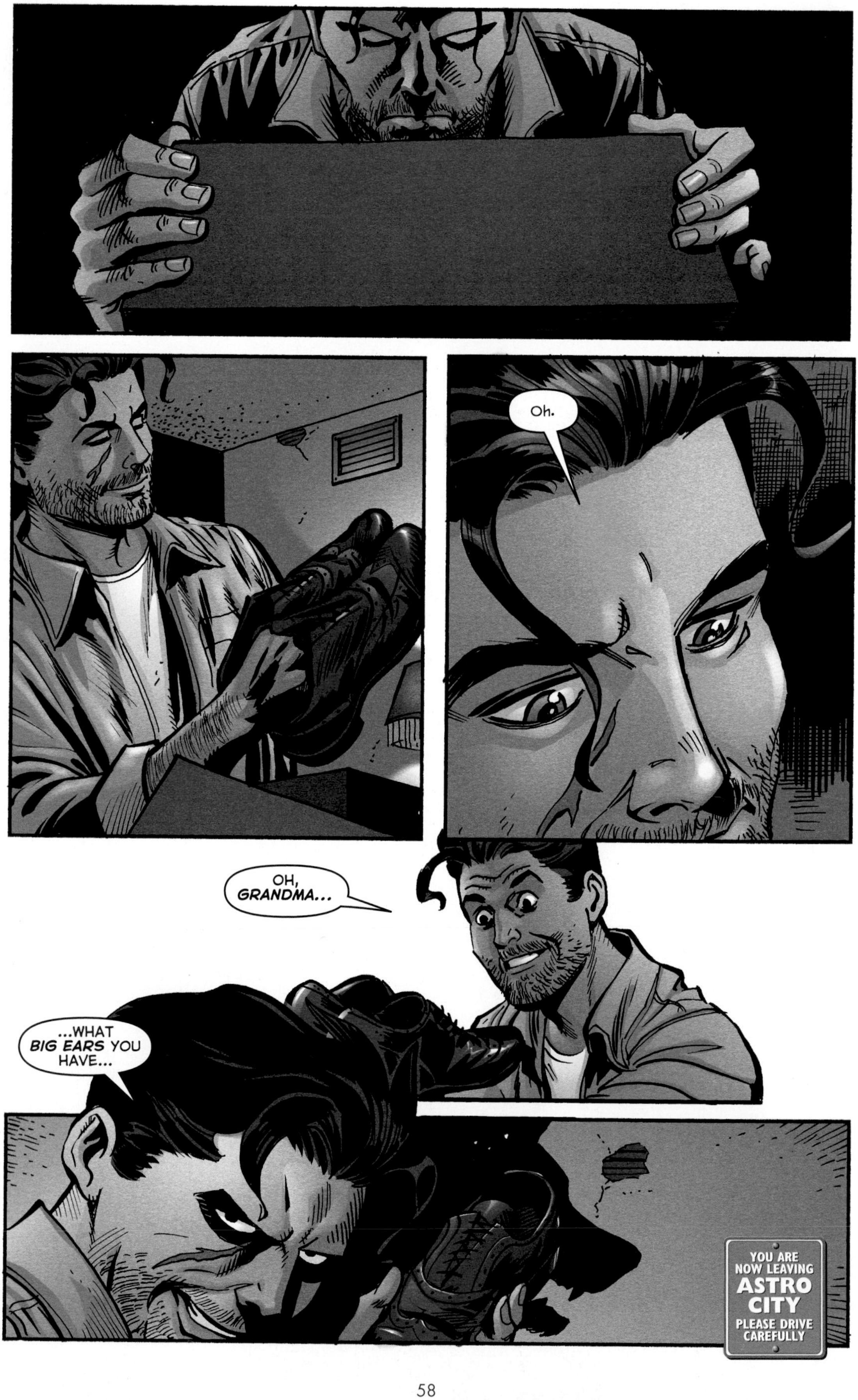
Oh.
OH, GRANDMA...
...WHAT BIG EARS YOU HAVE...
YOU ARE NOW LEAVING ASTRO CITY PLEASE DRIVE CAREFULLY

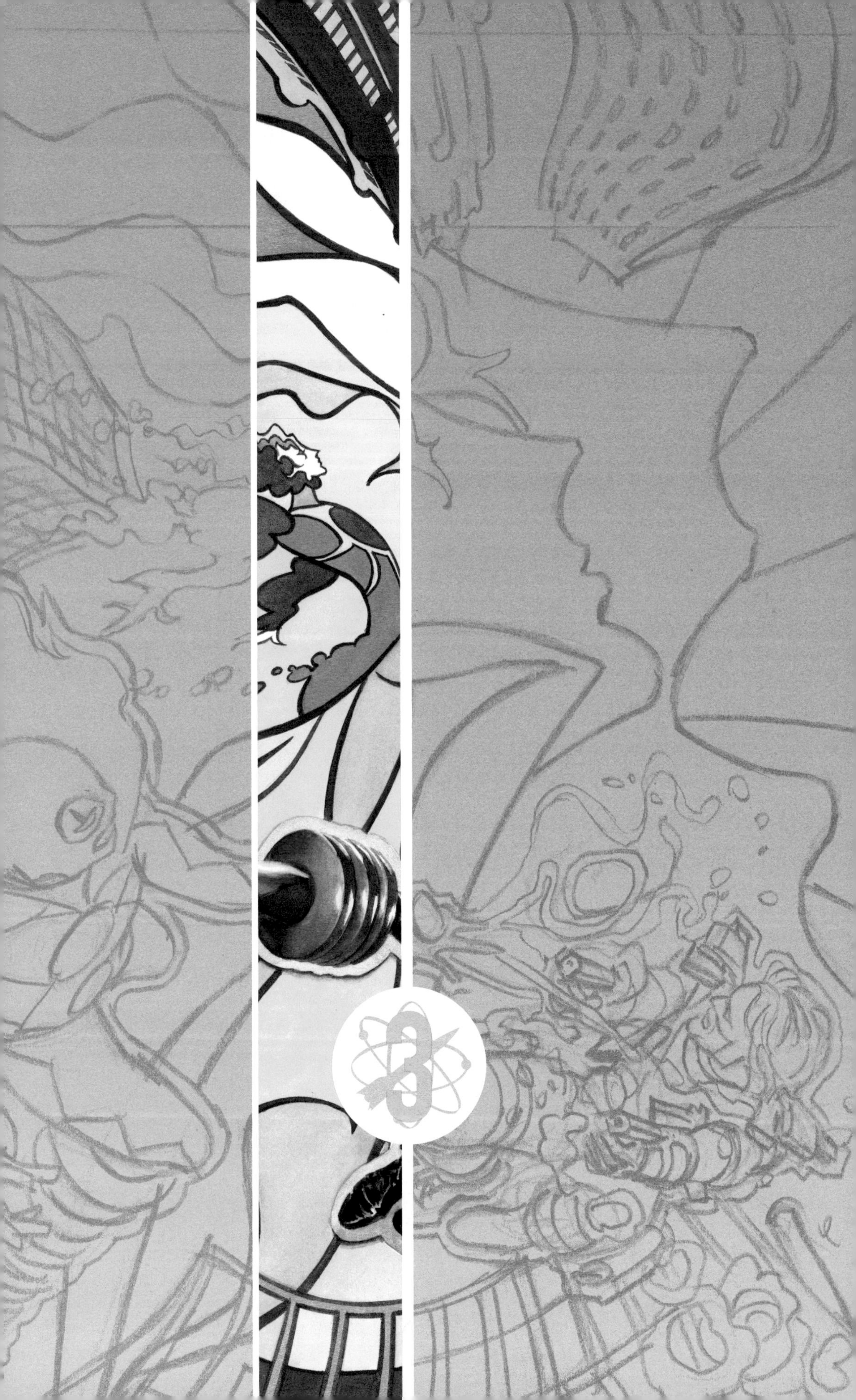
3

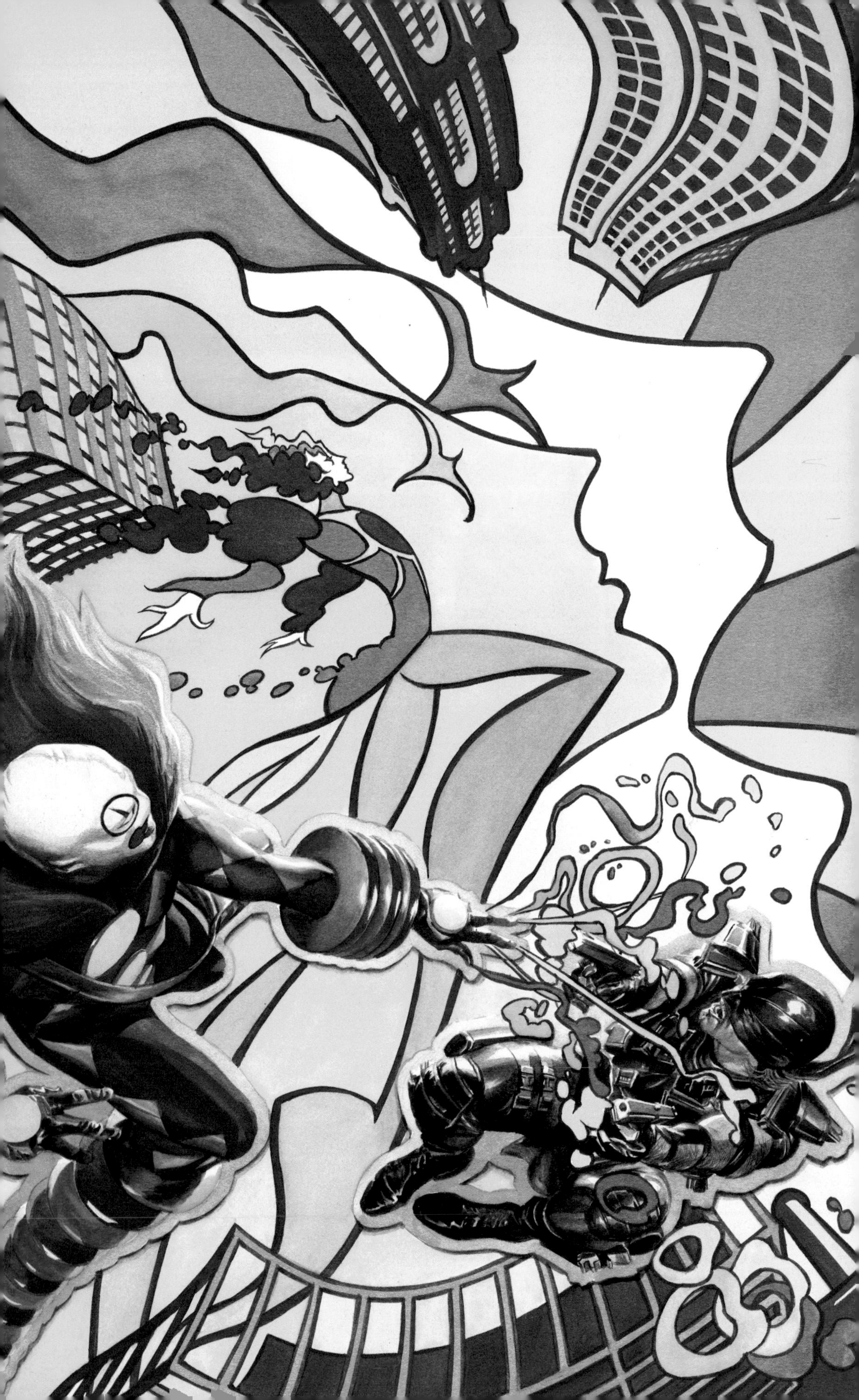

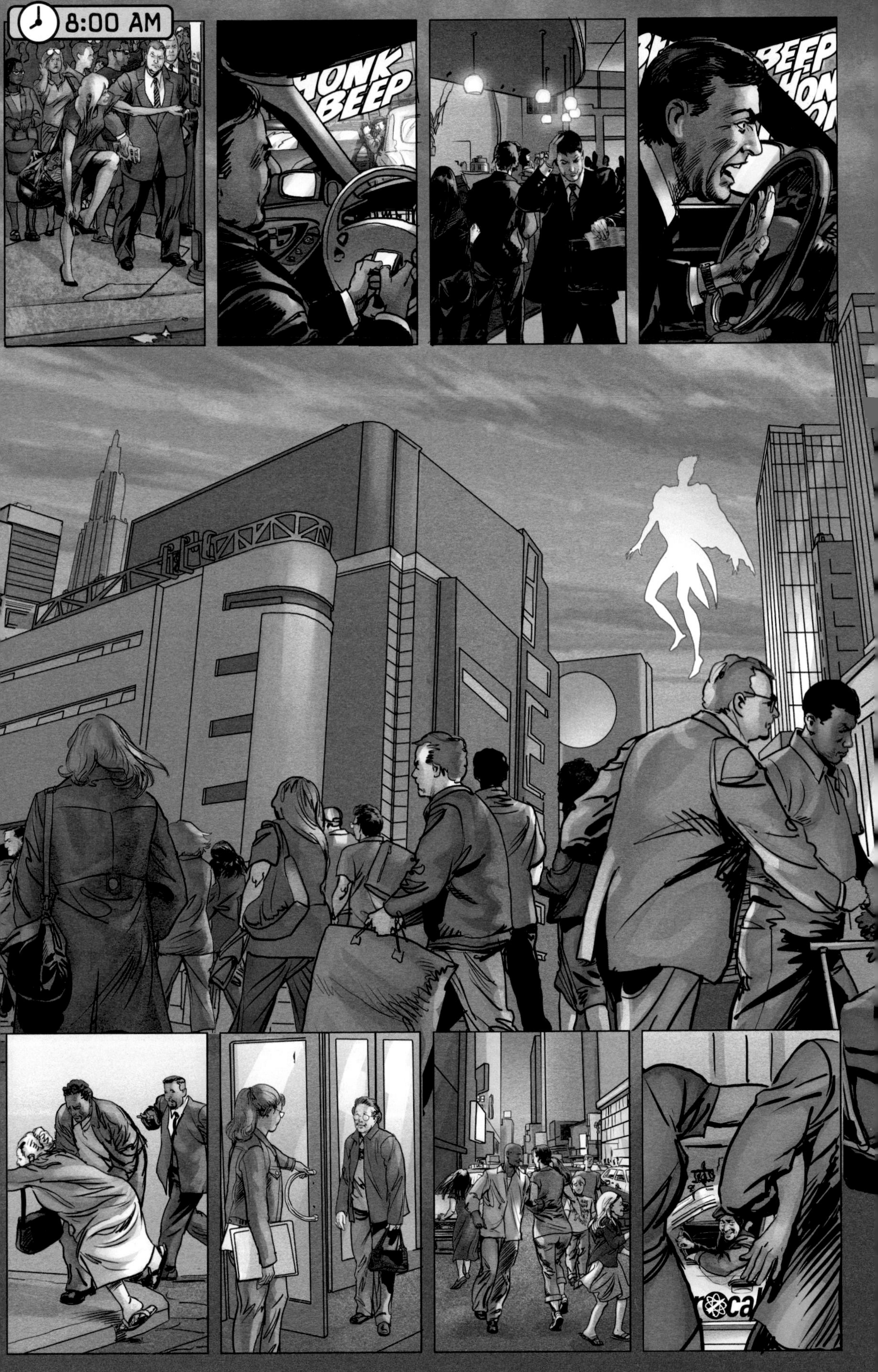
8:00 AM
HONK
BEEP
BEEP
HONK

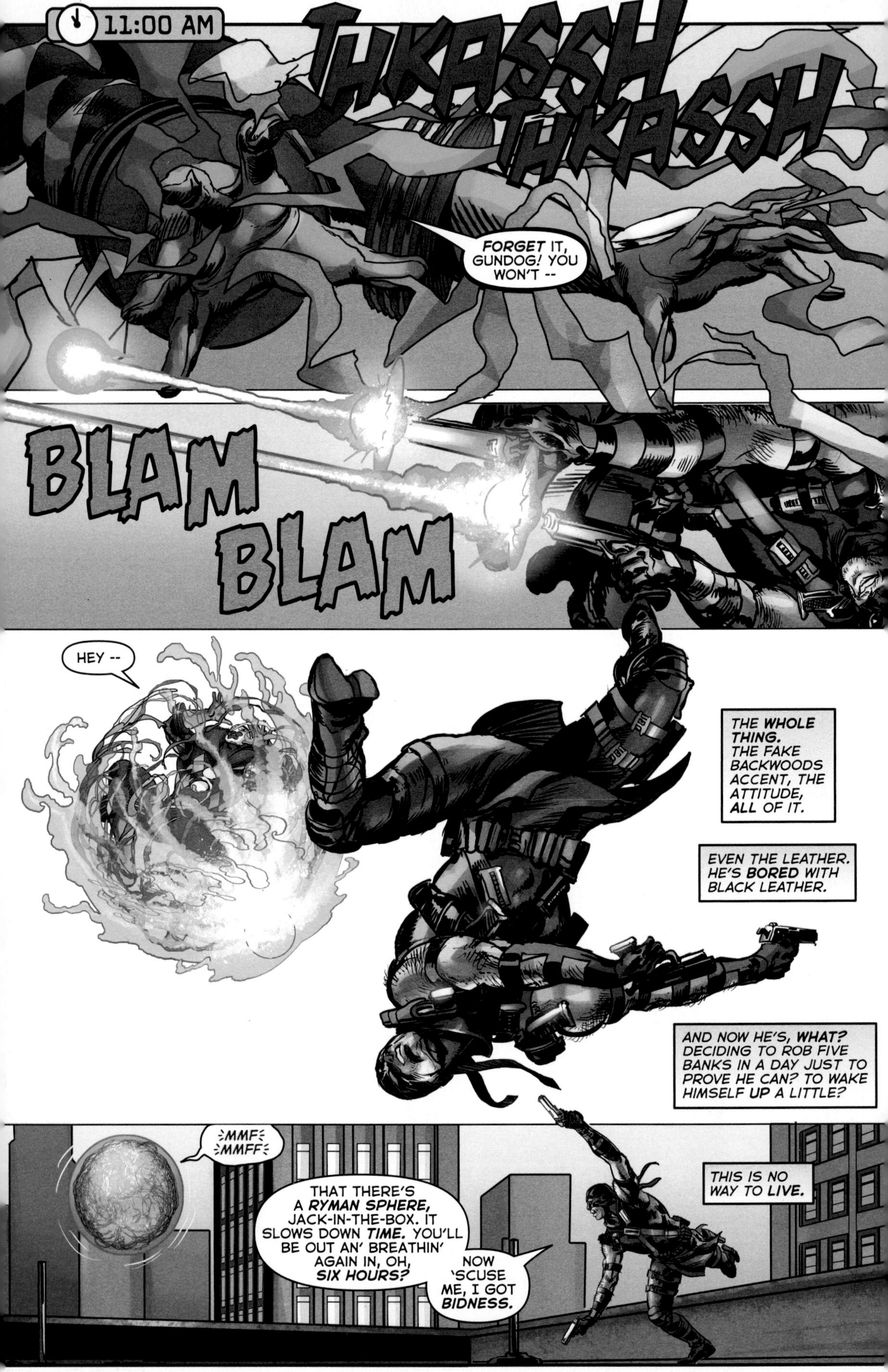
11:00 AM
THKASSH THKASSH
FORGET IT, GUNDOG! YOU WON'T --
BLAM BLAM
HEY --
THE WHOLE THING. THE FAKE BACKWOODS ACCENT, THE ATTITUDE, ALL OF IT.
EVEN THE LEATHER. HE'S BORED WITH BLACK LEATHER.
AND NOW HE'S, WHAT? DECIDING TO ROB FIVE BANKS IN A DAY JUST TO PROVE HE CAN? TO WAKE HIMSELF UP A LITTLE?
MMF MMFF
THAT THERE'S A RYMAN SPHERE, JACK-IN-THE-BOX. IT SLOWS DOWN TIME. YOU'LL BE OUT AN' BREATHIN' AGAIN IN, OH, SIX HOURS?
NOW 'SCUSE ME, I GOT BIDNESS.
THIS IS NO WAY TO LIVE.

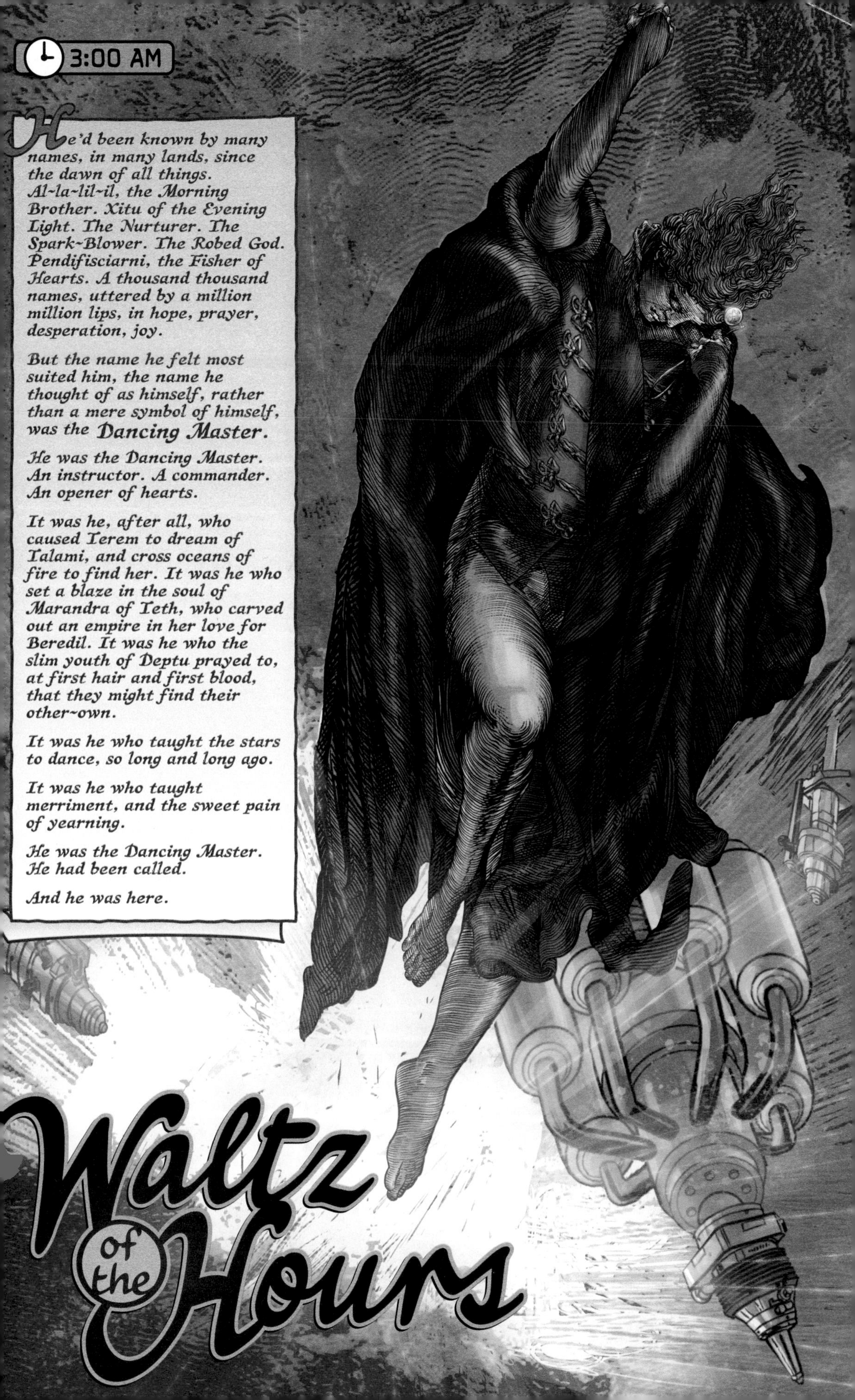

3:00 AM
He'd been known by many names, in many lands, since the dawn of all things. Al~la~lil~il, the Morning Brother. Xitu of the Evening Light. The Nurturer. The Spark~Blower. The Robed God. Pendifisciarni, the Fisher of Hearts. A thousand thousand names, uttered by a million million lips, in hope, prayer, desperation, joy.
But the name he felt most suited him, the name he thought of as himself, rather than a mere symbol of himself, was the Dancing Master.
He was the Dancing Master. An instructor. A commander. An opener of hearts.
It was he, after all, who caused Terem to dream of Talami, and cross oceans of fire to find her. It was he who set a blaze in the soul of Marandra of Teth, who carved out an empire in her love for Beredil. It was he who the slim youth of Deptu prayed to, at first hair and first blood, that they might find their other~own.
It was he who taught the stars to dance, so long and long ago.
It was he who taught merriment, and the sweet pain of yearning.
He was the Dancing Master. He had been called.
And he was here.
Waltz of the Hours

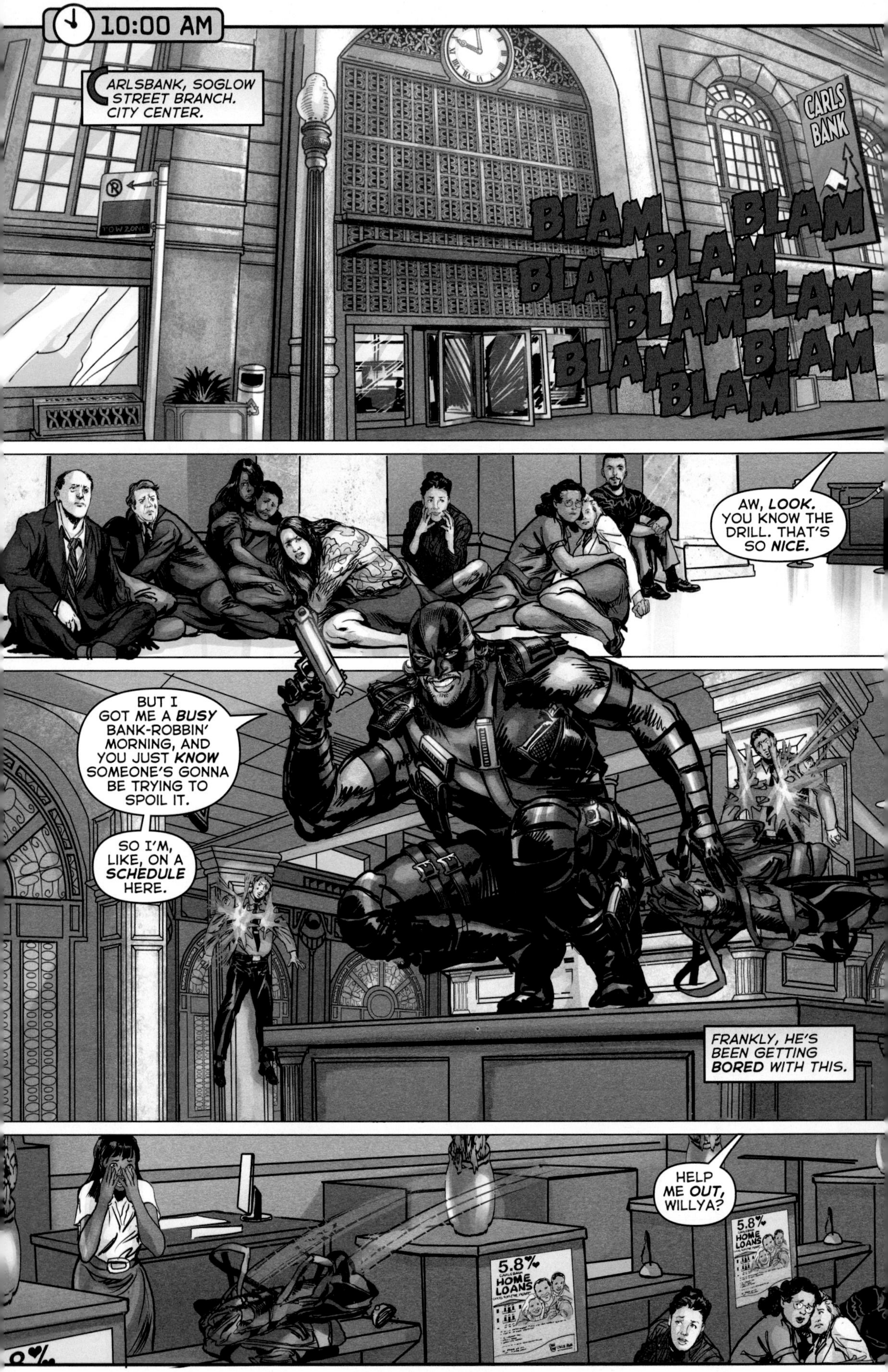
10:00 AM
CARLSBANK, SOGLOW STREET BRANCH. CITY CENTER.
TOW ZONE
CARLS BANK
BLAM BLAM
BLAMBLAM
BLAMBLAM
BLAM BLAM
BLAM
AW, LOOK. YOU KNOW THE DRILL. THAT'S SO NICE.
BUT I GOT ME A BUSY BANK-ROBBIN' MORNING, AND YOU JUST KNOW SOMEONE'S GONNA BE TRYING TO SPOIL IT.
SO I'M, LIKE, ON A SCHEDULE HERE.
FRANKLY, HE'S BEEN GETTING BORED WITH THIS.
HELP ME OUT, WILLYA?
5.8% HOME LOANS
5.8% HOME LOANS

R'D UNIT 7, ROUTCAULT CAMPUS, N.R. GISTICS INC.

EVER SINCE **ED NICHOLLS** AND **DAVISON ROYCE** HAD DISCOVERED THE **N-FIELD**, BACK IN THE 1950s, IT HAD BEEN A FASCINATING MYSTERY.

HOW DID SIGNALS TRANSMIT THROUGH THE FIELD IN APPARENT **VIOLATION** OF ANY KNOWN PHYSICS?

AND NOW --

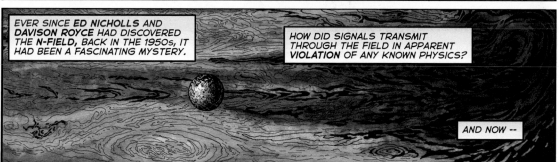

THE ROBOT WAS ON **IO**, IN ORBIT AROUND **JUPITER**.

THE SIGNALS -- THEY'RE **FINALLY** SEEING SOME DELAY. OR IS IT JUST **DEGRADATION?** IS IT TIME, DISTANCE OR --

GOT IT, GOT IT, GOT IT GOT IT GOT --

DAMMIT! DROPPED THE **SAMPLE!**

DEFINITE FLUCTUATION IN COMMAND FLOW.

BUT **VIDEO** IS UNINTERRUPTED. STILL COMING THROUGH THE INSTA-LINK CLEAN AND --

WHO'S CUSPING? BROUGHT YOU **COFFEE**. CHUCK, ALLISON, HERACLIO, THE **CAVALRY'S** HERE.

ZVI!

YOU CAN MAKE THIS DAMNED RIG WORK. I'M **OUTTA** HERE!

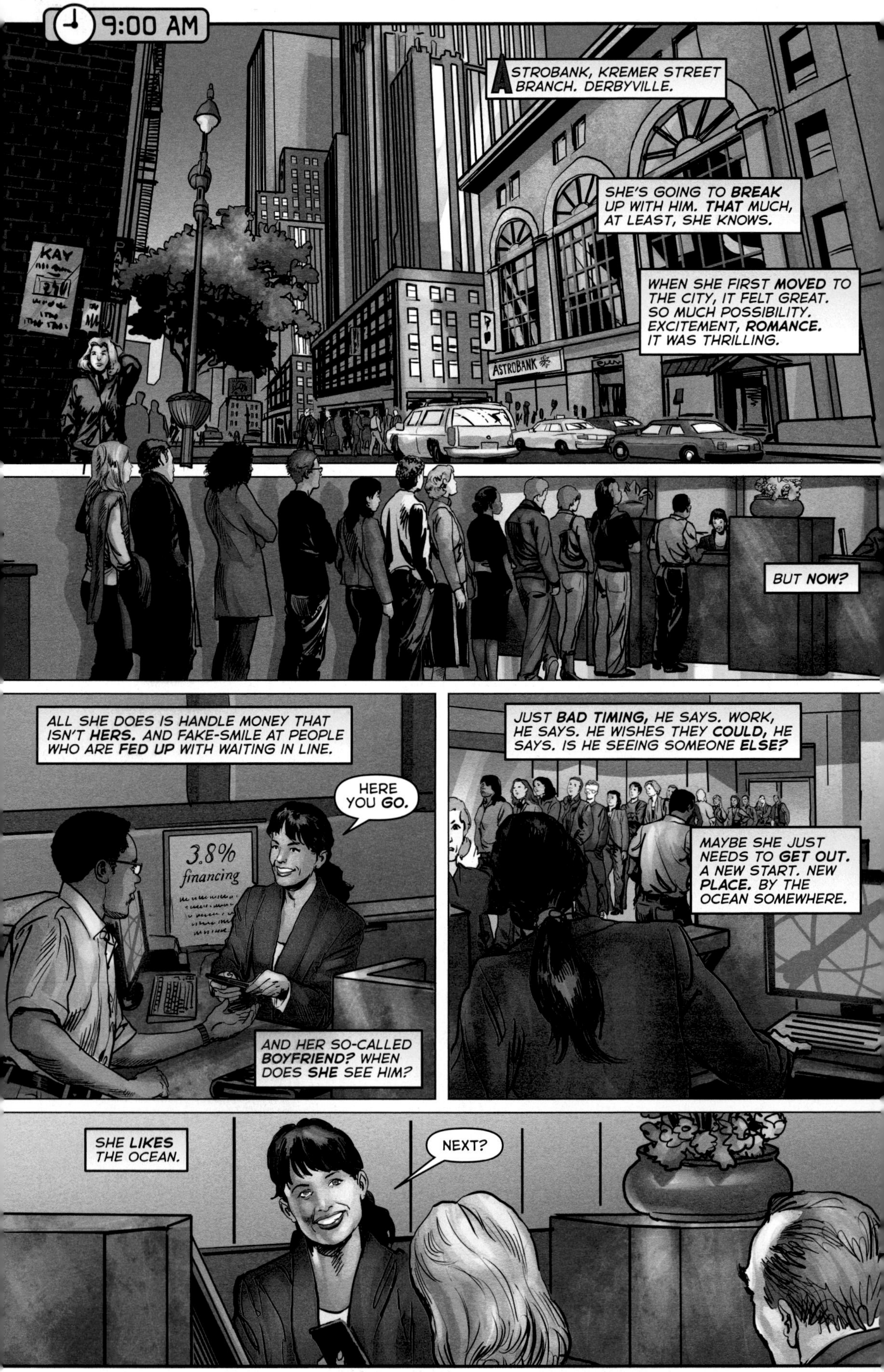
9:00 AM
ASTROBANK, KREMER STREET BRANCH. DERBYVILLE.
SHE'S GOING TO BREAK UP WITH HIM. THAT MUCH, AT LEAST, SHE KNOWS.
WHEN SHE FIRST MOVED TO THE CITY, IT FELT GREAT. SO MUCH POSSIBILITY. EXCITEMENT, ROMANCE. IT WAS THRILLING.
ASTROBANK
BUT NOW?
ALL SHE DOES IS HANDLE MONEY THAT ISN'T HERS. AND FAKE-SMILE AT PEOPLE WHO ARE FED UP WITH WAITING IN LINE.
HERE YOU GO.
3.8% financing
AND HER SO-CALLED BOYFRIEND? WHEN DOES SHE SEE HIM?
JUST BAD TIMING, HE SAYS. WORK, HE SAYS. HE WISHES THEY COULD, HE SAYS. IS HE SEEING SOMEONE ELSE?
MAYBE SHE JUST NEEDS TO GET OUT. A NEW START. NEW PLACE. BY THE OCEAN SOMEWHERE.
SHE LIKES THE OCEAN.
NEXT?

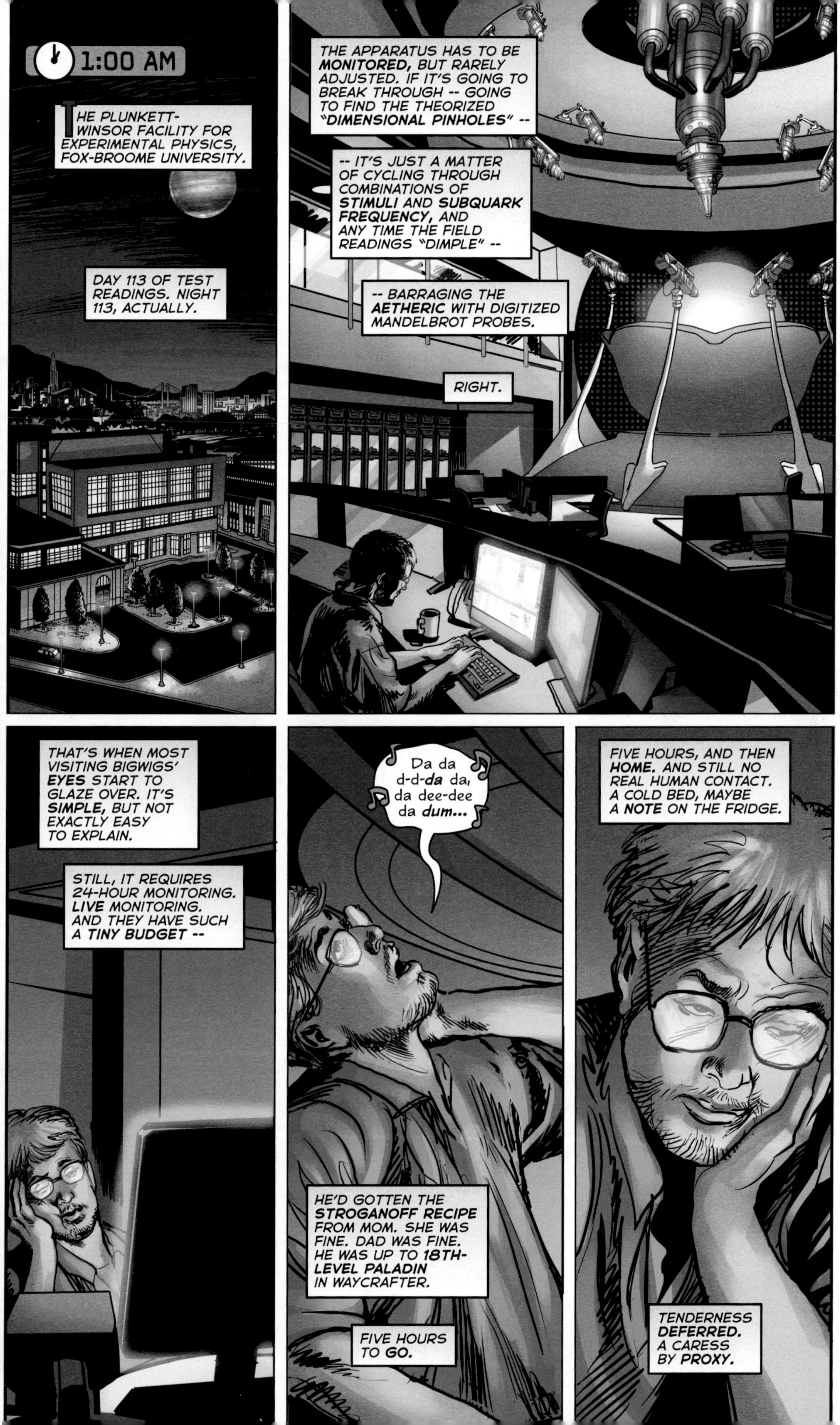
1:00 AM
THE PLUNKETT-WINSOR FACILITY FOR EXPERIMENTAL PHYSICS, FOX-BROOME UNIVERSITY.
DAY 113 OF TEST READINGS. NIGHT 113, ACTUALLY.
THE APPARATUS HAS TO BE **MONITORED,** BUT RARELY ADJUSTED. IF IT'S GOING TO BREAK THROUGH -- GOING TO FIND THE THEORIZED **"DIMENSIONAL PINHOLES"** --
-- IT'S JUST A MATTER OF CYCLING THROUGH COMBINATIONS OF **STIMULI** AND **SUBQUARK FREQUENCY,** AND ANY TIME THE FIELD READINGS "DIMPLE" --
-- BARRAGING THE **AETHERIC** WITH DIGITIZED MANDELBROT PROBES.
RIGHT.
THAT'S WHEN MOST VISITING BIGWIGS' **EYES** START TO GLAZE OVER. IT'S **SIMPLE,** BUT NOT EXACTLY EASY TO EXPLAIN.
STILL, IT REQUIRES 24-HOUR MONITORING. **LIVE** MONITORING. AND THEY HAVE SUCH A **TINY BUDGET** --
Da da d-d-*da* da, da dee-dee da *dum...*
HE'D GOTTEN THE **STROGANOFF RECIPE** FROM MOM. SHE WAS FINE. DAD WAS FINE. HE WAS UP TO **18TH-LEVEL PALADIN** IN WAYCRAFTER.
FIVE HOURS TO **GO.**
FIVE HOURS, AND THEN **HOME.** AND STILL NO REAL HUMAN CONTACT. A COLD BED, MAYBE A **NOTE** ON THE FRIDGE.
TENDERNESS **DEFERRED.** A CARESS BY **PROXY.**

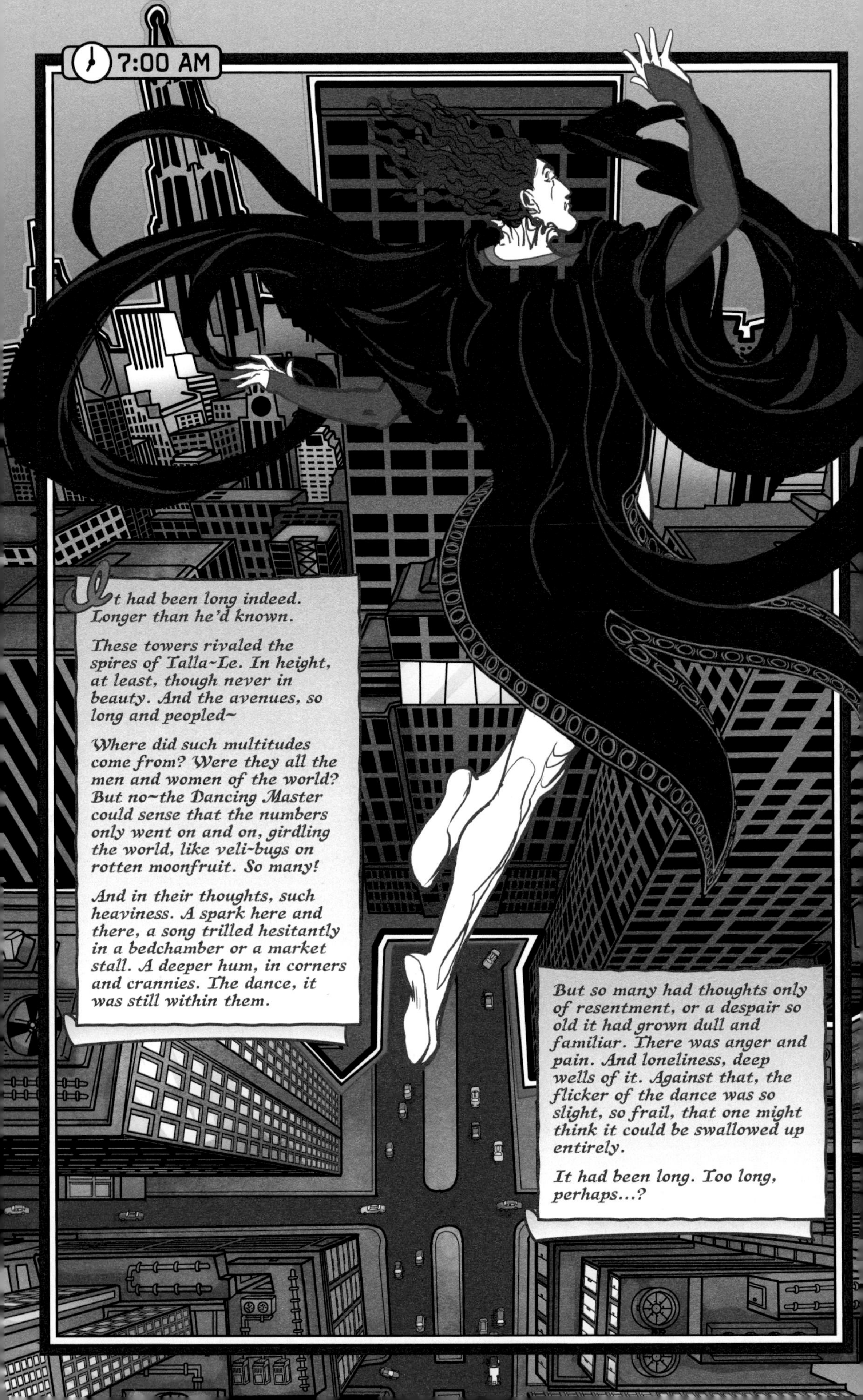
7:00 AM
It had been long indeed. Longer than he'd known.
These towers rivaled the spires of Talla~Le. In height, at least, though never in beauty. And the avenues, so long and peopled~
Where did such multitudes come from? Were they all the men and women of the world? But no~the Dancing Master could sense that the numbers only went on and on, girdling the world, like veli~bugs on rotten moonfruit. So many!
And in their thoughts, such heaviness. A spark here and there, a song trilled hesitantly in a bedchamber or a market stall. A deeper hum, in corners and crannies. The dance, it was still within them.
But so many had thoughts only of resentment, or a despair so old it had grown dull and familiar. There was anger and pain. And loneliness, deep wells of it. Against that, the flicker of the dance was so slight, so frail, that one might think it could be swallowed up entirely.
It had been long. Too long, perhaps...?

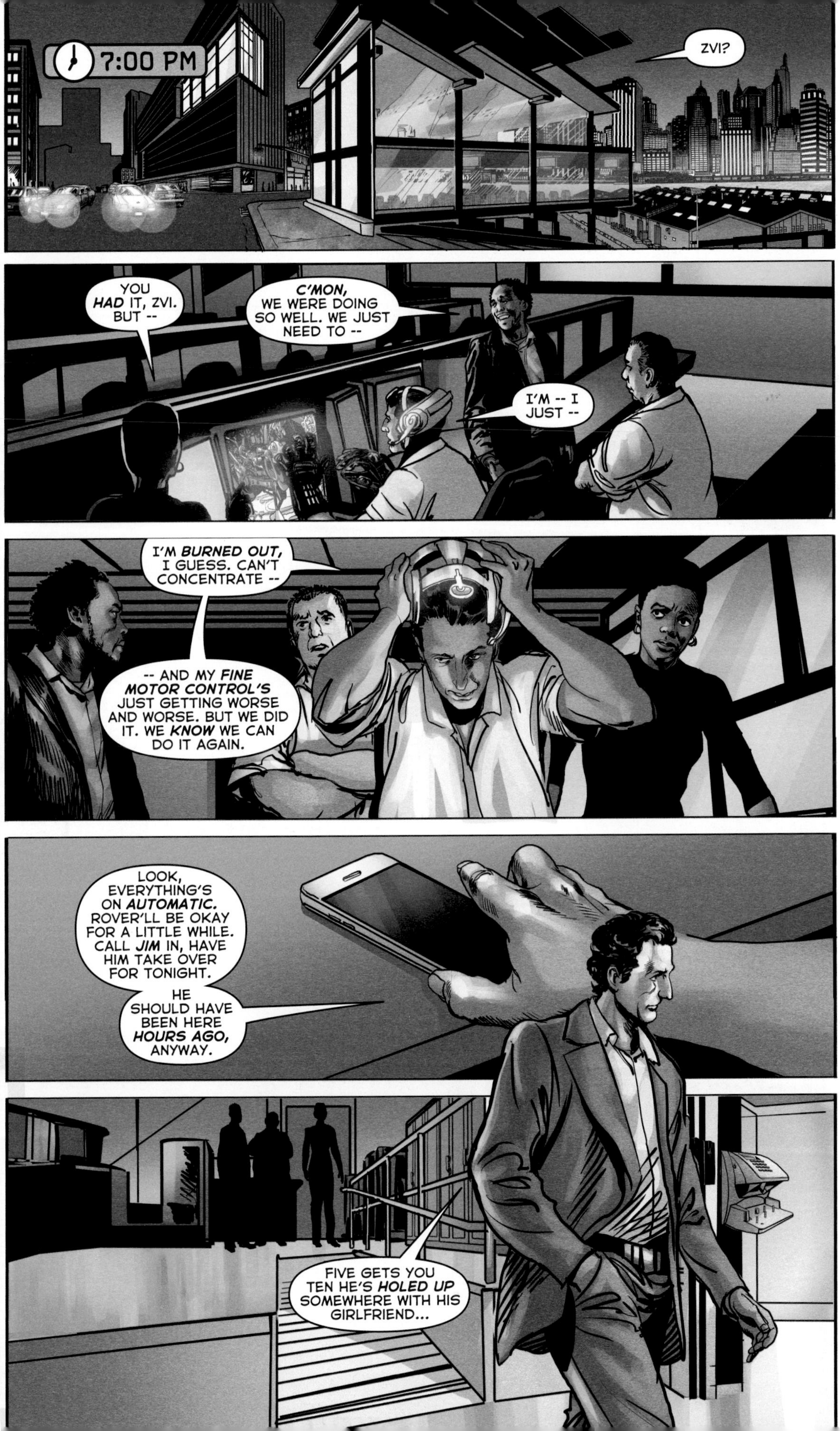
7:00 PM
ZVI?
YOU HAD IT, ZVI. BUT --
C'MON, WE WERE DOING SO WELL. WE JUST NEED TO --
I'M -- I JUST --
I'M BURNED OUT, I GUESS. CAN'T CONCENTRATE --
-- AND MY FINE MOTOR CONTROL'S JUST GETTING WORSE AND WORSE. BUT WE DID IT. WE KNOW WE CAN DO IT AGAIN.
LOOK, EVERYTHING'S ON AUTOMATIC. ROVER'LL BE OKAY FOR A LITTLE WHILE. CALL JIM IN, HAVE HIM TAKE OVER FOR TONIGHT.
HE SHOULD HAVE BEEN HERE HOURS AGO, ANYWAY.
FIVE GETS YOU TEN HE'S HOLED UP SOMEWHERE WITH HIS GIRLFRIEND...

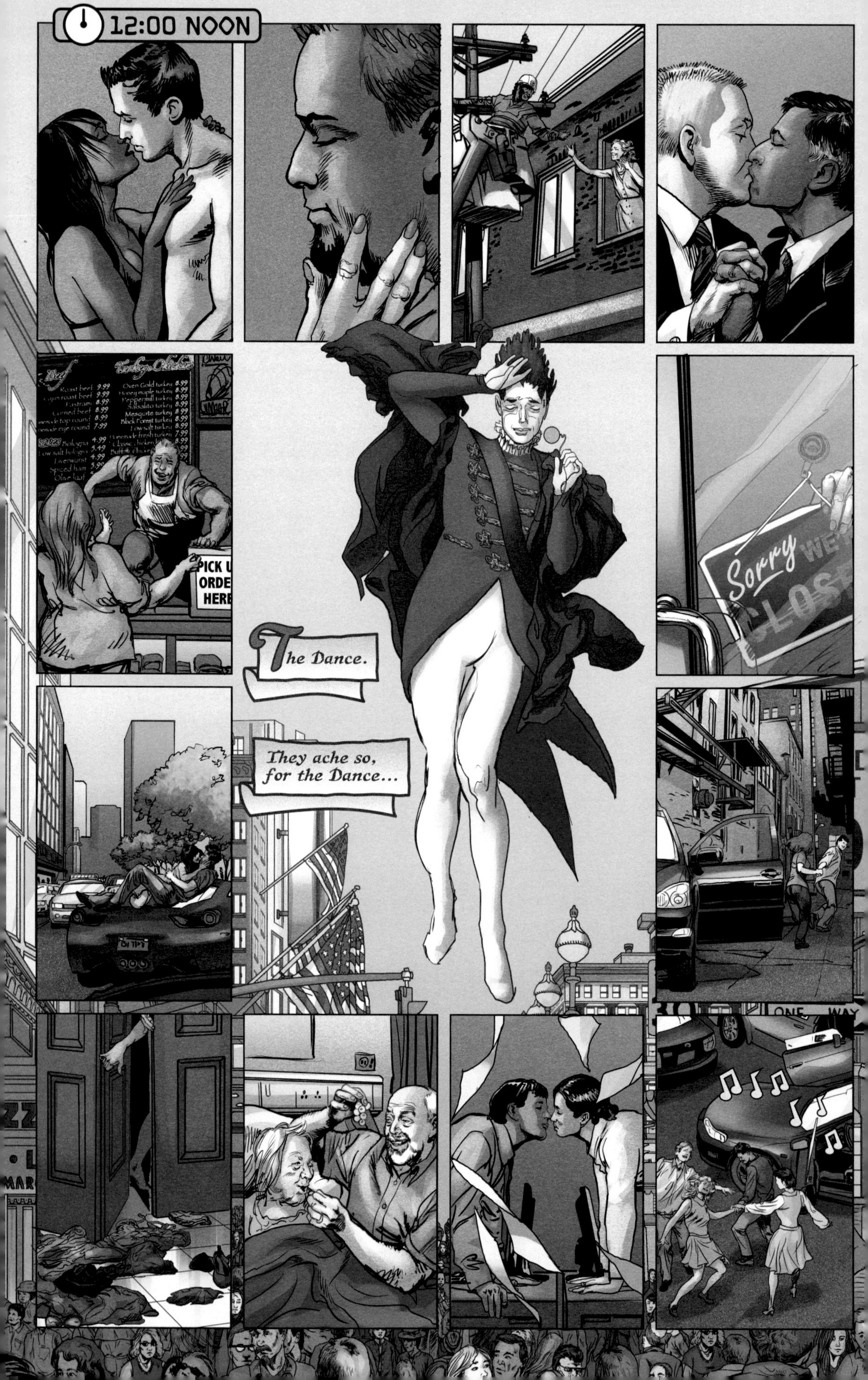
12:00 NOON
PICK U
ORDE
HERE
Sorry WE
CLOS
The Dance.
They ache so, for the Dance...
ONE WAY

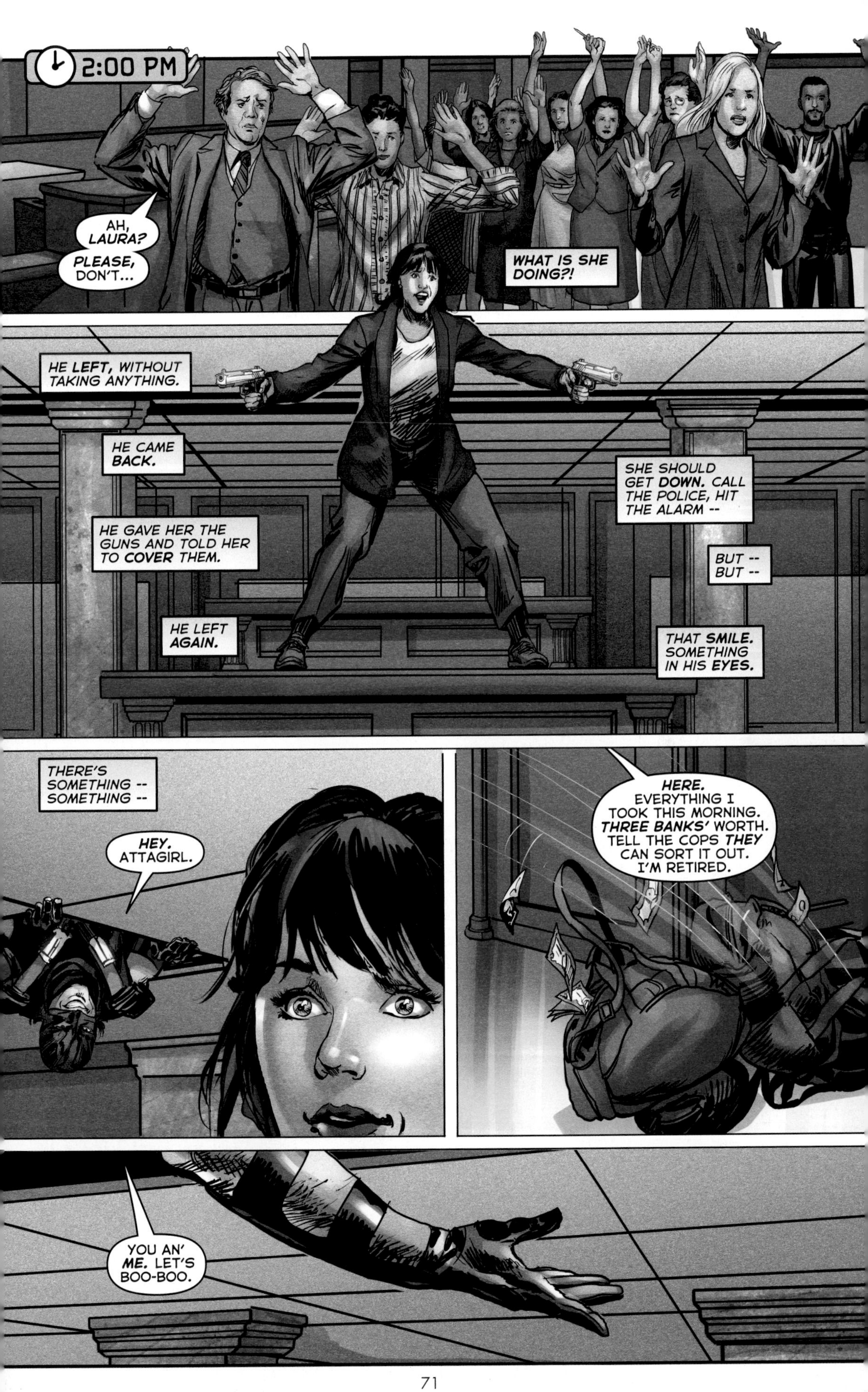
2:00 PM
AH, LAURA? PLEASE, DON'T...
WHAT IS SHE DOING?!
HE LEFT, WITHOUT TAKING ANYTHING.
HE CAME BACK.
HE GAVE HER THE GUNS AND TOLD HER TO COVER THEM.
HE LEFT AGAIN.
SHE SHOULD GET DOWN. CALL THE POLICE, HIT THE ALARM --
BUT -- BUT --
THAT SMILE. SOMETHING IN HIS EYES.
THERE'S SOMETHING -- SOMETHING --
HEY. ATTAGIRL.
HERE. EVERYTHING I TOOK THIS MORNING. THREE BANKS' WORTH. TELL THE COPS THEY CAN SORT IT OUT. I'M RETIRED.
YOU AN' ME. LET'S BOO-BOO.

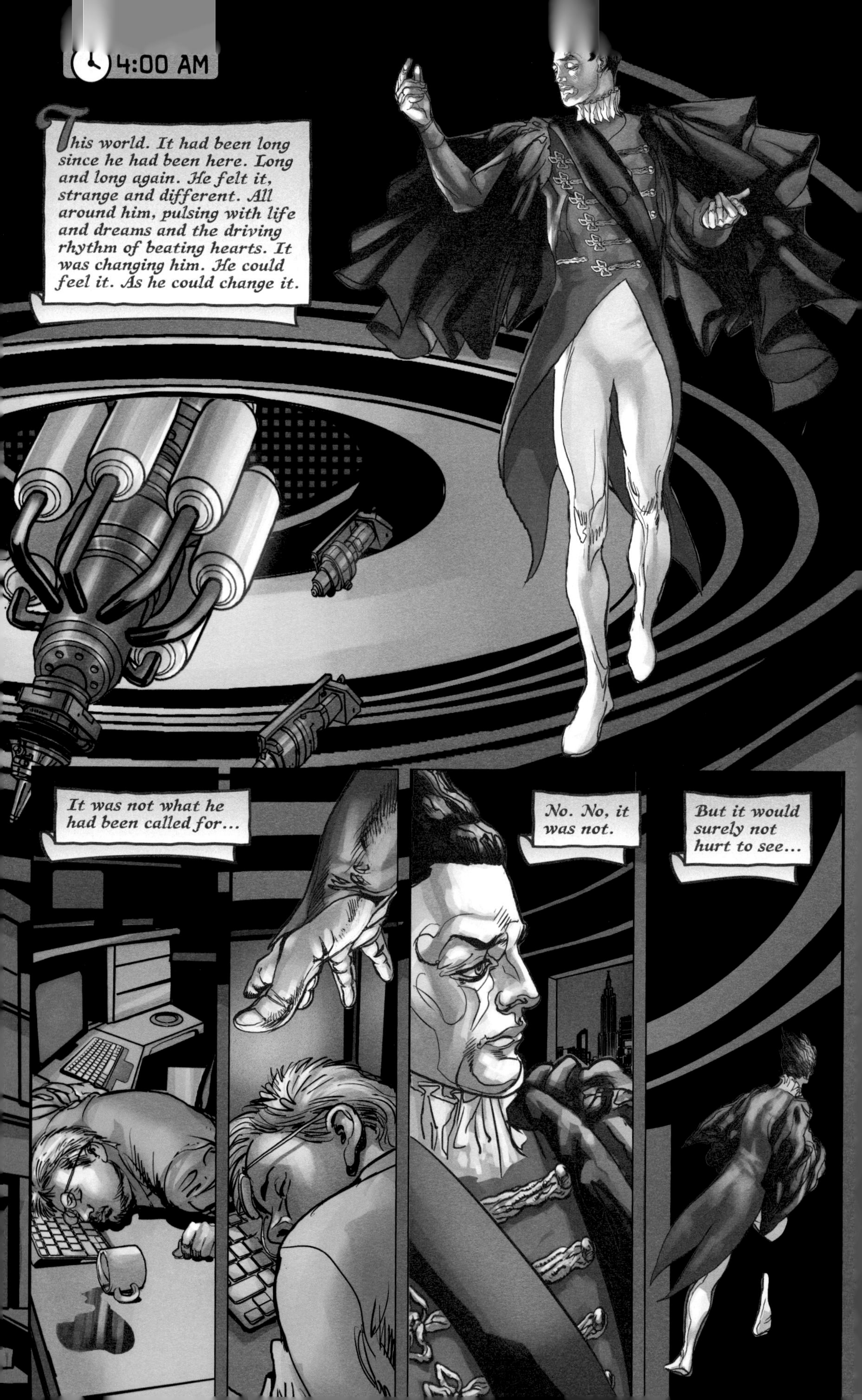

4:00 AM
This world. It had been long since he had been here. Long and long again. He felt it, strange and different. All around him, pulsing with life and dreams and the driving rhythm of beating hearts. It was changing him. He could feel it. As he could change it.
It was not what he had been called for...
No. No, it was not.
But it would surely not hurt to see...

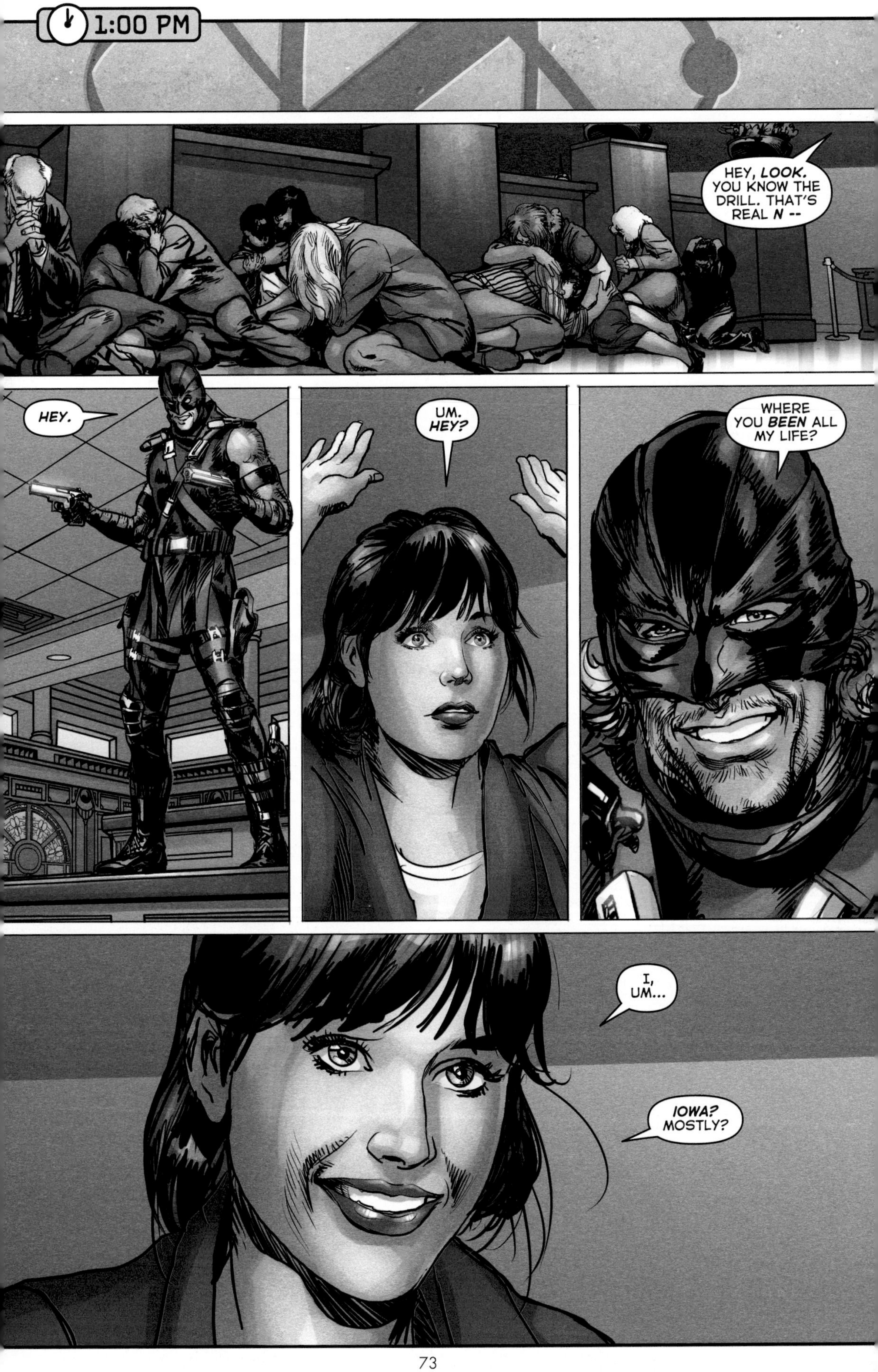
1:00 PM
HEY, LOOK. YOU KNOW THE DRILL. THAT'S REAL N --
HEY.
UM. HEY?
WHERE YOU BEEN ALL MY LIFE?
I, UM...
IOWA? MOSTLY?

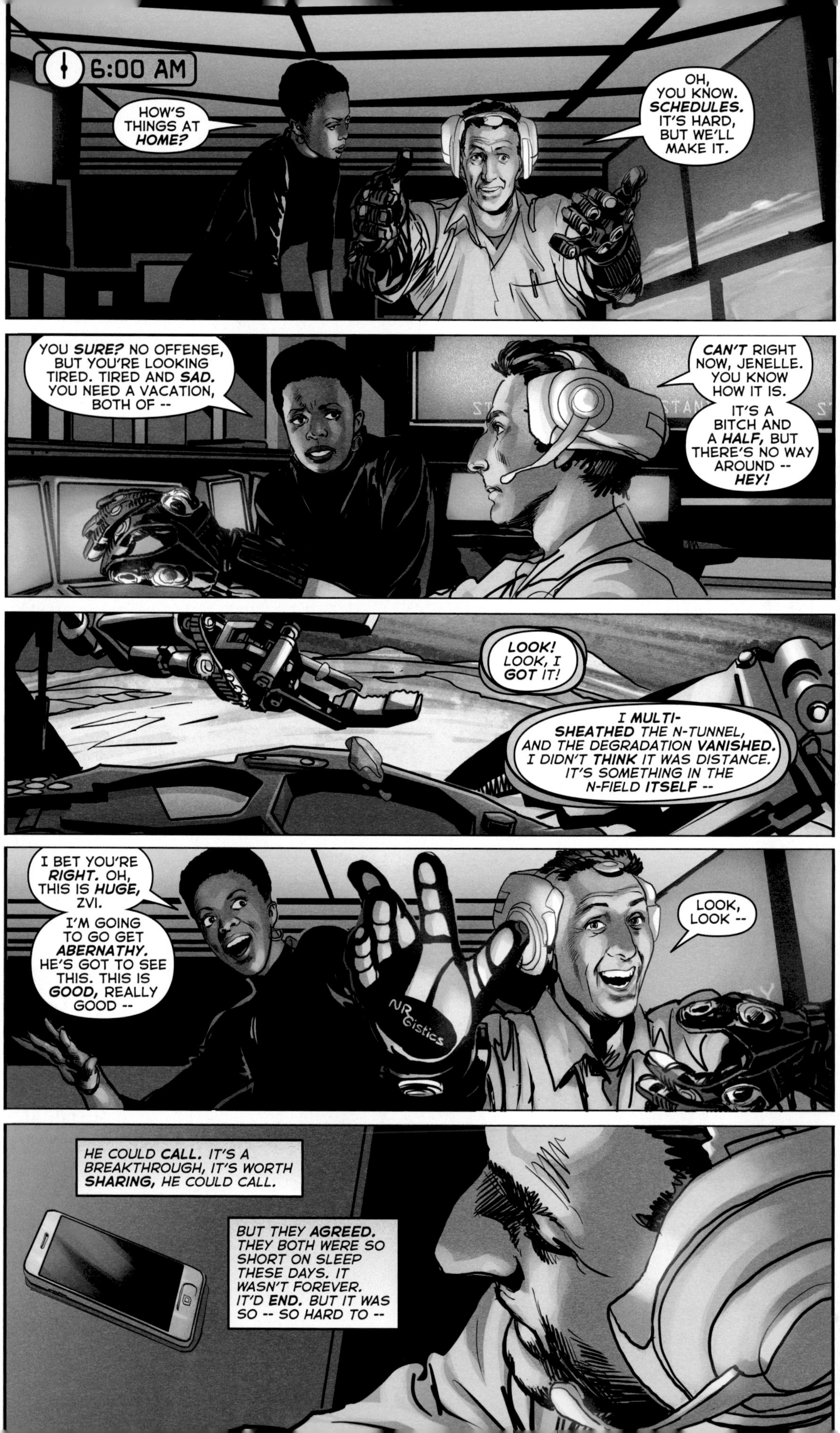
6:00 AM
HOW'S THINGS AT *HOME?*
OH, YOU KNOW. *SCHEDULES.* IT'S HARD, BUT WE'LL MAKE IT.
YOU *SURE?* NO OFFENSE, BUT YOU'RE LOOKING TIRED. TIRED AND *SAD.* YOU NEED A VACATION, BOTH OF --
CAN'T RIGHT NOW, JENELLE. YOU KNOW HOW IT IS.
IT'S A BITCH AND A *HALF,* BUT THERE'S NO WAY AROUND -- *HEY!*
LOOK! LOOK, I *GOT* IT!
I *MULTI-SHEATHED* THE N-TUNNEL, AND THE DEGRADATION *VANISHED.* I DIDN'T *THINK* IT WAS DISTANCE. IT'S SOMETHING IN THE N-FIELD *ITSELF* --
I BET YOU'RE *RIGHT.* OH, THIS IS *HUGE,* ZVI.
I'M GOING TO GO GET *ABERNATHY.* HE'S GOT TO SEE THIS. THIS IS *GOOD,* REALLY GOOD --
LOOK, LOOK --
NRGistics
HE COULD *CALL.* IT'S A BREAKTHROUGH, IT'S WORTH *SHARING,* HE COULD CALL.
BUT THEY *AGREED.* THEY BOTH WERE SO SHORT ON SLEEP THESE DAYS. IT WASN'T FOREVER. IT'D *END.* BUT IT WAS SO -- SO HARD TO --

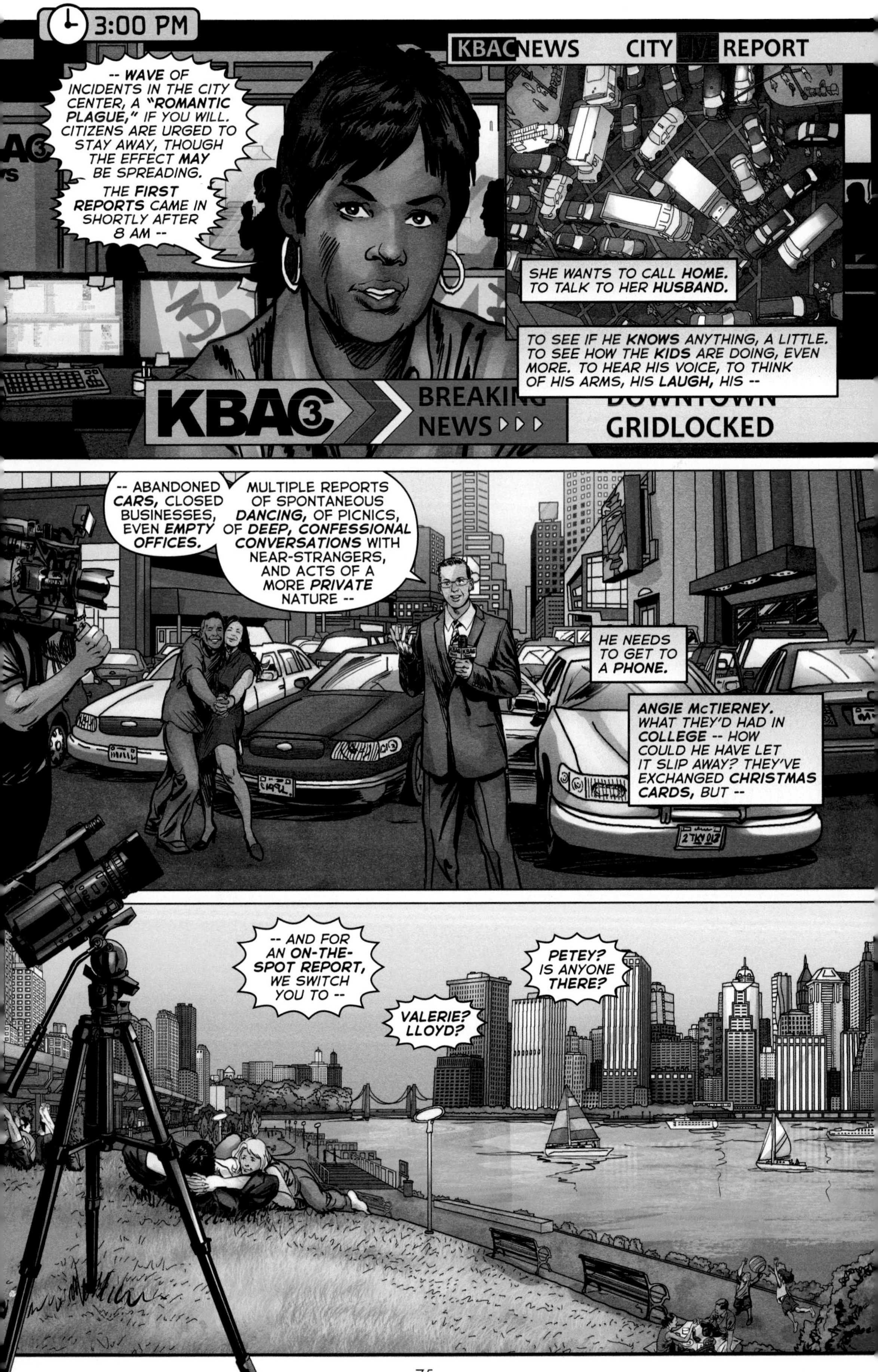
3:00 PM
KBAC NEWS CITY LIVE REPORT
-- WAVE OF INCIDENTS IN THE CITY CENTER, A "ROMANTIC PLAGUE," IF YOU WILL. CITIZENS ARE URGED TO STAY AWAY, THOUGH THE EFFECT MAY BE SPREADING.
THE FIRST REPORTS CAME IN SHORTLY AFTER 8 AM --
SHE WANTS TO CALL HOME. TO TALK TO HER HUSBAND.
TO SEE IF HE KNOWS ANYTHING, A LITTLE. TO SEE HOW THE KIDS ARE DOING, EVEN MORE. TO HEAR HIS VOICE, TO THINK OF HIS ARMS, HIS LAUGH, HIS --
KBAC 3 BREAKING NEWS
GRIDLOCKED
-- ABANDONED CARS, CLOSED BUSINESSES, EVEN EMPTY OFFICES.
MULTIPLE REPORTS OF SPONTANEOUS DANCING, OF PICNICS, OF DEEP, CONFESSIONAL CONVERSATIONS WITH NEAR-STRANGERS, AND ACTS OF A MORE PRIVATE NATURE --
HE NEEDS TO GET TO A PHONE.
ANGIE McTIERNEY. WHAT THEY'D HAD IN COLLEGE -- HOW COULD HE HAVE LET IT SLIP AWAY? THEY'VE EXCHANGED CHRISTMAS CARDS, BUT --
-- AND FOR AN ON-THE-SPOT REPORT, WE SWITCH YOU TO --
VALERIE? LLOYD?
PETEY? IS ANYONE THERE?

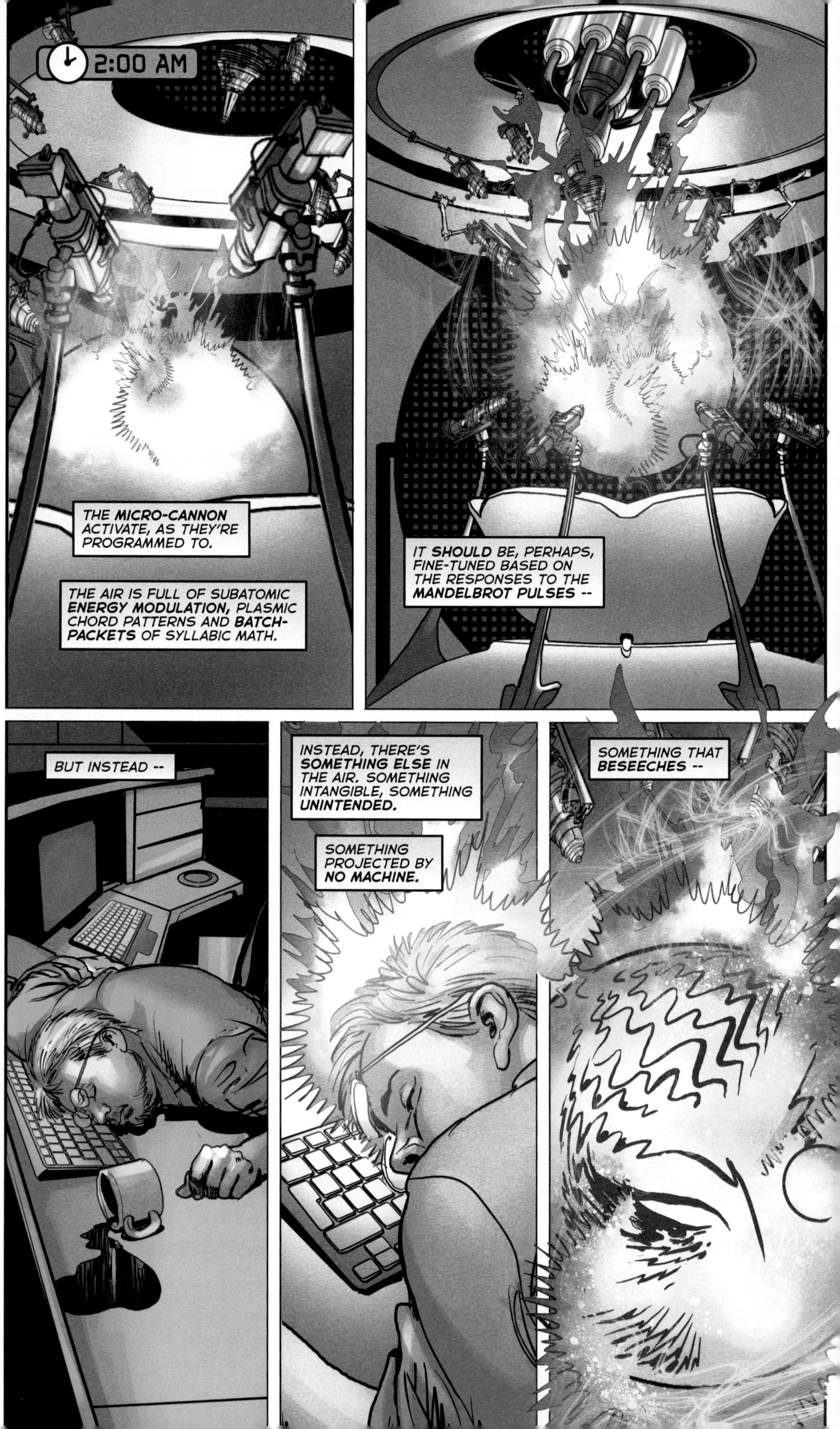
2:00 AM
THE MICRO-CANNON ACTIVATE, AS THEY'RE PROGRAMMED TO.
THE AIR IS FULL OF SUBATOMIC ENERGY MODULATION, PLASMIC CHORD PATTERNS AND BATCH-PACKETS OF SYLLABIC MATH.
IT SHOULD BE, PERHAPS, FINE-TUNED BASED ON THE RESPONSES TO THE MANDELBROT PULSES --
BUT INSTEAD --
INSTEAD, THERE'S SOMETHING ELSE IN THE AIR. SOMETHING INTANGIBLE, SOMETHING UNINTENDED.
SOMETHING PROJECTED BY NO MACHINE.
SOMETHING THAT BESEECHES --

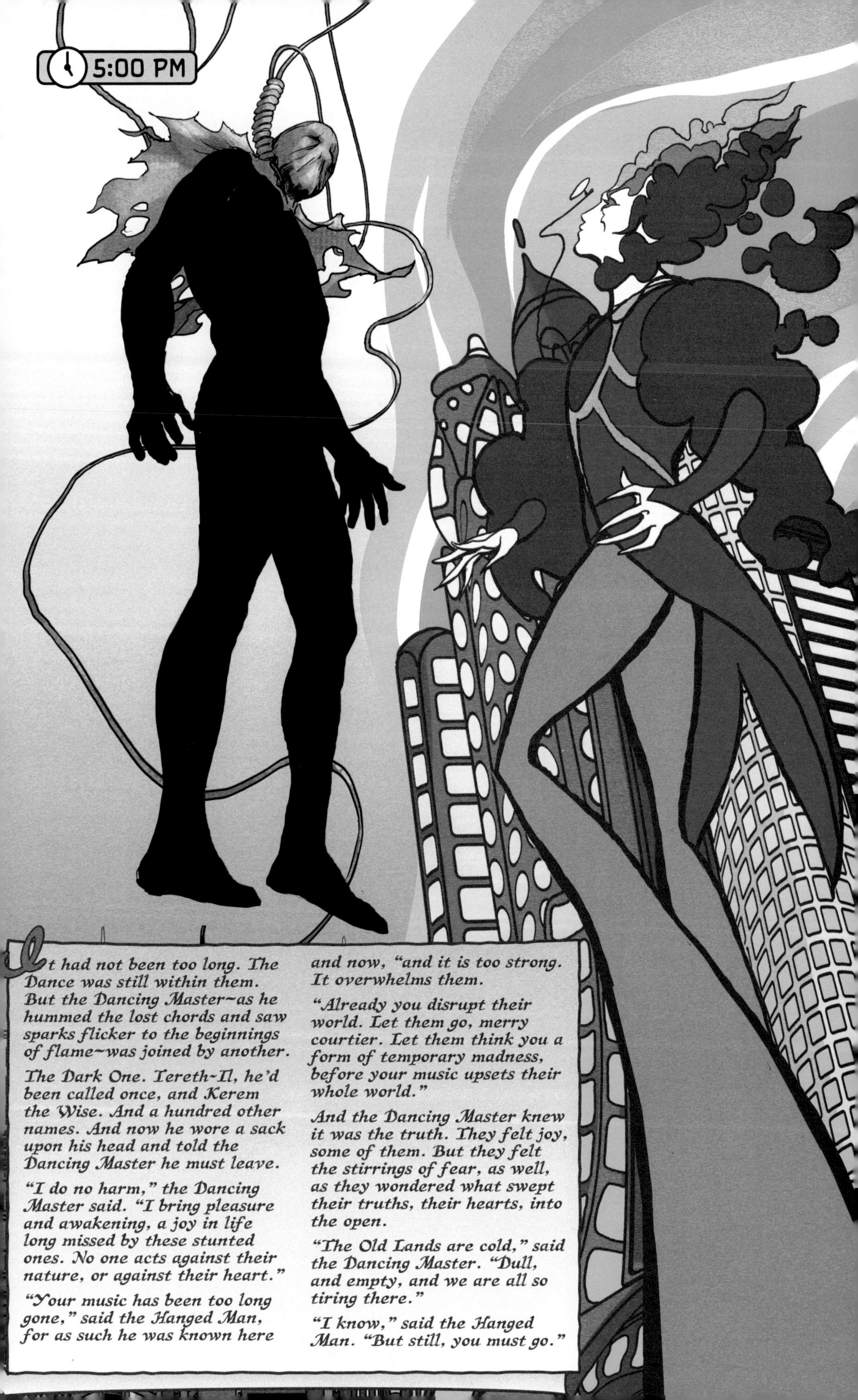
5:00 PM

It had not been too long. The Dance was still within them. But the Dancing Master~as he hummed the lost chords and saw sparks flicker to the beginnings of flame~was joined by another.

The Dark One. Tereth~Il, he'd been called once, and Kerem the Wise. And a hundred other names. And now he wore a sack upon his head and told the Dancing Master he must leave.

"I do no harm," the Dancing Master said. "I bring pleasure and awakening, a joy in life long missed by these stunted ones. No one acts against their nature, or against their heart."

"Your music has been too long gone," said the Hanged Man, for as such he was known here and now, "and it is too strong. It overwhelms them.

"Already you disrupt their world. Let them go, merry courtier. Let them think you a form of temporary madness, before your music upsets their whole world."

And the Dancing Master knew it was the truth. They felt joy, some of them. But they felt the stirrings of fear, as well, as they wondered what swept their truths, their hearts, into the open.

"The Old Lands are cold," said the Dancing Master. "Dull, and empty, and we are all so tiring there."

"I know," said the Hanged Man. "But still, you must go."

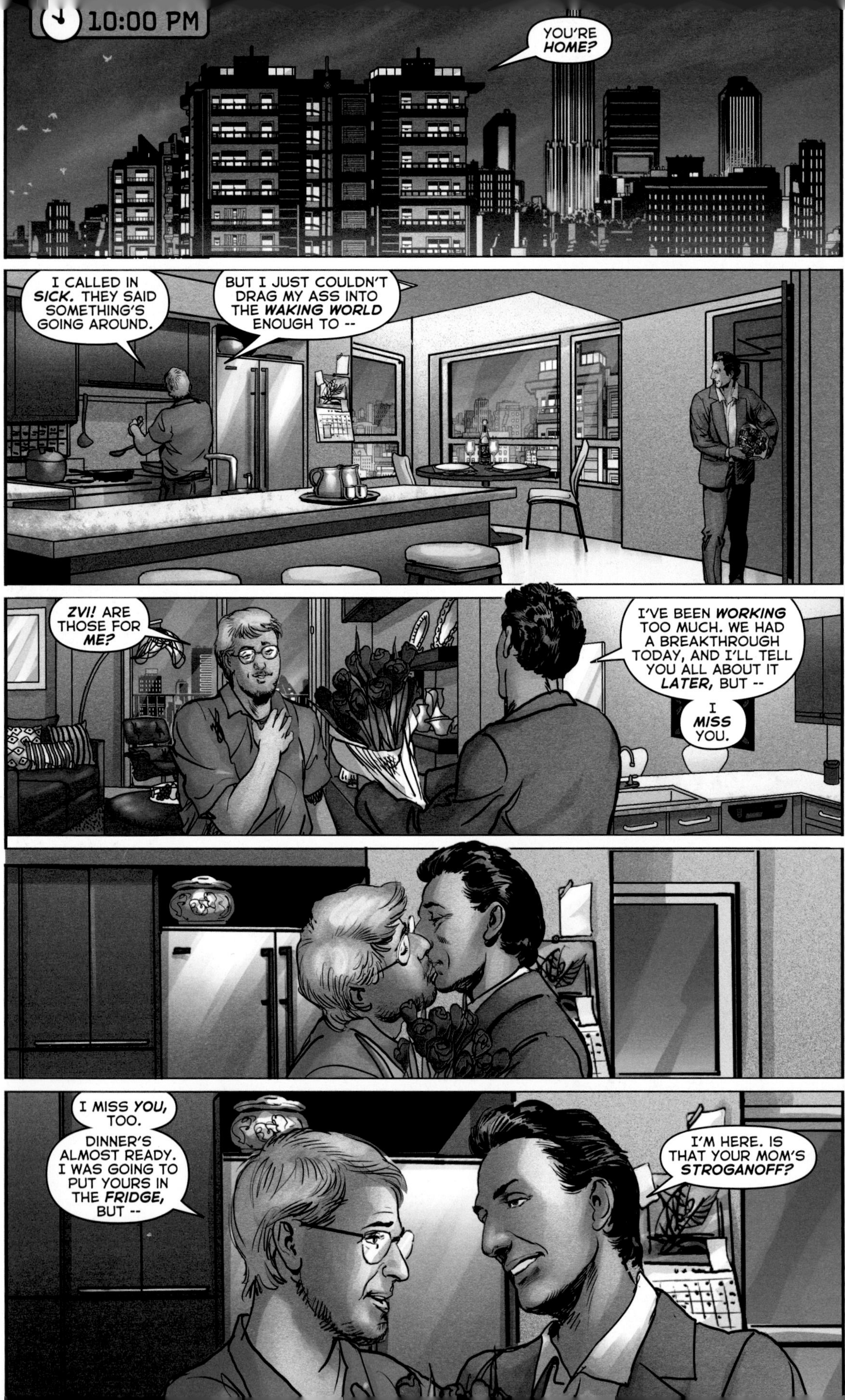
10:00 PM
YOU'RE HOME?
I CALLED IN SICK. THEY SAID SOMETHING'S GOING AROUND.
BUT I JUST COULDN'T DRAG MY ASS INTO THE WAKING WORLD ENOUGH TO --
ZVI! ARE THOSE FOR ME?
I'VE BEEN WORKING TOO MUCH. WE HAD A BREAKTHROUGH TODAY, AND I'LL TELL YOU ALL ABOUT IT LATER, BUT --
I MISS YOU.
I MISS YOU, TOO.
DINNER'S ALMOST READY. I WAS GOING TO PUT YOURS IN THE FRIDGE, BUT --
I'M HERE. IS THAT YOUR MOM'S STROGANOFF?

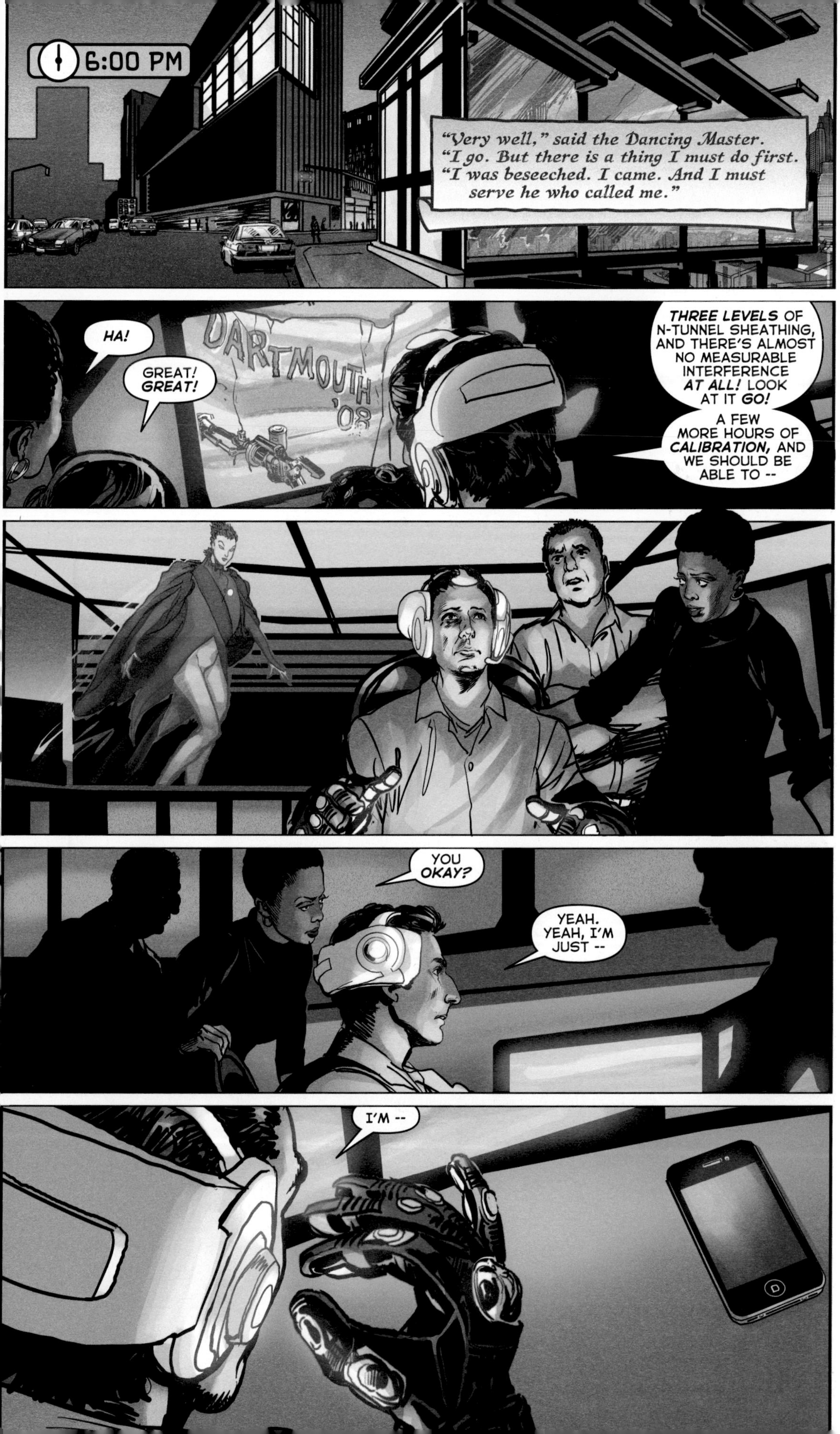

6:00 PM
"Very well," said the Dancing Master. "I go. But there is a thing I must do first. "I was beseeched. I came. And I must serve he who called me."
DARTMOUTH '08
HA!
GREAT! GREAT!
THREE LEVELS OF N-TUNNEL SHEATHING, AND THERE'S ALMOST NO MEASURABLE INTERFERENCE AT ALL! LOOK AT IT GO!
A FEW MORE HOURS OF CALIBRATION, AND WE SHOULD BE ABLE TO --
YOU OKAY?
YEAH. YEAH, I'M JUST --
I'M --

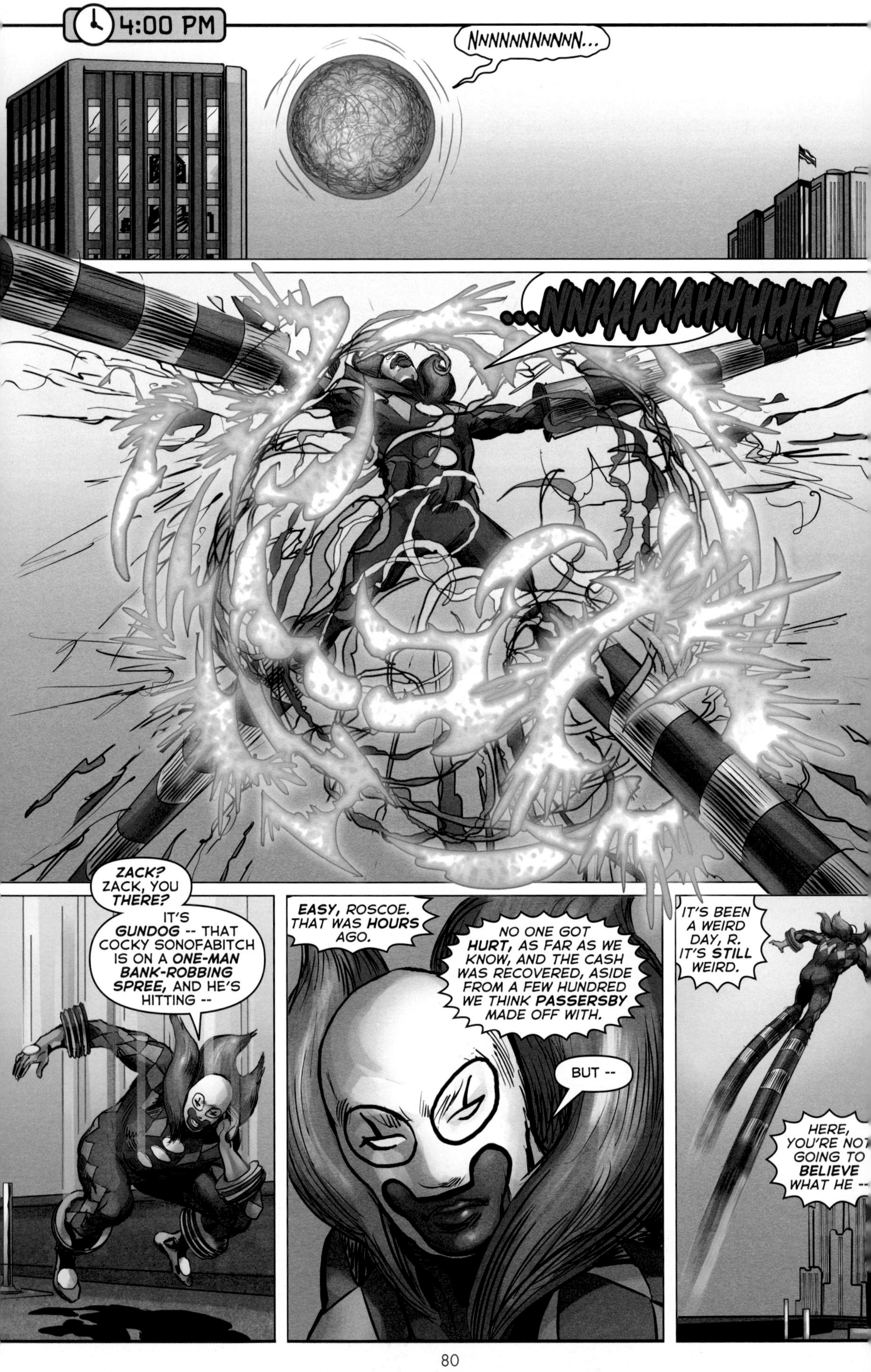
4:00 PM
NNNNNNNNNNN...
...NNAAAAAAHHHHHH!
ZACK? ZACK, YOU THERE?
IT'S GUNDOG -- THAT COCKY SONOFABITCH IS ON A ONE-MAN BANK-ROBBING SPREE, AND HE'S HITTING --
EASY, ROSCOE. THAT WAS HOURS AGO.
NO ONE GOT HURT, AS FAR AS WE KNOW, AND THE CASH WAS RECOVERED, ASIDE FROM A FEW HUNDRED WE THINK PASSERSBY MADE OFF WITH.
BUT --
IT'S BEEN A WEIRD DAY, R. IT'S STILL WEIRD.
HERE, YOU'RE NOT GOING TO BELIEVE WHAT HE --

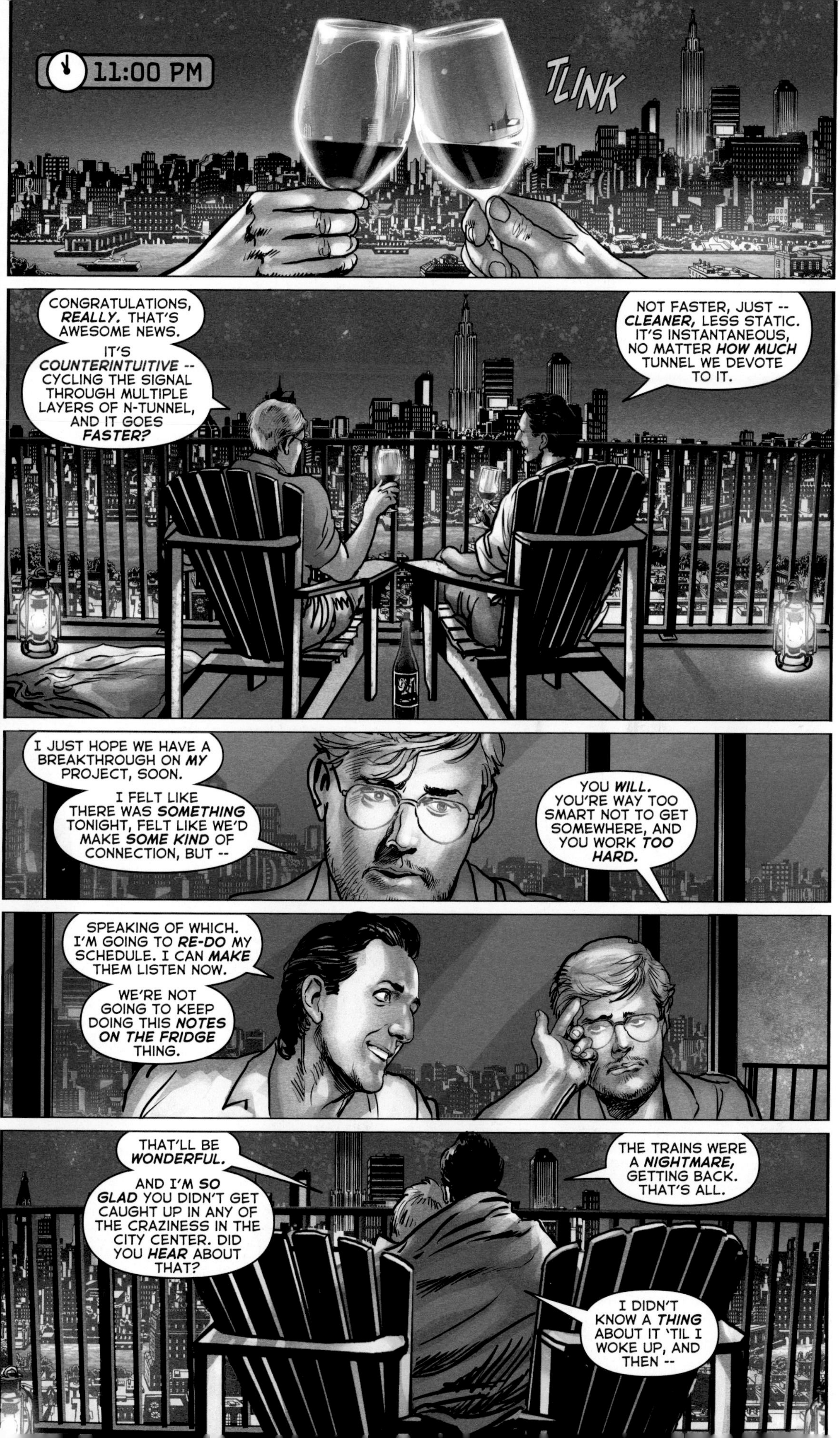
11:00 PM
TLINK
CONGRATULATIONS, REALLY. THAT'S AWESOME NEWS.
IT'S COUNTERINTUITIVE -- CYCLING THE SIGNAL THROUGH MULTIPLE LAYERS OF N-TUNNEL, AND IT GOES FASTER?
NOT FASTER, JUST -- CLEANER, LESS STATIC. IT'S INSTANTANEOUS, NO MATTER HOW MUCH TUNNEL WE DEVOTE TO IT.
I JUST HOPE WE HAVE A BREAKTHROUGH ON MY PROJECT, SOON.
I FELT LIKE THERE WAS SOMETHING TONIGHT, FELT LIKE WE'D MAKE SOME KIND OF CONNECTION, BUT --
YOU WILL. YOU'RE WAY TOO SMART NOT TO GET SOMEWHERE, AND YOU WORK TOO HARD.
SPEAKING OF WHICH. I'M GOING TO RE-DO MY SCHEDULE. I CAN MAKE THEM LISTEN NOW.
WE'RE NOT GOING TO KEEP DOING THIS NOTES ON THE FRIDGE THING.
THAT'LL BE WONDERFUL.
AND I'M SO GLAD YOU DIDN'T GET CAUGHT UP IN ANY OF THE CRAZINESS IN THE CITY CENTER. DID YOU HEAR ABOUT THAT?
THE TRAINS WERE A NIGHTMARE, GETTING BACK. THAT'S ALL.
I DIDN'T KNOW A THING ABOUT IT 'TIL I WOKE UP, AND THEN --

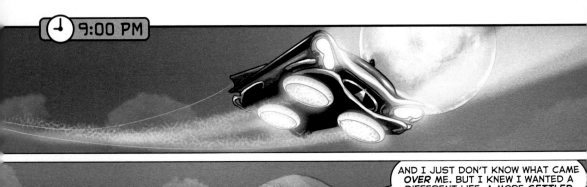

AND I JUST DON'T KNOW WHAT CAME *OVER* ME. BUT I KNEW I WANTED A DIFFERENT LIFE, A MORE *SETTLED* LIFE. AND I WANTED IT WITH *YOU.*

I KNOW. IT WAS LIKE -- A *LIGHT* COMING ON, WASN'T IT?

A LIGHT. OR *MUSIC,* MAYBE.

I LIKE YOUR *REAL VOICE,* BY THE WAY. WAY BETTER THAN THAT MOUNTAIN-BOY THING. BUT I DON'T -- WHERE ARE YOU *FROM?*

MAINE. I'M FROM *MAINE.*

I WAS THINKING. MY GREAT-UNCLE -- HE'S GOT NO *KIDS,* AND HE'S GOT THIS *LOBSTER JOINT* ON THE COAST, UP NEAR ROCKLAND.

HE BUGS ME TO COME *RUN* IT WITH HIM.

YOU LIKE *LOBSTER?*

ARE YOU KIDDING? I *LOVE* LOBSTER...

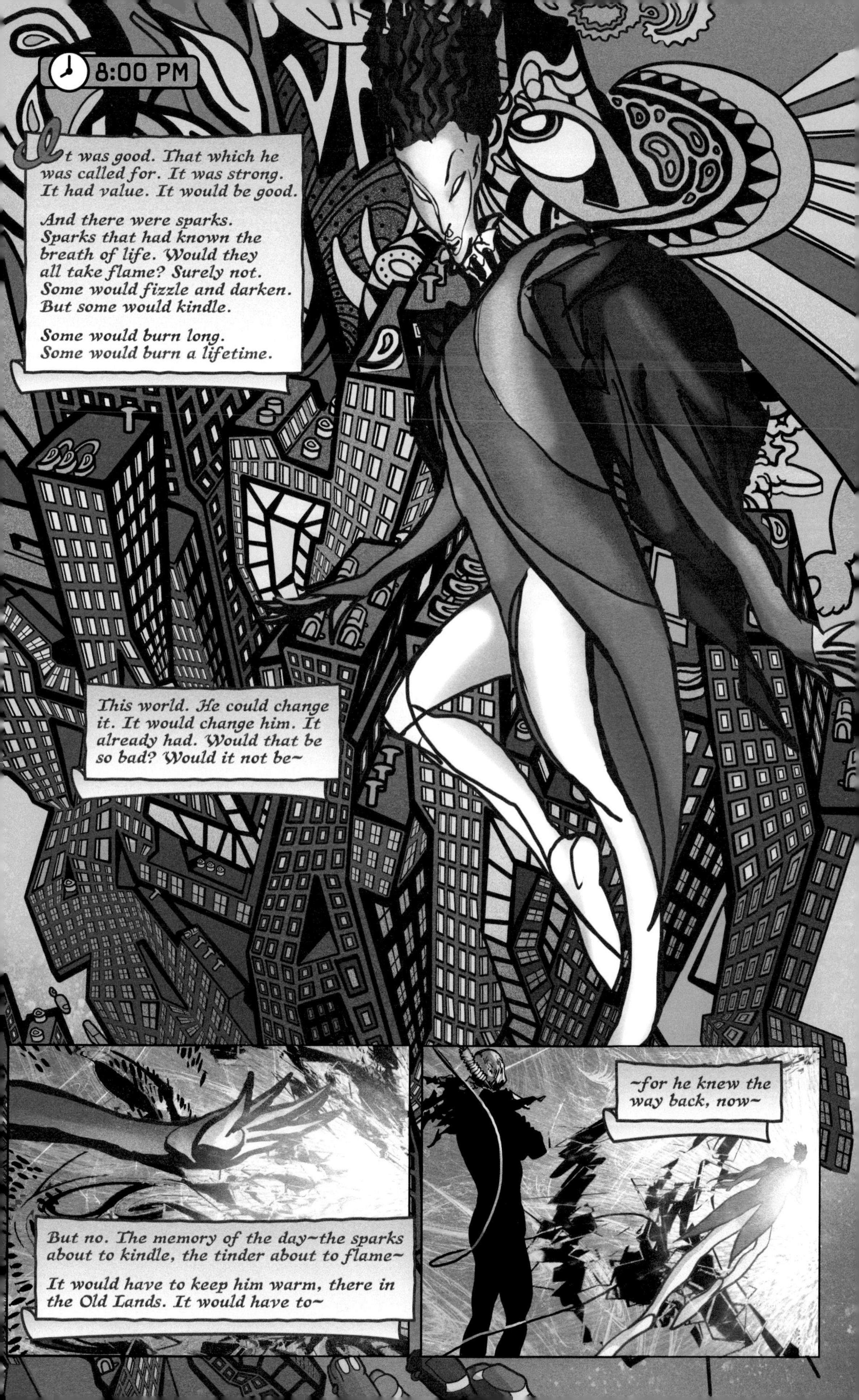
8:00 PM
It was good. That which he was called for. It was strong. It had value. It would be good.
And there were sparks. Sparks that had known the breath of life. Would they all take flame? Surely not. Some would fizzle and darken. But some would kindle.
Some would burn long. Some would burn a lifetime.
This world. He could change it. It would change him. It already had. Would that be so bad? Would it not be~
But no. The memory of the day~the sparks about to kindle, the tinder about to flame~
It would have to keep him warm, there in the Old Lands. It would have to~
~for he knew the way back, now~

MIDNIGHT

HAS ANYONE REACHED JIM YET? WHEN YOU *DO*, TELL HIM TO GET HIS ASS --

IT'S *OKAY*, PETE. ROVER'S JUST CYCLING THROUGH TESTS. IT'S BEEN A *CRAZY DAY* OUT THERE, SO LET'S JUST CUT EVERYONE SOME SLACK --

"-- AND FOCUS ON GETTING BACK TO *NORMAL*."

ROVER. ITS NAME IS ROVER.

ITS NAME IS ROVER AND THIS IS IO AND IT DOESN'T HEAR JIM'S VOICE AND IT DOESN'T HEAR ZVI'S VOICE AND IT'S **ALL ALONE**.

IT DOESN'T KNOW HOW IT KNOWS *ANY* OF THIS. BUT IT KNOWS IT.

ITS NAME IS ROVER AND THE MUSIC WENT RIGHT **THROUGH** IT --

AND JIM AND ZVI AND *CHUCK* ARE ALL GONE AND IT WANTS THEM **BACK**.

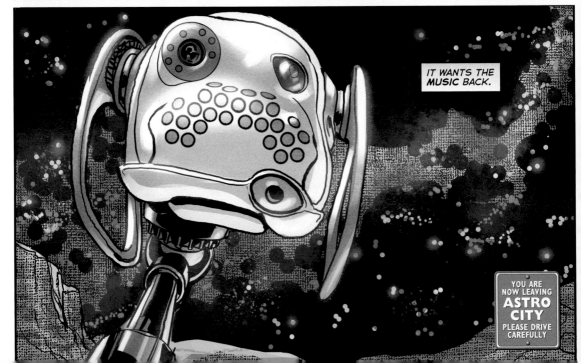

IT WANTS THE MUSIC BACK.

YOU ARE NOW LEAVING
ASTRO CITY
PLEASE DRIVE CAREFULLY

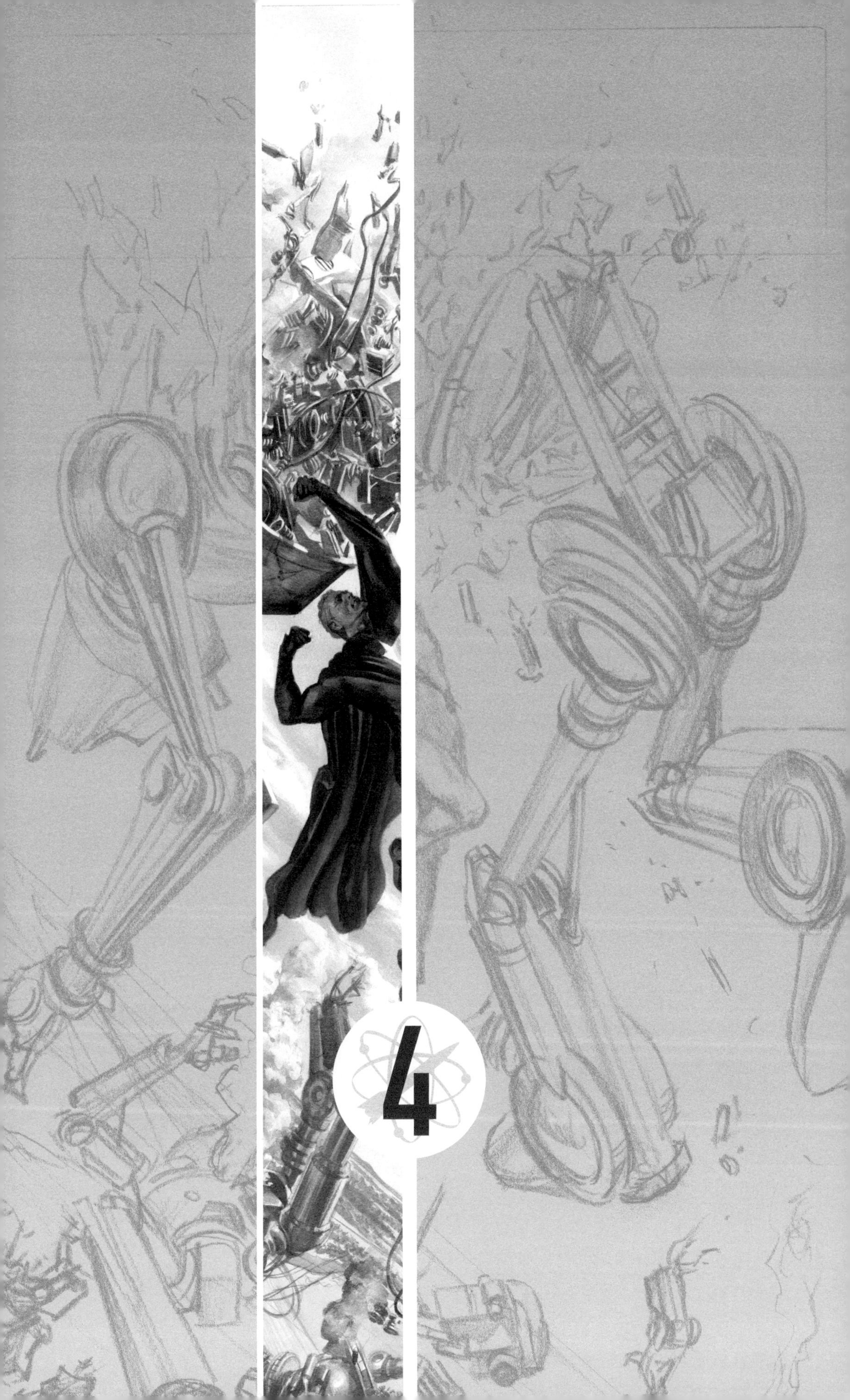
4

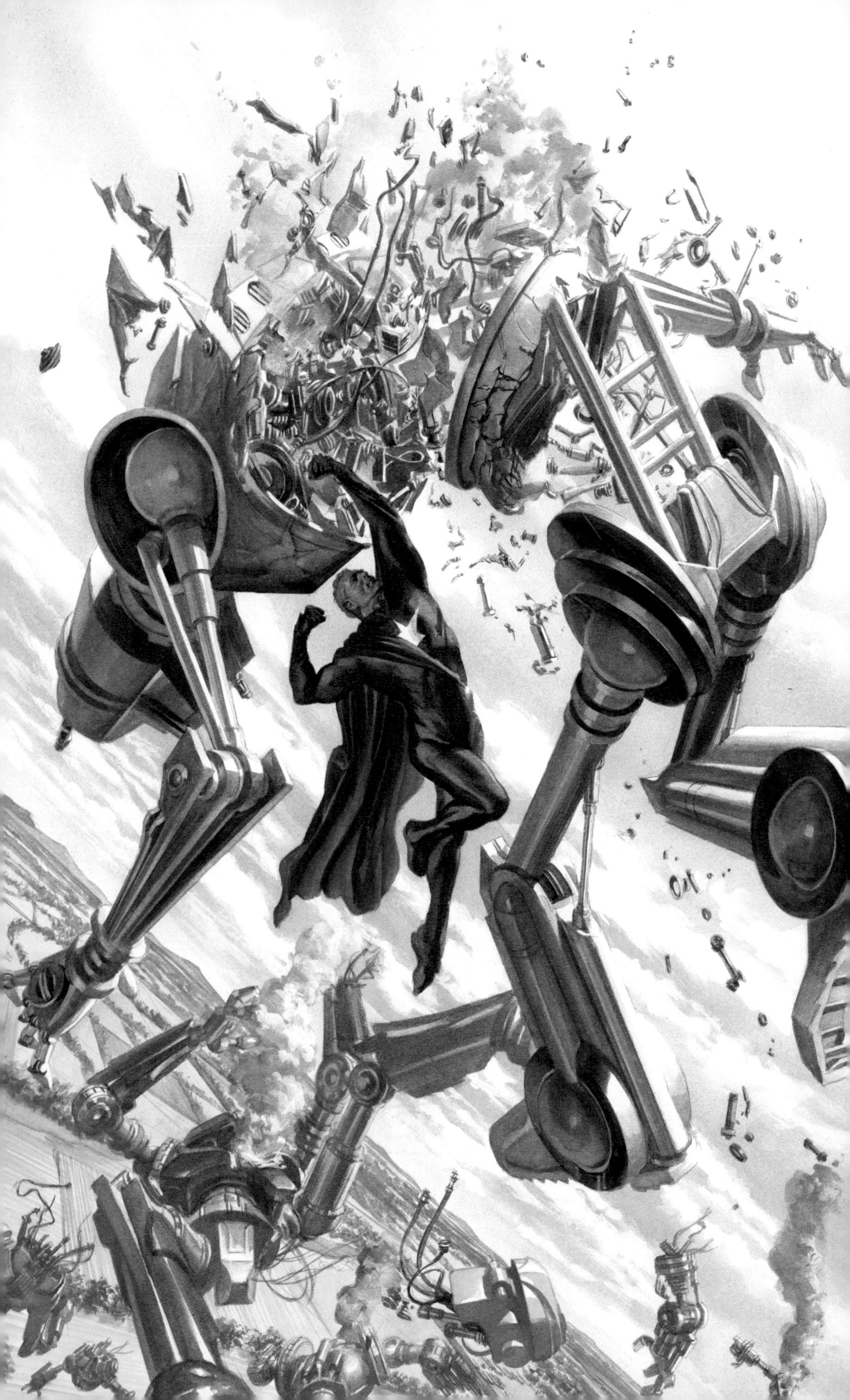

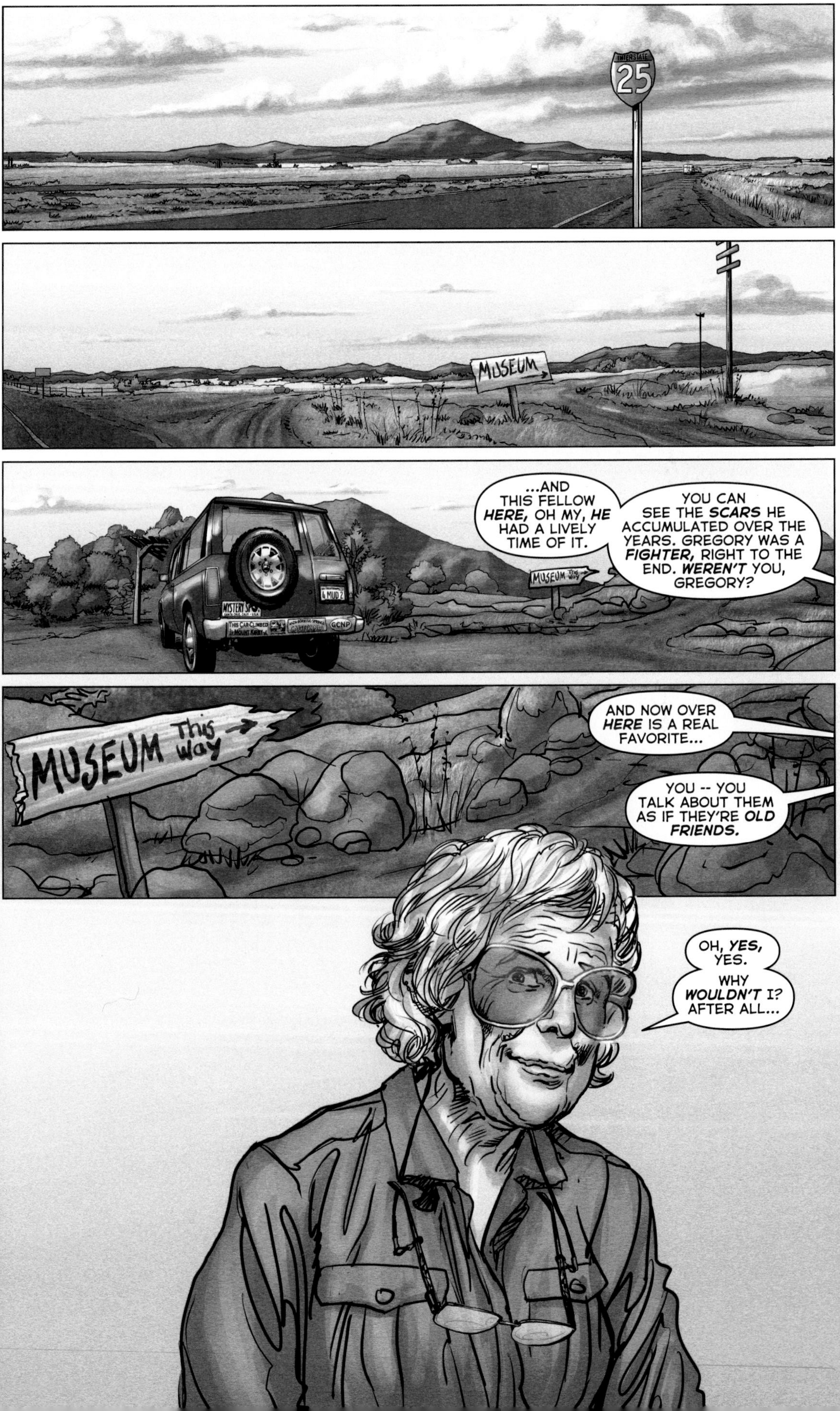

INTERSTATE
25
MUSEUM
MUSEUM This way
MYSTERY SPOT
4 MUD 2
GCNP
...AND THIS FELLOW HERE, OH MY, HE HAD A LIVELY TIME OF IT.
YOU CAN SEE THE SCARS HE ACCUMULATED OVER THE YEARS. GREGORY WAS A FIGHTER, RIGHT TO THE END. WEREN'T YOU, GREGORY?
MUSEUM This way
AND NOW OVER HERE IS A REAL FAVORITE...
YOU -- YOU TALK ABOUT THEM AS IF THEY'RE OLD FRIENDS.
OH, YES, YES.
WHY WOULDN'T I? AFTER ALL...

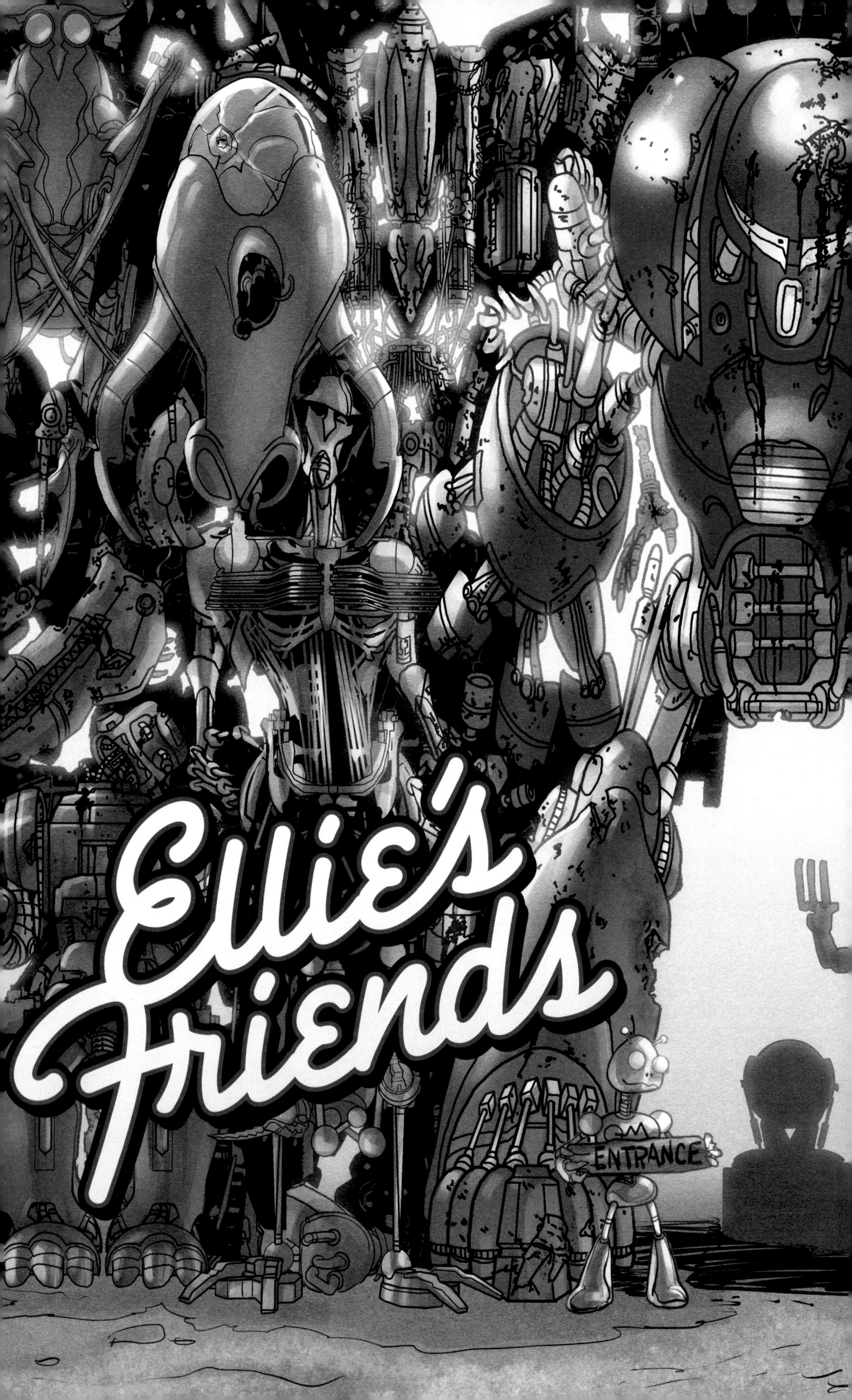
Ellie's Friends
ENTRANCE

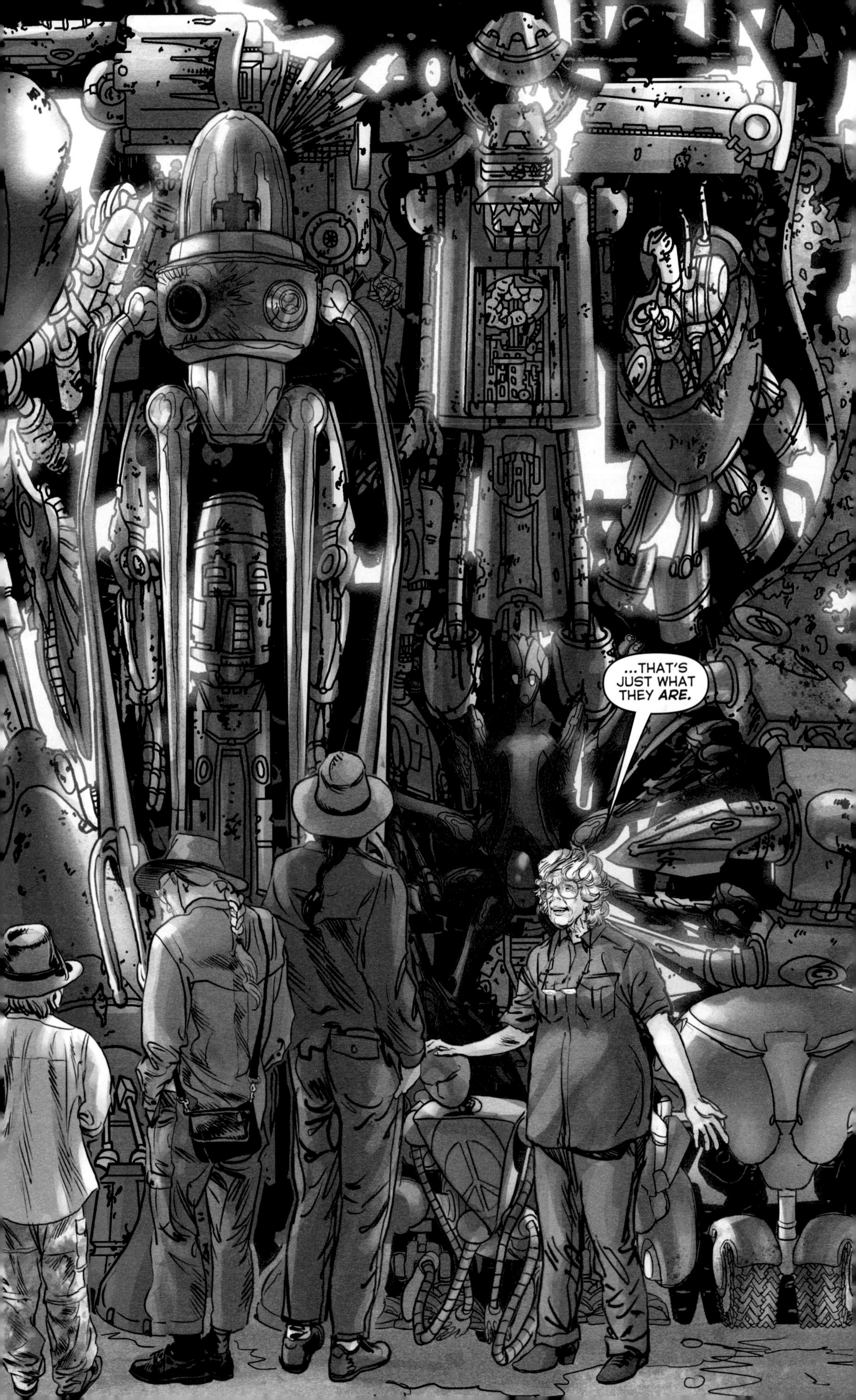
...THAT'S JUST WHAT THEY ARE.

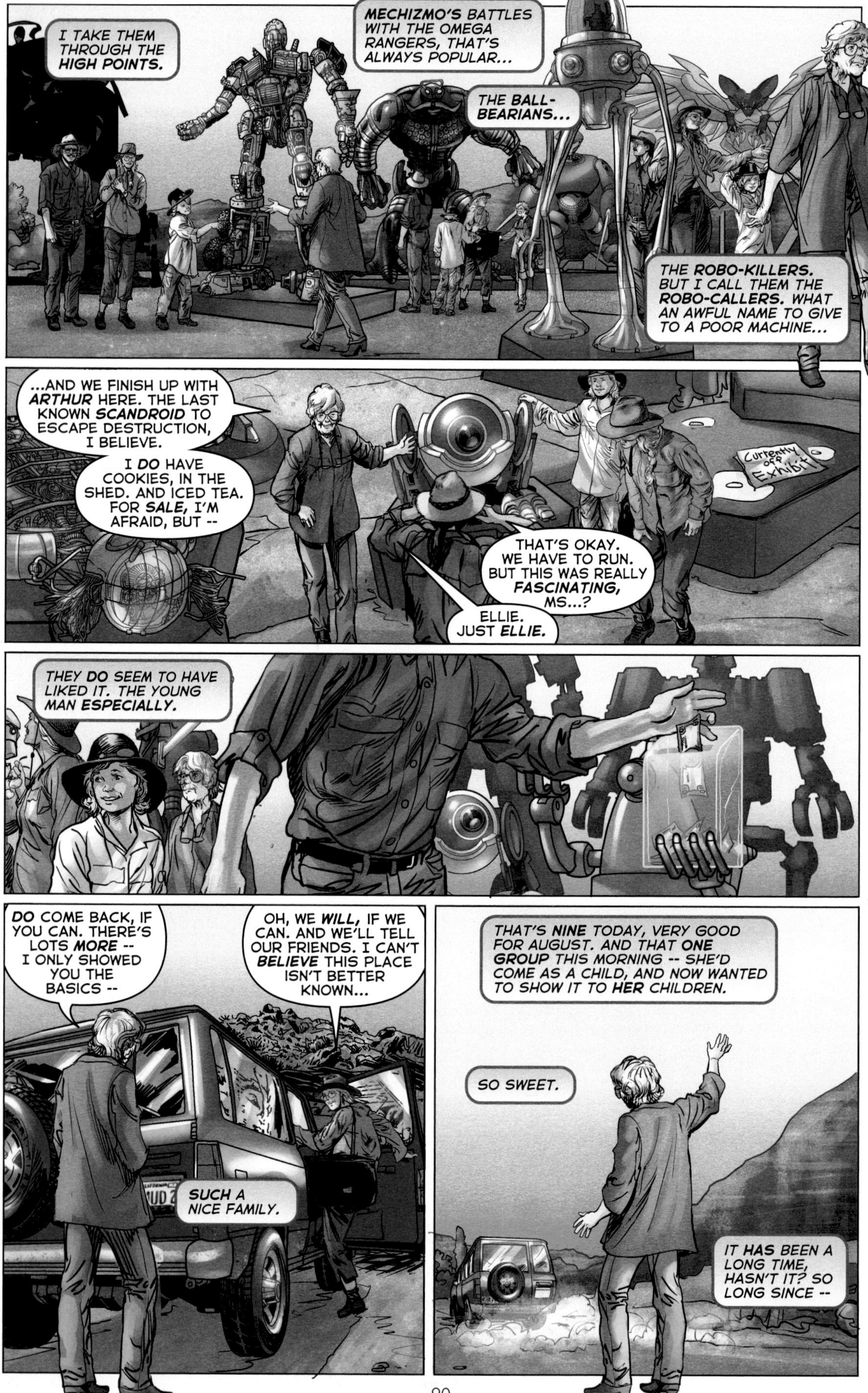
I TAKE THEM THROUGH THE HIGH POINTS.
MECHIZMO'S BATTLES WITH THE OMEGA RANGERS, THAT'S ALWAYS POPULAR...
THE BALL-BEARIANS...
THE ROBO-KILLERS. BUT I CALL THEM THE ROBO-CALLERS. WHAT AN AWFUL NAME TO GIVE TO A POOR MACHINE...
...AND WE FINISH UP WITH ARTHUR HERE. THE LAST KNOWN SCANDROID TO ESCAPE DESTRUCTION, I BELIEVE.
I DO HAVE COOKIES, IN THE SHED. AND ICED TEA. FOR SALE, I'M AFRAID, BUT --
Currently off Exhibit
THAT'S OKAY. WE HAVE TO RUN. BUT THIS WAS REALLY FASCINATING, MS...?
ELLIE. JUST ELLIE.
THEY DO SEEM TO HAVE LIKED IT. THE YOUNG MAN ESPECIALLY.
DO COME BACK, IF YOU CAN. THERE'S LOTS MORE -- I ONLY SHOWED YOU THE BASICS --
OH, WE WILL, IF WE CAN. AND WE'LL TELL OUR FRIENDS. I CAN'T BELIEVE THIS PLACE ISN'T BETTER KNOWN...
SUCH A NICE FAMILY.
THAT'S NINE TODAY, VERY GOOD FOR AUGUST. AND THAT ONE GROUP THIS MORNING -- SHE'D COME AS A CHILD, AND NOW WANTED TO SHOW IT TO HER CHILDREN.
SO SWEET.
IT HAS BEEN A LONG TIME, HASN'T IT? SO LONG SINCE --

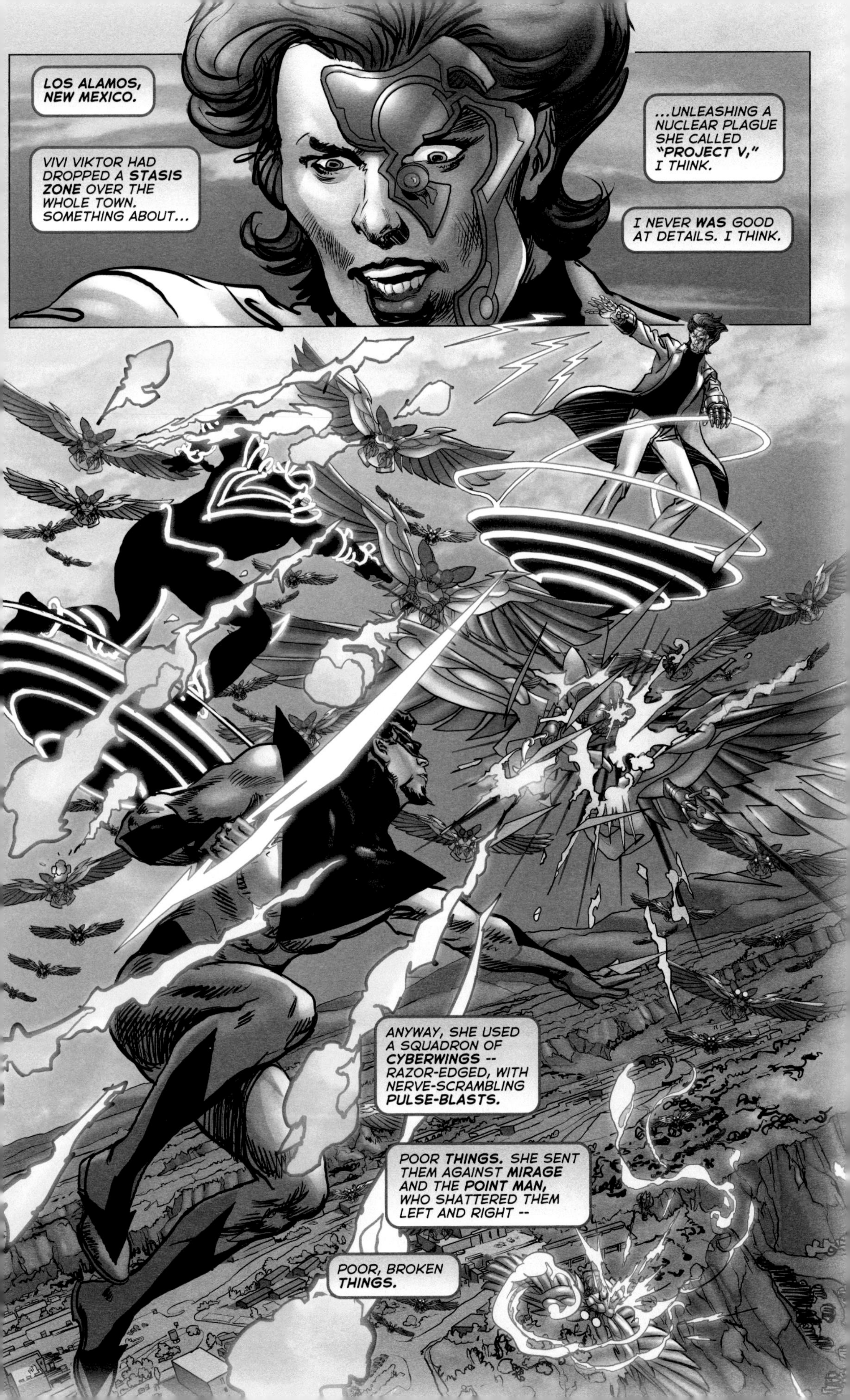
LOS ALAMOS, NEW MEXICO.
VIVI VIKTOR HAD DROPPED A STASIS ZONE OVER THE WHOLE TOWN. SOMETHING ABOUT...
...UNLEASHING A NUCLEAR PLAGUE SHE CALLED "PROJECT V," I THINK.
I NEVER WAS GOOD AT DETAILS. I THINK.
ANYWAY, SHE USED A SQUADRON OF CYBERWINGS -- RAZOR-EDGED, WITH NERVE-SCRAMBLING PULSE-BLASTS.
POOR THINGS. SHE SENT THEM AGAINST MIRAGE AND THE POINT MAN, WHO SHATTERED THEM LEFT AND RIGHT --
POOR, BROKEN THINGS.

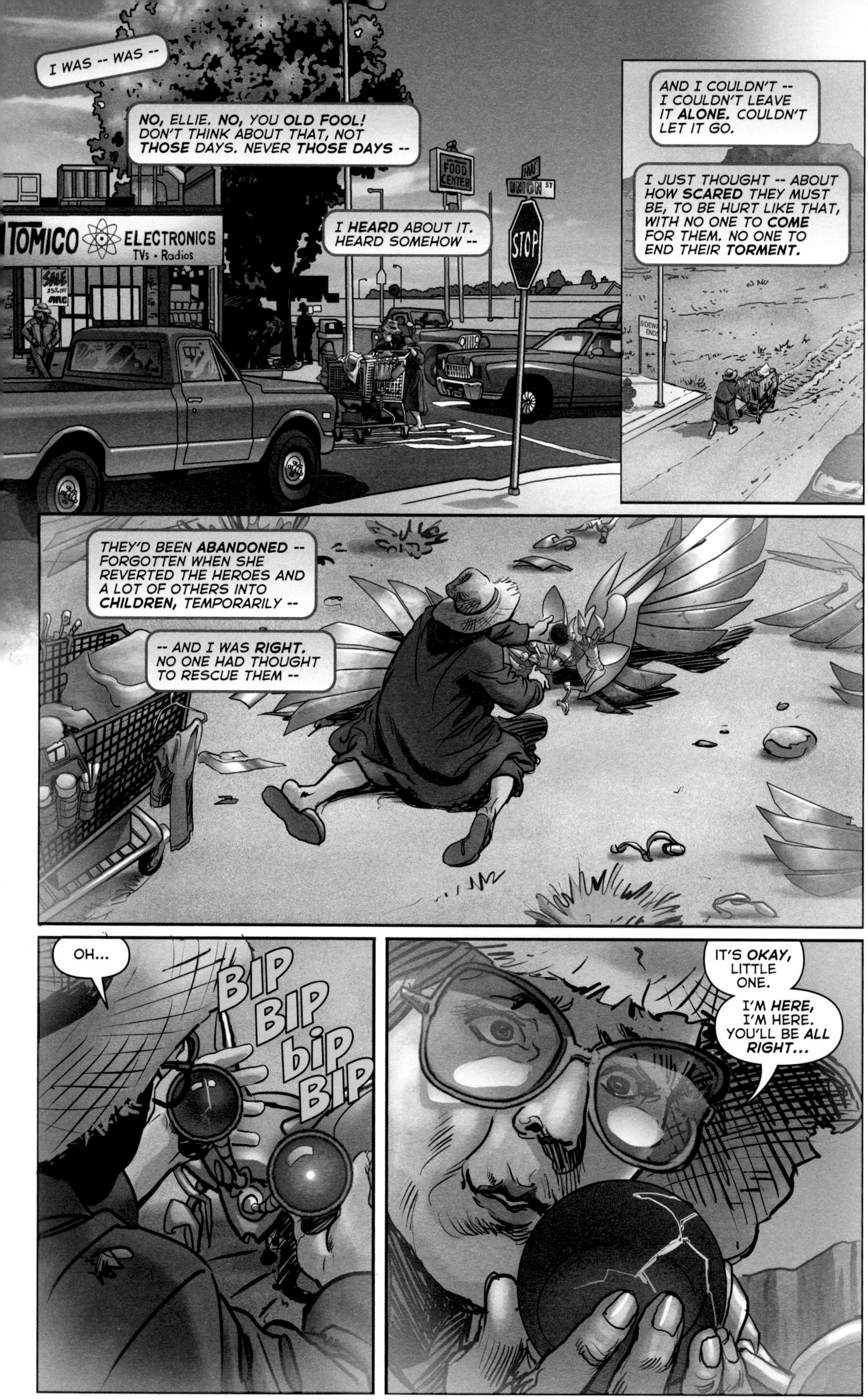
I WAS -- WAS --
NO, ELLIE. NO, YOU OLD FOOL! DON'T THINK ABOUT THAT, NOT THOSE DAYS. NEVER THOSE DAYS --
FOOD CENTER
UNION ST
STOP
ATOMICO ELECTRONICS TVs • Radios
SALE
I HEARD ABOUT IT. HEARD SOMEHOW --
AND I COULDN'T -- I COULDN'T LEAVE IT ALONE. COULDN'T LET IT GO.
I JUST THOUGHT -- ABOUT HOW SCARED THEY MUST BE, TO BE HURT LIKE THAT, WITH NO ONE TO COME FOR THEM. NO ONE TO END THEIR TORMENT.
THEY'D BEEN ABANDONED -- FORGOTTEN WHEN SHE REVERTED THE HEROES AND A LOT OF OTHERS INTO CHILDREN, TEMPORARILY --
-- AND I WAS RIGHT. NO ONE HAD THOUGHT TO RESCUE THEM --
OH...
BIP BIP bip BIP
IT'S OKAY, LITTLE ONE.
I'M HERE, I'M HERE. YOU'LL BE ALL RIGHT...

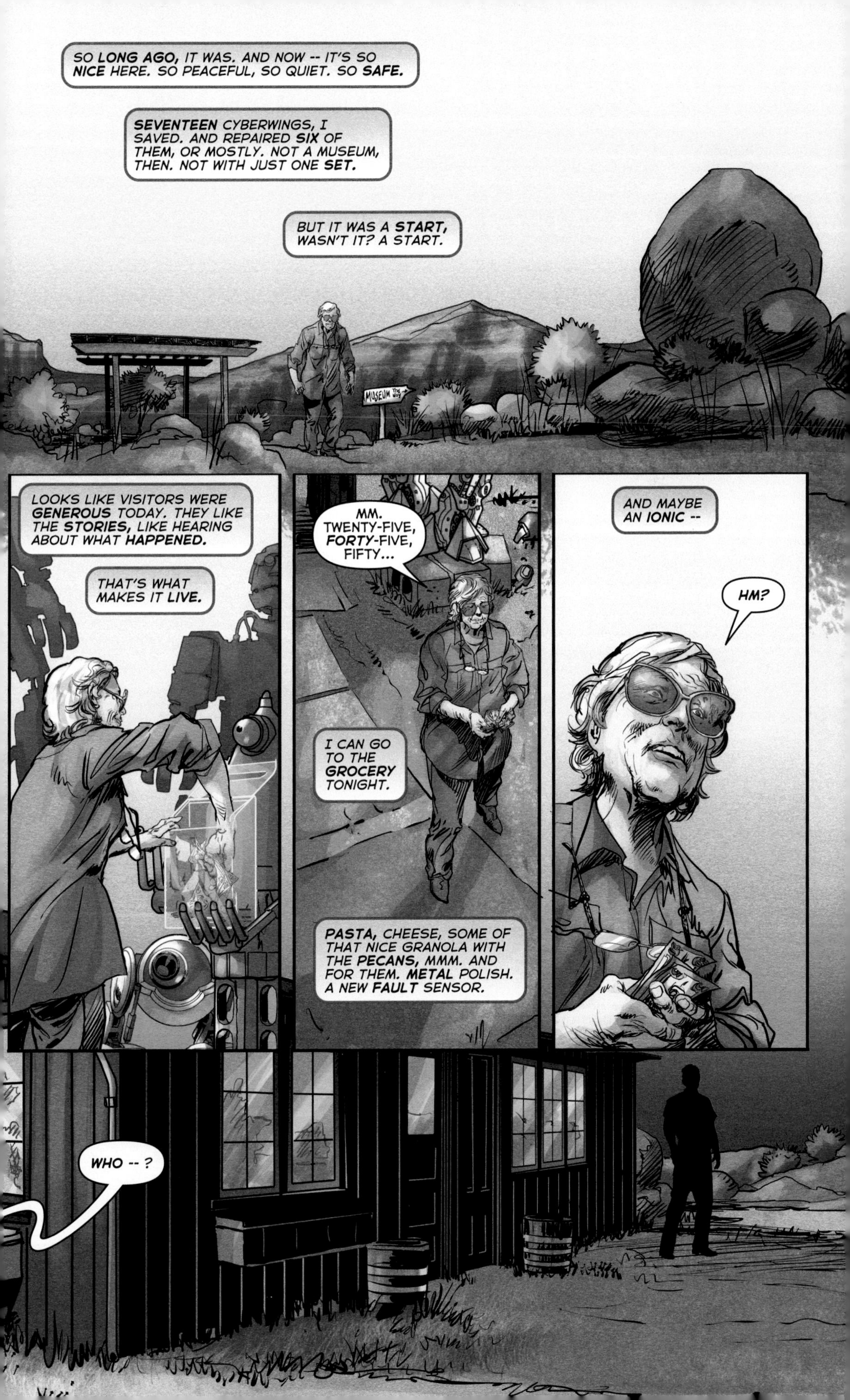
SO LONG AGO, IT WAS. AND NOW -- IT'S SO NICE HERE. SO PEACEFUL, SO QUIET. SO SAFE.
SEVENTEEN CYBERWINGS, I SAVED. AND REPAIRED SIX OF THEM, OR MOSTLY. NOT A MUSEUM, THEN. NOT WITH JUST ONE SET.
BUT IT WAS A START, WASN'T IT? A START.
MUSEUM
LOOKS LIKE VISITORS WERE GENEROUS TODAY. THEY LIKE THE STORIES, LIKE HEARING ABOUT WHAT HAPPENED.
THAT'S WHAT MAKES IT LIVE.
MM. TWENTY-FIVE, FORTY-FIVE, FIFTY...
I CAN GO TO THE GROCERY TONIGHT.
PASTA, CHEESE, SOME OF THAT NICE GRANOLA WITH THE PECANS, MMM. AND FOR THEM. METAL POLISH. A NEW FAULT SENSOR.
AND MAYBE AN IONIC --
HM?
WHO -- ?

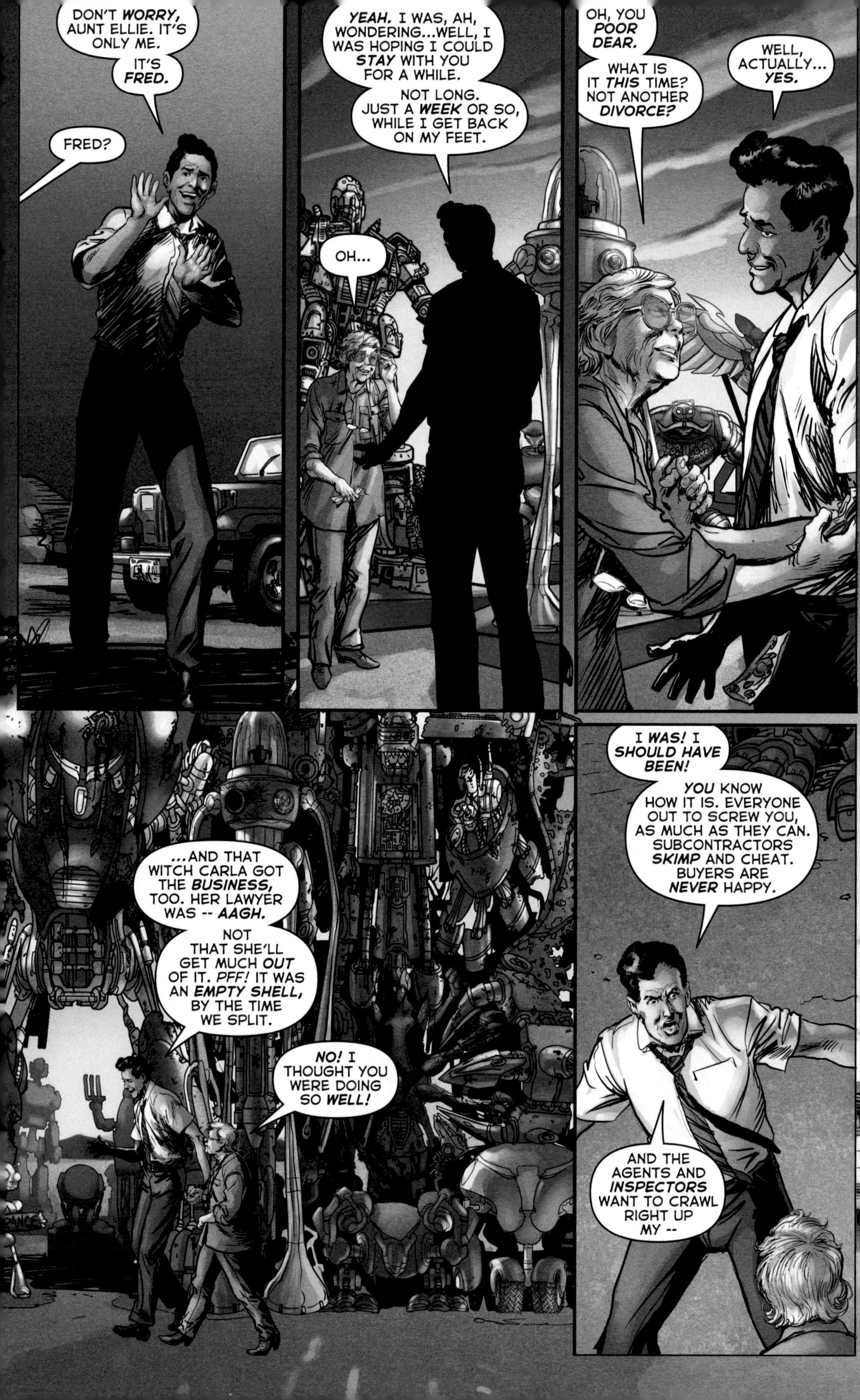

DON'T WORRY, AUNT ELLIE. IT'S ONLY ME.
IT'S FRED.
FRED?
YEAH. I WAS, AH, WONDERING...WELL, I WAS HOPING I COULD STAY WITH YOU FOR A WHILE.
NOT LONG. JUST A WEEK OR SO, WHILE I GET BACK ON MY FEET.
OH...
OH, YOU POOR DEAR.
WHAT IS IT THIS TIME? NOT ANOTHER DIVORCE?
WELL, ACTUALLY... YES.
...AND THAT WITCH CARLA GOT THE BUSINESS, TOO. HER LAWYER WAS -- AAGH.
NOT THAT SHE'LL GET MUCH OUT OF IT. PFF! IT WAS AN EMPTY SHELL, BY THE TIME WE SPLIT.
NO! I THOUGHT YOU WERE DOING SO WELL!
I WAS! I SHOULD HAVE BEEN!
YOU KNOW HOW IT IS. EVERYONE OUT TO SCREW YOU, AS MUCH AS THEY CAN. SUBCONTRACTORS SKIMP AND CHEAT. BUYERS ARE NEVER HAPPY.
AND THE AGENTS AND INSPECTORS WANT TO CRAWL RIGHT UP MY --

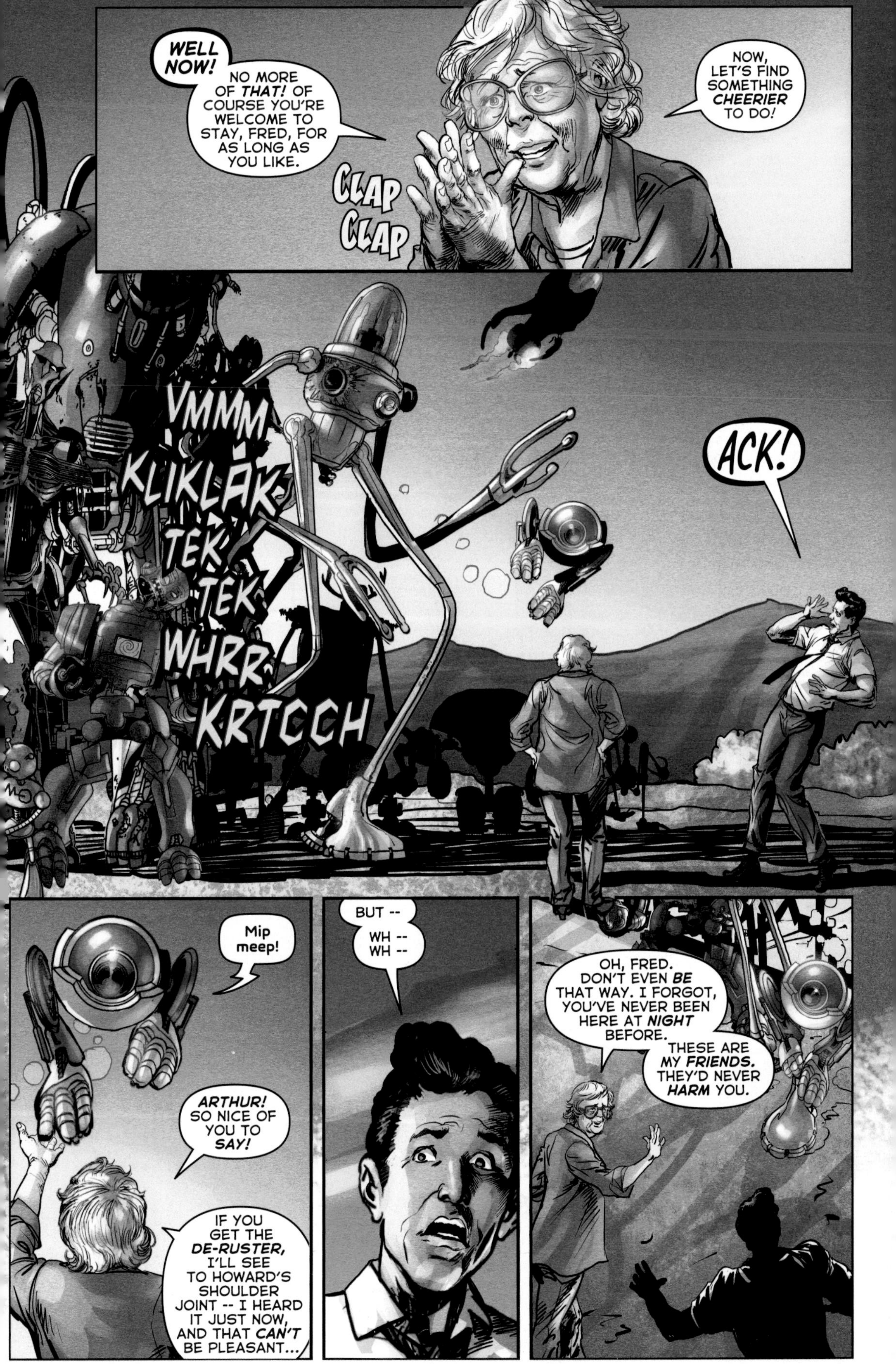
WELL NOW!
NO MORE OF THAT! OF COURSE YOU'RE WELCOME TO STAY, FRED, FOR AS LONG AS YOU LIKE.
CLAP CLAP
NOW, LET'S FIND SOMETHING CHEERIER TO DO!
VMMM KLIKLAK TEK TEK WHRR KRTCCH
ACK!
Mip meep!
ARTHUR! SO NICE OF YOU TO SAY!
IF YOU GET THE DE-RUSTER, I'LL SEE TO HOWARD'S SHOULDER JOINT -- I HEARD IT JUST NOW, AND THAT CAN'T BE PLEASANT...
BUT --
WH -- WH --
OH, FRED. DON'T EVEN BE THAT WAY. I FORGOT, YOU'VE NEVER BEEN HERE AT NIGHT BEFORE.
THESE ARE MY FRIENDS. THEY'D NEVER HARM YOU.

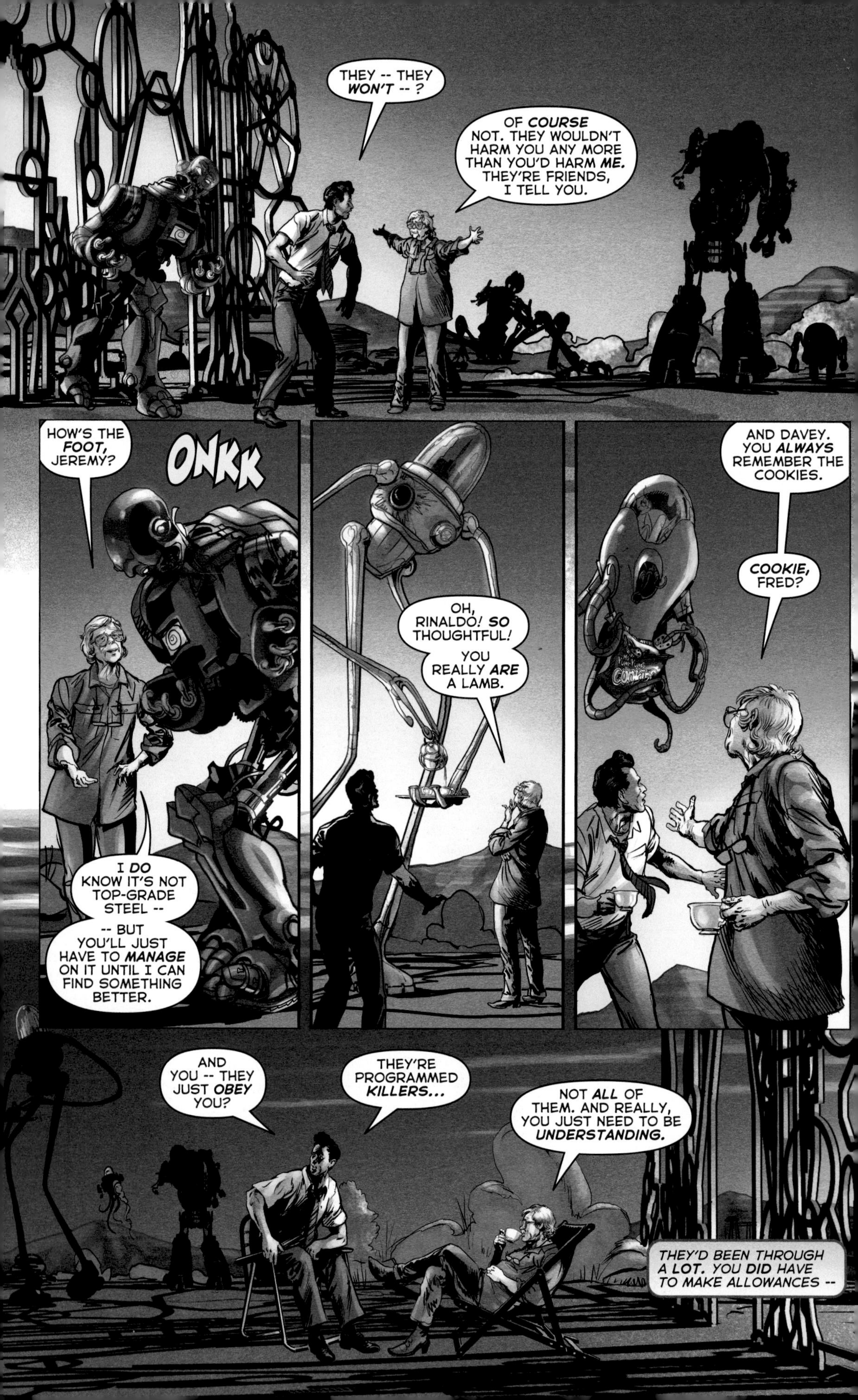
THEY -- THEY WON'T -- ?
OF COURSE NOT. THEY WOULDN'T HARM YOU ANY MORE THAN YOU'D HARM ME. THEY'RE FRIENDS, I TELL YOU.
HOW'S THE FOOT, JEREMY?
ONKK
I DO KNOW IT'S NOT TOP-GRADE STEEL --
-- BUT YOU'LL JUST HAVE TO MANAGE ON IT UNTIL I CAN FIND SOMETHING BETTER.
OH, RINALDO! SO THOUGHTFUL!
YOU REALLY ARE A LAMB.
AND DAVEY. YOU ALWAYS REMEMBER THE COOKIES.
COOKIE, FRED?
AND YOU -- THEY JUST OBEY YOU?
THEY'RE PROGRAMMED KILLERS...
NOT ALL OF THEM. AND REALLY, YOU JUST NEED TO BE UNDERSTANDING.
THEY'D BEEN THROUGH A LOT. YOU DID HAVE TO MAKE ALLOWANCES --

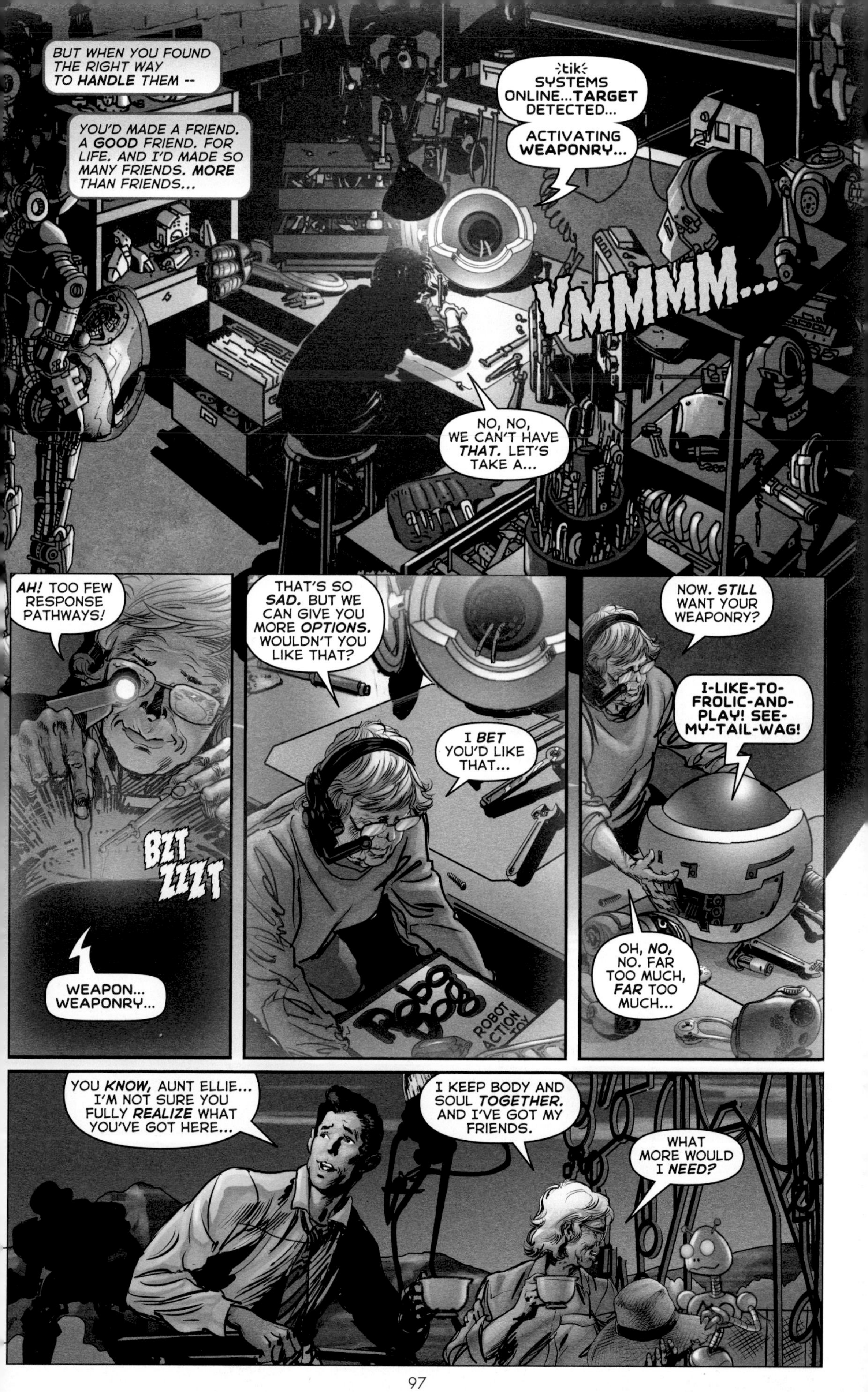

BUT WHEN YOU FOUND THE RIGHT WAY TO HANDLE THEM --
YOU'D MADE A FRIEND. A GOOD FRIEND. FOR LIFE. AND I'D MADE SO MANY FRIENDS. MORE THAN FRIENDS...
tik
SYSTEMS ONLINE...TARGET DETECTED...
ACTIVATING WEAPONRY...
VMMMM...
NO, NO, WE CAN'T HAVE THAT. LET'S TAKE A...
AH! TOO FEW RESPONSE PATHWAYS!
BZT ZZZT
WEAPON... WEAPONRY...
THAT'S SO SAD. BUT WE CAN GIVE YOU MORE OPTIONS. WOULDN'T YOU LIKE THAT?
I BET YOU'D LIKE THAT...
ROBOT ACTION TOY
NOW. STILL WANT YOUR WEAPONRY?
I-LIKE-TO-FROLIC-AND-PLAY! SEE-MY-TAIL-WAG!
OH, NO, NO. FAR TOO MUCH, FAR TOO MUCH...
YOU KNOW, AUNT ELLIE... I'M NOT SURE YOU FULLY REALIZE WHAT YOU'VE GOT HERE...
I KEEP BODY AND SOUL TOGETHER. AND I'VE GOT MY FRIENDS.
WHAT MORE WOULD I NEED?

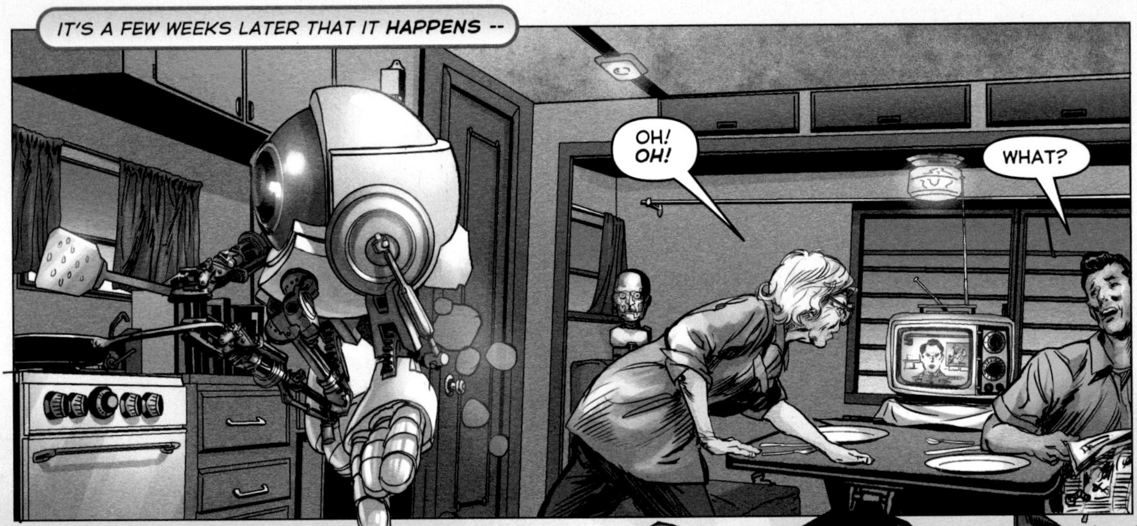
IT'S A FEW WEEKS LATER THAT IT HAPPENS --
OH! OH!
WHAT?

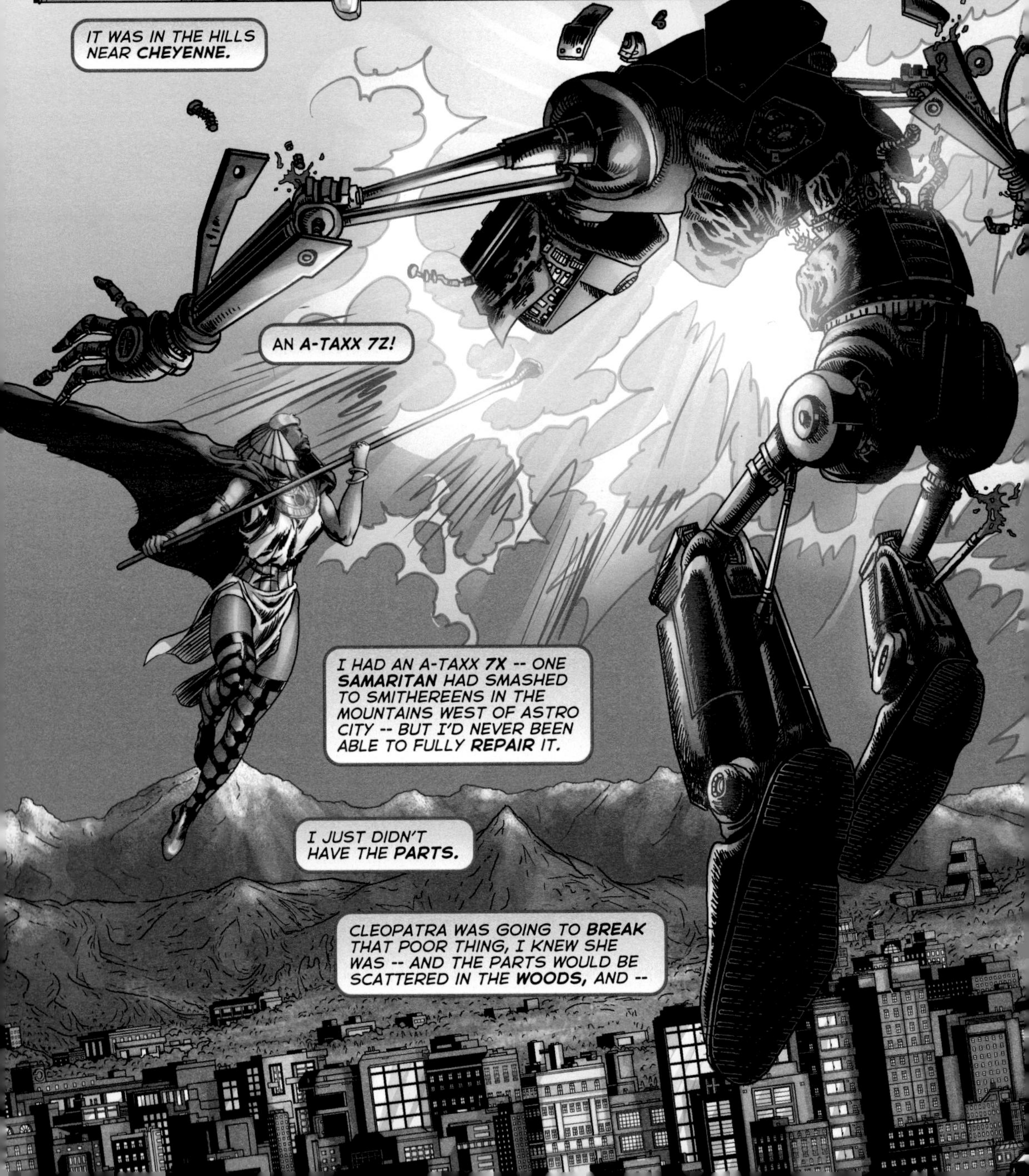
IT WAS IN THE HILLS NEAR CHEYENNE.
AN A-TAXX 7Z!
I HAD AN A-TAXX 7X -- ONE SAMARITAN HAD SMASHED TO SMITHEREENS IN THE MOUNTAINS WEST OF ASTRO CITY -- BUT I'D NEVER BEEN ABLE TO FULLY REPAIR IT.
I JUST DIDN'T HAVE THE PARTS.
CLEOPATRA WAS GOING TO BREAK THAT POOR THING, I KNEW SHE WAS -- AND THE PARTS WOULD BE SCATTERED IN THE WOODS, AND --

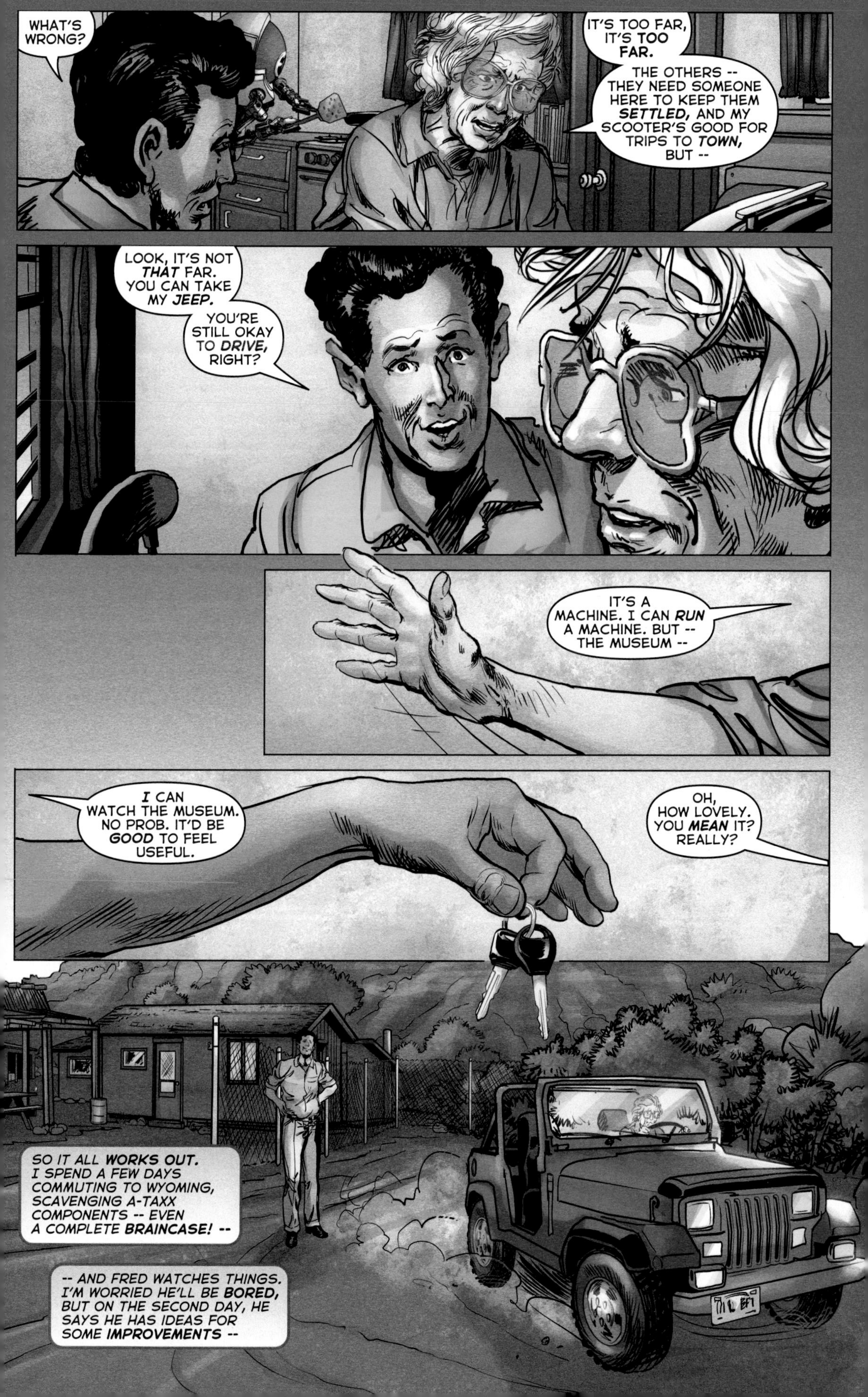
WHAT'S WRONG?
IT'S TOO FAR, IT'S TOO FAR.
THE OTHERS -- THEY NEED SOMEONE HERE TO KEEP THEM SETTLED, AND MY SCOOTER'S GOOD FOR TRIPS TO TOWN, BUT --
LOOK, IT'S NOT THAT FAR. YOU CAN TAKE MY JEEP.
YOU'RE STILL OKAY TO DRIVE, RIGHT?
IT'S A MACHINE. I CAN RUN A MACHINE. BUT -- THE MUSEUM --
I CAN WATCH THE MUSEUM. NO PROB. IT'D BE GOOD TO FEEL USEFUL.
OH, HOW LOVELY. YOU MEAN IT? REALLY?
SO IT ALL WORKS OUT. I SPEND A FEW DAYS COMMUTING TO WYOMING, SCAVENGING A-TAXX COMPONENTS -- EVEN A COMPLETE BRAINCASE! --
-- AND FRED WATCHES THINGS. I'M WORRIED HE'LL BE BORED, BUT ON THE SECOND DAY, HE SAYS HE HAS IDEAS FOR SOME IMPROVEMENTS --

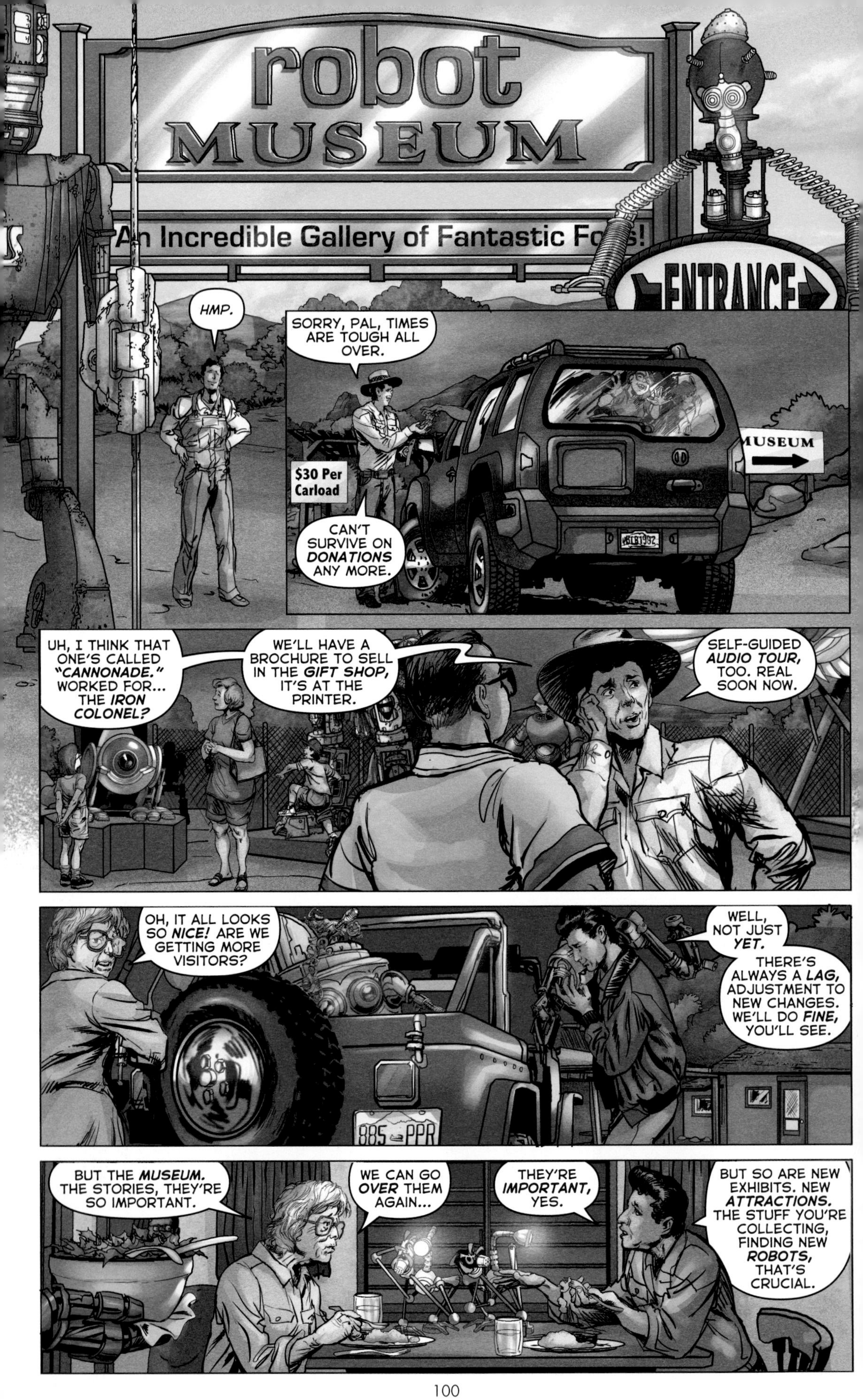
robot MUSEUM
An Incredible Gallery of Fantastic Fo s!
ENTRANCE
HMP.
SORRY, PAL, TIMES ARE TOUGH ALL OVER.
$30 Per Carload
MUSEUM
CAN'T SURVIVE ON *DONATIONS* ANY MORE.
UH, I THINK THAT ONE'S CALLED *"CANNONADE."* WORKED FOR... THE *IRON COLONEL?*
WE'LL HAVE A BROCHURE TO SELL IN THE *GIFT SHOP,* IT'S AT THE PRINTER.
SELF-GUIDED *AUDIO TOUR,* TOO. REAL SOON NOW.
OH, IT ALL LOOKS SO *NICE!* ARE WE GETTING MORE VISITORS?
WELL, NOT JUST *YET.*
THERE'S ALWAYS A *LAG,* ADJUSTMENT TO NEW CHANGES. WE'LL DO *FINE,* YOU'LL SEE.
885 PPR
BUT THE *MUSEUM.* THE STORIES, THEY'RE SO IMPORTANT.
WE CAN GO *OVER* THEM AGAIN...
THEY'RE *IMPORTANT,* YES.
BUT SO ARE NEW EXHIBITS. NEW *ATTRACTIONS.* THE STUFF YOU'RE COLLECTING, FINDING NEW *ROBOTS,* THAT'S CRUCIAL.

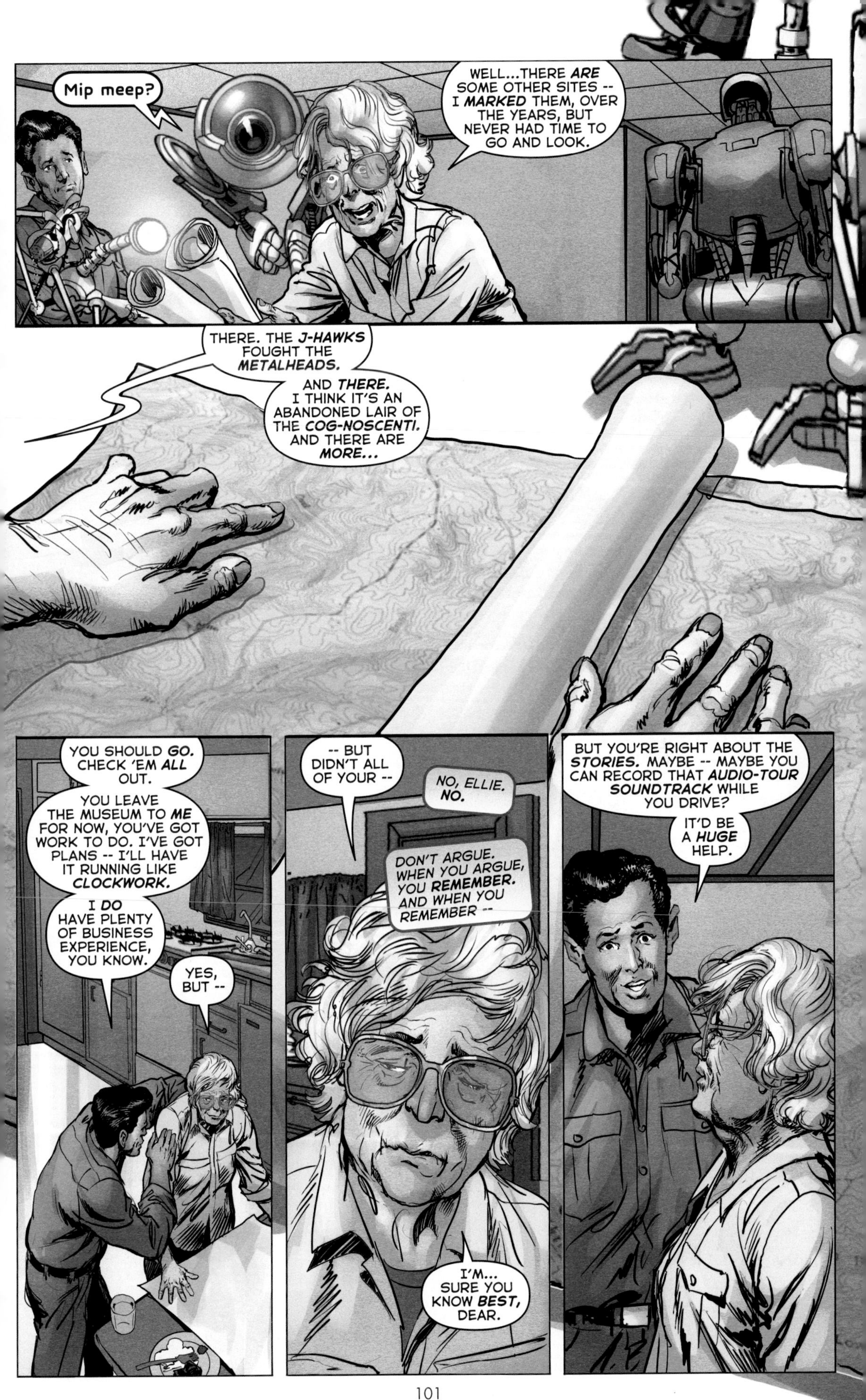

Mip meep?
WELL...THERE ARE SOME OTHER SITES -- I MARKED THEM, OVER THE YEARS, BUT NEVER HAD TIME TO GO AND LOOK.
THERE. THE J-HAWKS FOUGHT THE METALHEADS.
AND THERE. I THINK IT'S AN ABANDONED LAIR OF THE COG-NOSCENTI. AND THERE ARE MORE...
YOU SHOULD GO. CHECK 'EM ALL OUT.
YOU LEAVE THE MUSEUM TO ME FOR NOW, YOU'VE GOT WORK TO DO. I'VE GOT PLANS -- I'LL HAVE IT RUNNING LIKE CLOCKWORK.
I DO HAVE PLENTY OF BUSINESS EXPERIENCE, YOU KNOW.
YES, BUT --
-- BUT DIDN'T ALL OF YOUR --
NO, ELLIE. NO.
DON'T ARGUE. WHEN YOU ARGUE, YOU REMEMBER. AND WHEN YOU REMEMBER --
I'M... SURE YOU KNOW BEST, DEAR.
BUT YOU'RE RIGHT ABOUT THE STORIES. MAYBE -- MAYBE YOU CAN RECORD THAT AUDIO-TOUR SOUNDTRACK WHILE YOU DRIVE?
IT'D BE A HUGE HELP.

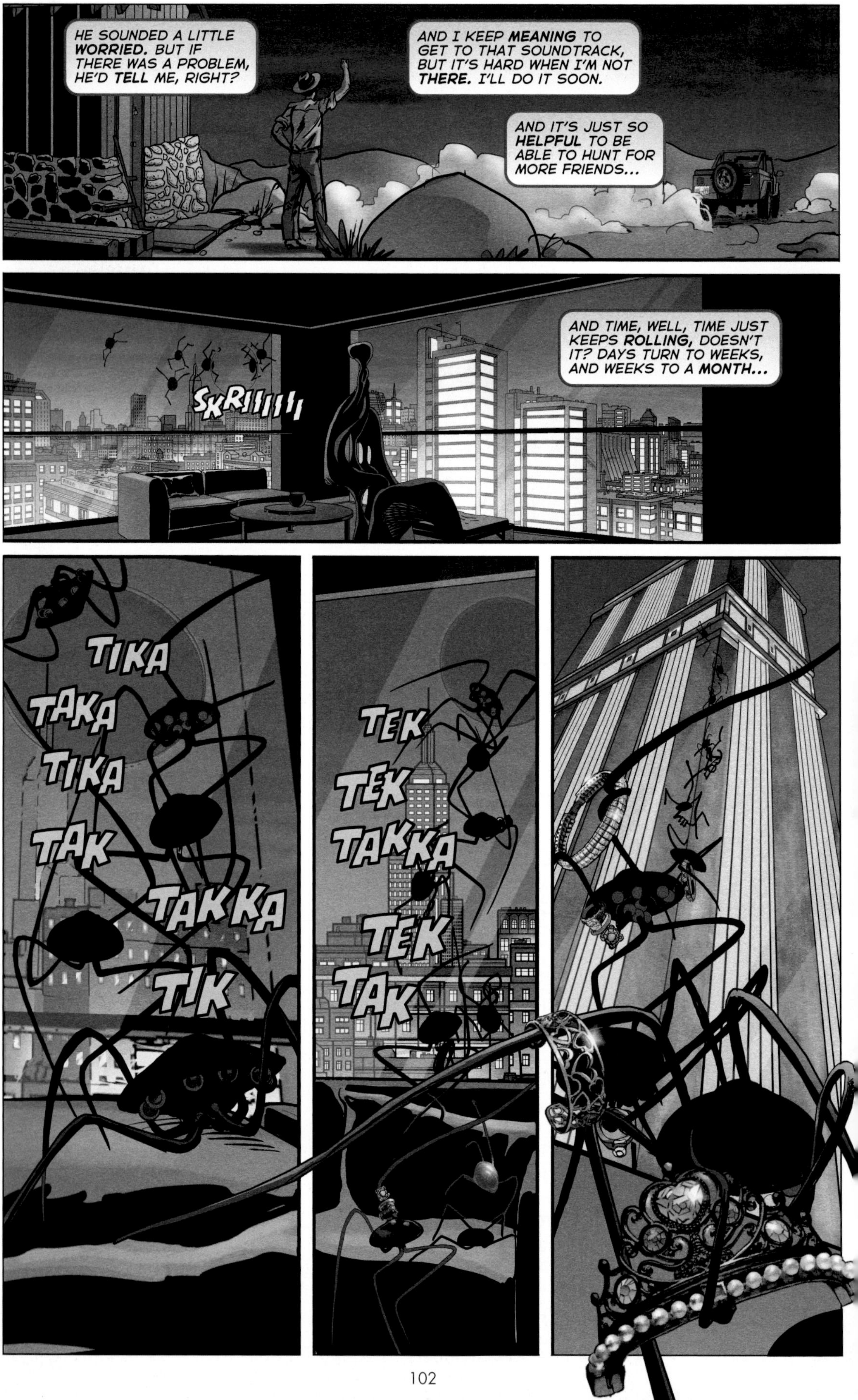

HE SOUNDED A LITTLE WORRIED. BUT IF THERE WAS A PROBLEM, HE'D TELL ME, RIGHT?
AND I KEEP MEANING TO GET TO THAT SOUNDTRACK, BUT IT'S HARD WHEN I'M NOT THERE. I'LL DO IT SOON.
AND IT'S JUST SO HELPFUL TO BE ABLE TO HUNT FOR MORE FRIENDS...
AND TIME, WELL, TIME JUST KEEPS ROLLING, DOESN'T IT? DAYS TURN TO WEEKS, AND WEEKS TO A MONTH...
SKRIIIIII
TIKA
TAKA
TIKA
TAK
TAKKA
TIK
TEK
TEK
TAKKA
TEK
TAK

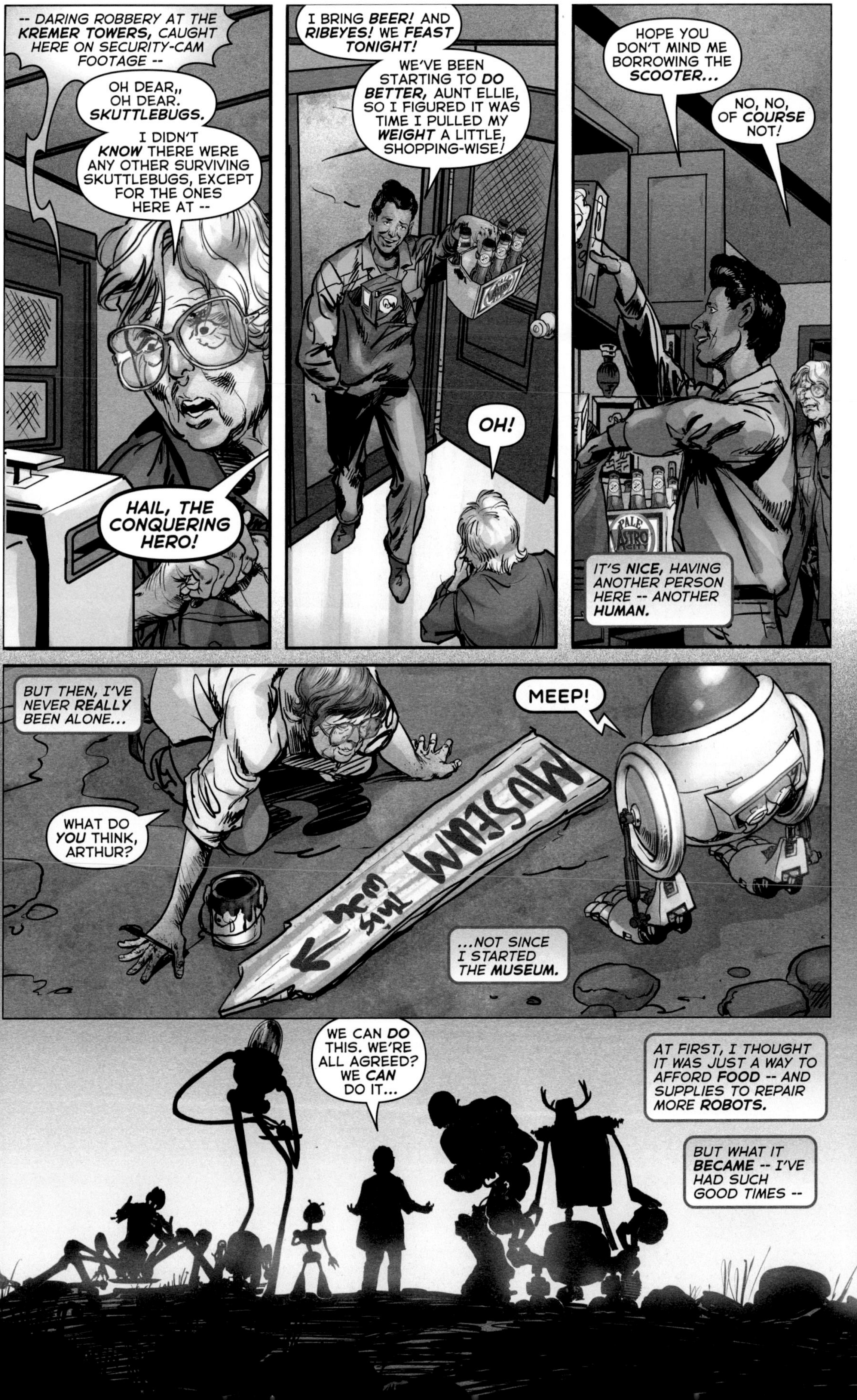
-- DARING ROBBERY AT THE KREMER TOWERS, CAUGHT HERE ON SECURITY-CAM FOOTAGE --
OH DEAR,, OH DEAR. SKUTTLEBUGS.
I DIDN'T KNOW THERE WERE ANY OTHER SURVIVING SKUTTLEBUGS, EXCEPT FOR THE ONES HERE AT --
HAIL, THE CONQUERING HERO!
I BRING BEER! AND RIBEYES! WE FEAST TONIGHT!
WE'VE BEEN STARTING TO DO BETTER, AUNT ELLIE, SO I FIGURED IT WAS TIME I PULLED MY WEIGHT A LITTLE, SHOPPING-WISE!
OH!
HOPE YOU DON'T MIND ME BORROWING THE SCOOTER...
NO, NO, OF COURSE NOT!
PALE ASTRO
IT'S NICE, HAVING ANOTHER PERSON HERE -- ANOTHER HUMAN.
BUT THEN, I'VE NEVER REALLY BEEN ALONE...
MEEP!
MUSEUM
THIS WAY
WHAT DO YOU THINK, ARTHUR?
...NOT SINCE I STARTED THE MUSEUM.
WE CAN DO THIS. WE'RE ALL AGREED? WE CAN DO IT...
AT FIRST, I THOUGHT IT WAS JUST A WAY TO AFFORD FOOD -- AND SUPPLIES TO REPAIR MORE ROBOTS.
BUT WHAT IT BECAME -- I'VE HAD SUCH GOOD TIMES --

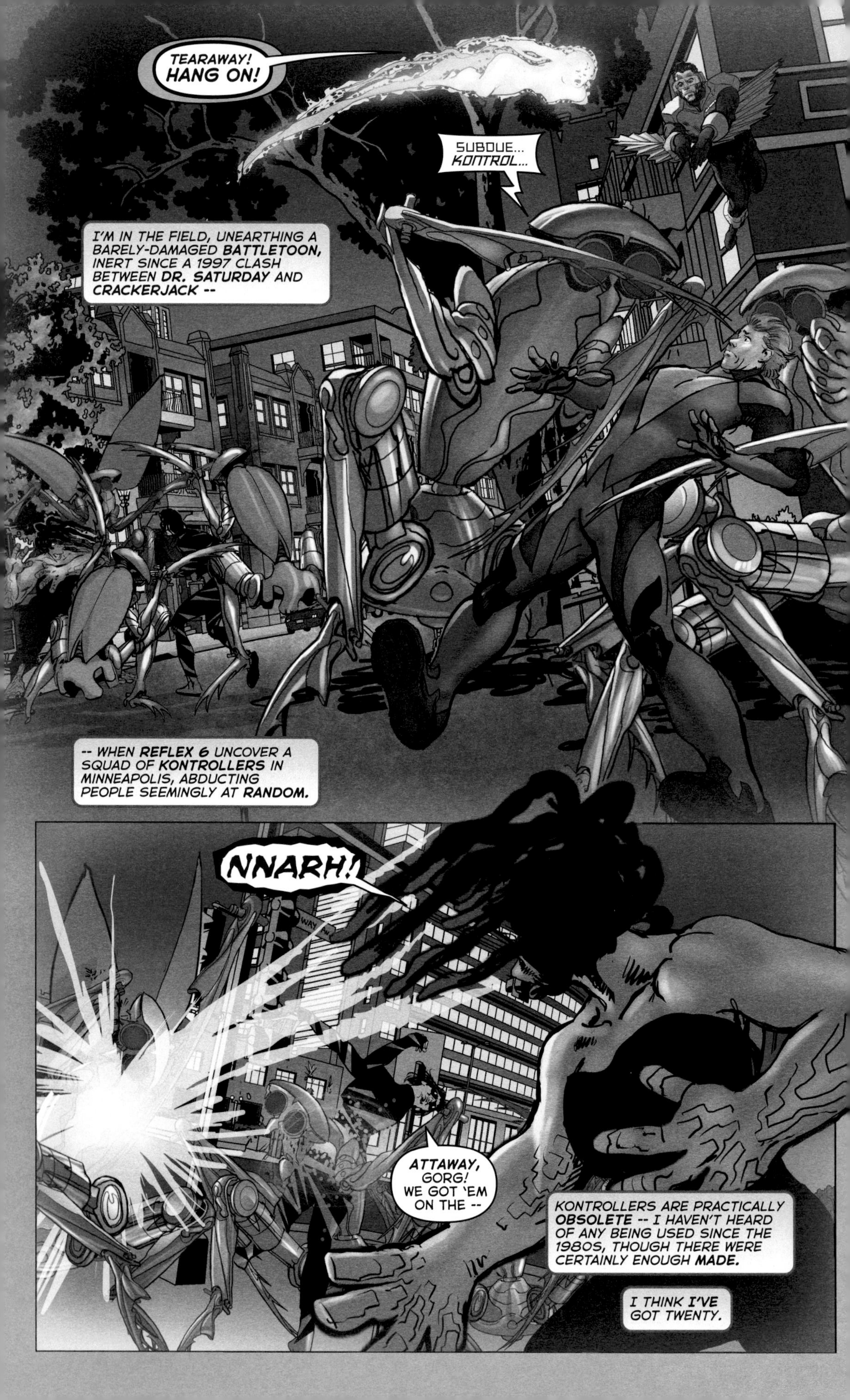
TEARAWAY! HANG ON!
SUBDUE... KONTROL...
I'M IN THE FIELD, UNEARTHING A BARELY-DAMAGED BATTLETOON, INERT SINCE A 1997 CLASH BETWEEN DR. SATURDAY AND CRACKERJACK --
-- WHEN REFLEX 6 UNCOVER A SQUAD OF KONTROLLERS IN MINNEAPOLIS, ABDUCTING PEOPLE SEEMINGLY AT RANDOM.
NNARH!
ATTAWAY, GORG! WE GOT 'EM ON THE --
KONTROLLERS ARE PRACTICALLY OBSOLETE -- I HAVEN'T HEARD OF ANY BEING USED SINCE THE 1980S, THOUGH THERE WERE CERTAINLY ENOUGH MADE.
I THINK I'VE GOT TWENTY.

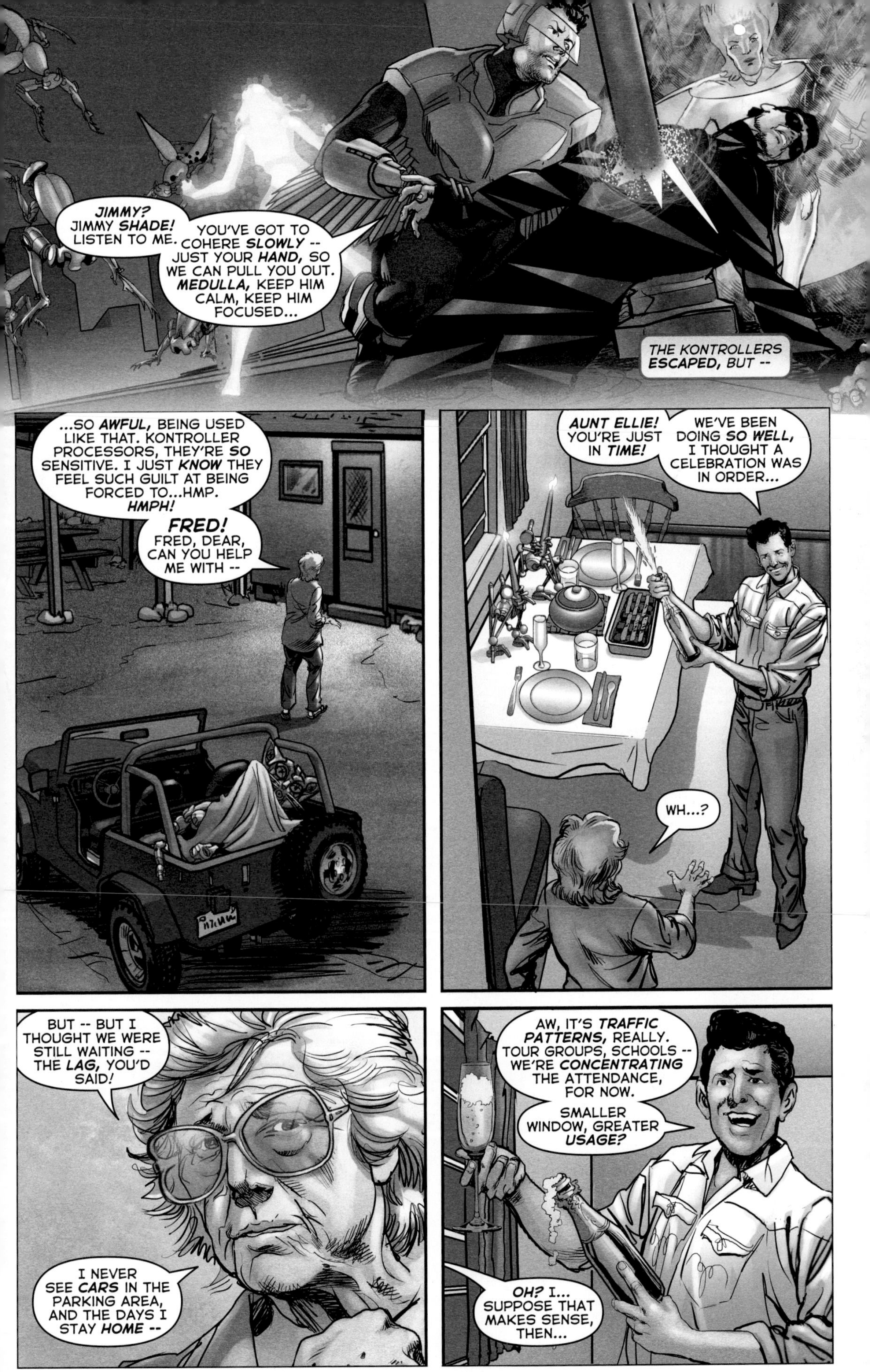
JIMMY? JIMMY SHADE! LISTEN TO ME.
YOU'VE GOT TO COHERE SLOWLY -- JUST YOUR HAND, SO WE CAN PULL YOU OUT. MEDULLA, KEEP HIM CALM, KEEP HIM FOCUSED...
THE KONTROLLERS ESCAPED, BUT --
...SO AWFUL, BEING USED LIKE THAT. KONTROLLER PROCESSORS, THEY'RE SO SENSITIVE. I JUST KNOW THEY FEEL SUCH GUILT AT BEING FORCED TO...HMP. HMPH!
FRED! FRED, DEAR, CAN YOU HELP ME WITH --
AUNT ELLIE! YOU'RE JUST IN TIME!
WE'VE BEEN DOING SO WELL, I THOUGHT A CELEBRATION WAS IN ORDER...
WH...?
BUT -- BUT I THOUGHT WE WERE STILL WAITING -- THE LAG, YOU'D SAID!
I NEVER SEE CARS IN THE PARKING AREA, AND THE DAYS I STAY HOME --
AW, IT'S TRAFFIC PATTERNS, REALLY. TOUR GROUPS, SCHOOLS -- WE'RE CONCENTRATING THE ATTENDANCE, FOR NOW.
SMALLER WINDOW, GREATER USAGE?
OH? I... SUPPOSE THAT MAKES SENSE, THEN...

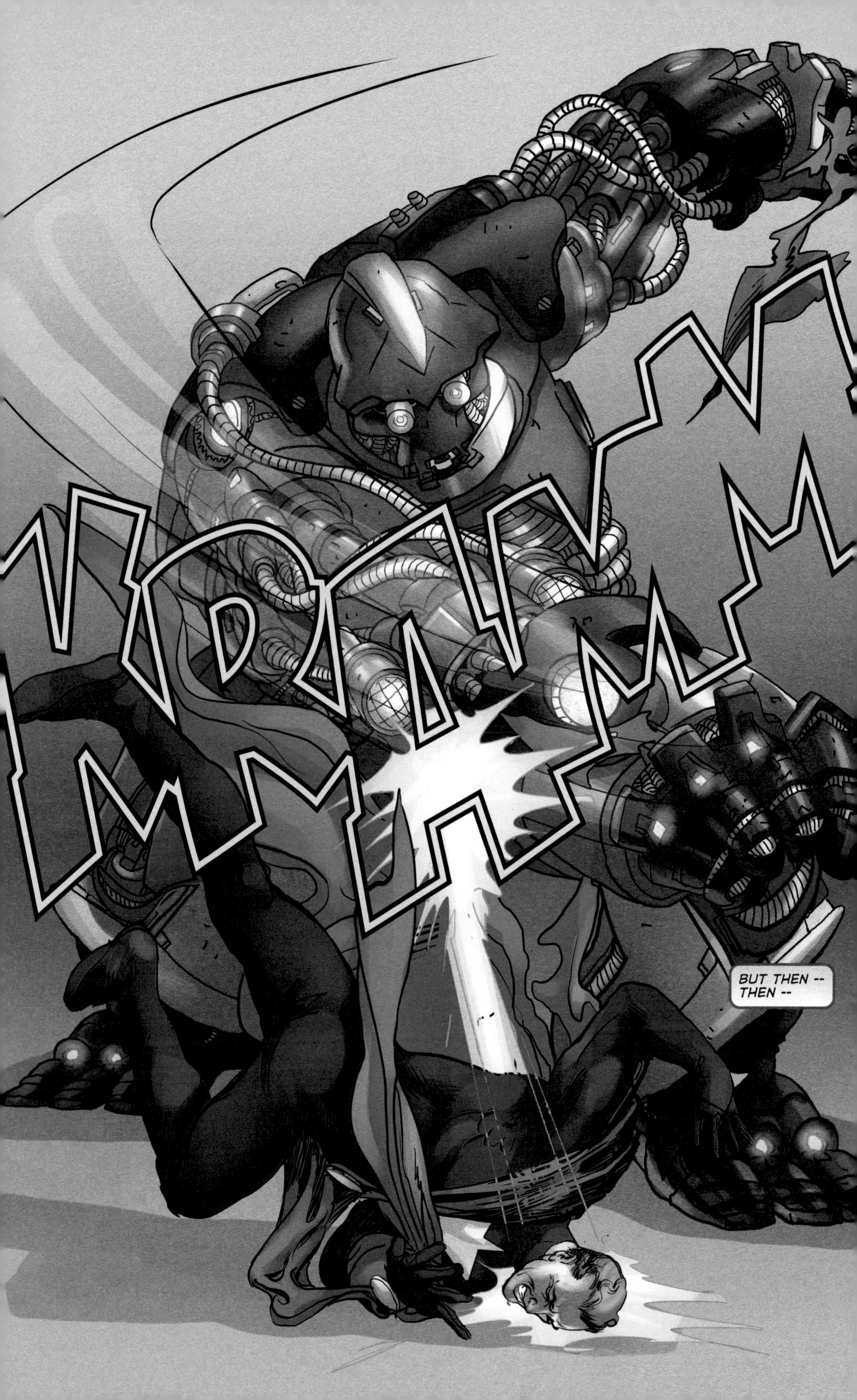
WHAM
BUT THEN --
THEN --

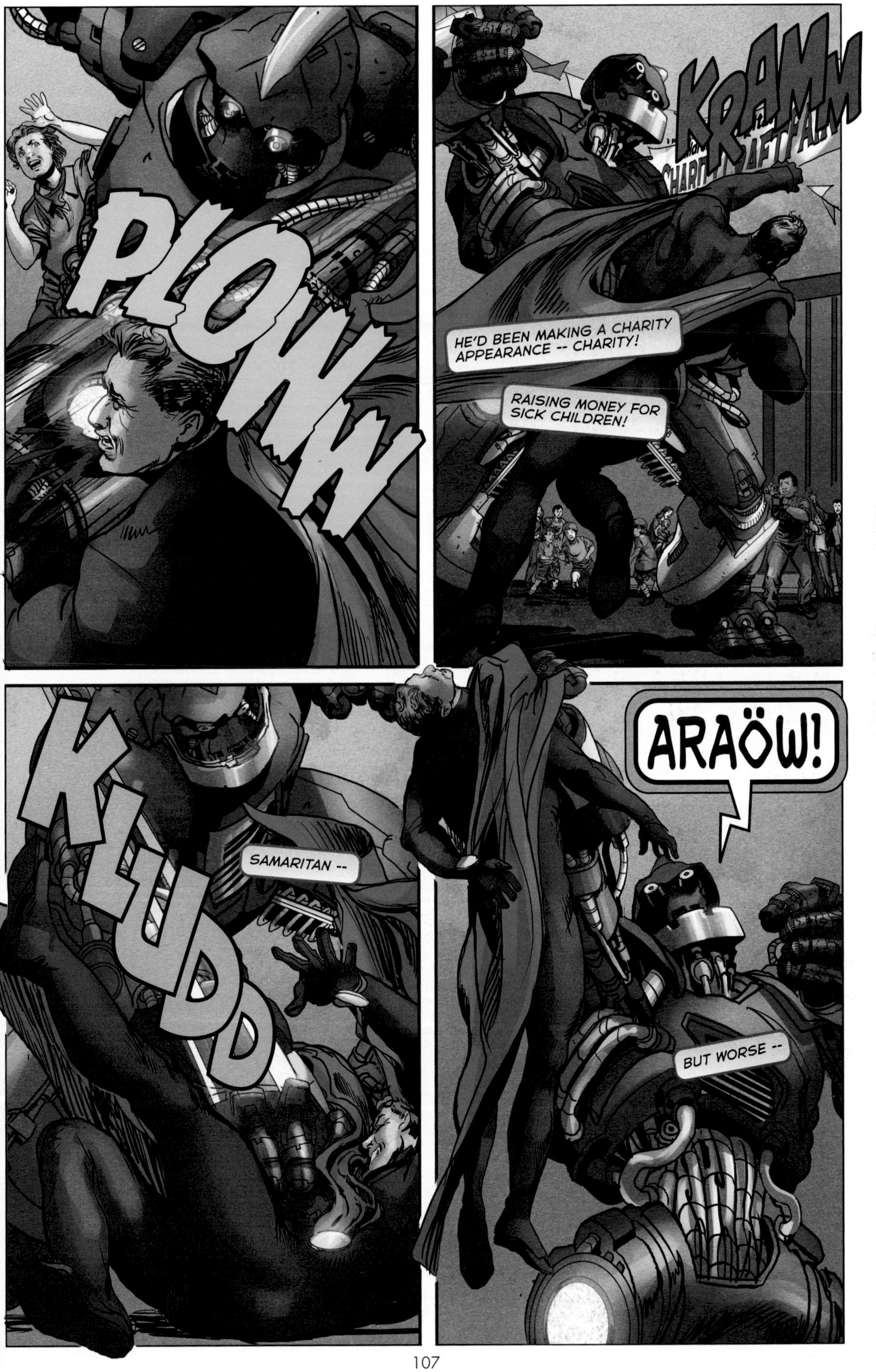
PLOWW
KRAMM
HE'D BEEN MAKING A CHARITY APPEARANCE -- CHARITY!
RAISING MONEY FOR SICK CHILDREN!
KLUDD
SAMARITAN --
ARAÖW!
BUT WORSE --

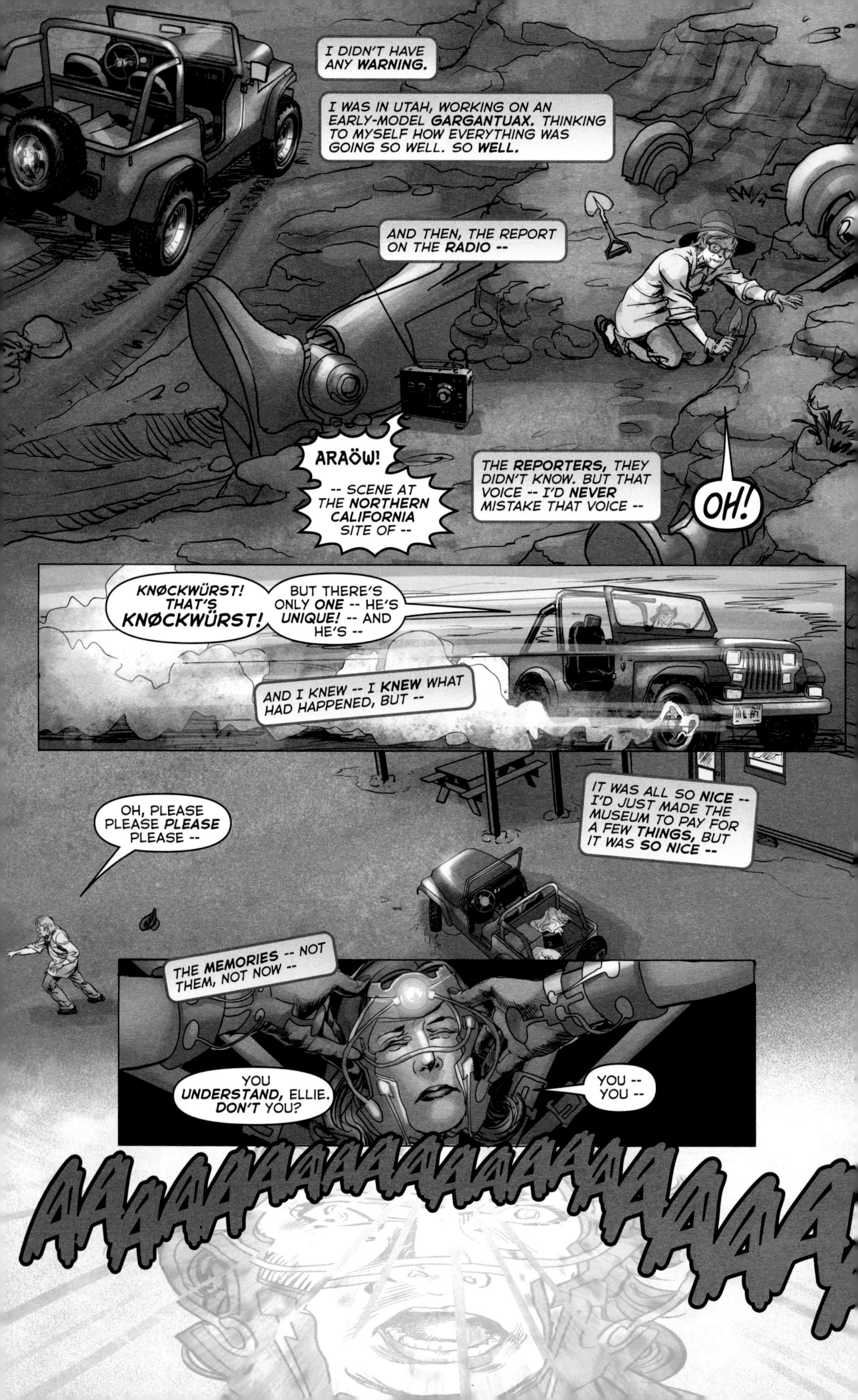
I DIDN'T HAVE ANY WARNING.
I WAS IN UTAH, WORKING ON AN EARLY-MODEL GARGANTUAX. THINKING TO MYSELF HOW EVERYTHING WAS GOING SO WELL. SO WELL.
AND THEN, THE REPORT ON THE RADIO --
ARAÖW!
-- SCENE AT THE NORTHERN CALIFORNIA SITE OF --
THE REPORTERS, THEY DIDN'T KNOW. BUT THAT VOICE -- I'D NEVER MISTAKE THAT VOICE --
OH!
KNØCKWÜRST! THAT'S KNØCKWÜRST!
BUT THERE'S ONLY ONE -- HE'S UNIQUE! -- AND HE'S --
AND I KNEW -- I KNEW WHAT HAD HAPPENED, BUT --
OH, PLEASE PLEASE PLEASE PLEASE --
IT WAS ALL SO NICE -- I'D JUST MADE THE MUSEUM TO PAY FOR A FEW THINGS, BUT IT WAS SO NICE --
THE MEMORIES -- NOT THEM, NOT NOW --
YOU UNDERSTAND, ELLIE. DON'T YOU?
YOU -- YOU --
AAAAAAAAAAAAAAAAAAAAAA

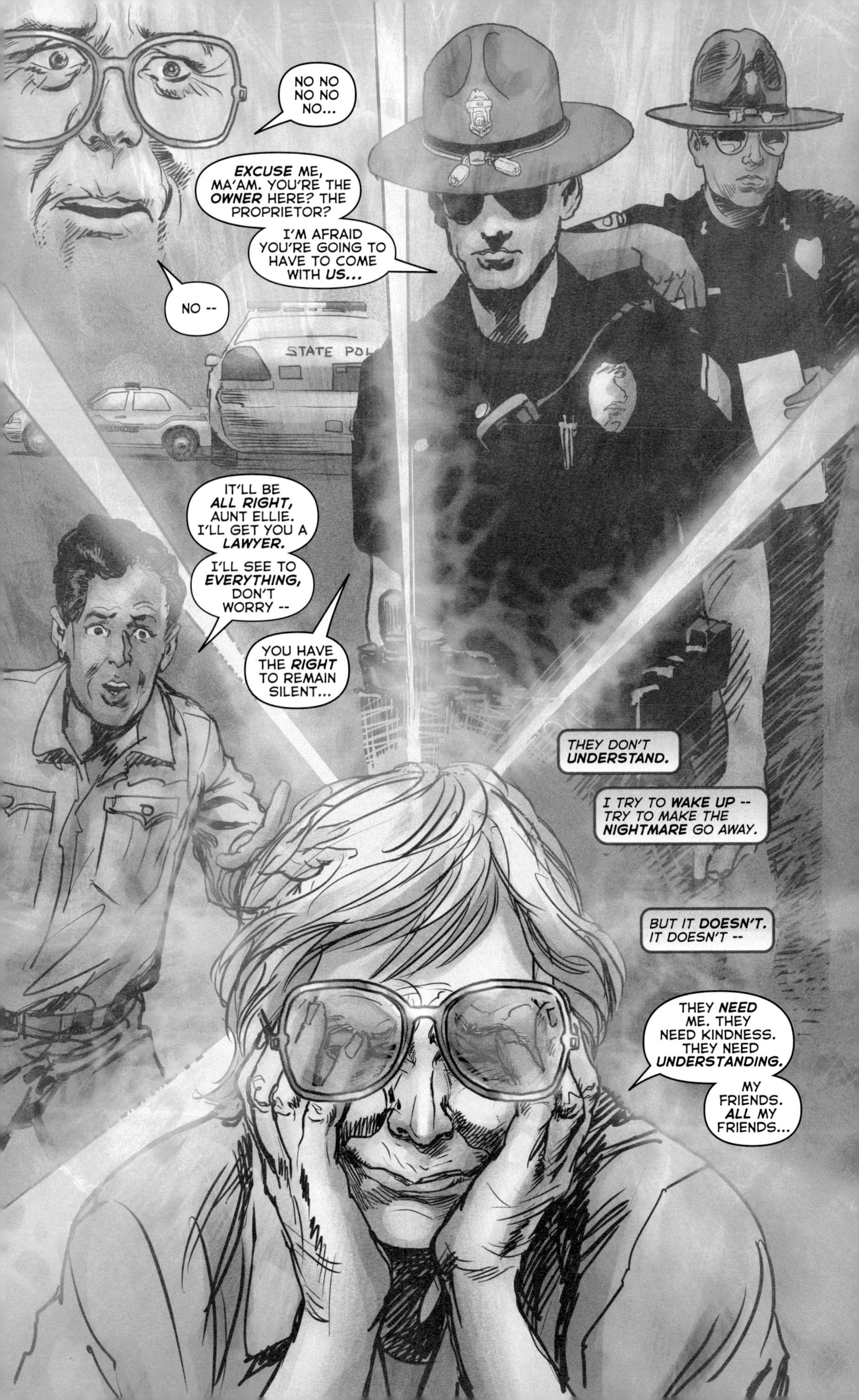

NO NO NO NO NO...
EXCUSE ME, MA'AM. YOU'RE THE OWNER HERE? THE PROPRIETOR?
I'M AFRAID YOU'RE GOING TO HAVE TO COME WITH US...
NO --
STATE POL
IT'LL BE ALL RIGHT, AUNT ELLIE. I'LL GET YOU A LAWYER.
I'LL SEE TO EVERYTHING, DON'T WORRY --
YOU HAVE THE RIGHT TO REMAIN SILENT...
THEY DON'T UNDERSTAND.
I TRY TO WAKE UP -- TRY TO MAKE THE NIGHTMARE GO AWAY.
BUT IT DOESN'T. IT DOESN'T --
THEY NEED ME. THEY NEED KINDNESS. THEY NEED UNDERSTANDING.
MY FRIENDS. ALL MY FRIENDS...

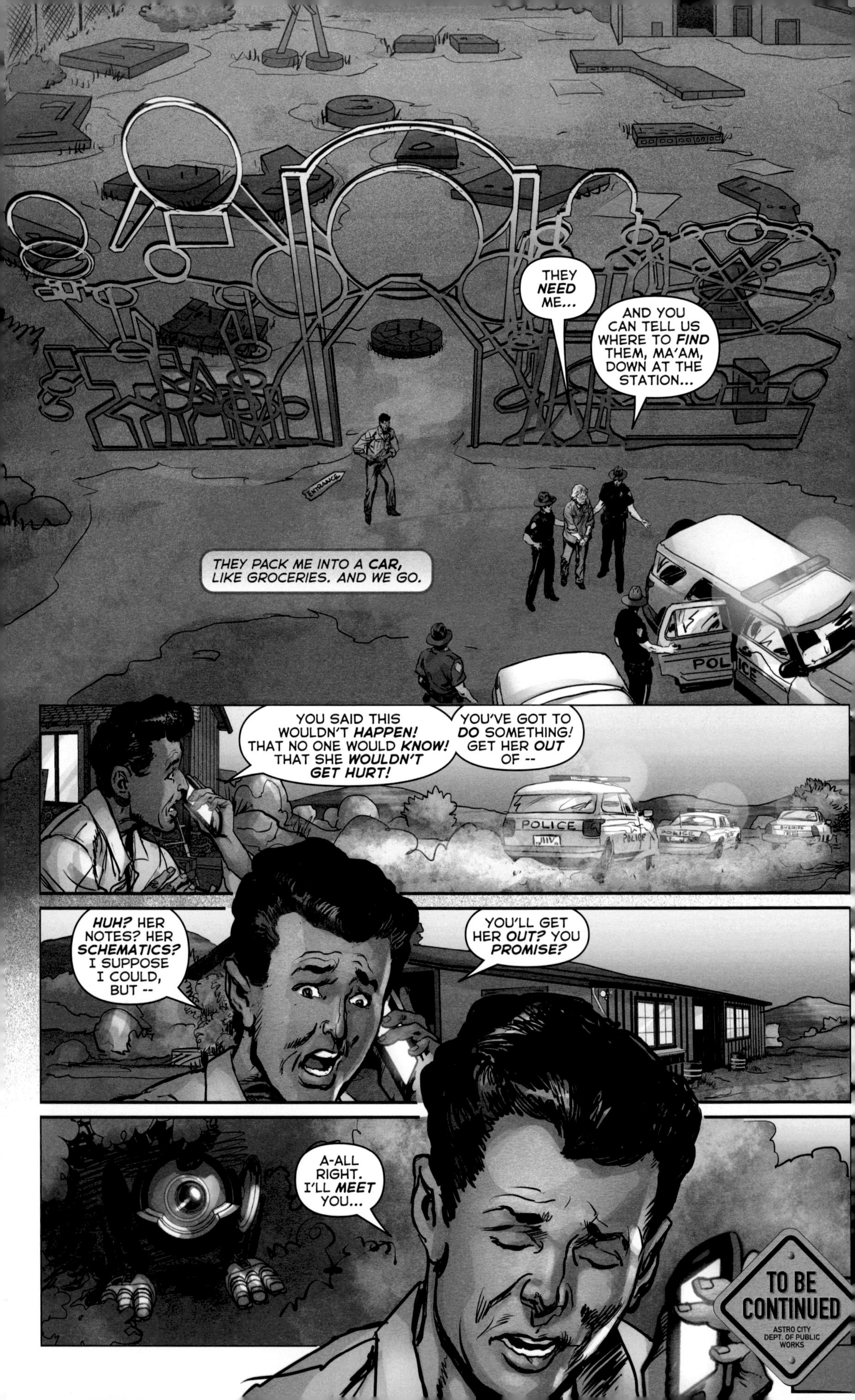
THEY NEED ME...
AND YOU CAN TELL US WHERE TO FIND THEM, MA'AM, DOWN AT THE STATION...
ENTRANCE
THEY PACK ME INTO A CAR, LIKE GROCERIES. AND WE GO.
POLICE
YOU SAID THIS WOULDN'T HAPPEN! THAT NO ONE WOULD KNOW! THAT SHE WOULDN'T GET HURT!
YOU'VE GOT TO DO SOMETHING! GET HER OUT OF --
POLICE
HUH? HER NOTES? HER SCHEMATICS? I SUPPOSE I COULD, BUT --
YOU'LL GET HER OUT? YOU PROMISE?
A-ALL RIGHT. I'LL MEET YOU...
TO BE CONTINUED
ASTRO CITY DEPT. OF PUBLIC WORKS

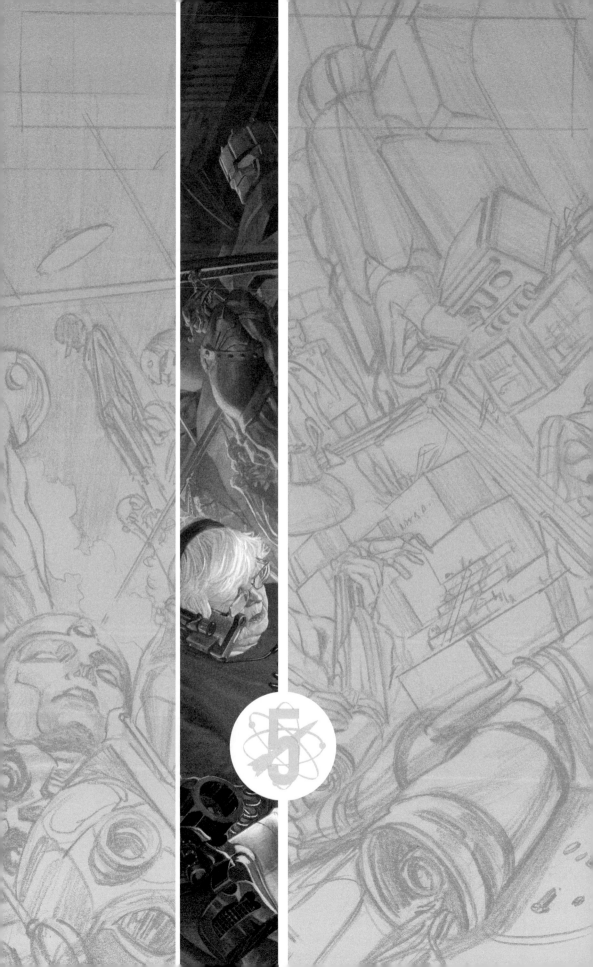

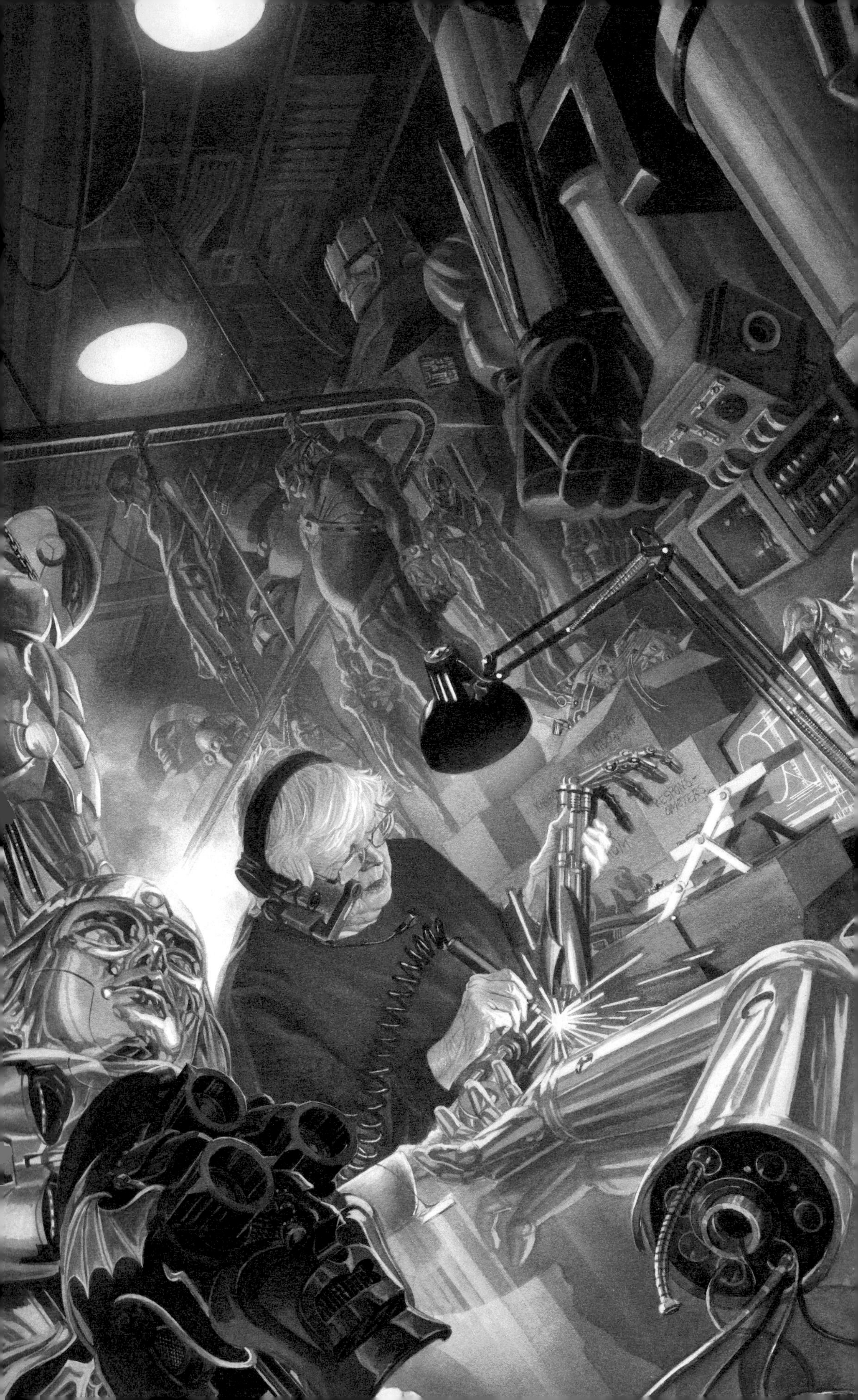

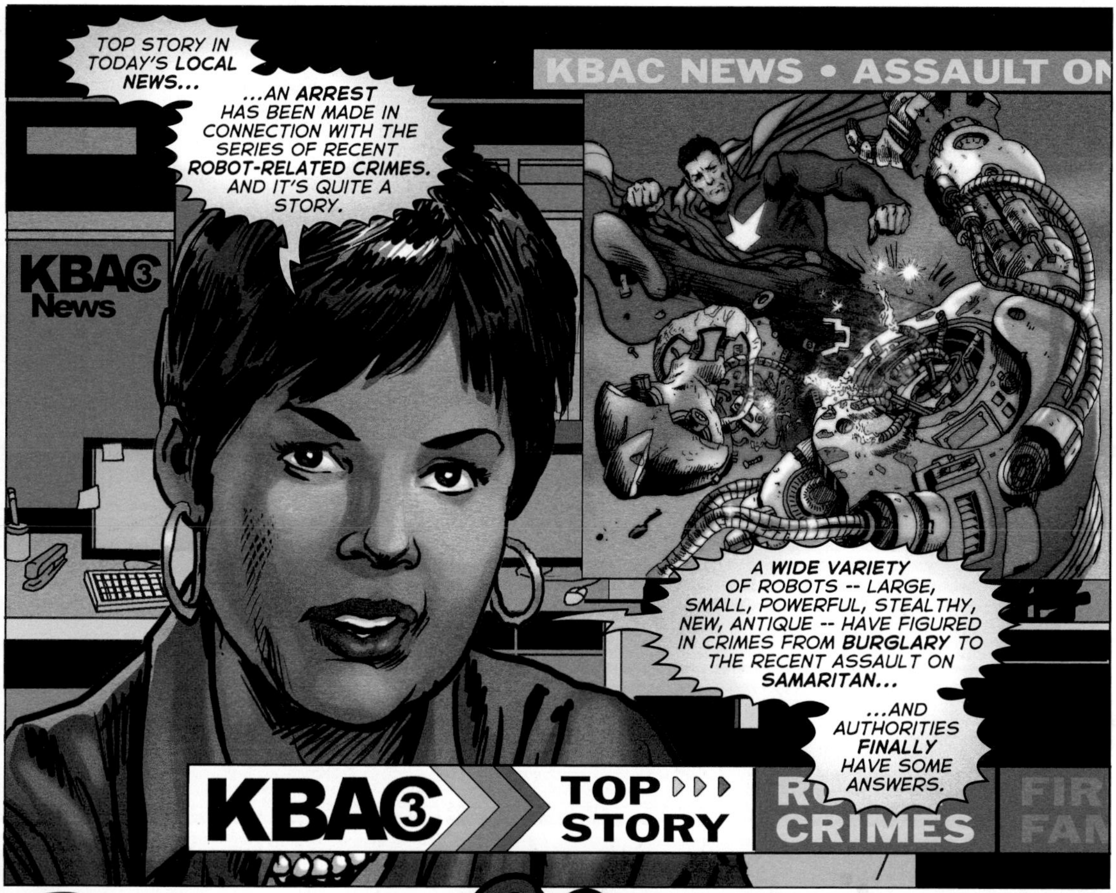
TOP STORY IN TODAY'S LOCAL NEWS...
...AN ARREST HAS BEEN MADE IN CONNECTION WITH THE SERIES OF RECENT ROBOT-RELATED CRIMES. AND IT'S QUITE A STORY.
KBAC NEWS • ASSAULT ON
KBAC 3 News
A WIDE VARIETY OF ROBOTS -- LARGE, SMALL, POWERFUL, STEALTHY, NEW, ANTIQUE -- HAVE FIGURED IN CRIMES FROM BURGLARY TO THE RECENT ASSAULT ON SAMARITAN...
...AND AUTHORITIES FINALLY HAVE SOME ANSWERS.
KBAC 3
TOP STORY
CRIMES

Friends & Relations

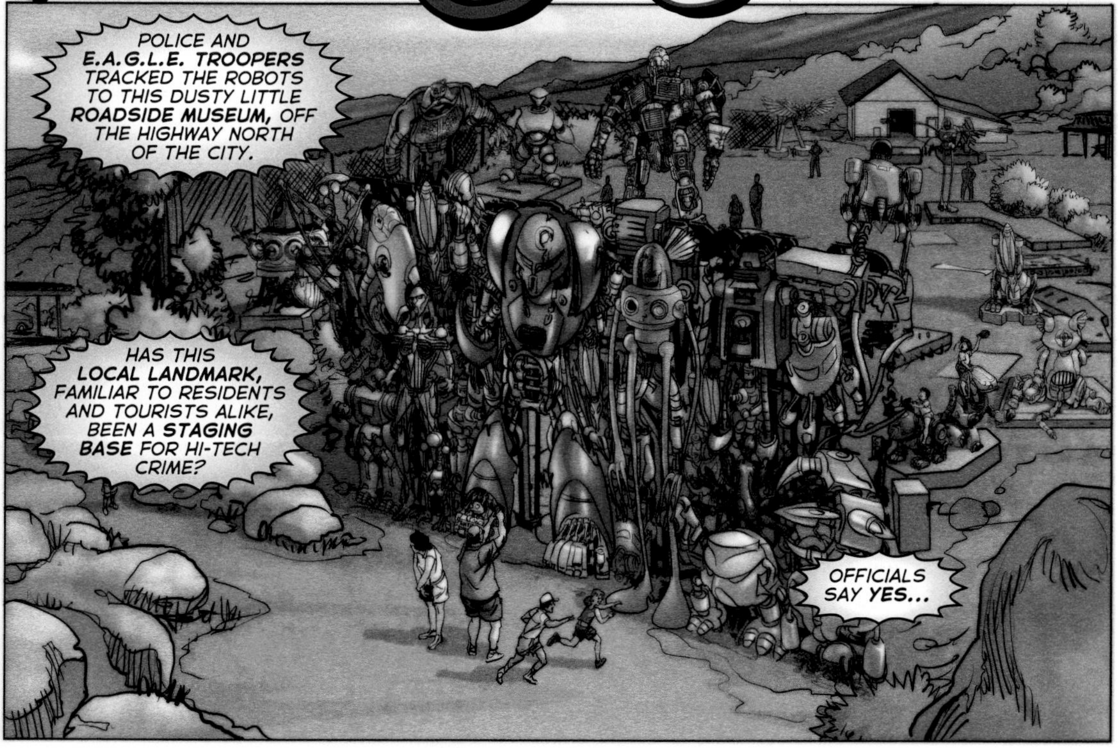
POLICE AND E.A.G.L.E. TROOPERS TRACKED THE ROBOTS TO THIS DUSTY LITTLE ROADSIDE MUSEUM, OFF THE HIGHWAY NORTH OF THE CITY.
HAS THIS LOCAL LANDMARK, FAMILIAR TO RESIDENTS AND TOURISTS ALIKE, BEEN A STAGING BASE FOR HI-TECH CRIME?
OFFICIALS SAY YES...

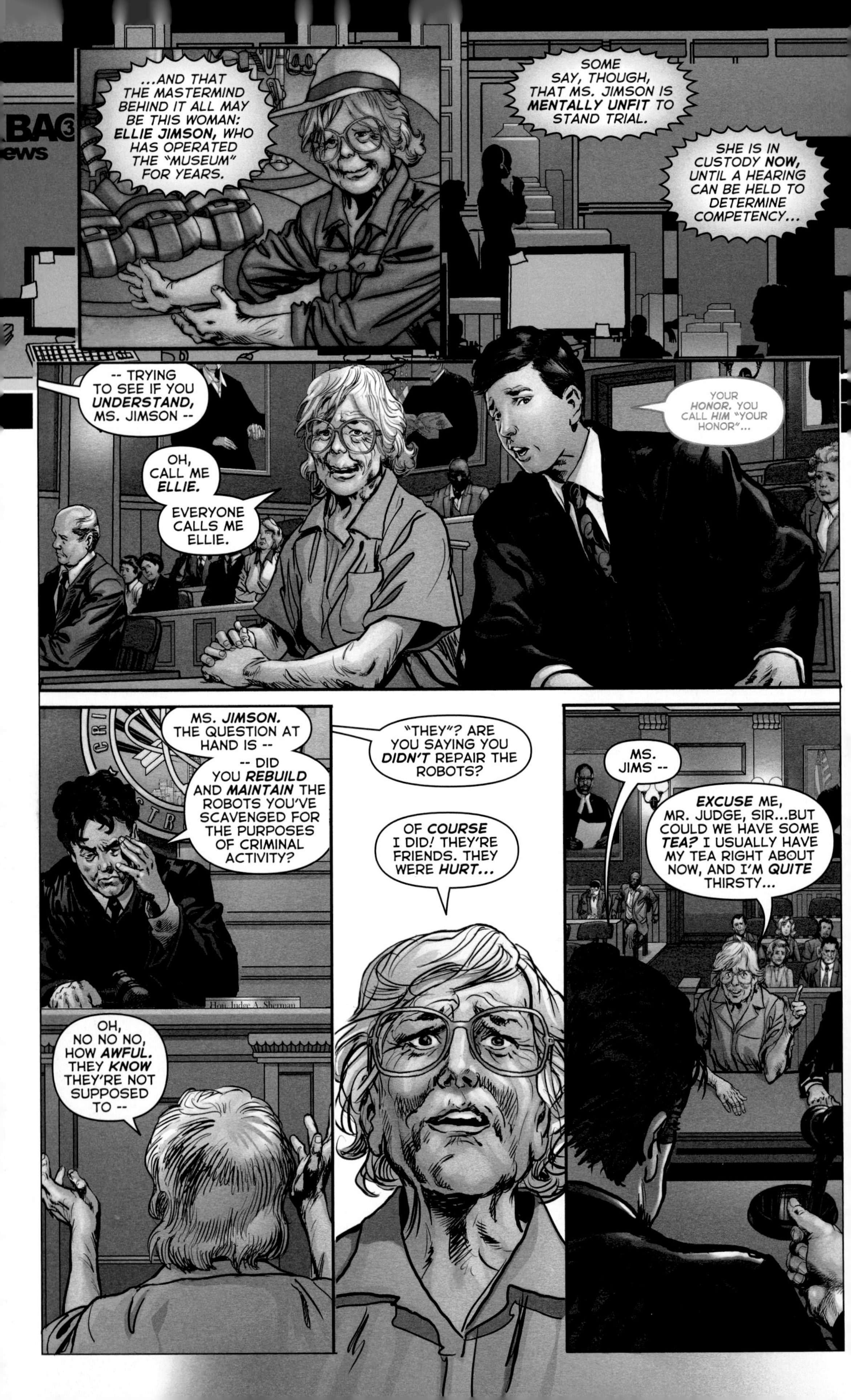

...AND THAT THE MASTERMIND BEHIND IT ALL MAY BE THIS WOMAN: ELLIE JIMSON, WHO HAS OPERATED THE "MUSEUM" FOR YEARS.
SOME SAY, THOUGH, THAT MS. JIMSON IS MENTALLY UNFIT TO STAND TRIAL.
SHE IS IN CUSTODY NOW, UNTIL A HEARING CAN BE HELD TO DETERMINE COMPETENCY...
-- TRYING TO SEE IF YOU UNDERSTAND, MS. JIMSON --
OH, CALL ME ELLIE.
EVERYONE CALLS ME ELLIE.
YOUR HONOR. YOU CALL HIM "YOUR HONOR"...
MS. JIMSON. THE QUESTION AT HAND IS --
-- DID YOU REBUILD AND MAINTAIN THE ROBOTS YOU'VE SCAVENGED FOR THE PURPOSES OF CRIMINAL ACTIVITY?
Hon. Judge A. Sherman
OH, NO NO NO, HOW AWFUL. THEY KNOW THEY'RE NOT SUPPOSED TO --
"THEY"? ARE YOU SAYING YOU DIDN'T REPAIR THE ROBOTS?
OF COURSE I DID! THEY'RE FRIENDS. THEY WERE HURT...
MS. JIMS --
EXCUSE ME, MR. JUDGE, SIR...BUT COULD WE HAVE SOME TEA? I USUALLY HAVE MY TEA RIGHT ABOUT NOW, AND I'M QUITE THIRSTY...

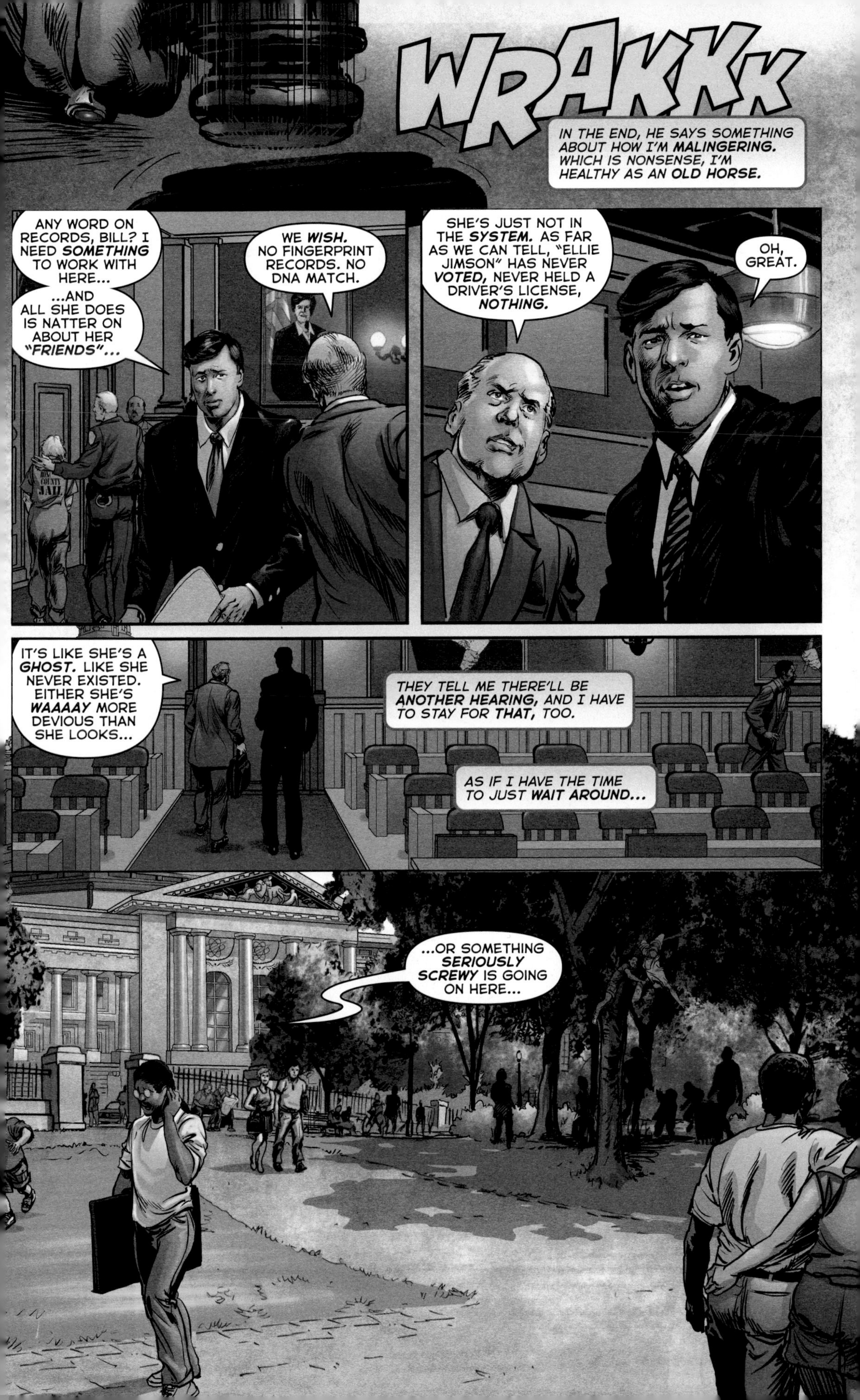
WRAKKK
IN THE END, HE SAYS SOMETHING ABOUT HOW I'M MALINGERING. WHICH IS NONSENSE, I'M HEALTHY AS AN OLD HORSE.
ANY WORD ON RECORDS, BILL? I NEED SOMETHING TO WORK WITH HERE...
...AND ALL SHE DOES IS NATTER ON ABOUT HER "FRIENDS"...
WE WISH. NO FINGERPRINT RECORDS. NO DNA MATCH.
COUNTY JAIL
SHE'S JUST NOT IN THE SYSTEM. AS FAR AS WE CAN TELL, "ELLIE JIMSON" HAS NEVER VOTED, NEVER HELD A DRIVER'S LICENSE, NOTHING.
OH, GREAT.
IT'S LIKE SHE'S A GHOST. LIKE SHE NEVER EXISTED. EITHER SHE'S WAAAAY MORE DEVIOUS THAN SHE LOOKS...
THEY TELL ME THERE'LL BE ANOTHER HEARING, AND I HAVE TO STAY FOR THAT, TOO.
AS IF I HAVE THE TIME TO JUST WAIT AROUND...
...OR SOMETHING SERIOUSLY SCREWY IS GOING ON HERE...

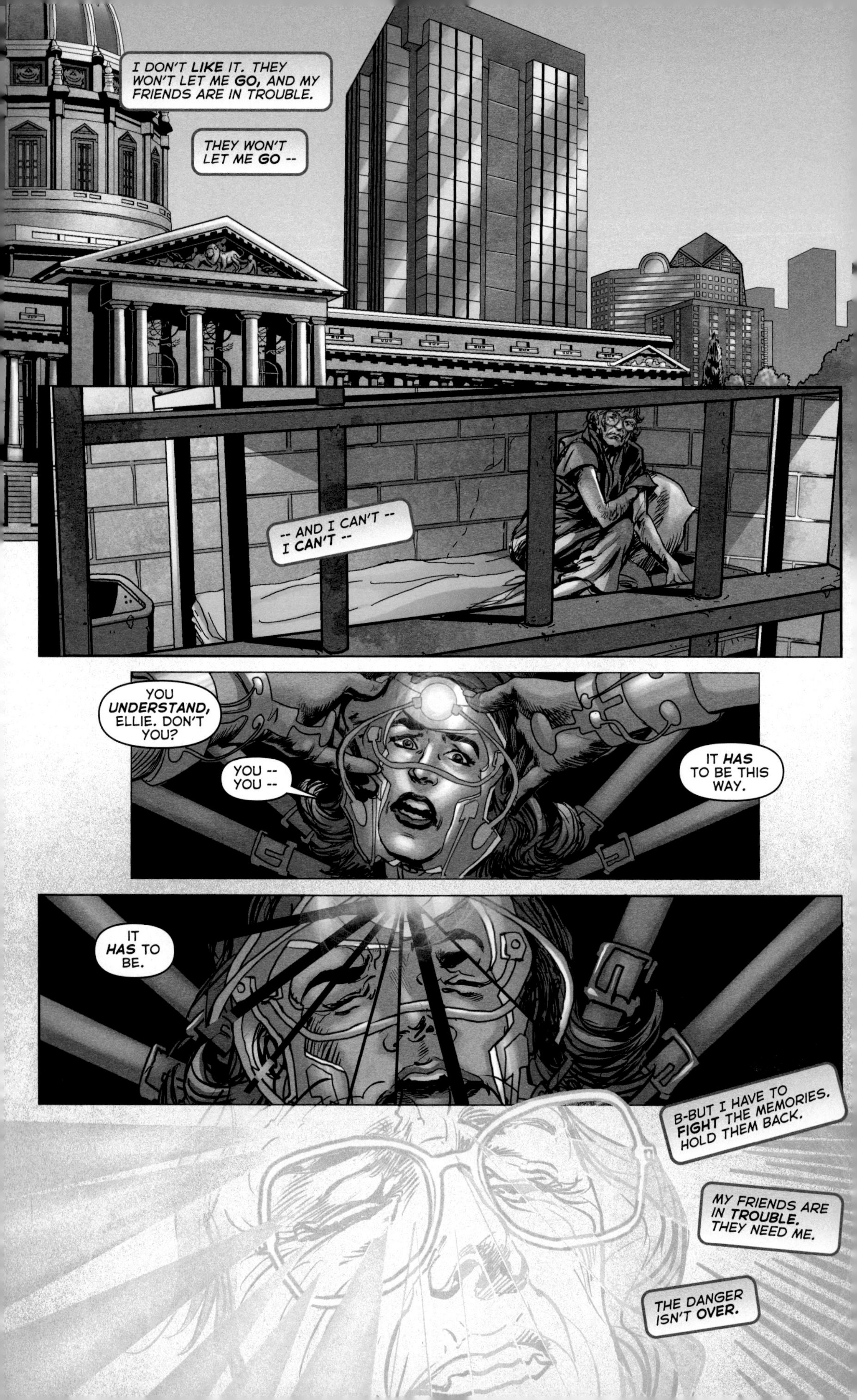
I DON'T LIKE IT. THEY WON'T LET ME GO, AND MY FRIENDS ARE IN TROUBLE.
THEY WON'T LET ME GO --
-- AND I CAN'T -- I CAN'T --
YOU UNDERSTAND, ELLIE. DON'T YOU?
YOU -- YOU --
IT HAS TO BE THIS WAY.
IT HAS TO BE.
B-BUT I HAVE TO FIGHT THE MEMORIES. HOLD THEM BACK.
MY FRIENDS ARE IN TROUBLE. THEY NEED ME.
THE DANGER ISN'T OVER.

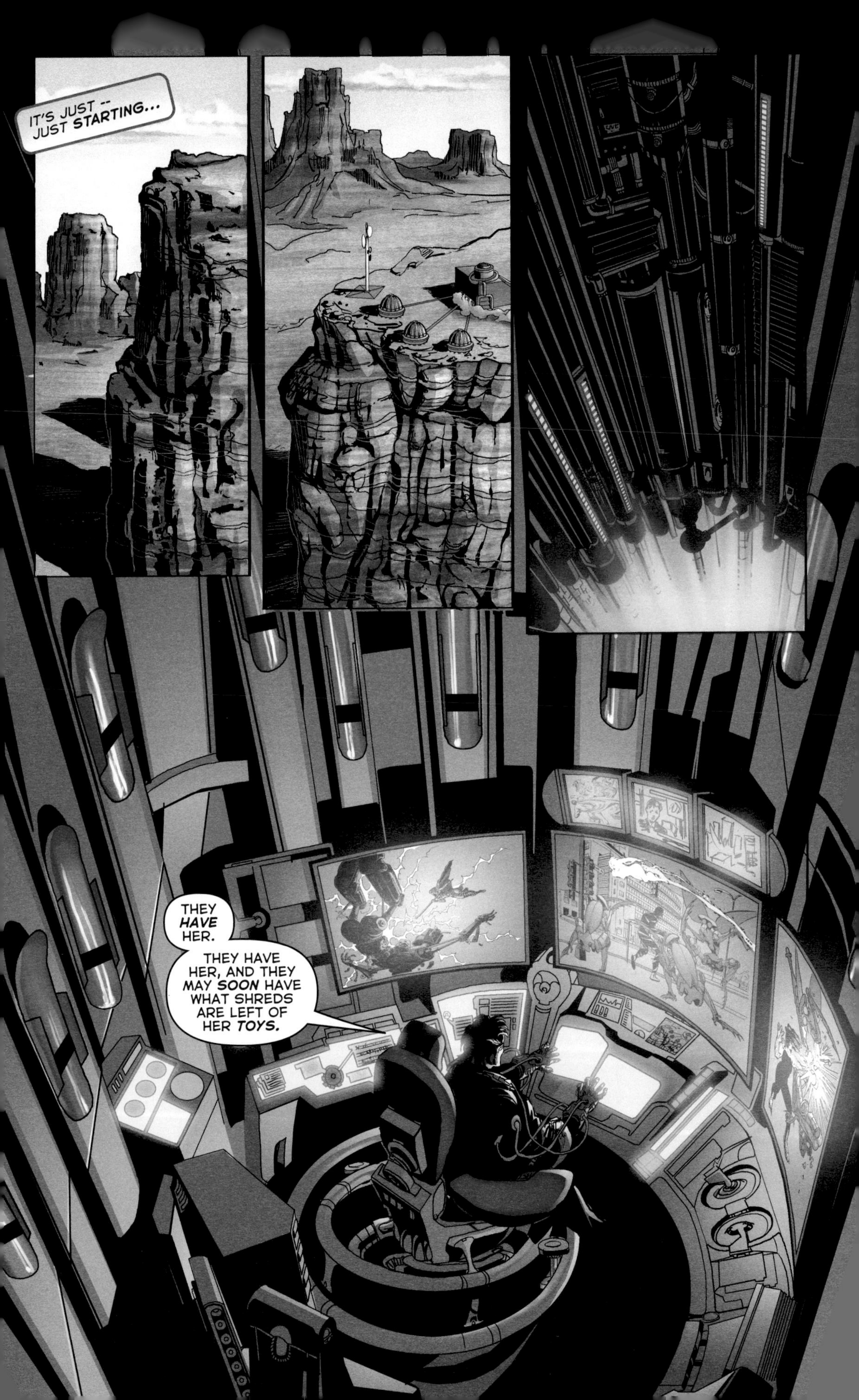
IT'S JUST -- JUST STARTING...
THEY HAVE HER.
THEY HAVE HER, AND THEY MAY SOON HAVE WHAT SHREDS ARE LEFT OF HER TOYS.

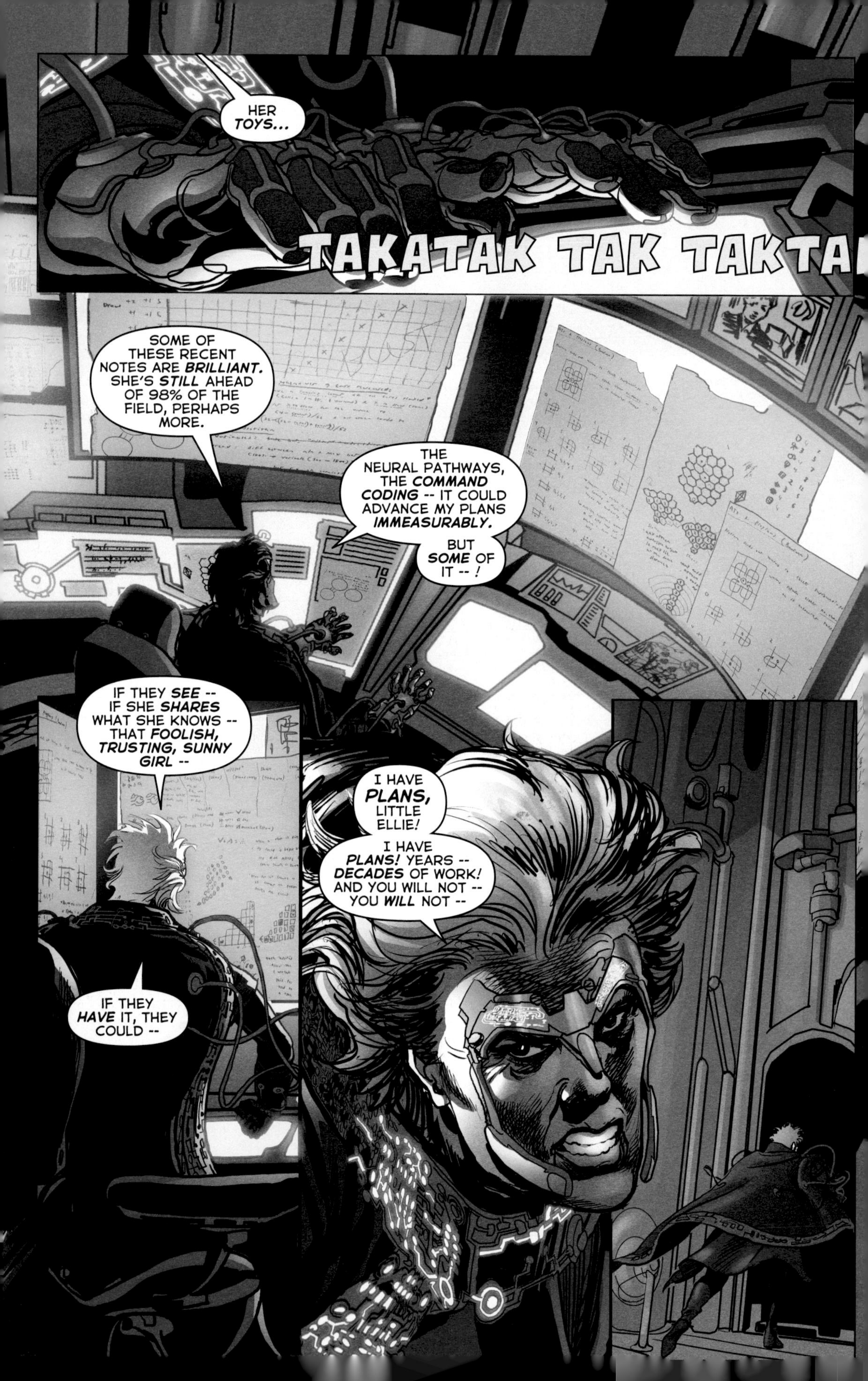
HER TOYS...
TAKATAK TAK TAKTA
SOME OF THESE RECENT NOTES ARE BRILLIANT. SHE'S STILL AHEAD OF 98% OF THE FIELD, PERHAPS MORE.
THE NEURAL PATHWAYS, THE COMMAND CODING -- IT COULD ADVANCE MY PLANS IMMEASURABLY.
BUT SOME OF IT -- !
IF THEY SEE -- IF SHE SHARES WHAT SHE KNOWS -- THAT FOOLISH, TRUSTING, SUNNY GIRL --
IF THEY HAVE IT, THEY COULD --
I HAVE PLANS, LITTLE ELLIE!
I HAVE PLANS! YEARS -- DECADES OF WORK! AND YOU WILL NOT -- YOU WILL NOT --

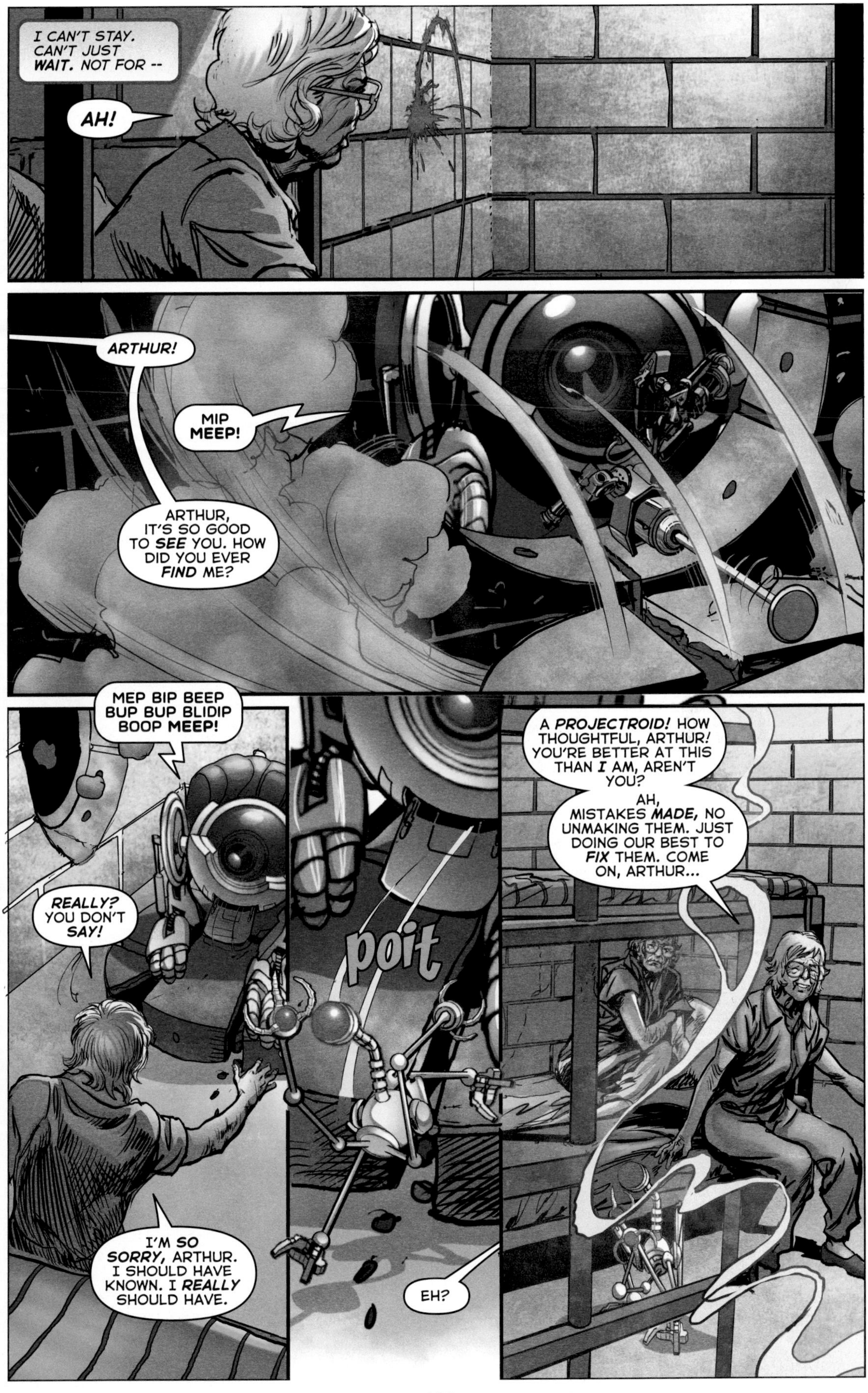
I CAN'T STAY. CAN'T JUST WAIT. NOT FOR --
AH!
ARTHUR!
MIP MEEP!
ARTHUR, IT'S SO GOOD TO SEE YOU. HOW DID YOU EVER FIND ME?
MEP BIP BEEP BUP BUP BLIDIP BOOP MEEP!
REALLY? YOU DON'T SAY!
I'M SO SORRY, ARTHUR. I SHOULD HAVE KNOWN. I REALLY SHOULD HAVE.
poit
EH?
A PROJECTROID! HOW THOUGHTFUL, ARTHUR! YOU'RE BETTER AT THIS THAN I AM, AREN'T YOU?
AH, MISTAKES MADE, NO UNMAKING THEM. JUST DOING OUR BEST TO FIX THEM. COME ON, ARTHUR...

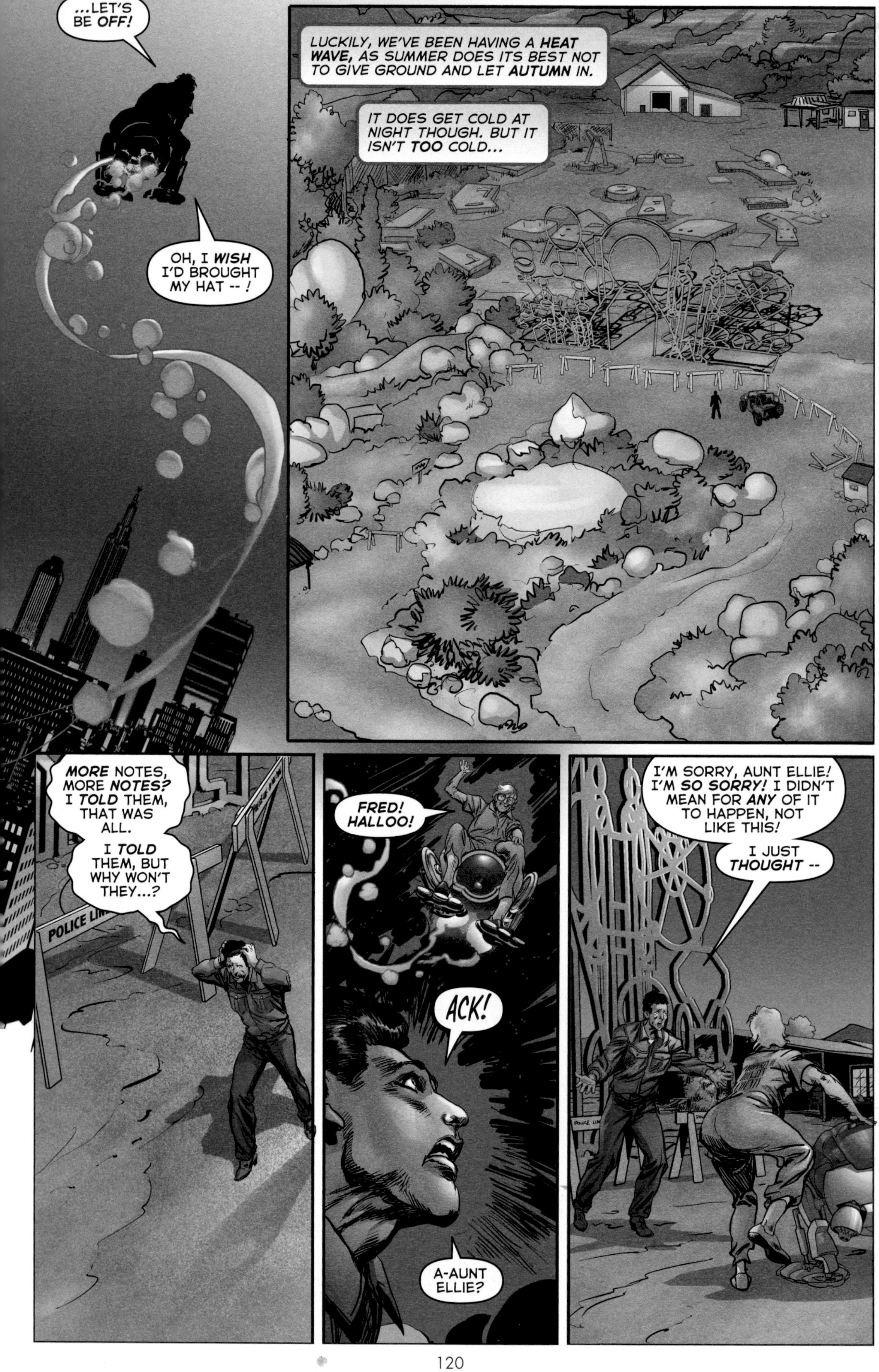
...LET'S BE OFF!
OH, I WISH I'D BROUGHT MY HAT -- !
LUCKILY, WE'VE BEEN HAVING A HEAT WAVE, AS SUMMER DOES ITS BEST NOT TO GIVE GROUND AND LET AUTUMN IN.
IT DOES GET COLD AT NIGHT THOUGH. BUT IT ISN'T TOO COLD...
MORE NOTES, MORE NOTES? I TOLD THEM, THAT WAS ALL.
I TOLD THEM, BUT WHY WON'T THEY...?
FRED! HALLOO!
ACK!
A-AUNT ELLIE?
I'M SORRY, AUNT ELLIE! I'M SO SORRY! I DIDN'T MEAN FOR ANY OF IT TO HAPPEN, NOT LIKE THIS!
I JUST THOUGHT --

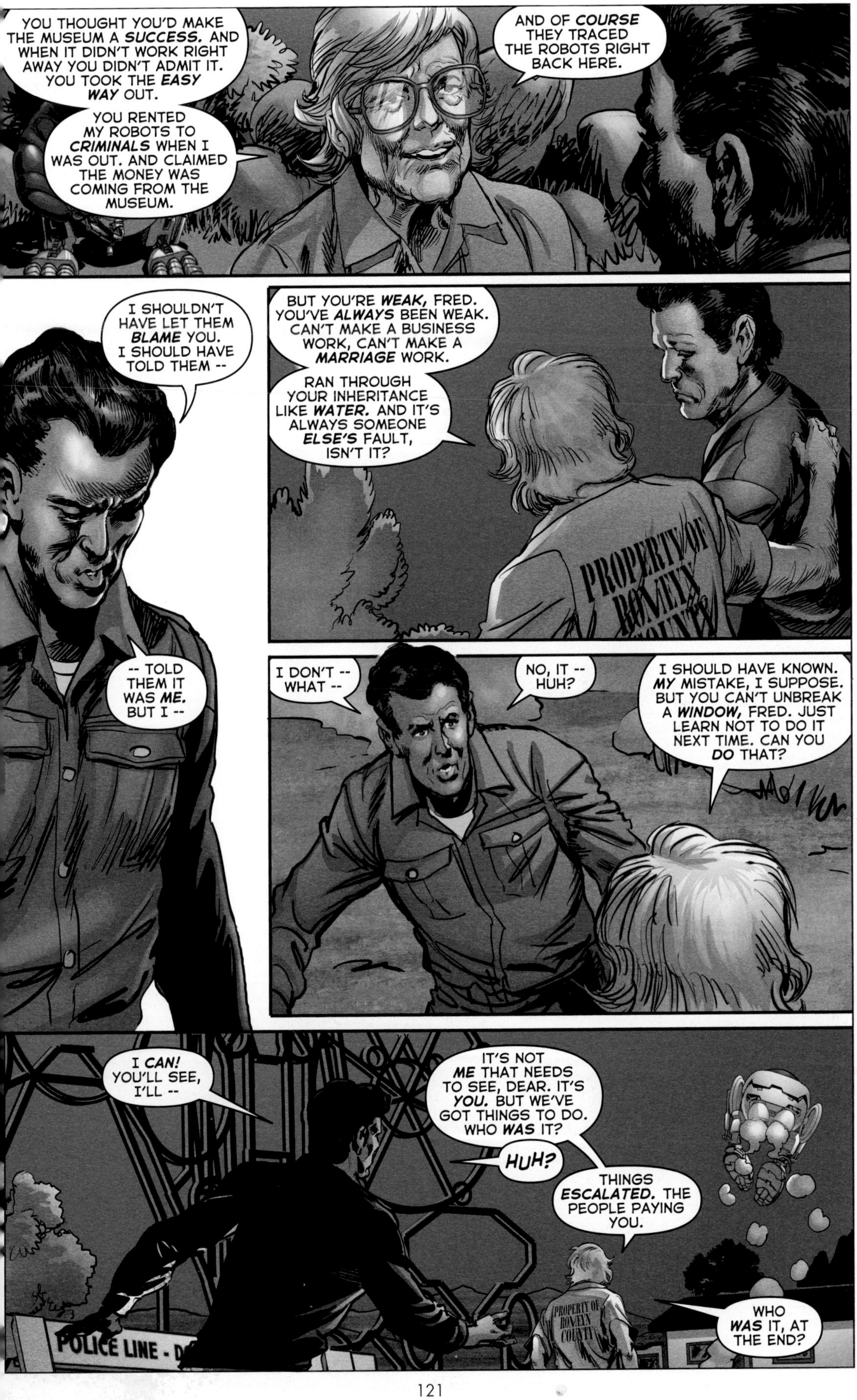
YOU THOUGHT YOU'D MAKE THE MUSEUM A SUCCESS. AND WHEN IT DIDN'T WORK RIGHT AWAY YOU DIDN'T ADMIT IT. YOU TOOK THE EASY WAY OUT.
YOU RENTED MY ROBOTS TO CRIMINALS WHEN I WAS OUT. AND CLAIMED THE MONEY WAS COMING FROM THE MUSEUM.
AND OF COURSE THEY TRACED THE ROBOTS RIGHT BACK HERE.
I SHOULDN'T HAVE LET THEM BLAME YOU. I SHOULD HAVE TOLD THEM --
BUT YOU'RE WEAK, FRED. YOU'VE ALWAYS BEEN WEAK. CAN'T MAKE A BUSINESS WORK, CAN'T MAKE A MARRIAGE WORK.
RAN THROUGH YOUR INHERITANCE LIKE WATER. AND IT'S ALWAYS SOMEONE ELSE'S FAULT, ISN'T IT?
PROPERTY OF ROMEYN COUNTY
-- TOLD THEM IT WAS ME. BUT I --
I DON'T -- WHAT --
NO, IT -- HUH?
I SHOULD HAVE KNOWN. MY MISTAKE, I SUPPOSE. BUT YOU CAN'T UNBREAK A WINDOW, FRED. JUST LEARN NOT TO DO IT NEXT TIME. CAN YOU DO THAT?
I CAN! YOU'LL SEE, I'LL --
IT'S NOT ME THAT NEEDS TO SEE, DEAR. IT'S YOU. BUT WE'VE GOT THINGS TO DO. WHO WAS IT?
HUH?
THINGS ESCALATED. THE PEOPLE PAYING YOU.
WHO WAS IT, AT THE END?
PROPERTY OF ROMEYN COUNTY
POLICE LINE - D

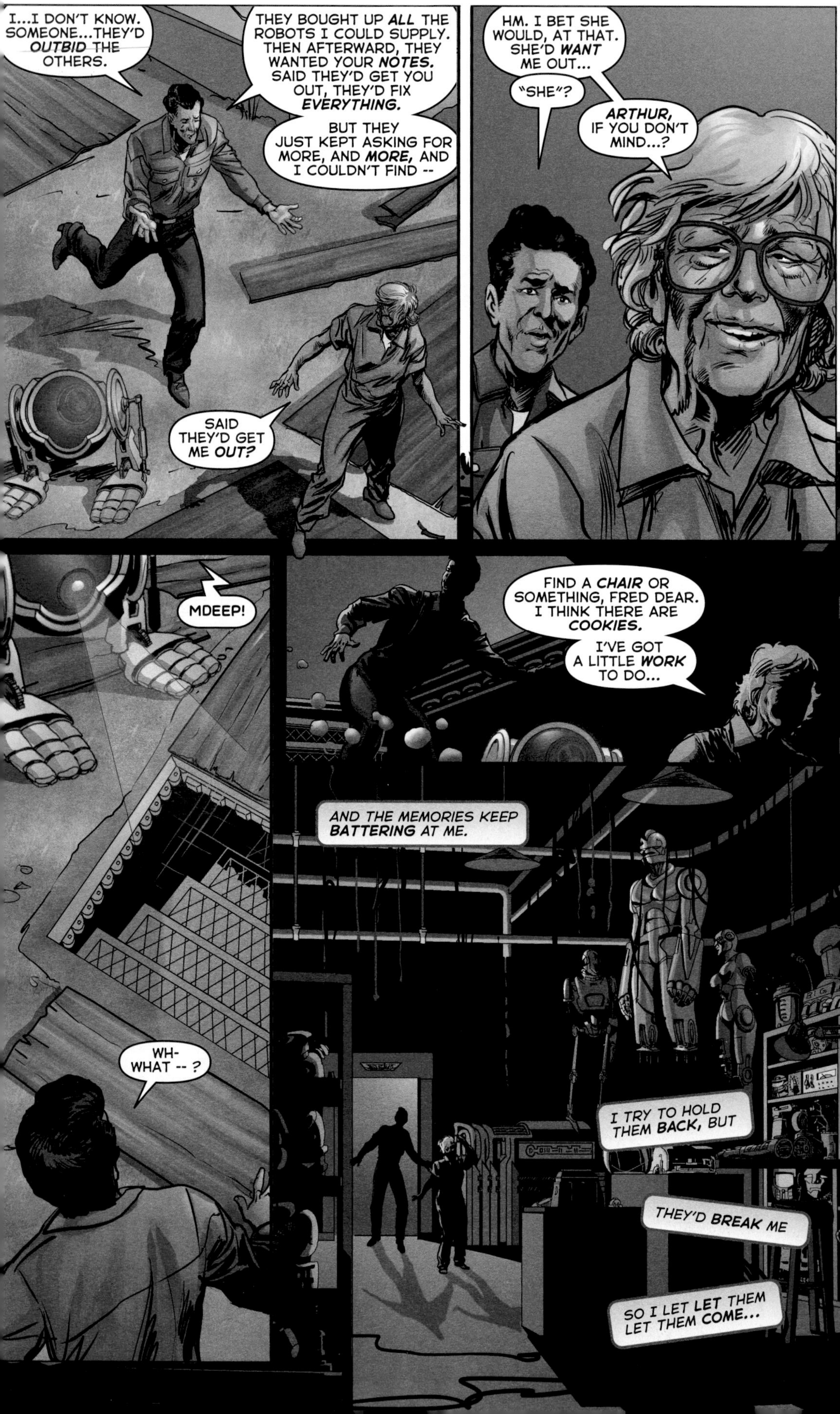
I...I DON'T KNOW. SOMEONE...THEY'D OUTBID THE OTHERS.
THEY BOUGHT UP ALL THE ROBOTS I COULD SUPPLY. THEN AFTERWARD, THEY WANTED YOUR NOTES. SAID THEY'D GET YOU OUT, THEY'D FIX EVERYTHING.
BUT THEY JUST KEPT ASKING FOR MORE, AND MORE, AND I COULDN'T FIND --
SAID THEY'D GET ME OUT?
HM. I BET SHE WOULD, AT THAT. SHE'D WANT ME OUT...
"SHE"?
ARTHUR, IF YOU DON'T MIND...?
MDEEP!
WH- WHAT -- ?
FIND A CHAIR OR SOMETHING, FRED DEAR. I THINK THERE ARE COOKIES.
I'VE GOT A LITTLE WORK TO DO...
AND THE MEMORIES KEEP BATTERING AT ME.
I TRY TO HOLD THEM BACK, BUT
THEY'D BREAK ME
SO I LET LET THEM LET THEM COME...

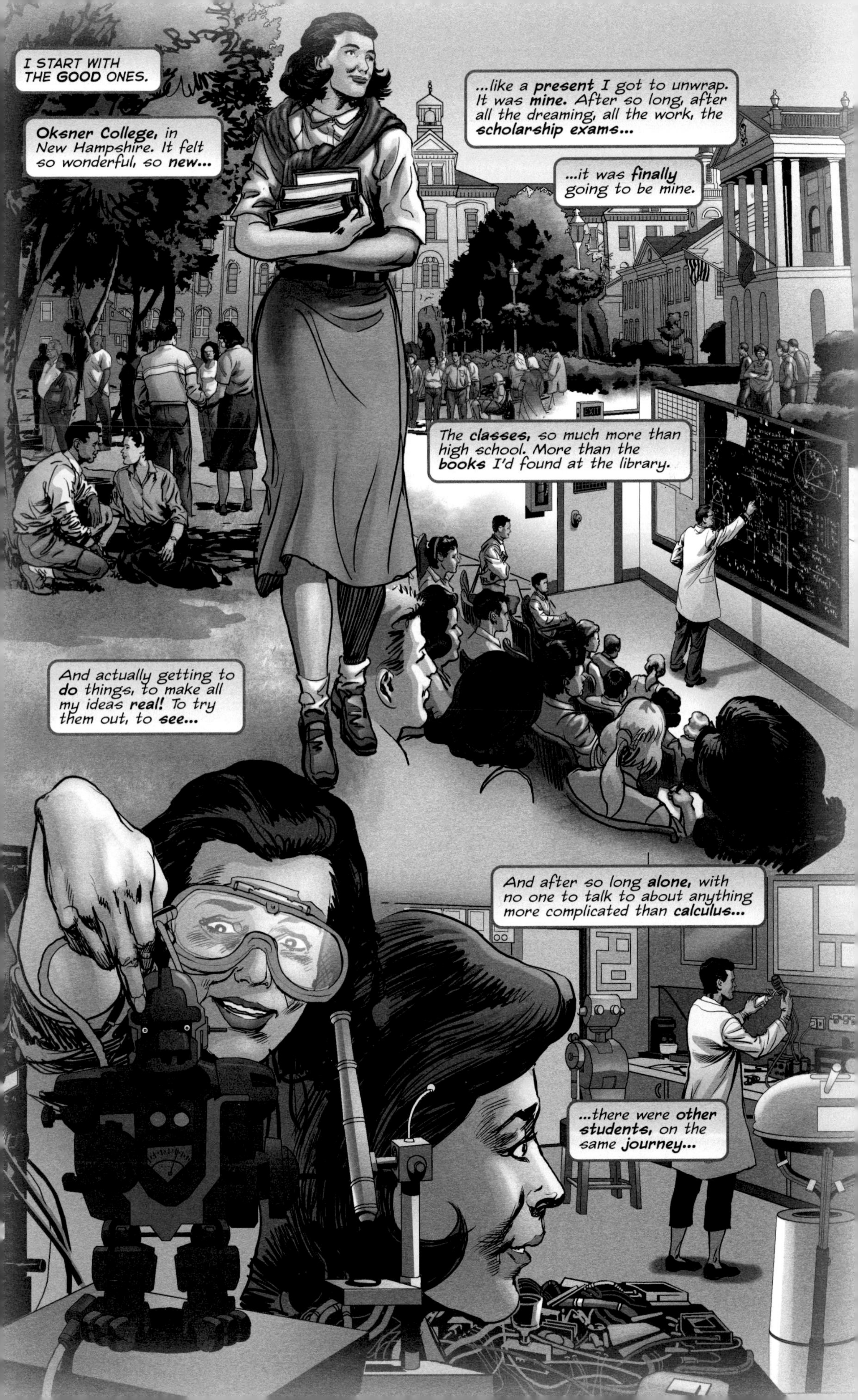
I START WITH THE GOOD ONES.
Oksner College, in New Hampshire. It felt so wonderful, so new...
...like a present I got to unwrap. It was mine. After so long, after all the dreaming, all the work, the scholarship exams...
...it was finally going to be mine.
EXIT
The classes, so much more than high school. More than the books I'd found at the library.
And actually getting to do things, to make all my ideas real! To try them out, to see...
And after so long alone, with no one to talk to about anything more complicated than calculus...
...there were other students, on the same journey...

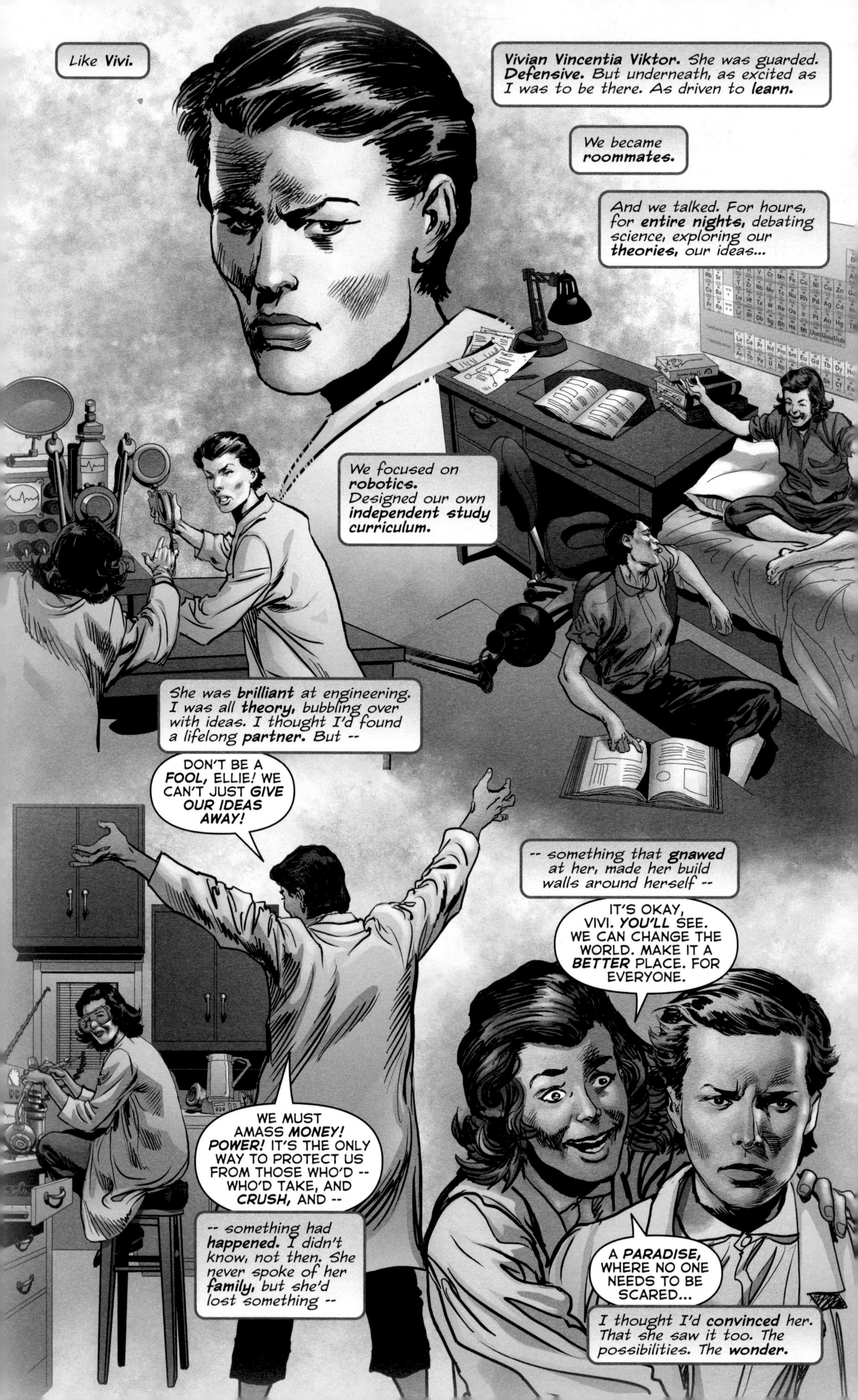
Like Vivi.
Vivian Vincentia Viktor. She was guarded. Defensive. But underneath, as excited as I was to be there. As driven to learn.
We became roommates.
And we talked. For hours, for entire nights, debating science, exploring our theories, our ideas...
We focused on robotics. Designed our own independent study curriculum.
She was brilliant at engineering. I was all theory, bubbling over with ideas. I thought I'd found a lifelong partner. But --
DON'T BE A FOOL, ELLIE! WE CAN'T JUST GIVE OUR IDEAS AWAY!
WE MUST AMASS MONEY! POWER! IT'S THE ONLY WAY TO PROTECT US FROM THOSE WHO'D -- WHO'D TAKE, AND CRUSH, AND --
-- something had happened. I didn't know, not then. She never spoke of her family, but she'd lost something --
-- something that gnawed at her, made her build walls around herself --
IT'S OKAY, VIVI. YOU'LL SEE. WE CAN CHANGE THE WORLD. MAKE IT A BETTER PLACE. FOR EVERYONE.
A PARADISE, WHERE NO ONE NEEDS TO BE SCARED...
I thought I'd convinced her. That she saw it too. The possibilities. The wonder.

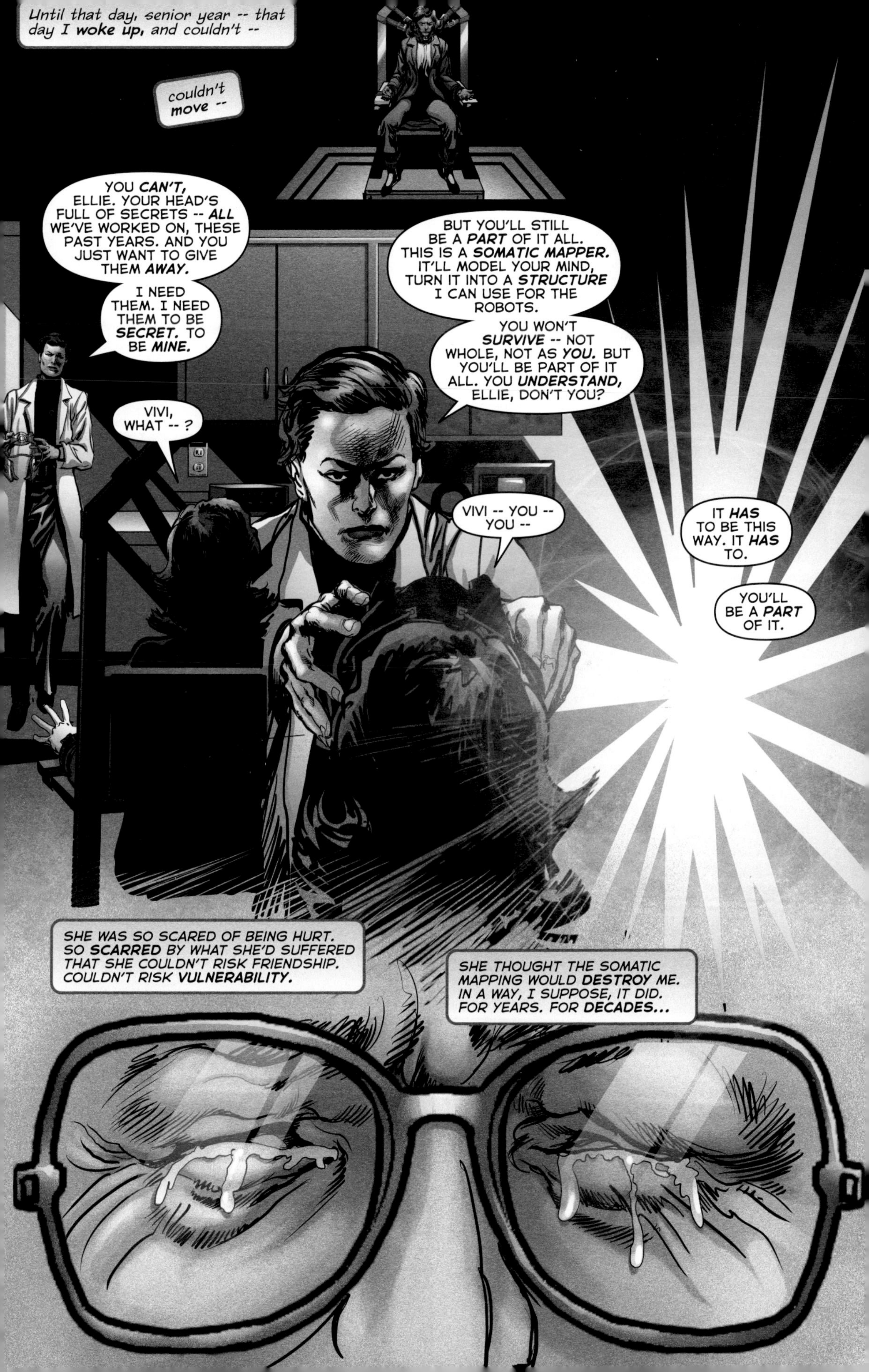
Until that day, senior year -- that day I woke up, and couldn't --
couldn't move --
YOU CAN'T, ELLIE. YOUR HEAD'S FULL OF SECRETS -- ALL WE'VE WORKED ON, THESE PAST YEARS. AND YOU JUST WANT TO GIVE THEM AWAY.
I NEED THEM. I NEED THEM TO BE SECRET. TO BE MINE.
BUT YOU'LL STILL BE A PART OF IT ALL. THIS IS A SOMATIC MAPPER. IT'LL MODEL YOUR MIND, TURN IT INTO A STRUCTURE I CAN USE FOR THE ROBOTS.
YOU WON'T SURVIVE -- NOT WHOLE, NOT AS YOU. BUT YOU'LL BE PART OF IT ALL. YOU UNDERSTAND, ELLIE, DON'T YOU?
VIVI, WHAT -- ?
VIVI -- YOU -- YOU --
IT HAS TO BE THIS WAY. IT HAS TO.
YOU'LL BE A PART OF IT.
SHE WAS SO SCARED OF BEING HURT. SO SCARRED BY WHAT SHE'D SUFFERED THAT SHE COULDN'T RISK FRIENDSHIP. COULDN'T RISK VULNERABILITY.
SHE THOUGHT THE SOMATIC MAPPING WOULD DESTROY ME. IN A WAY, I SUPPOSE, IT DID. FOR YEARS. FOR DECADES...

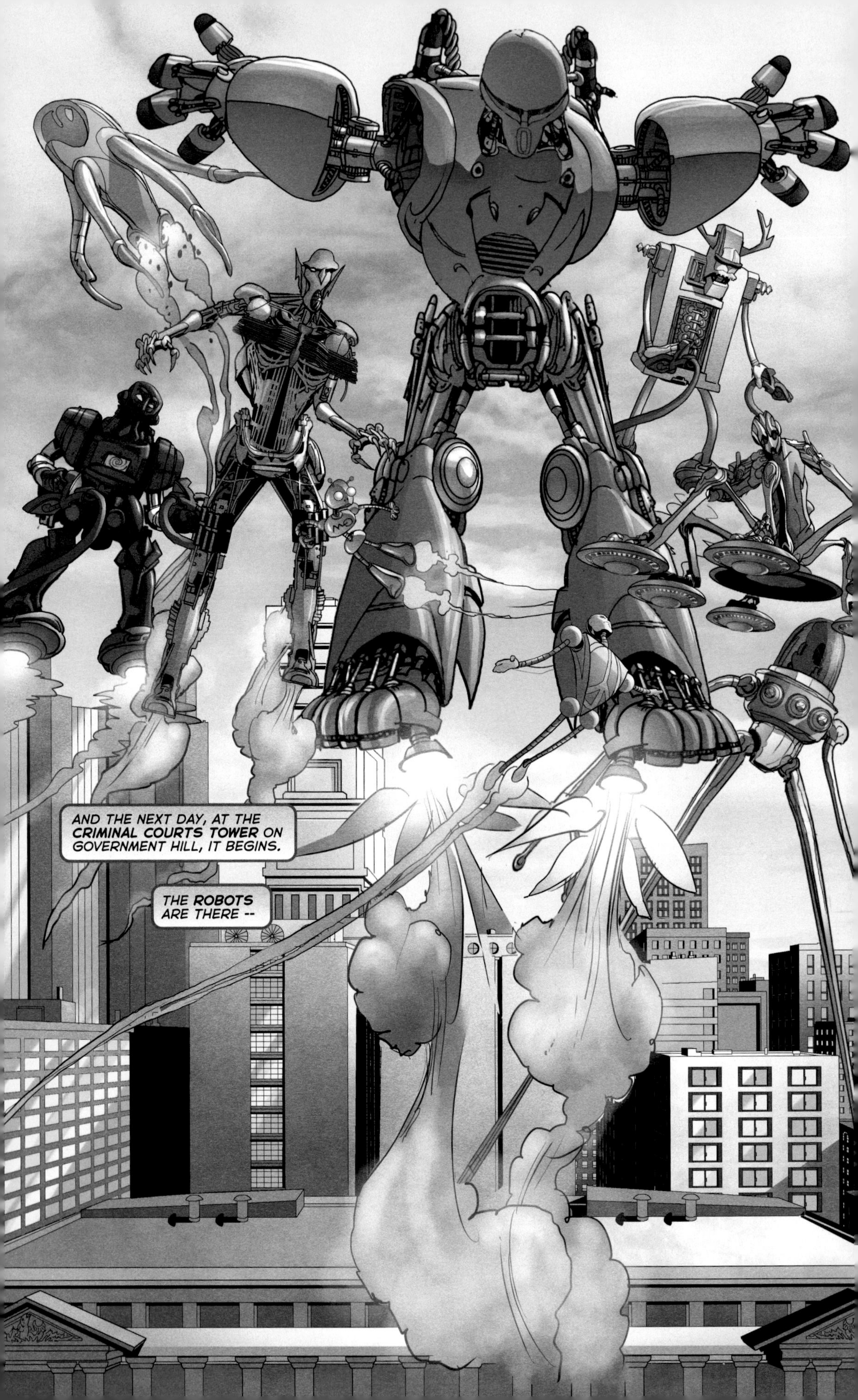
AND THE NEXT DAY, AT THE CRIMINAL COURTS TOWER ON GOVERNMENT HILL, IT BEGINS.
THE ROBOTS ARE THERE --

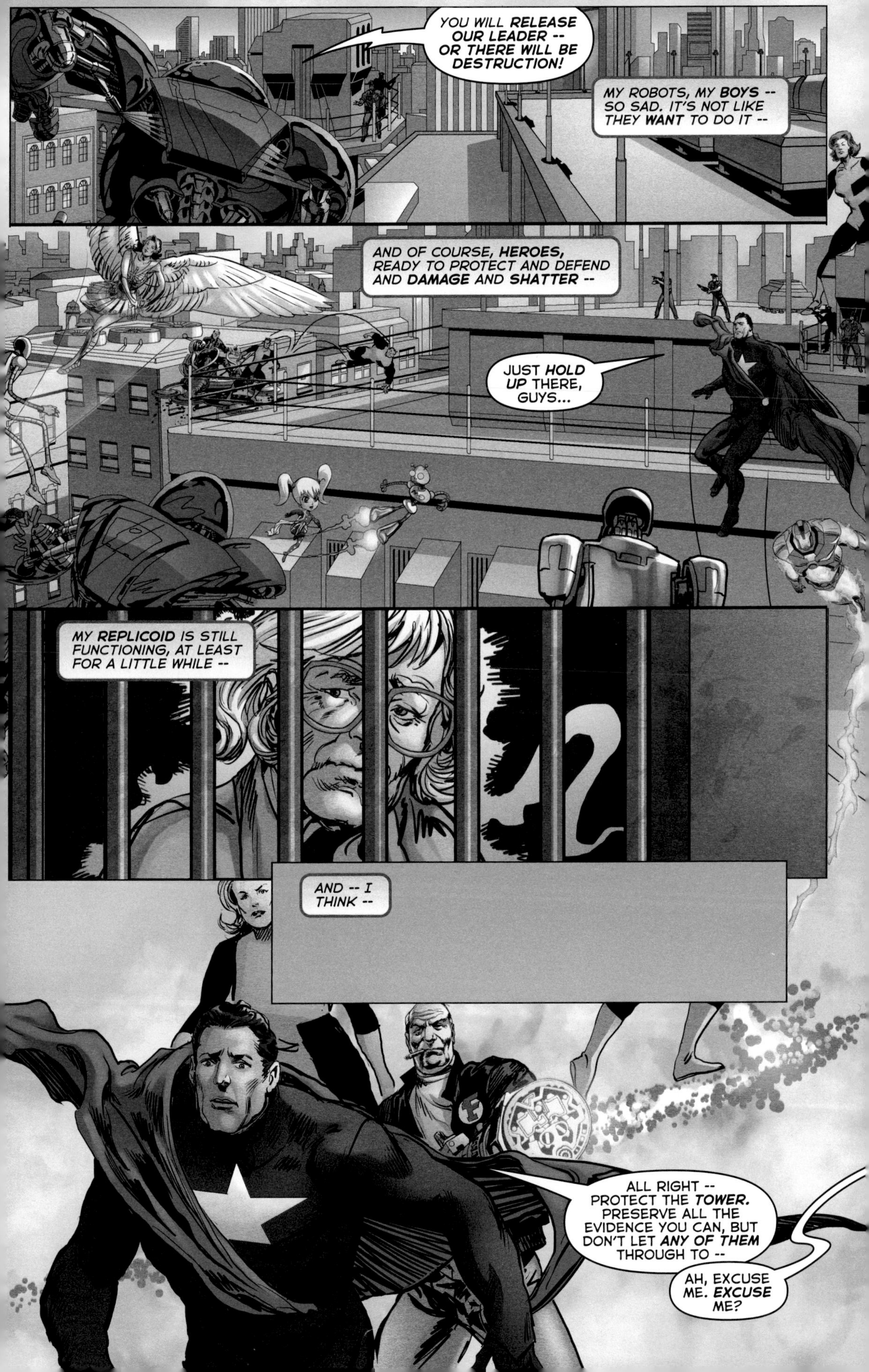
YOU WILL RELEASE OUR LEADER -- OR THERE WILL BE DESTRUCTION!
MY ROBOTS, MY BOYS -- SO SAD. IT'S NOT LIKE THEY WANT TO DO IT --
AND OF COURSE, HEROES, READY TO PROTECT AND DEFEND AND DAMAGE AND SHATTER --
JUST HOLD UP THERE, GUYS...
MY REPLICOID IS STILL FUNCTIONING, AT LEAST FOR A LITTLE WHILE --
AND -- I THINK --
ALL RIGHT -- PROTECT THE TOWER. PRESERVE ALL THE EVIDENCE YOU CAN, BUT DON'T LET ANY OF THEM THROUGH TO --
AH, EXCUSE ME. EXCUSE ME?

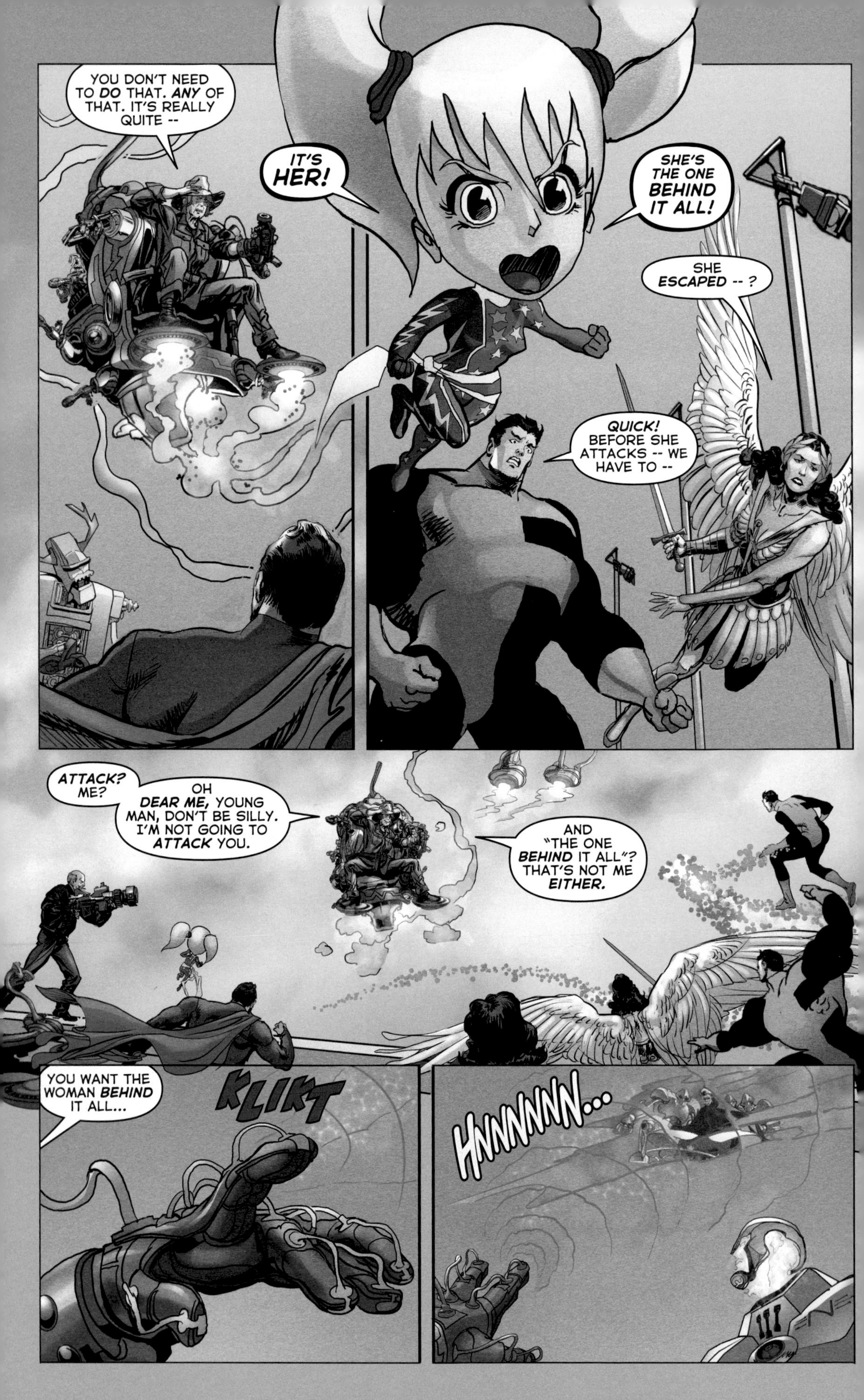

YOU DON'T NEED TO DO THAT. ANY OF THAT. IT'S REALLY QUITE --
IT'S HER!
SHE'S THE ONE BEHIND IT ALL!
SHE ESCAPED -- ?
QUICK! BEFORE SHE ATTACKS -- WE HAVE TO --
ATTACK? ME?
OH DEAR ME, YOUNG MAN, DON'T BE SILLY. I'M NOT GOING TO ATTACK YOU.
AND "THE ONE BEHIND IT ALL"? THAT'S NOT ME EITHER.
YOU WANT THE WOMAN BEHIND IT ALL...
KLIKT
HNNNNNN...

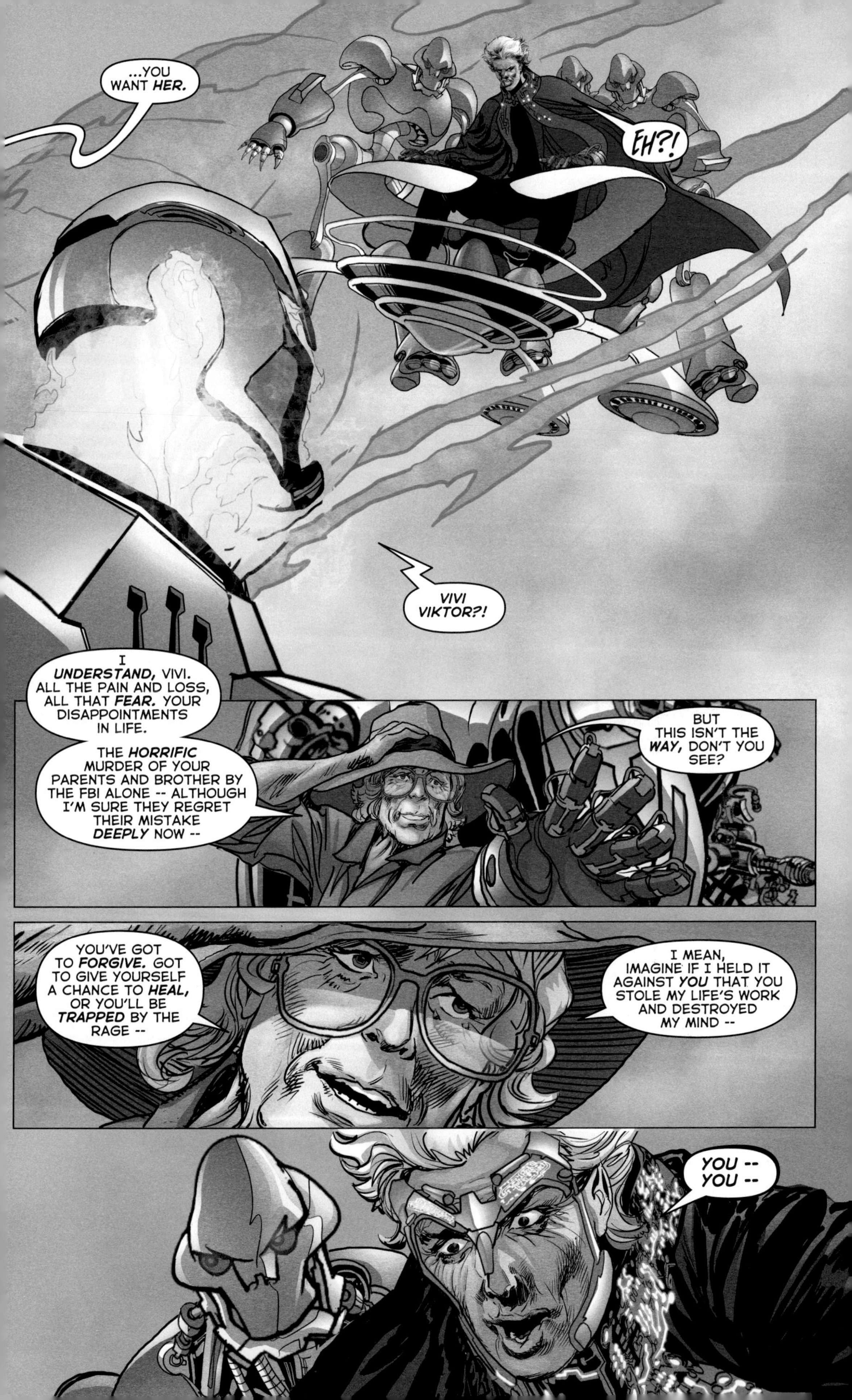
...YOU WANT HER.
EH?!
VIVI VIKTOR?!
I UNDERSTAND, VIVI. ALL THE PAIN AND LOSS, ALL THAT FEAR. YOUR DISAPPOINTMENTS IN LIFE.
THE HORRIFIC MURDER OF YOUR PARENTS AND BROTHER BY THE FBI ALONE -- ALTHOUGH I'M SURE THEY REGRET THEIR MISTAKE DEEPLY NOW --
BUT THIS ISN'T THE WAY, DON'T YOU SEE?
YOU'VE GOT TO FORGIVE. GOT TO GIVE YOURSELF A CHANCE TO HEAL, OR YOU'LL BE TRAPPED BY THE RAGE --
I MEAN, IMAGINE IF I HELD IT AGAINST YOU THAT YOU STOLE MY LIFE'S WORK AND DESTROYED MY MIND --
YOU -- YOU --

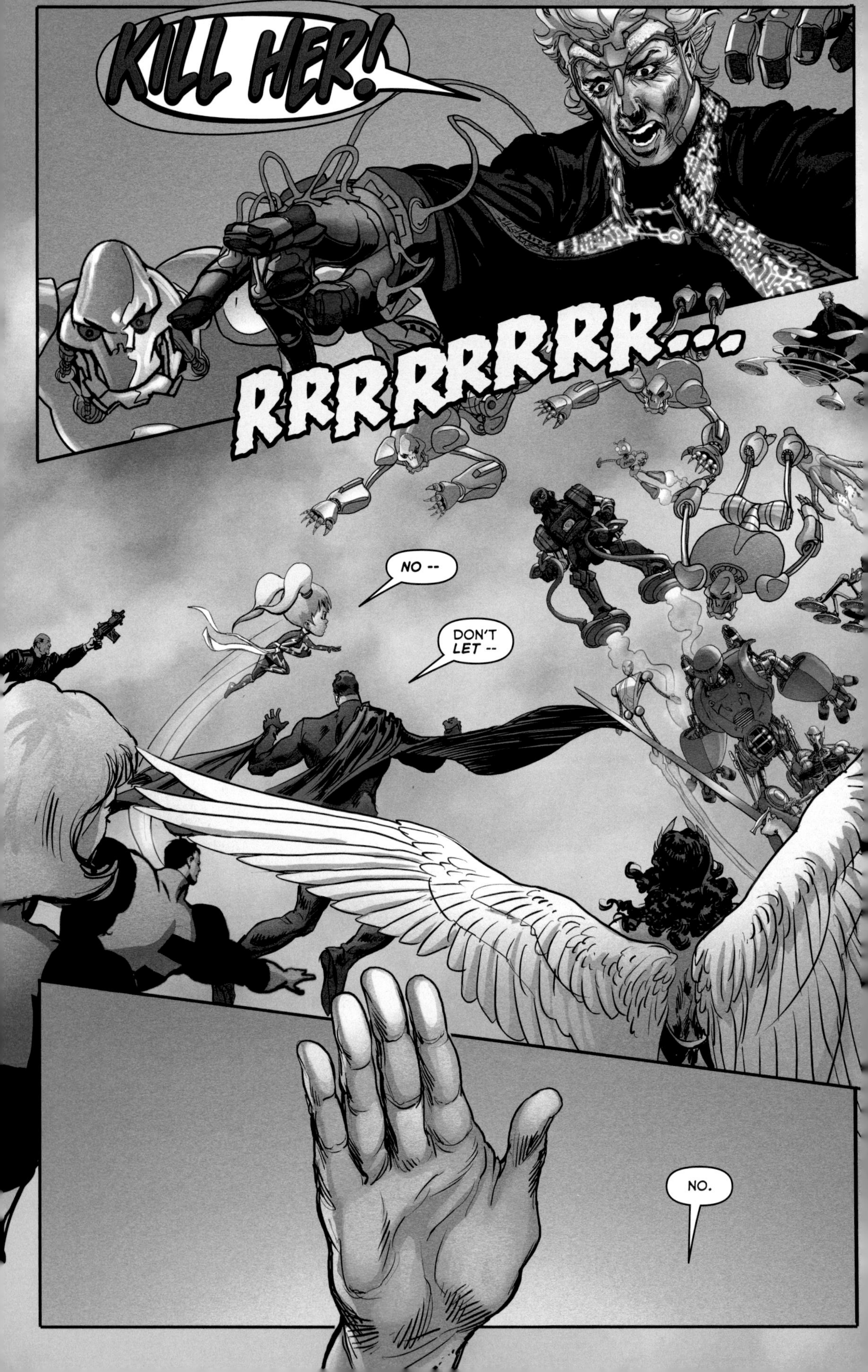
KILL HER!
RRRRRRRR...
NO --
DON'T LET --
NO.

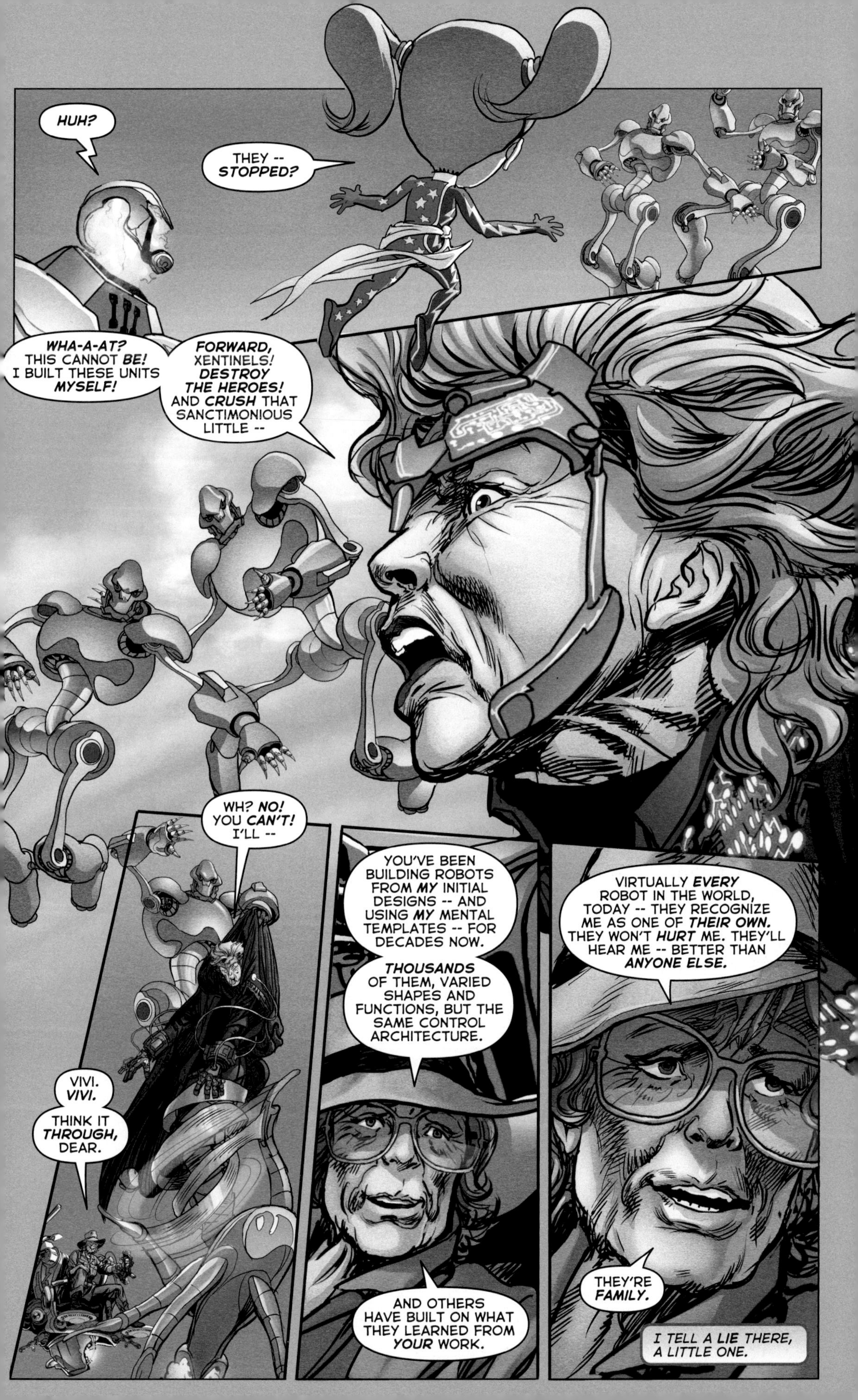
HUH?
THEY -- STOPPED?
WHA-A-AT? THIS CANNOT BE! I BUILT THESE UNITS MYSELF!
FORWARD, XENTINELS! DESTROY THE HEROES! AND CRUSH THAT SANCTIMONIOUS LITTLE --
WH? NO! YOU CAN'T! I'LL --
VIVI. VIVI.
THINK IT THROUGH, DEAR.
YOU'VE BEEN BUILDING ROBOTS FROM MY INITIAL DESIGNS -- AND USING MY MENTAL TEMPLATES -- FOR DECADES NOW.
THOUSANDS OF THEM, VARIED SHAPES AND FUNCTIONS, BUT THE SAME CONTROL ARCHITECTURE.
AND OTHERS HAVE BUILT ON WHAT THEY LEARNED FROM YOUR WORK.
VIRTUALLY EVERY ROBOT IN THE WORLD, TODAY -- THEY RECOGNIZE ME AS ONE OF THEIR OWN. THEY WON'T HURT ME. THEY'LL HEAR ME -- BETTER THAN ANYONE ELSE.
THEY'RE FAMILY.
I TELL A LIE THERE, A LITTLE ONE.

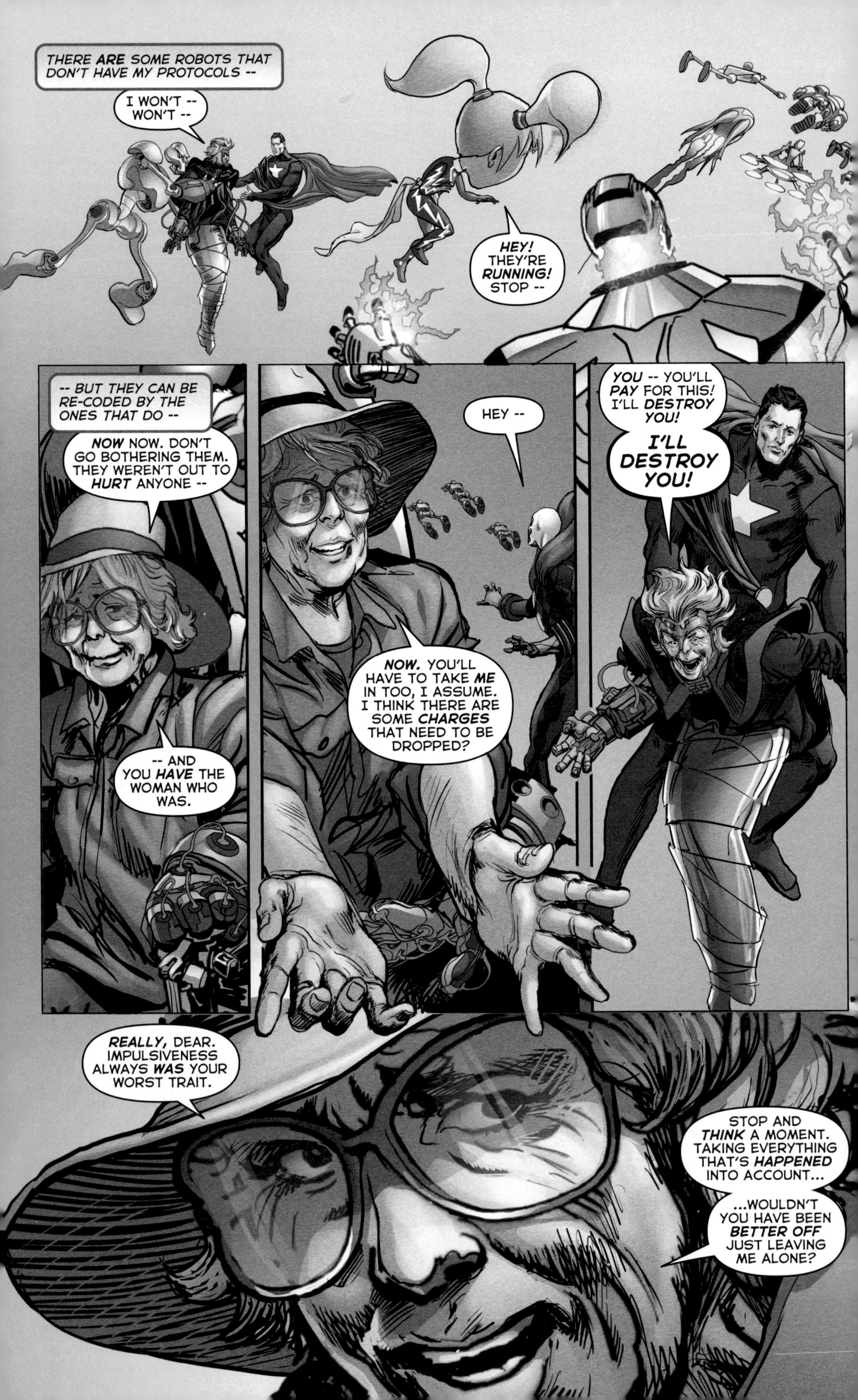
THERE ARE SOME ROBOTS THAT DON'T HAVE MY PROTOCOLS --
I WON'T -- WON'T --
HEY! THEY'RE RUNNING! STOP --
-- BUT THEY CAN BE RE-CODED BY THE ONES THAT DO --
NOW NOW. DON'T GO BOTHERING THEM. THEY WEREN'T OUT TO HURT ANYONE --
-- AND YOU HAVE THE WOMAN WHO WAS.
HEY --
NOW. YOU'LL HAVE TO TAKE ME IN TOO, I ASSUME. I THINK THERE ARE SOME CHARGES THAT NEED TO BE DROPPED?
YOU -- YOU'LL PAY FOR THIS! I'LL DESTROY YOU!
I'LL DESTROY YOU!
REALLY, DEAR. IMPULSIVENESS ALWAYS WAS YOUR WORST TRAIT.
STOP AND THINK A MOMENT. TAKING EVERYTHING THAT'S HAPPENED INTO ACCOUNT...
...WOULDN'T YOU HAVE BEEN BETTER OFF JUST LEAVING ME ALONE?

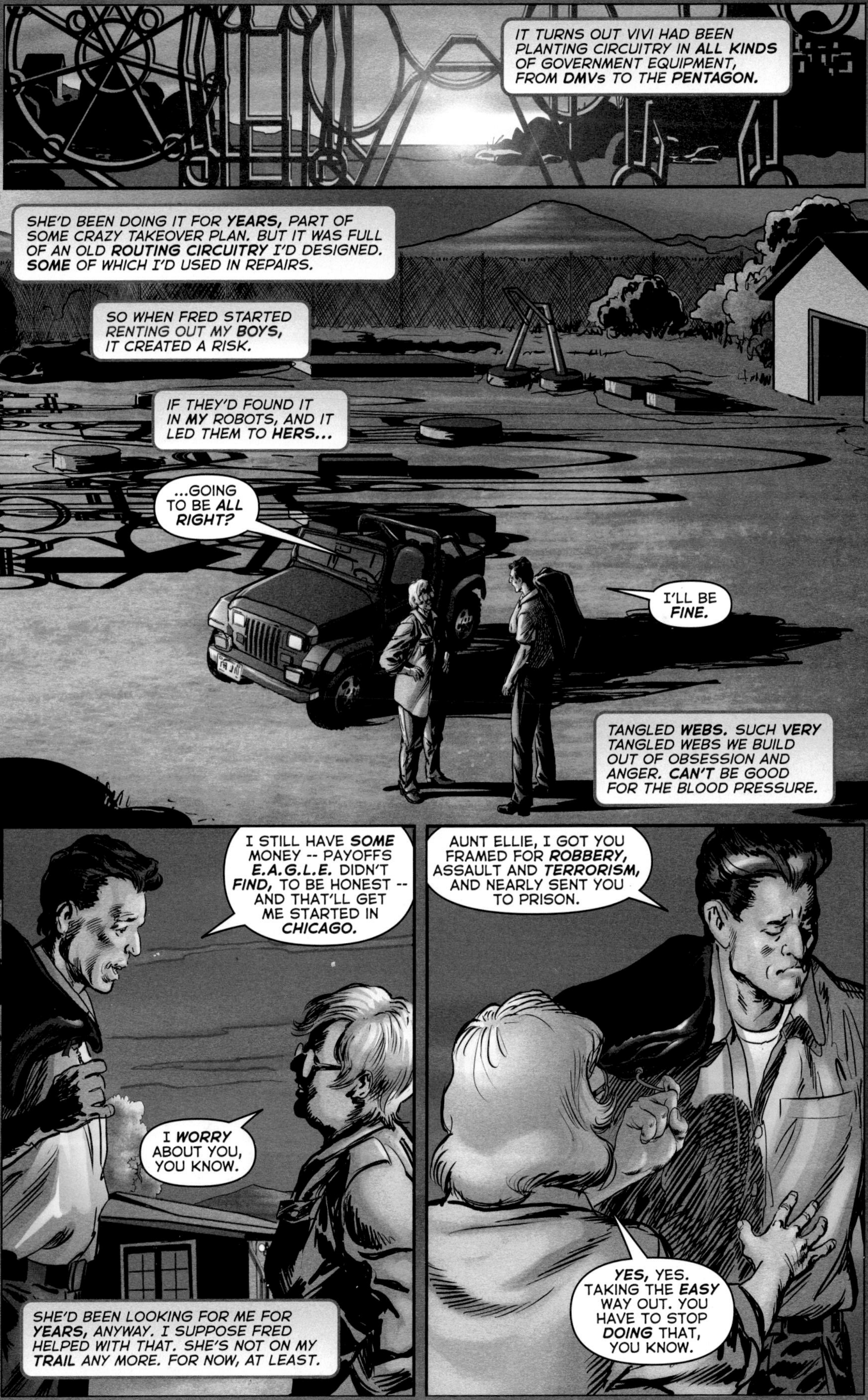
IT TURNS OUT VIVI HAD BEEN PLANTING CIRCUITRY IN ALL KINDS OF GOVERNMENT EQUIPMENT, FROM DMVs TO THE PENTAGON.
SHE'D BEEN DOING IT FOR YEARS, PART OF SOME CRAZY TAKEOVER PLAN. BUT IT WAS FULL OF AN OLD ROUTING CIRCUITRY I'D DESIGNED. SOME OF WHICH I'D USED IN REPAIRS.
SO WHEN FRED STARTED RENTING OUT MY BOYS, IT CREATED A RISK.
IF THEY'D FOUND IT IN MY ROBOTS, AND IT LED THEM TO HERS...
...GOING TO BE ALL RIGHT?
I'LL BE FINE.
TANGLED WEBS. SUCH VERY TANGLED WEBS WE BUILD OUT OF OBSESSION AND ANGER. CAN'T BE GOOD FOR THE BLOOD PRESSURE.
I STILL HAVE SOME MONEY -- PAYOFFS E.A.G.L.E. DIDN'T FIND, TO BE HONEST -- AND THAT'LL GET ME STARTED IN CHICAGO.
I WORRY ABOUT YOU, YOU KNOW.
SHE'D BEEN LOOKING FOR ME FOR YEARS, ANYWAY. I SUPPOSE FRED HELPED WITH THAT. SHE'S NOT ON MY TRAIL ANY MORE. FOR NOW, AT LEAST.
AUNT ELLIE, I GOT YOU FRAMED FOR ROBBERY, ASSAULT AND TERRORISM, AND NEARLY SENT YOU TO PRISON.
YES, YES. TAKING THE EASY WAY OUT. YOU HAVE TO STOP DOING THAT, YOU KNOW.

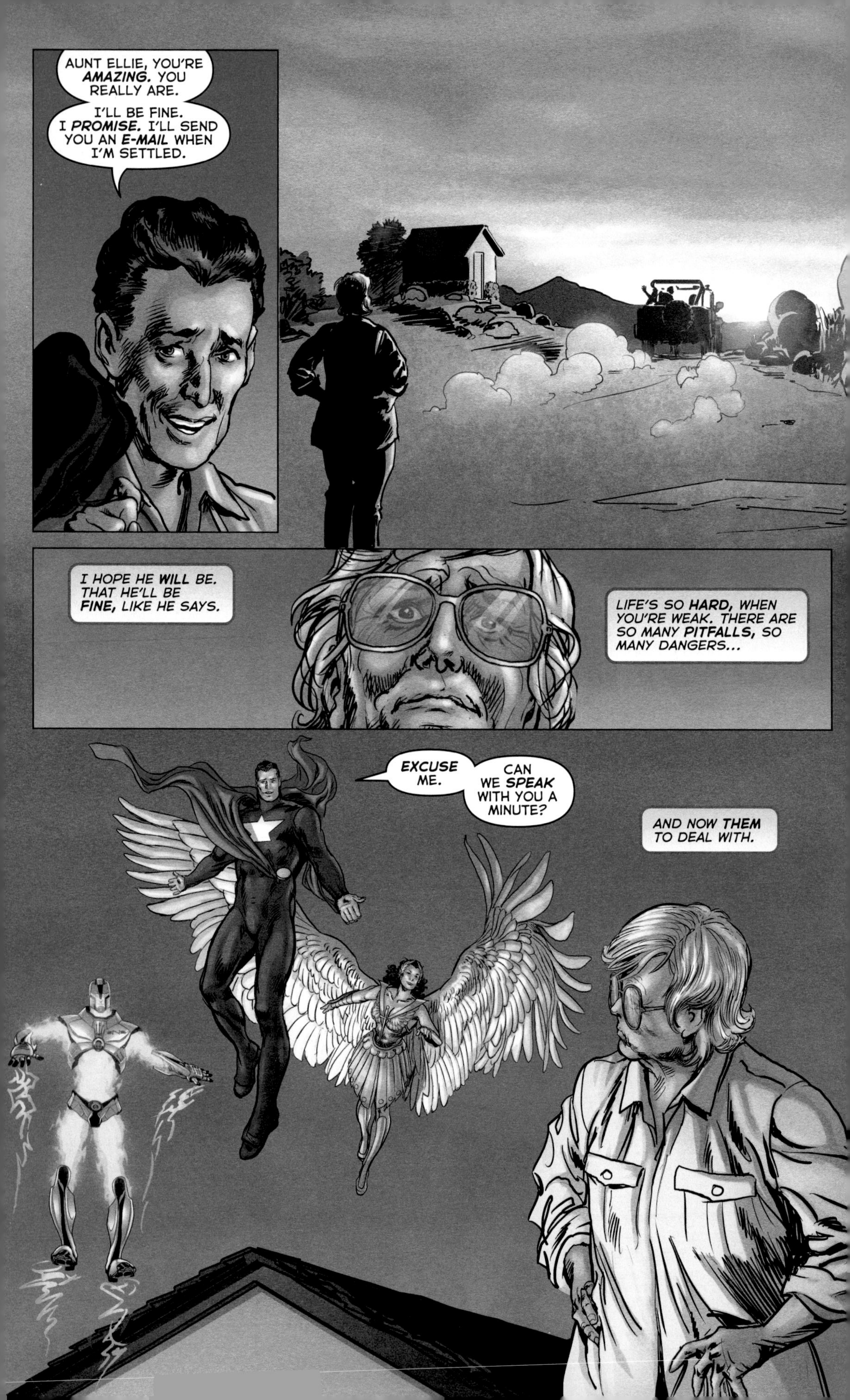
AUNT ELLIE, YOU'RE AMAZING. YOU REALLY ARE.
I'LL BE FINE. I PROMISE. I'LL SEND YOU AN E-MAIL WHEN I'M SETTLED.
I HOPE HE WILL BE. THAT HE'LL BE FINE, LIKE HE SAYS.
LIFE'S SO HARD, WHEN YOU'RE WEAK. THERE ARE SO MANY PITFALLS, SO MANY DANGERS...
EXCUSE ME.
CAN WE SPEAK WITH YOU A MINUTE?
AND NOW THEM TO DEAL WITH.

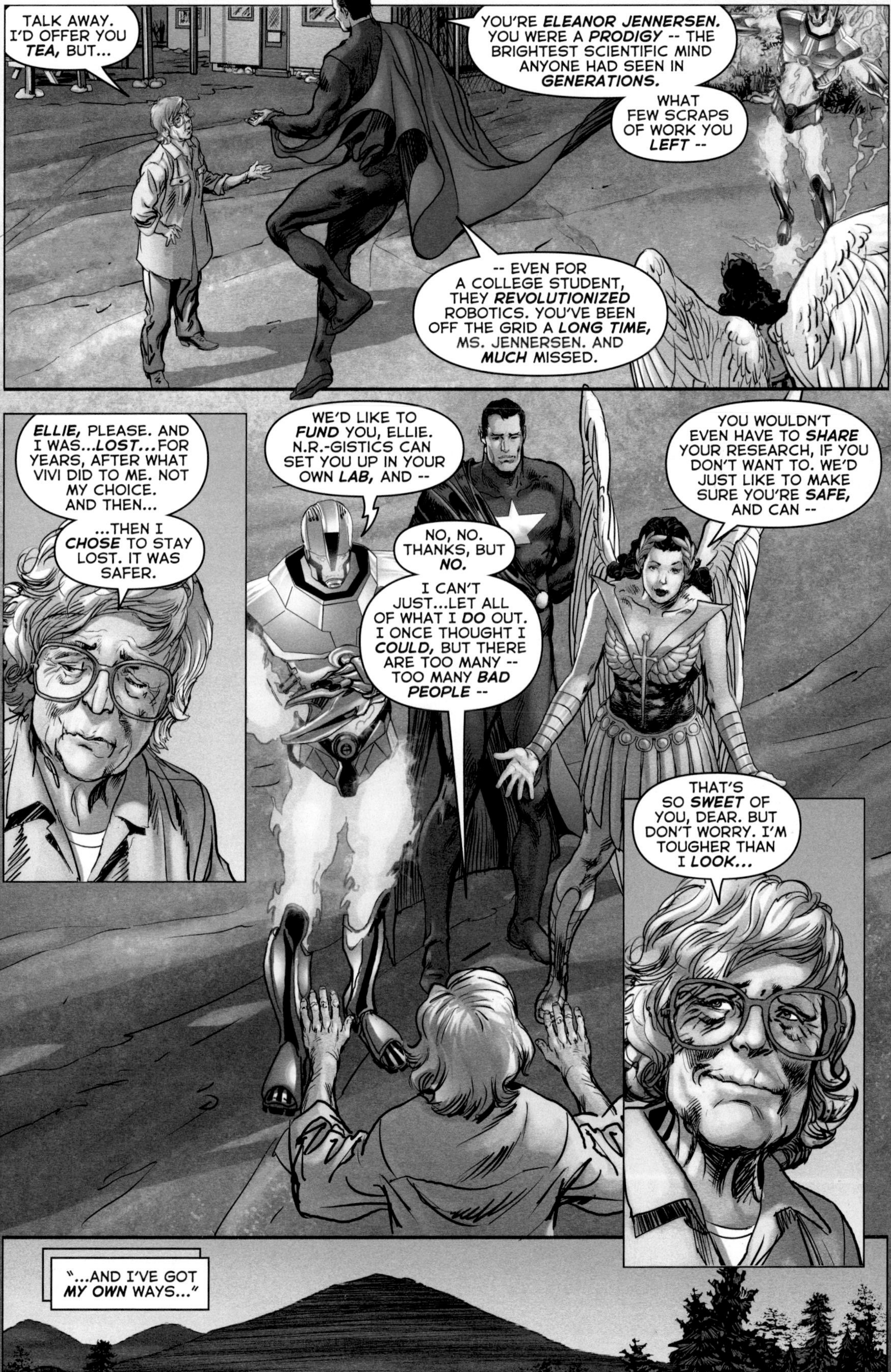
TALK AWAY. I'D OFFER YOU TEA, BUT...
YOU'RE ELEANOR JENNERSEN. YOU WERE A PRODIGY -- THE BRIGHTEST SCIENTIFIC MIND ANYONE HAD SEEN IN GENERATIONS.
WHAT FEW SCRAPS OF WORK YOU LEFT --
-- EVEN FOR A COLLEGE STUDENT, THEY REVOLUTIONIZED ROBOTICS. YOU'VE BEEN OFF THE GRID A LONG TIME, MS. JENNERSEN. AND MUCH MISSED.
ELLIE, PLEASE. AND I WAS...LOST...FOR YEARS, AFTER WHAT VIVI DID TO ME. NOT MY CHOICE. AND THEN...
...THEN I CHOSE TO STAY LOST. IT WAS SAFER.
WE'D LIKE TO FUND YOU, ELLIE. N.R.-GISTICS CAN SET YOU UP IN YOUR OWN LAB, AND --
YOU WOULDN'T EVEN HAVE TO SHARE YOUR RESEARCH, IF YOU DON'T WANT TO. WE'D JUST LIKE TO MAKE SURE YOU'RE SAFE, AND CAN --
NO, NO. THANKS, BUT NO.
I CAN'T JUST...LET ALL OF WHAT I DO OUT. I ONCE THOUGHT I COULD, BUT THERE ARE TOO MANY -- TOO MANY BAD PEOPLE --
THAT'S SO SWEET OF YOU, DEAR. BUT DON'T WORRY. I'M TOUGHER THAN I LOOK...
"...AND I'VE GOT MY OWN WAYS..."

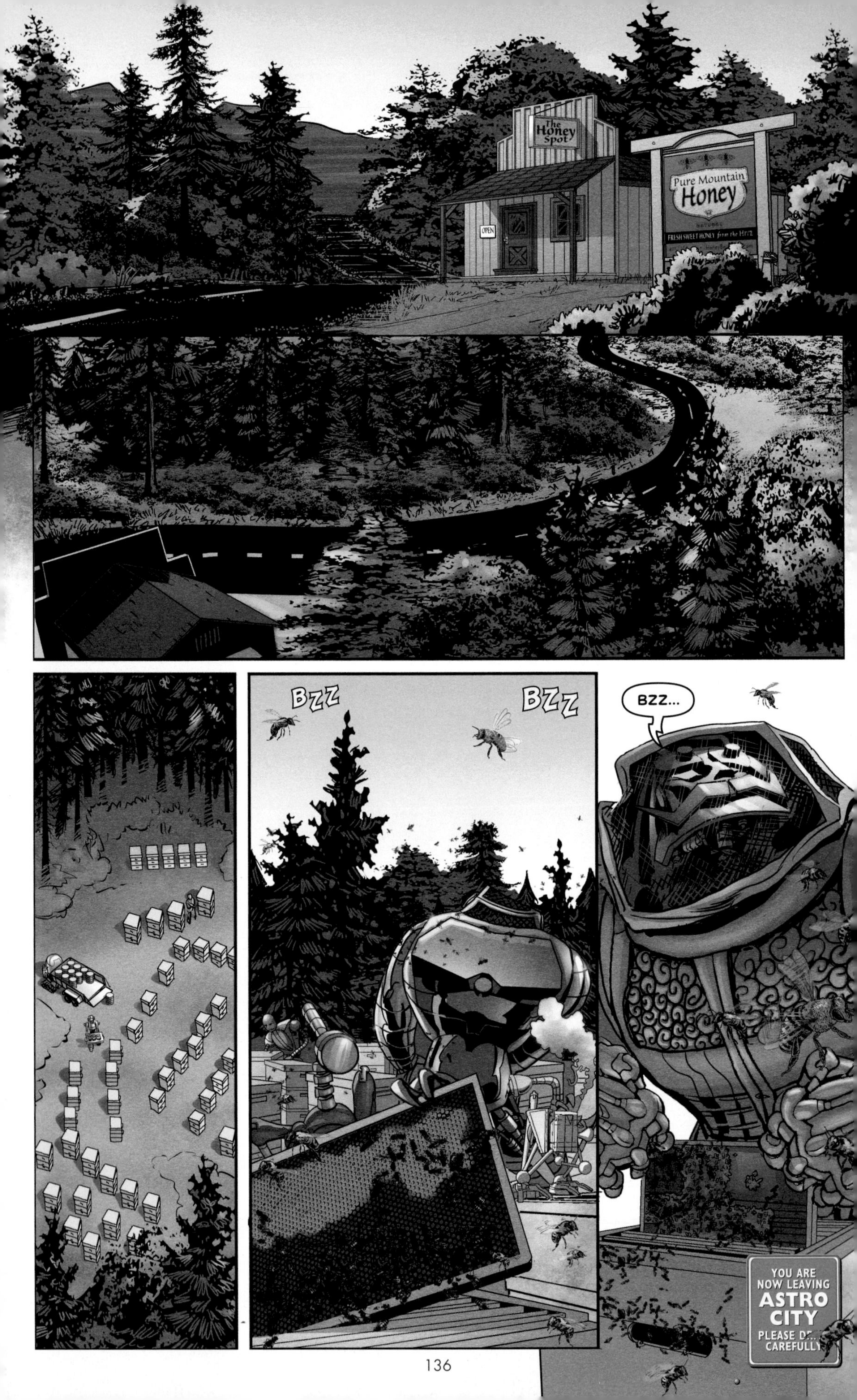
The Honey Spot
OPEN
Pure Mountain Honey
FRESH SWEET HONEY from the HIVE
BZZ
BZZ
BZZ...
YOU ARE NOW LEAVING
ASTRO CITY
PLEASE D
CAREFULLY

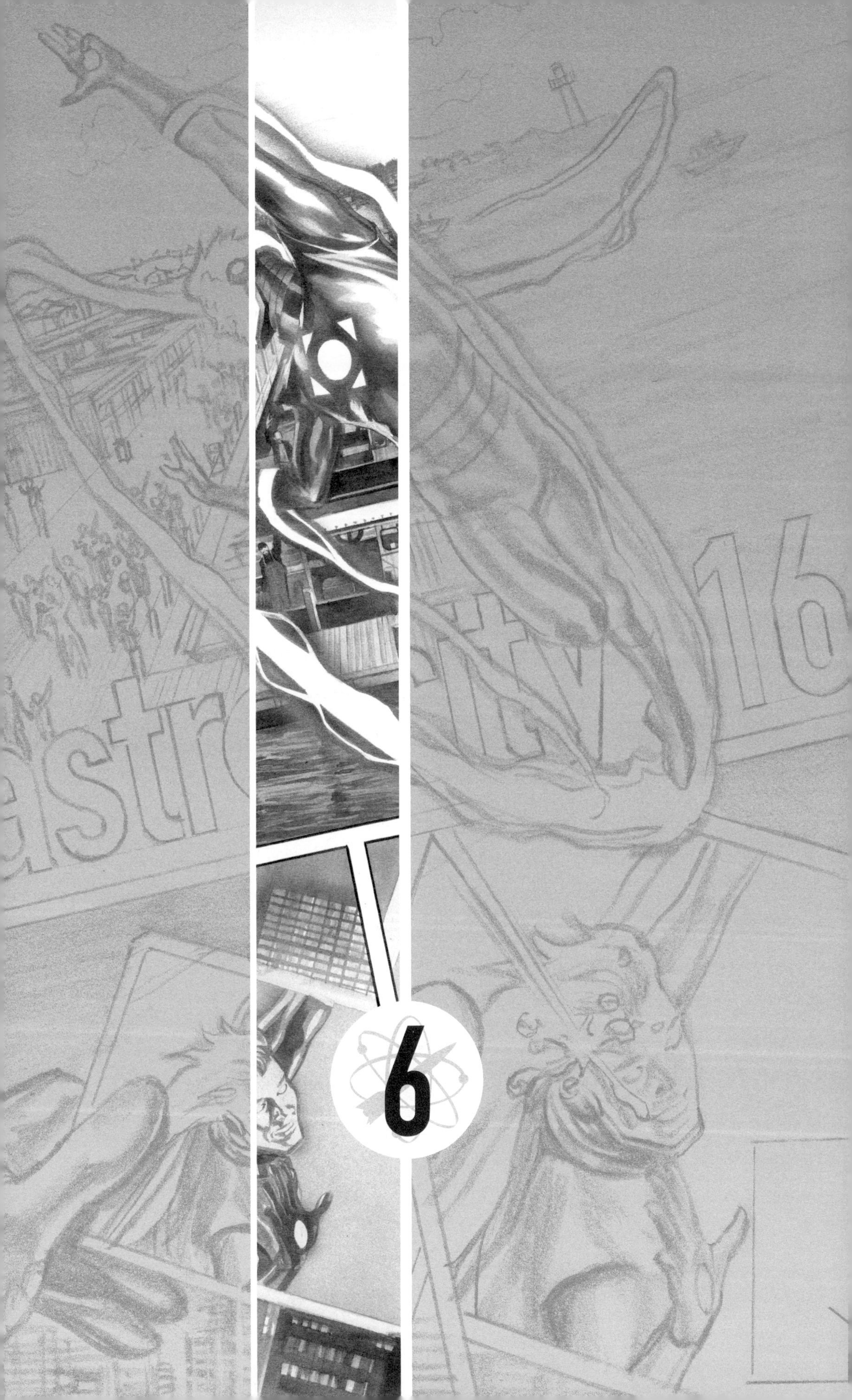
6

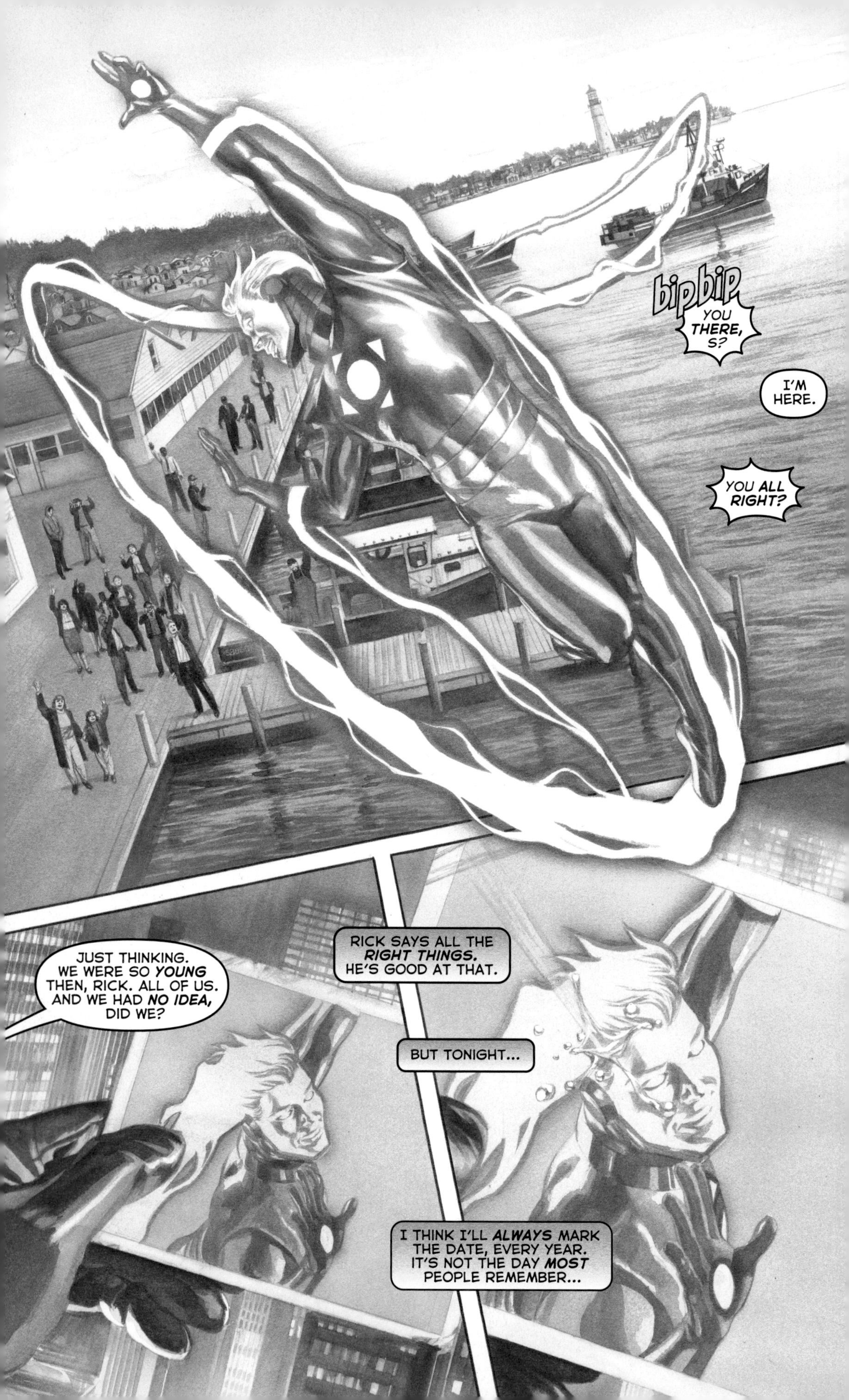
bipbip
YOU THERE, S?
I'M HERE.
YOU ALL RIGHT?
JUST THINKING. WE WERE SO YOUNG THEN, RICK. ALL OF US. AND WE HAD NO IDEA, DID WE?
RICK SAYS ALL THE RIGHT THINGS. HE'S GOOD AT THAT.
BUT TONIGHT...
I THINK I'LL ALWAYS MARK THE DATE, EVERY YEAR. IT'S NOT THE DAY MOST PEOPLE REMEMBER...

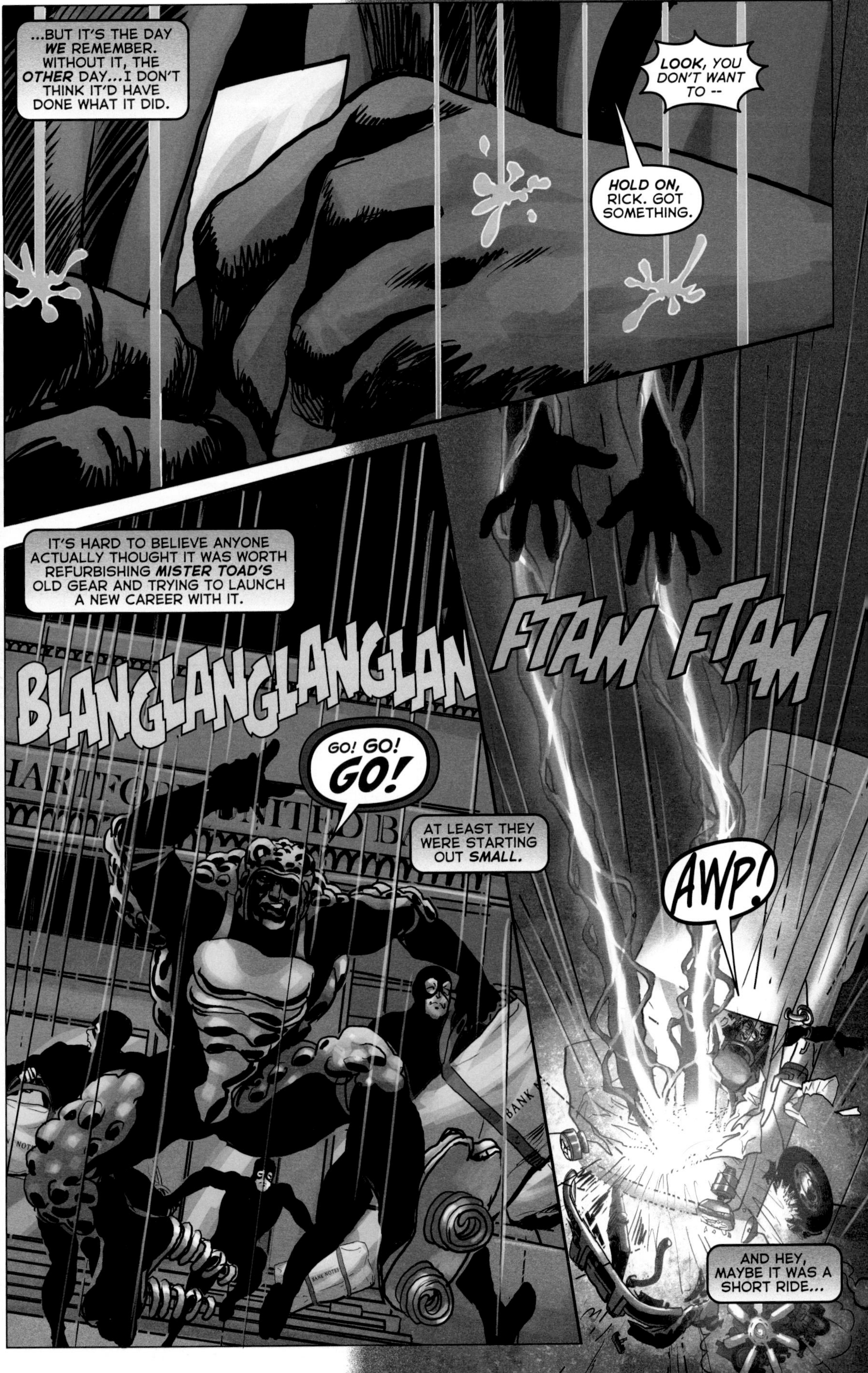
...BUT IT'S THE DAY WE REMEMBER. WITHOUT IT, THE OTHER DAY...I DON'T THINK IT'D HAVE DONE WHAT IT DID.
LOOK, YOU DON'T WANT TO --
HOLD ON, RICK. GOT SOMETHING.
IT'S HARD TO BELIEVE ANYONE ACTUALLY THOUGHT IT WAS WORTH REFURBISHING MISTER TOAD'S OLD GEAR AND TRYING TO LAUNCH A NEW CAREER WITH IT.
BLANGLANGLANGLAN
FTAM FTAM
GO! GO! GO!
AT LEAST THEY WERE STARTING OUT SMALL.
AWP!
AND HEY, MAYBE IT WAS A SHORT RIDE...

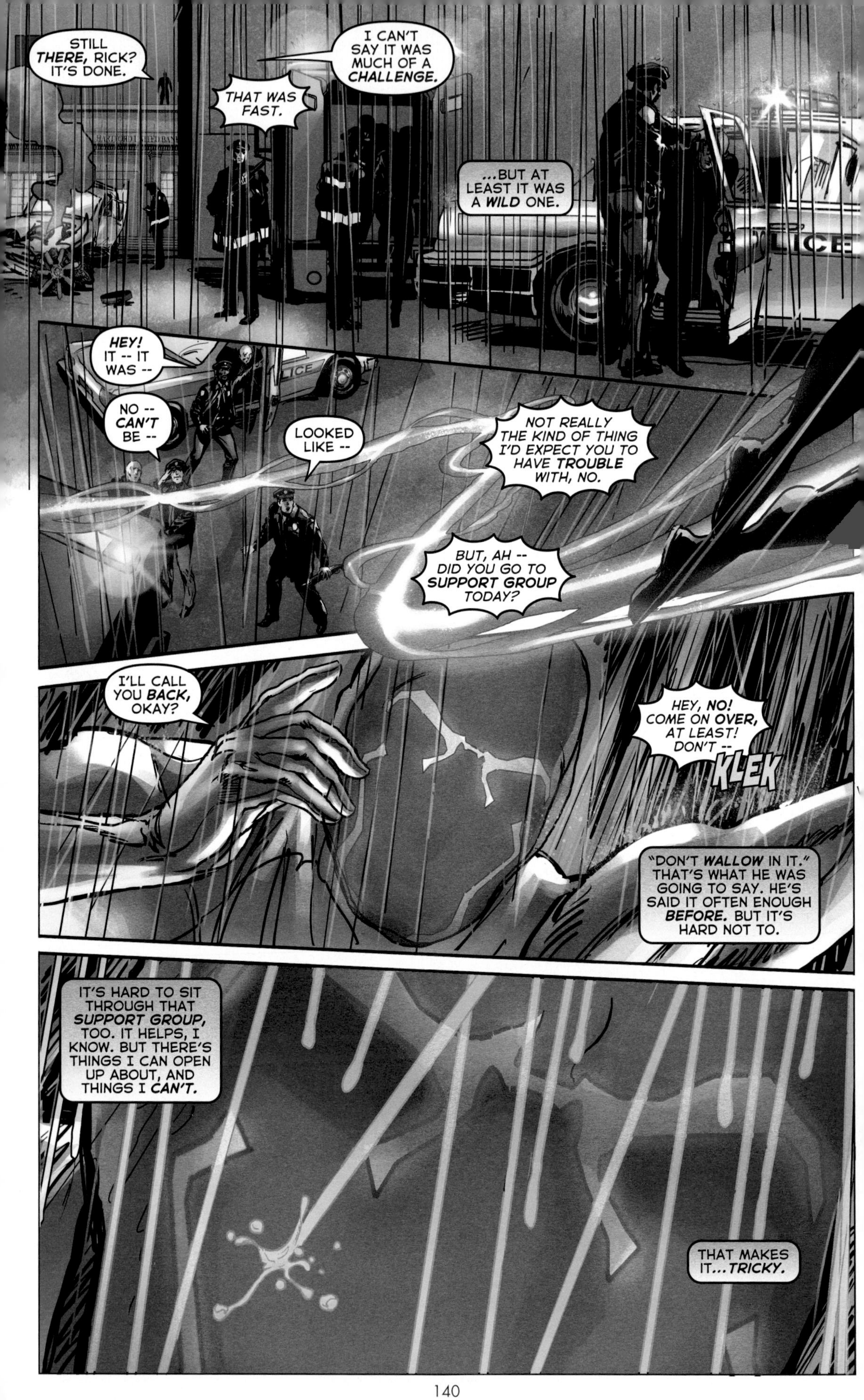
STILL THERE, RICK? IT'S DONE.
THAT WAS FAST.
I CAN'T SAY IT WAS MUCH OF A CHALLENGE.
...BUT AT LEAST IT WAS A WILD ONE.
HEY! IT -- IT WAS --
NO -- CAN'T BE --
LOOKED LIKE --
NOT REALLY THE KIND OF THING I'D EXPECT YOU TO HAVE TROUBLE WITH, NO.
BUT, AH -- DID YOU GO TO SUPPORT GROUP TODAY?
I'LL CALL YOU BACK, OKAY?
HEY, NO! COME ON OVER, AT LEAST! DON'T --
KLEK
"DON'T WALLOW IN IT." THAT'S WHAT HE WAS GOING TO SAY. HE'S SAID IT OFTEN ENOUGH BEFORE. BUT IT'S HARD NOT TO.
IT'S HARD TO SIT THROUGH THAT SUPPORT GROUP, TOO. IT HELPS, I KNOW. BUT THERE'S THINGS I CAN OPEN UP ABOUT, AND THINGS I CAN'T.
THAT MAKES IT...TRICKY.

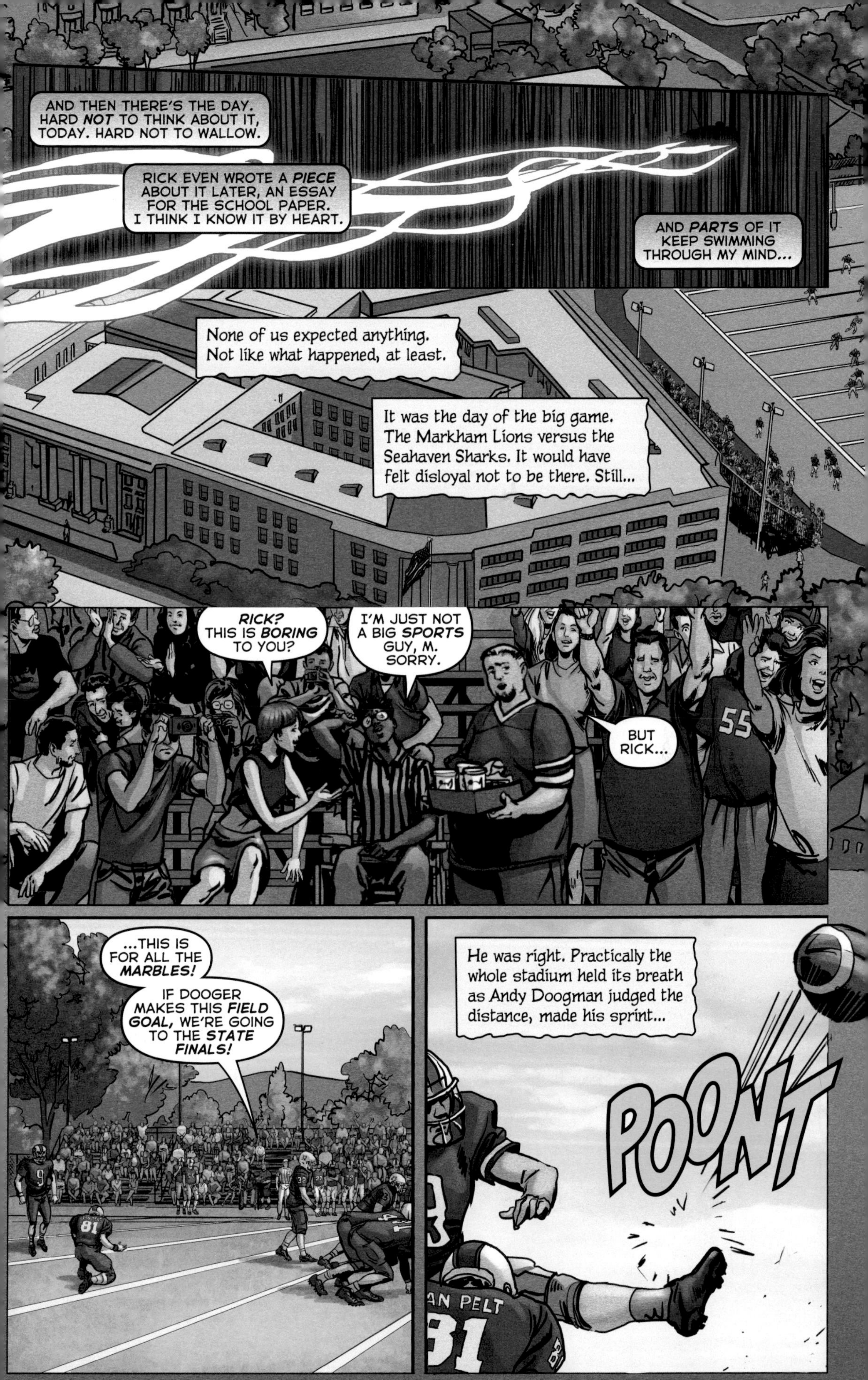

AND THEN THERE'S THE DAY. HARD *NOT* TO THINK ABOUT IT, TODAY. HARD NOT TO WALLOW.
RICK EVEN WROTE A *PIECE* ABOUT IT LATER, AN ESSAY FOR THE SCHOOL PAPER. I THINK I KNOW IT BY HEART.
AND *PARTS* OF IT KEEP SWIMMING THROUGH MY MIND...
None of us expected anything. Not like what happened, at least.
It was the day of the big game. The Markham Lions versus the Seahaven Sharks. It would have felt disloyal not to be there. Still...
RICK? THIS IS *BORING* TO YOU?
I'M JUST NOT A BIG *SPORTS* GUY, M. SORRY.
BUT RICK...
...THIS IS FOR ALL THE *MARBLES!*
IF DOOGER MAKES THIS *FIELD GOAL,* WE'RE GOING TO THE *STATE FINALS!*
He was right. Practically the whole stadium held its breath as Andy Doogman judged the distance, made his sprint...
POONT

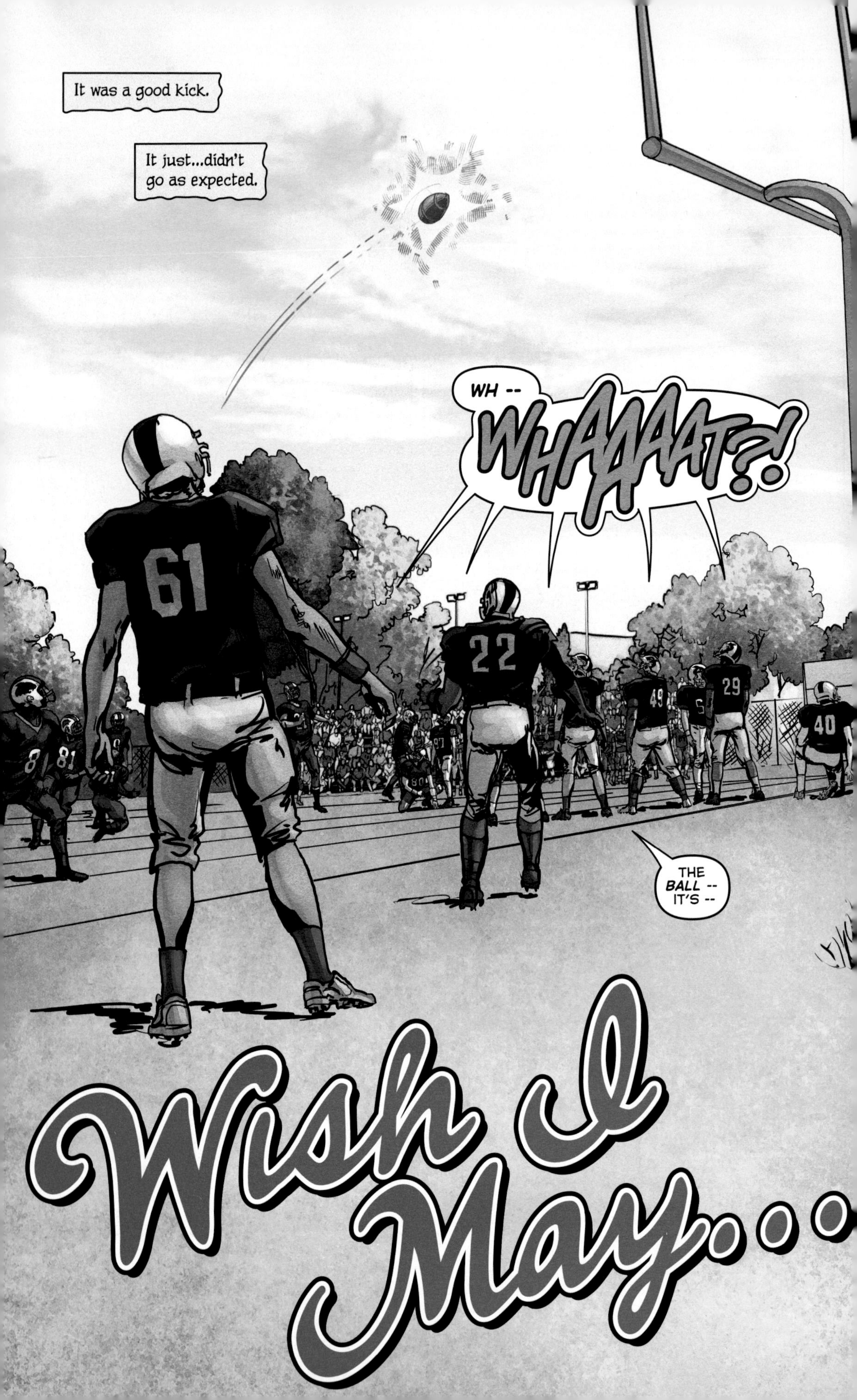
It was a good kick.
It just...didn't go as expected.
WH -- WHAAAAAT?!
THE BALL -- IT'S --
Wish I May...

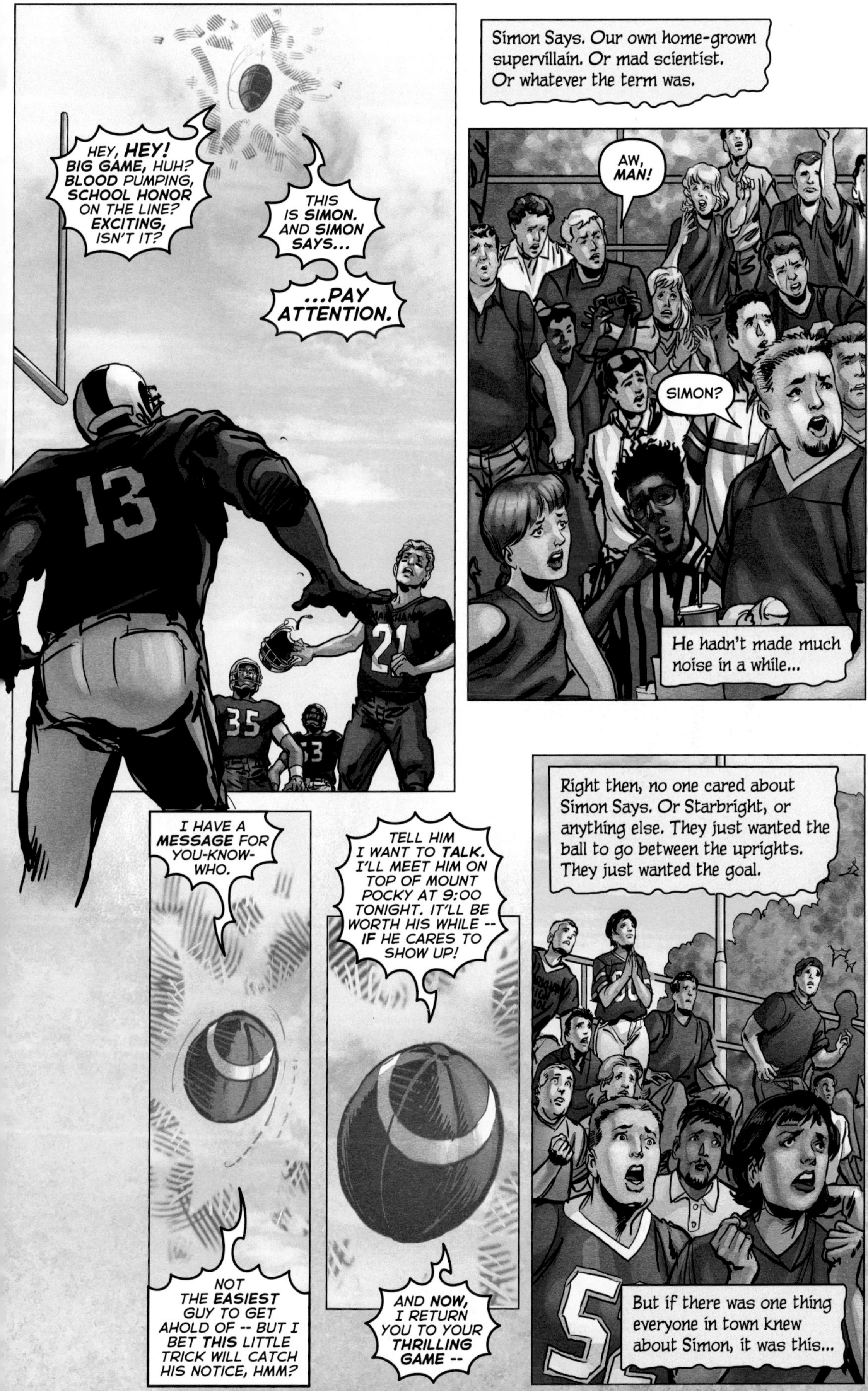
HEY, HEY! BIG GAME, HUH? BLOOD PUMPING, SCHOOL HONOR ON THE LINE? EXCITING, ISN'T IT?
THIS IS SIMON. AND SIMON SAYS...
...PAY ATTENTION.
Simon Says. Our own home-grown supervillain. Or mad scientist. Or whatever the term was.
AW, MAN!
SIMON?
He hadn't made much noise in a while...
I HAVE A MESSAGE FOR YOU-KNOW-WHO.
NOT THE EASIEST GUY TO GET AHOLD OF -- BUT I BET THIS LITTLE TRICK WILL CATCH HIS NOTICE, HMM?
TELL HIM I WANT TO TALK. I'LL MEET HIM ON TOP OF MOUNT POCKY AT 9:00 TONIGHT. IT'LL BE WORTH HIS WHILE -- IF HE CARES TO SHOW UP!
AND NOW, I RETURN YOU TO YOUR THRILLING GAME --
Right then, no one cared about Simon Says. Or Starbright, or anything else. They just wanted the ball to go between the uprights. They just wanted the goal.
But if there was one thing everyone in town knew about Simon, it was this...

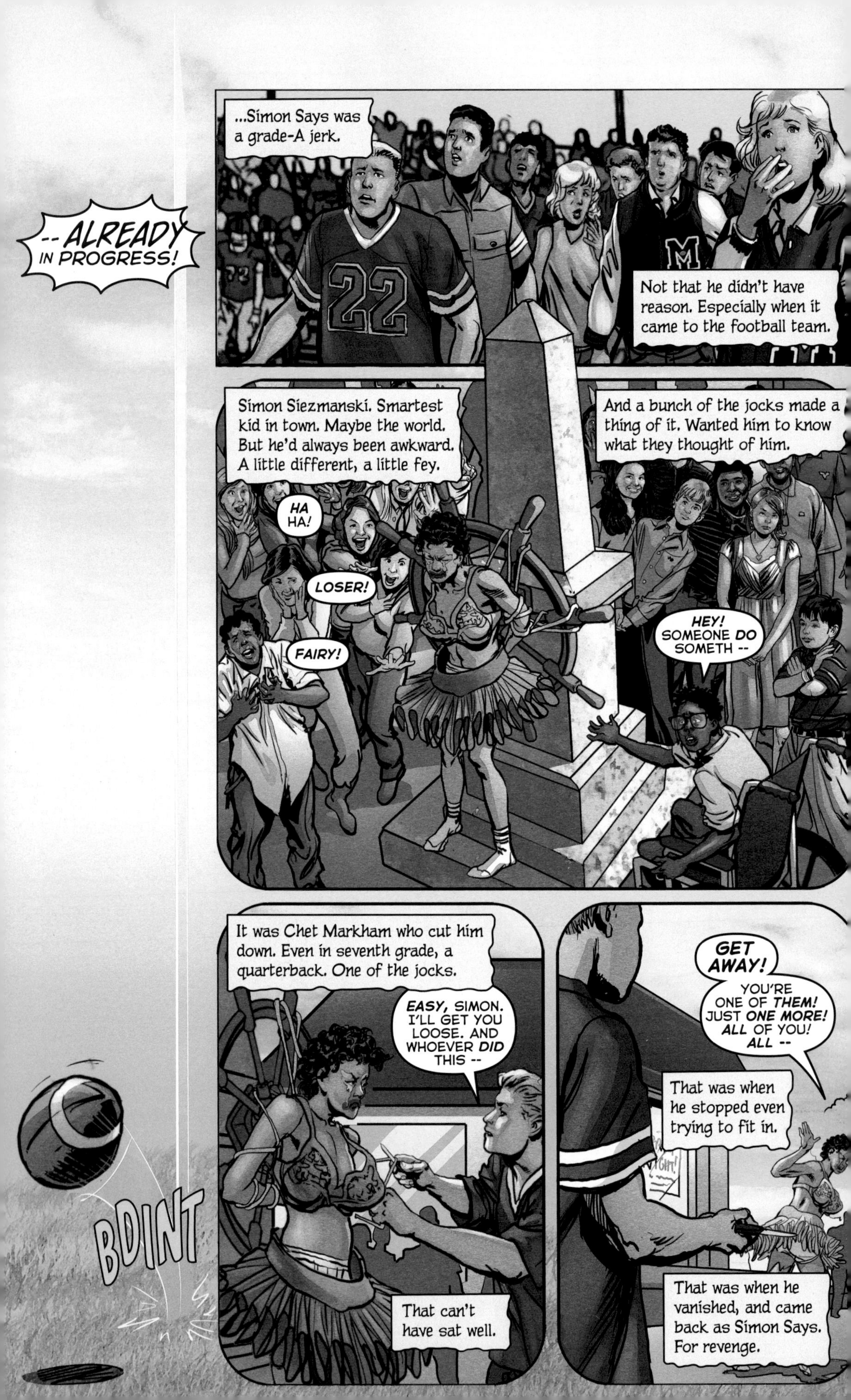
-- ALREADY IN PROGRESS!
...Simon Says was a grade-A jerk.
Not that he didn't have reason. Especially when it came to the football team.
Simon Siezmanski. Smartest kid in town. Maybe the world. But he'd always been awkward. A little different, a little fey.
And a bunch of the jocks made a thing of it. Wanted him to know what they thought of him.
HA HA!
LOSER!
FAIRY!
HEY! SOMEONE DO SOMETH --
It was Chet Markham who cut him down. Even in seventh grade, a quarterback. One of the jocks.
EASY, SIMON. I'LL GET YOU LOOSE. AND WHOEVER DID THIS --
That can't have sat well.
GET AWAY!
YOU'RE ONE OF THEM! JUST ONE MORE! ALL OF YOU! ALL --
That was when he stopped even trying to fit in.
That was when he vanished, and came back as Simon Says. For revenge.
BDINT

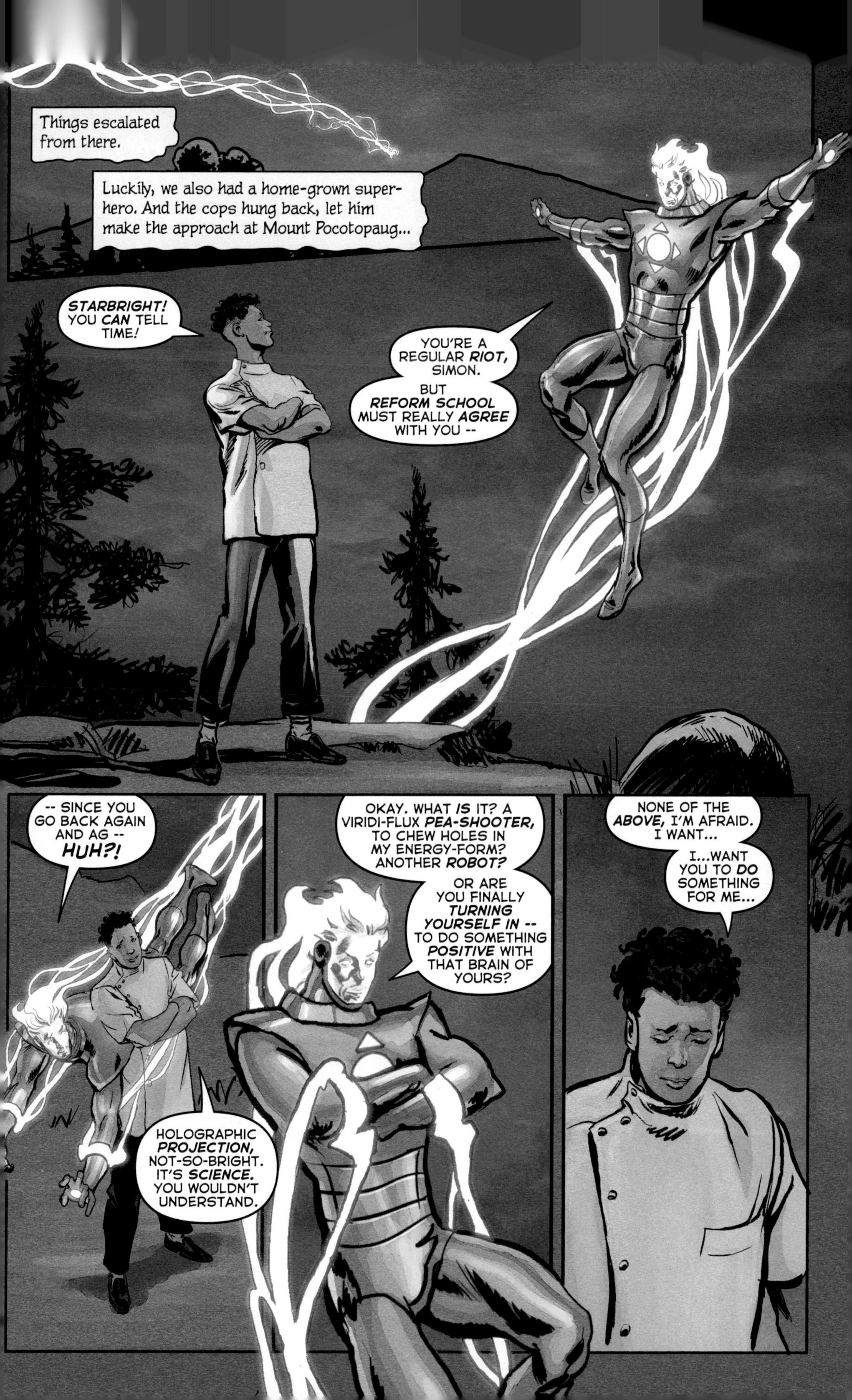
Things escalated from there.
Luckily, we also had a home-grown super-hero. And the cops hung back, let him make the approach at Mount Pocotopaug...
STARBRIGHT! YOU CAN TELL TIME!
YOU'RE A REGULAR RIOT, SIMON.
BUT REFORM SCHOOL MUST REALLY AGREE WITH YOU --
-- SINCE YOU GO BACK AGAIN AND AG -- HUH?!
HOLOGRAPHIC PROJECTION, NOT-SO-BRIGHT. IT'S SCIENCE. YOU WOULDN'T UNDERSTAND.
OKAY. WHAT IS IT? A VIRIDI-FLUX PEA-SHOOTER, TO CHEW HOLES IN MY ENERGY-FORM? ANOTHER ROBOT?
OR ARE YOU FINALLY TURNING YOURSELF IN -- TO DO SOMETHING POSITIVE WITH THAT BRAIN OF YOURS?
NONE OF THE ABOVE, I'M AFRAID. I WANT...
I...WANT YOU TO DO SOMETHING FOR ME...

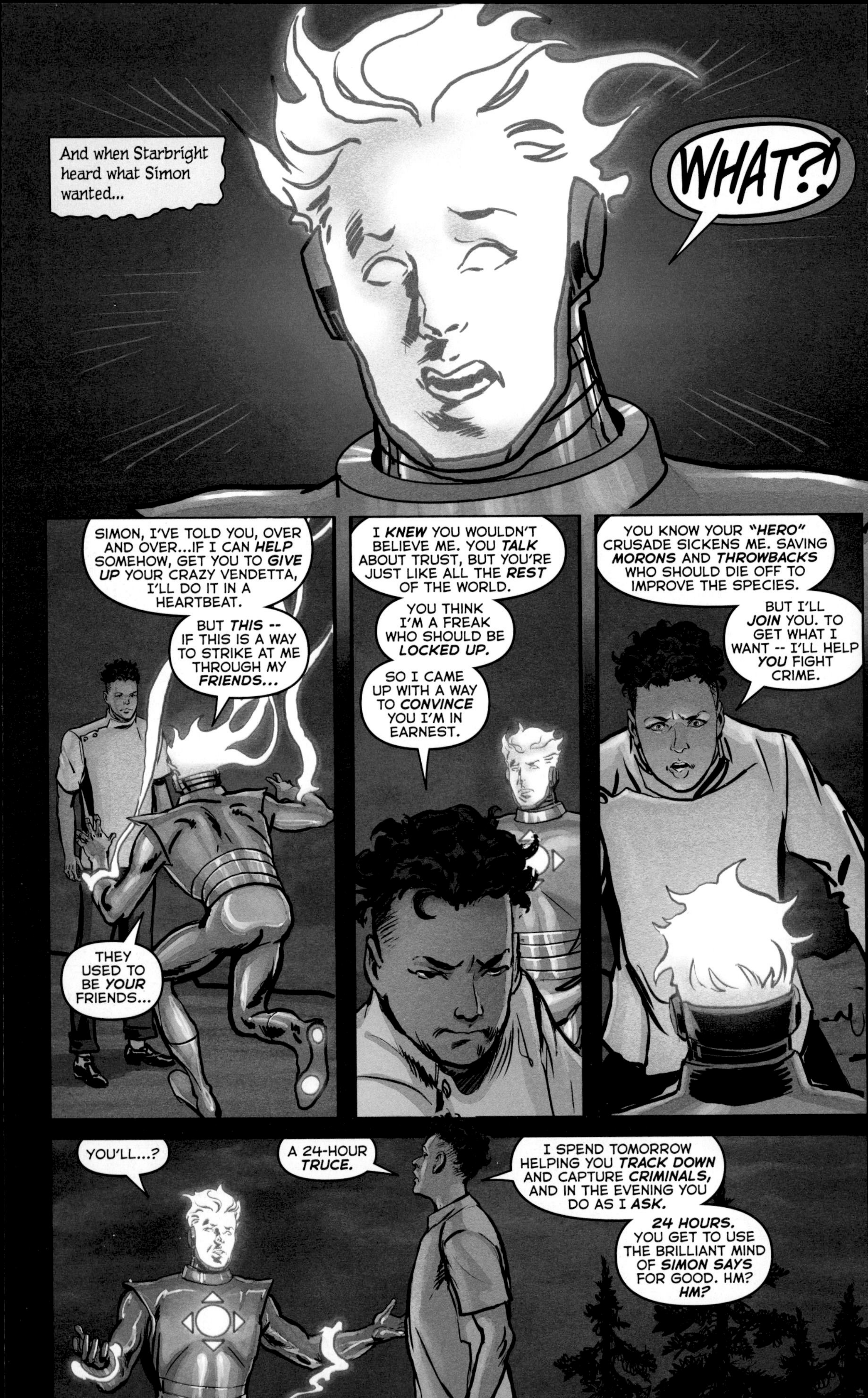
And when Starbright heard what Simon wanted...
WHAT?!
SIMON, I'VE TOLD YOU, OVER AND OVER...IF I CAN HELP SOMEHOW, GET YOU TO GIVE UP YOUR CRAZY VENDETTA, I'LL DO IT IN A HEARTBEAT.
BUT THIS -- IF THIS IS A WAY TO STRIKE AT ME THROUGH MY FRIENDS...
THEY USED TO BE YOUR FRIENDS...
I KNEW YOU WOULDN'T BELIEVE ME. YOU TALK ABOUT TRUST, BUT YOU'RE JUST LIKE ALL THE REST OF THE WORLD.
YOU THINK I'M A FREAK WHO SHOULD BE LOCKED UP.
SO I CAME UP WITH A WAY TO CONVINCE YOU I'M IN EARNEST.
YOU KNOW YOUR "HERO" CRUSADE SICKENS ME. SAVING MORONS AND THROWBACKS WHO SHOULD DIE OFF TO IMPROVE THE SPECIES.
BUT I'LL JOIN YOU. TO GET WHAT I WANT -- I'LL HELP YOU FIGHT CRIME.
YOU'LL...?
A 24-HOUR TRUCE.
I SPEND TOMORROW HELPING YOU TRACK DOWN AND CAPTURE CRIMINALS, AND IN THE EVENING YOU DO AS I ASK.
24 HOURS. YOU GET TO USE THE BRILLIANT MIND OF SIMON SAYS FOR GOOD. HM? HM?

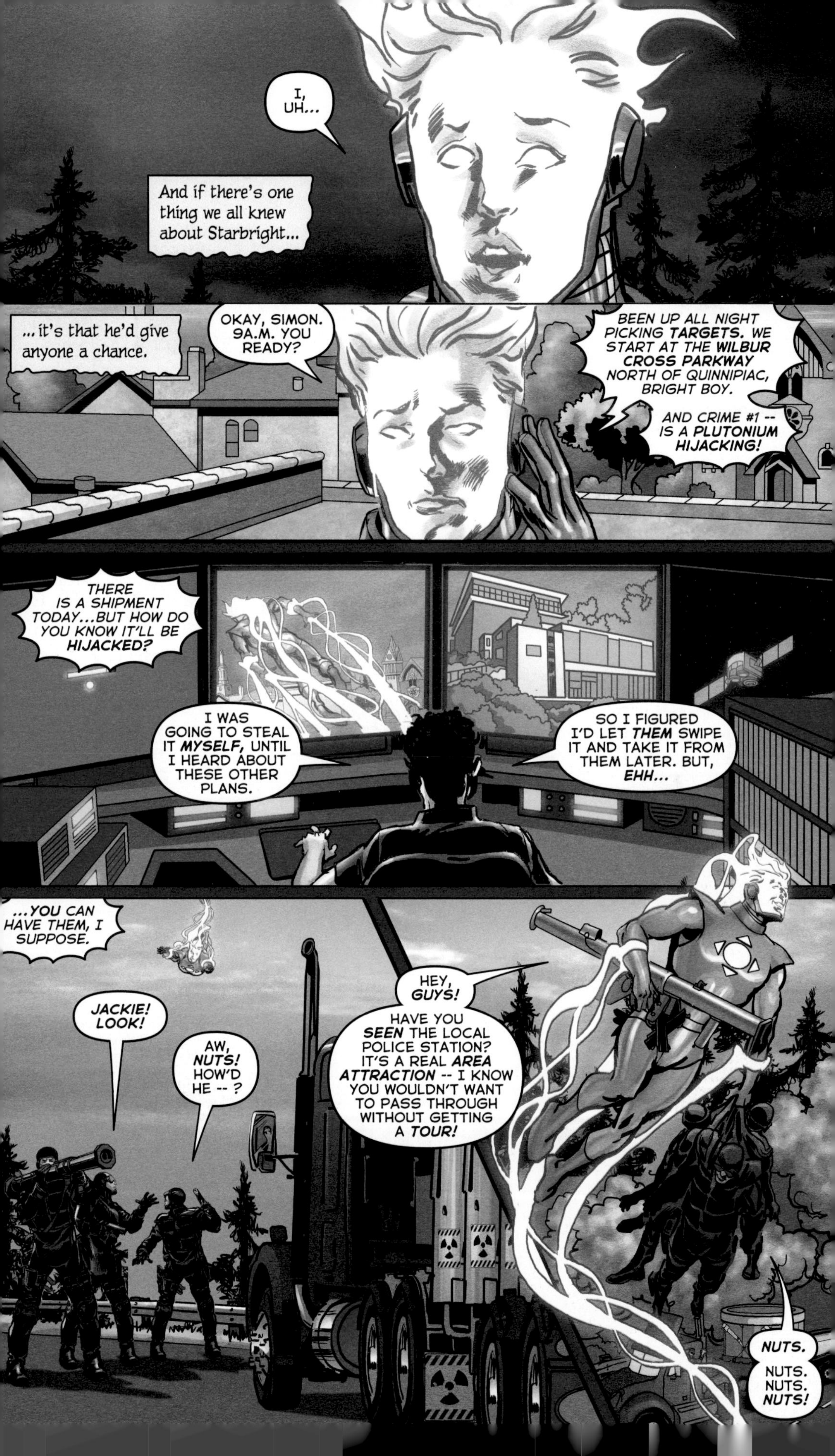

I, UH...
And if there's one thing we all knew about Starbright...
...it's that he'd give anyone a chance.
OKAY, SIMON. 9A.M. YOU READY?
BEEN UP ALL NIGHT PICKING TARGETS. WE START AT THE WILBUR CROSS PARKWAY NORTH OF QUINNIPIAC, BRIGHT BOY.
AND CRIME #1 -- IS A PLUTONIUM HIJACKING!
THERE IS A SHIPMENT TODAY...BUT HOW DO YOU KNOW IT'LL BE HIJACKED?
I WAS GOING TO STEAL IT MYSELF, UNTIL I HEARD ABOUT THESE OTHER PLANS.
SO I FIGURED I'D LET THEM SWIPE IT AND TAKE IT FROM THEM LATER. BUT, EHH...
...YOU CAN HAVE THEM, I SUPPOSE.
JACKIE! LOOK!
AW, NUTS! HOW'D HE -- ?
HEY, GUYS!
HAVE YOU SEEN THE LOCAL POLICE STATION? IT'S A REAL AREA ATTRACTION -- I KNOW YOU WOULDN'T WANT TO PASS THROUGH WITHOUT GETTING A TOUR!
NUTS.
NUTS. NUTS. NUTS!

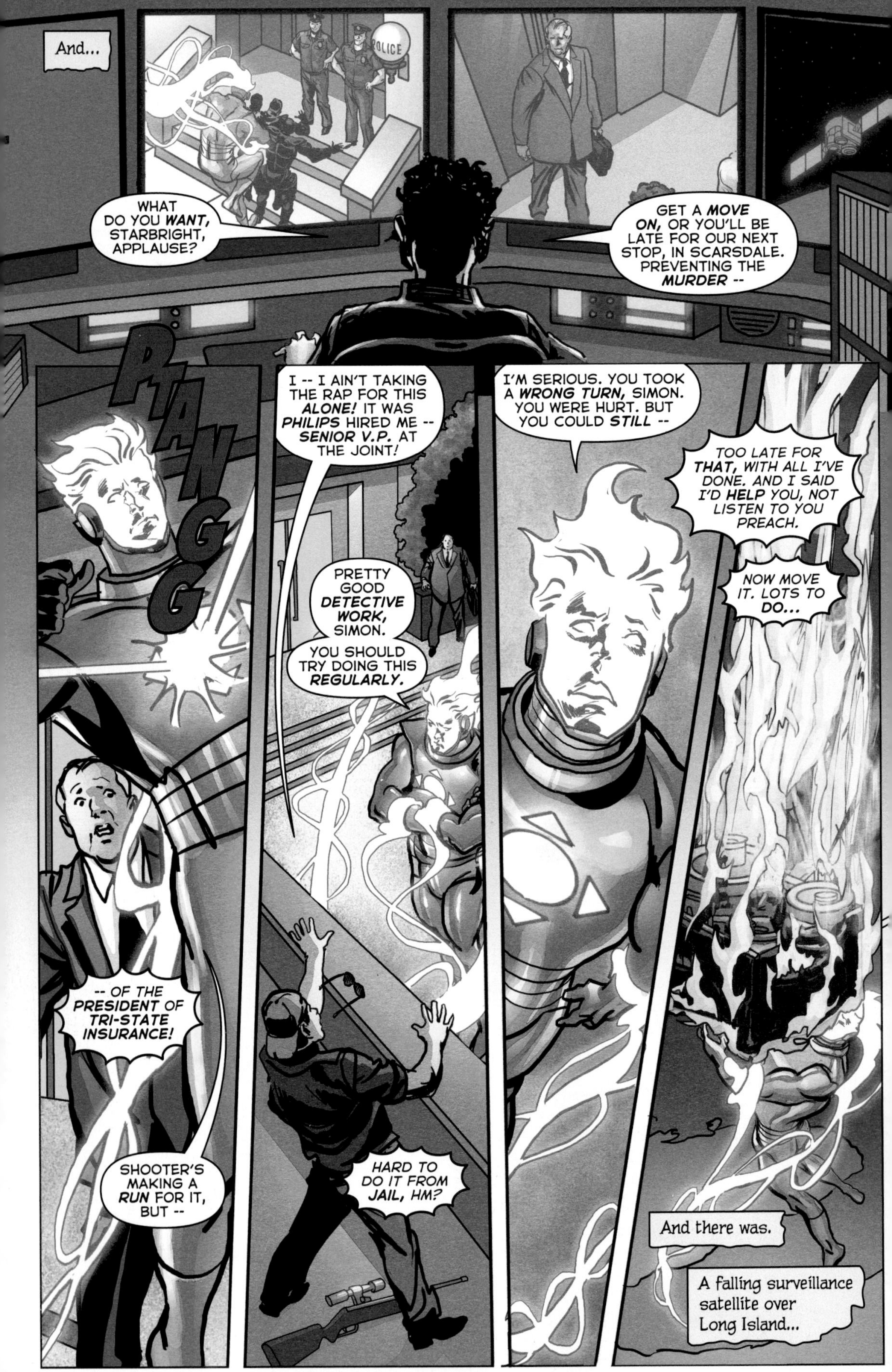

And...
WHAT DO YOU WANT, STARBRIGHT, APPLAUSE?
GET A MOVE ON, OR YOU'LL BE LATE FOR OUR NEXT STOP, IN SCARSDALE. PREVENTING THE MURDER --
PTANGG
-- OF THE PRESIDENT OF TRI-STATE INSURANCE!
SHOOTER'S MAKING A RUN FOR IT, BUT --
I -- I AIN'T TAKING THE RAP FOR THIS ALONE! IT WAS PHILIPS HIRED ME -- SENIOR V.P. AT THE JOINT!
PRETTY GOOD DETECTIVE WORK, SIMON.
YOU SHOULD TRY DOING THIS REGULARLY.
HARD TO DO IT FROM JAIL, HM?
I'M SERIOUS. YOU TOOK A WRONG TURN, SIMON. YOU WERE HURT. BUT YOU COULD STILL --
TOO LATE FOR THAT, WITH ALL I'VE DONE. AND I SAID I'D HELP YOU, NOT LISTEN TO YOU PREACH.
NOW MOVE IT. LOTS TO DO...
And there was.
A falling surveillance satellite over Long Island...

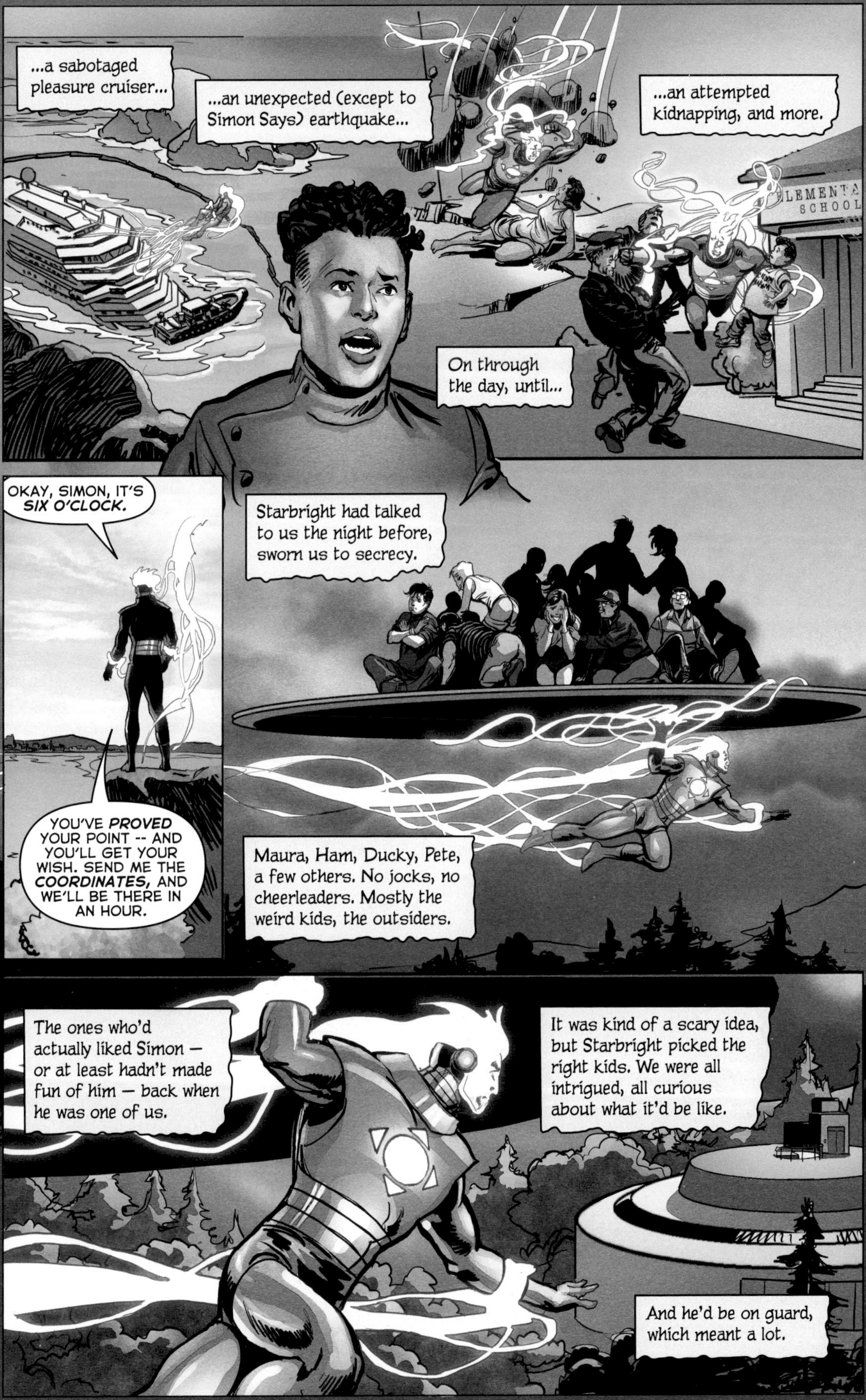
...a sabotaged pleasure cruiser...
...an unexpected (except to Simon Says) earthquake...
...an attempted kidnapping, and more.
ELEMENTA SCHOOL
On through the day, until...
OKAY, SIMON, IT'S *SIX O'CLOCK.*
Starbright had talked to us the night before, sworn us to secrecy.
YOU'VE *PROVED* YOUR POINT -- AND YOU'LL GET YOUR WISH. SEND ME THE *COORDINATES,* AND WE'LL BE THERE IN AN HOUR.
Maura, Ham, Ducky, Pete, a few others. No jocks, no cheerleaders. Mostly the weird kids, the outsiders.
The ones who'd actually liked Simon — or at least hadn't made fun of him — back when he was one of us.
It was kind of a scary idea, but Starbright picked the right kids. We were all intrigued, all curious about what it'd be like.
And he'd be on guard, which meant a lot.

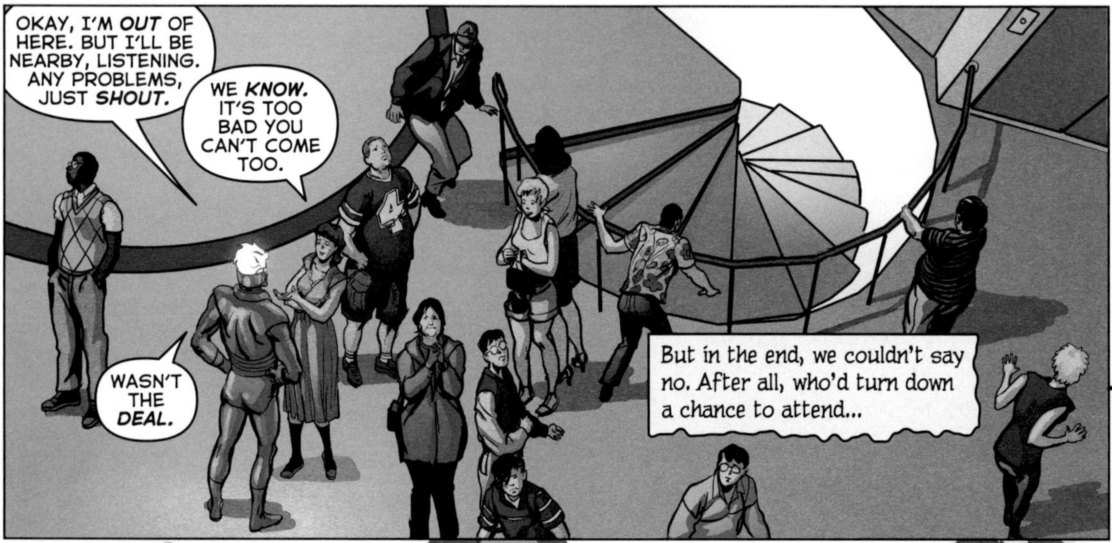
OKAY, I'M *OUT* OF HERE. BUT I'LL BE NEARBY, LISTENING. ANY PROBLEMS, JUST *SHOUT.*
WE *KNOW.* IT'S TOO BAD YOU CAN'T COME TOO.
WASN'T THE *DEAL.*
But in the end, we couldn't say no. After all, who'd turn down a chance to attend...

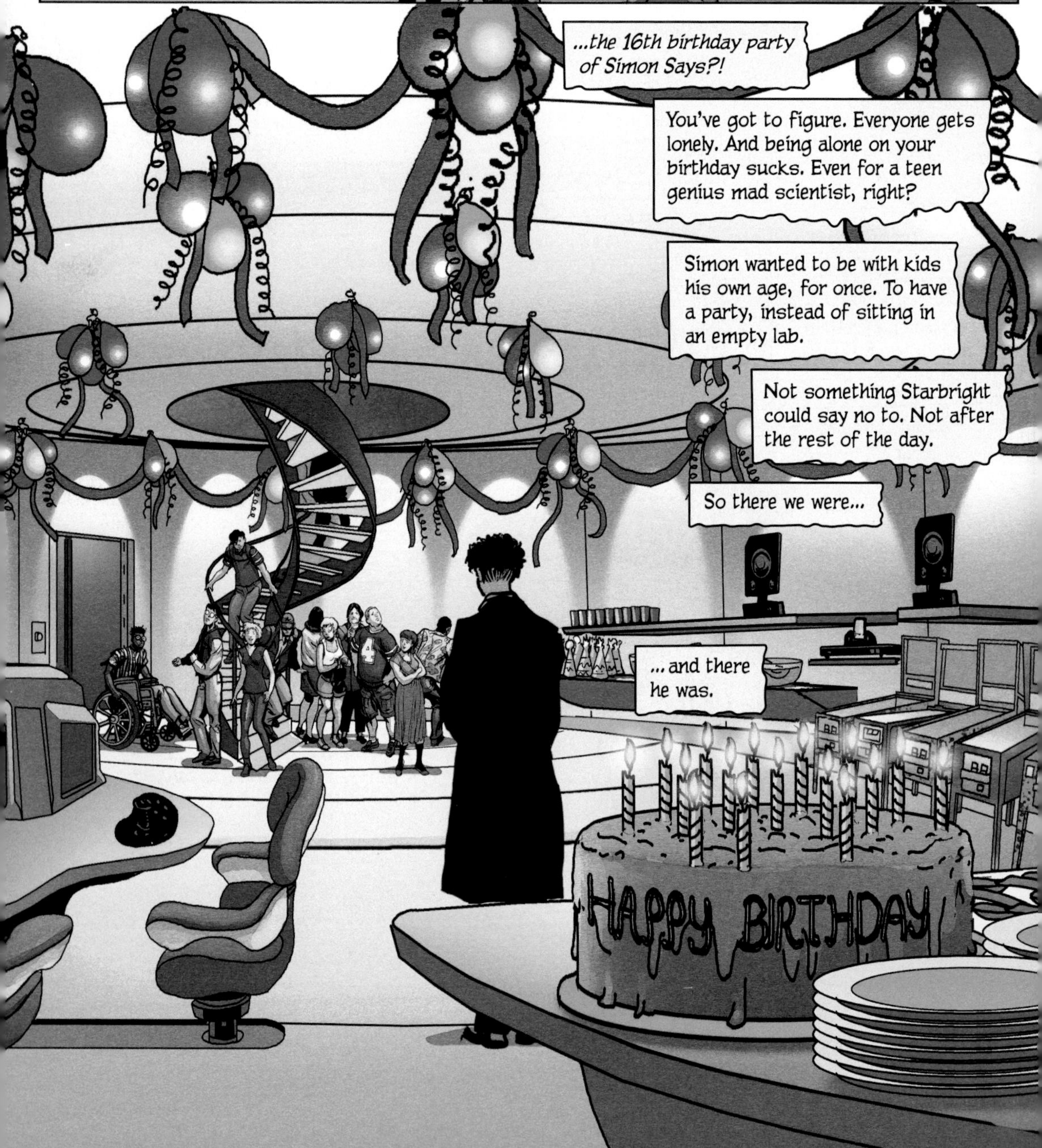
...the 16th birthday party of Simon Says?!
You've got to figure. Everyone gets lonely. And being alone on your birthday sucks. Even for a teen genius mad scientist, right?
Simon wanted to be with kids his own age, for once. To have a party, instead of sitting in an empty lab.
Not something Starbright could say no to. Not after the rest of the day.
So there we were...
...and there he was.
HAPPY BIRTHDAY

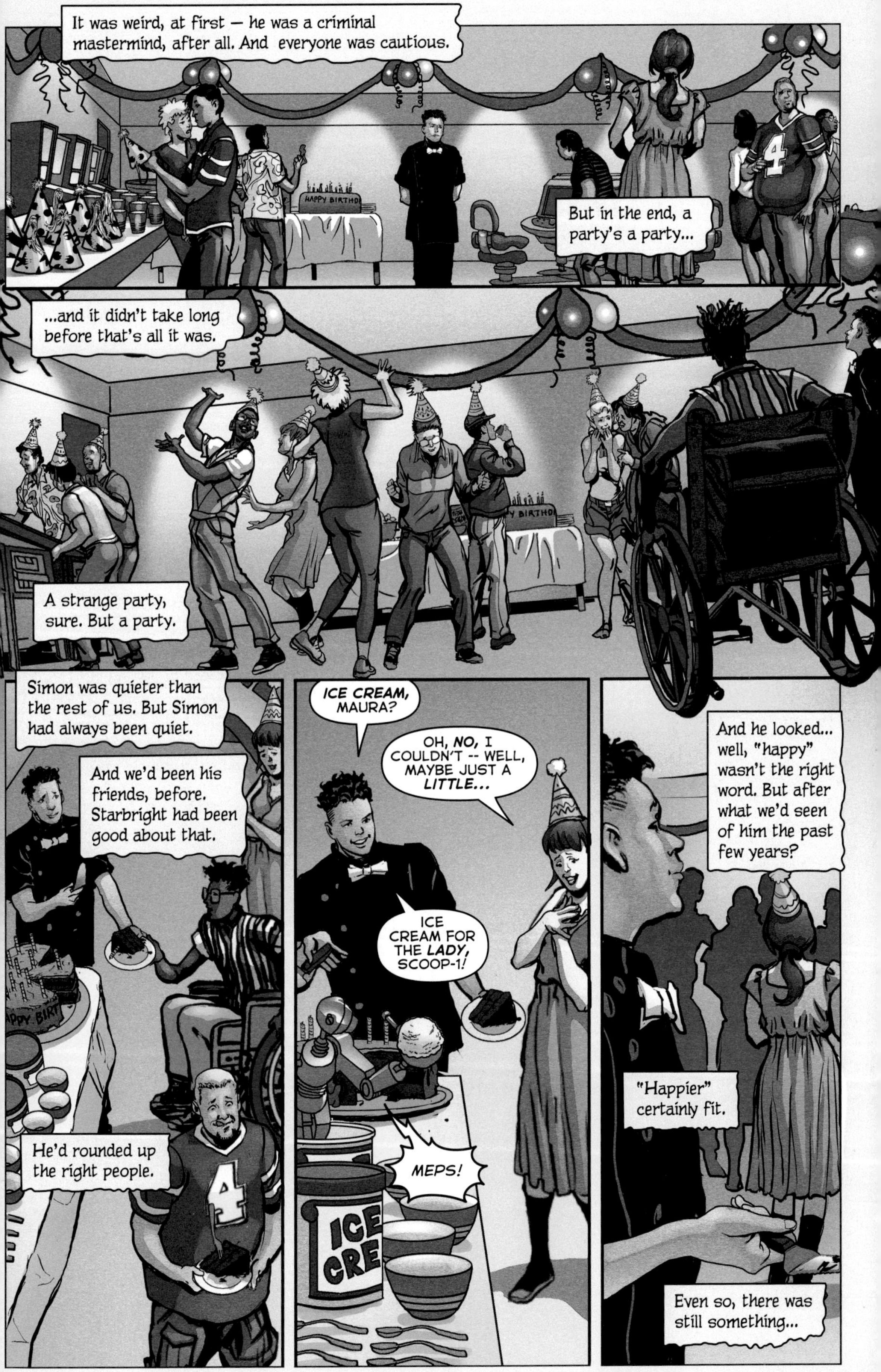
It was weird, at first — he was a criminal mastermind, after all. And everyone was cautious.
HAPPY BIRTHD
But in the end, a party's a party...
...and it didn't take long before that's all it was.
A strange party, sure. But a party.
Simon was quieter than the rest of us. But Simon had always been quiet.
And we'd been his friends, before. Starbright had been good about that.
He'd rounded up the right people.
ICE CREAM, MAURA?
OH, NO, I COULDN'T -- WELL, MAYBE JUST A LITTLE...
ICE CREAM FOR THE LADY, SCOOP-1!
MEPS!
ICE CRE
And he looked... well, "happy" wasn't the right word. But after what we'd seen of him the past few years?
"Happier" certainly fit.
Even so, there was still something...

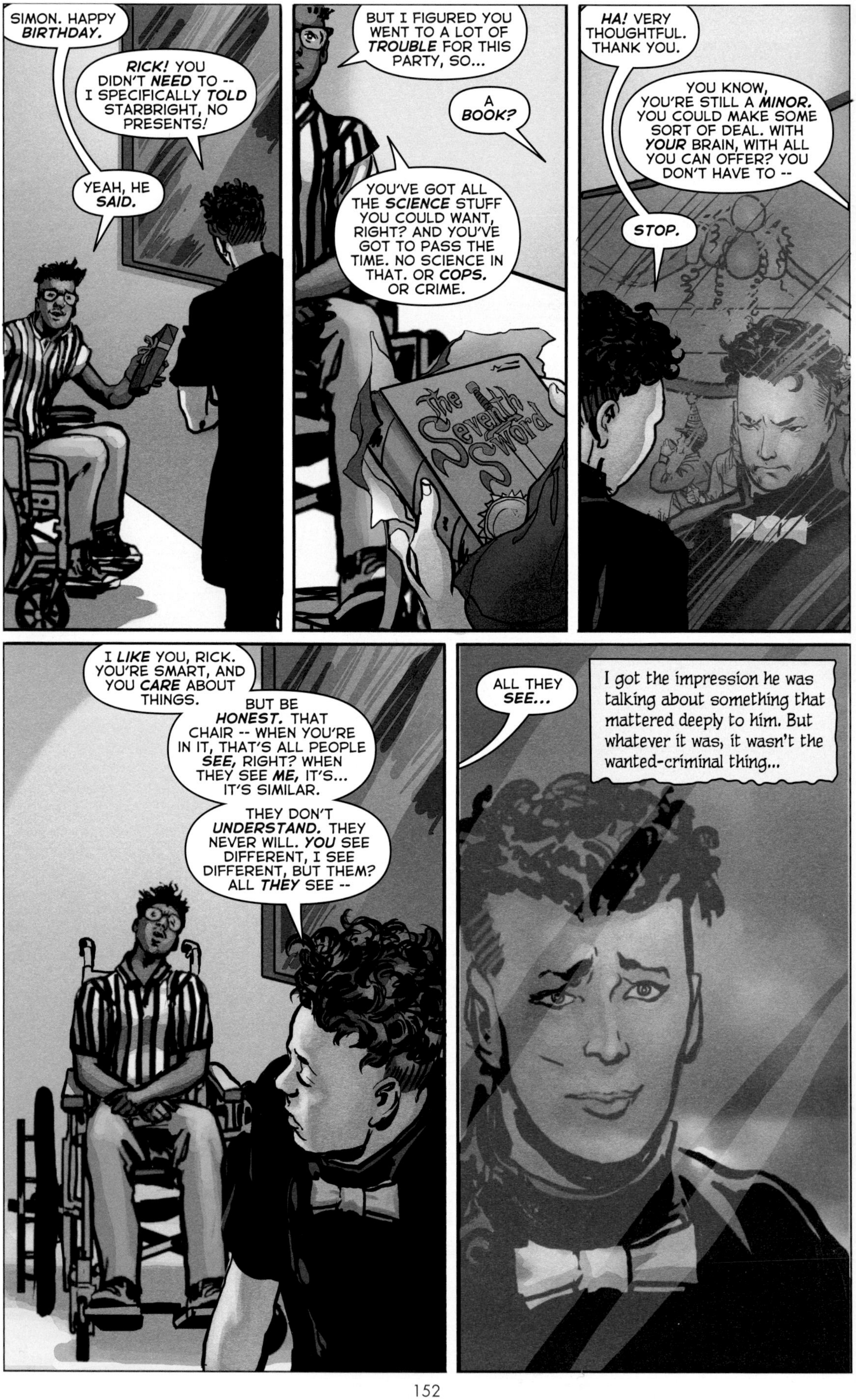
SIMON. HAPPY BIRTHDAY.
RICK! YOU DIDN'T NEED TO -- I SPECIFICALLY TOLD STARBRIGHT, NO PRESENTS!
YEAH, HE SAID.
BUT I FIGURED YOU WENT TO A LOT OF TROUBLE FOR THIS PARTY, SO...
A BOOK?
YOU'VE GOT ALL THE SCIENCE STUFF YOU COULD WANT, RIGHT? AND YOU'VE GOT TO PASS THE TIME. NO SCIENCE IN THAT. OR COPS. OR CRIME.
The Seventh Sword
HA! VERY THOUGHTFUL. THANK YOU.
YOU KNOW, YOU'RE STILL A MINOR. YOU COULD MAKE SOME SORT OF DEAL. WITH YOUR BRAIN, WITH ALL YOU CAN OFFER? YOU DON'T HAVE TO --
STOP.
I LIKE YOU, RICK. YOU'RE SMART, AND YOU CARE ABOUT THINGS.
BUT BE HONEST. THAT CHAIR -- WHEN YOU'RE IN IT, THAT'S ALL PEOPLE SEE, RIGHT? WHEN THEY SEE ME, IT'S... IT'S SIMILAR.
THEY DON'T UNDERSTAND. THEY NEVER WILL. YOU SEE DIFFERENT, I SEE DIFFERENT, BUT THEM? ALL THEY SEE --
ALL THEY SEE...
I got the impression he was talking about something that mattered deeply to him. But whatever it was, it wasn't the wanted-criminal thing...

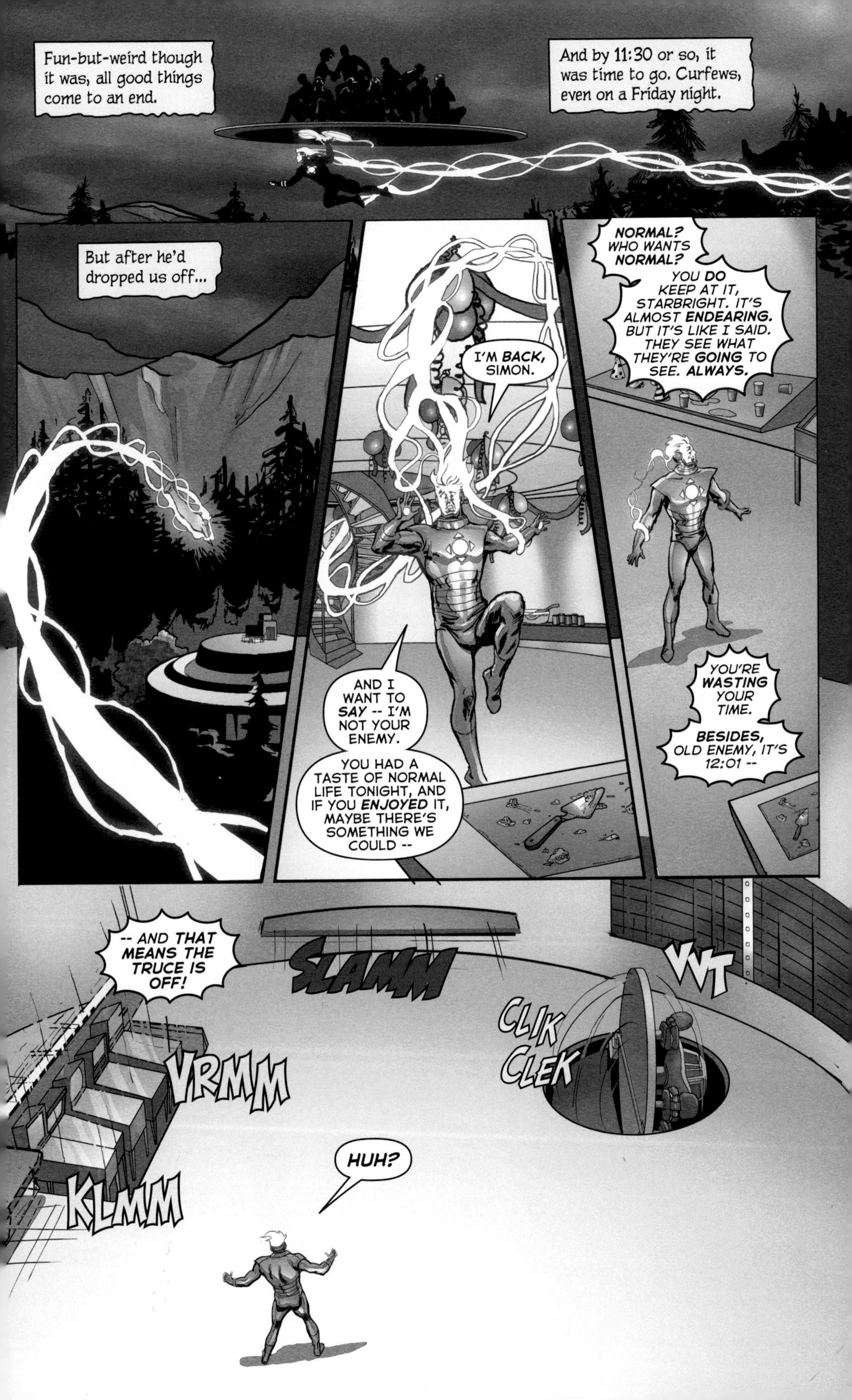
Fun-but-weird though it was, all good things come to an end.
And by 11:30 or so, it was time to go. Curfews, even on a Friday night.
But after he'd dropped us off...
I'M BACK, SIMON.
AND I WANT TO SAY -- I'M NOT YOUR ENEMY.
YOU HAD A TASTE OF NORMAL LIFE TONIGHT, AND IF YOU ENJOYED IT, MAYBE THERE'S SOMETHING WE COULD --
NORMAL? WHO WANTS NORMAL?
YOU DO KEEP AT IT, STARBRIGHT. IT'S ALMOST ENDEARING. BUT IT'S LIKE I SAID. THEY SEE WHAT THEY'RE GOING TO SEE. ALWAYS.
YOU'RE WASTING YOUR TIME.
BESIDES, OLD ENEMY, IT'S 12:01 --
-- AND THAT MEANS THE TRUCE IS OFF!
SLAMM
VVT
CLIK CLEK
VRMM
KLMM
HUH?

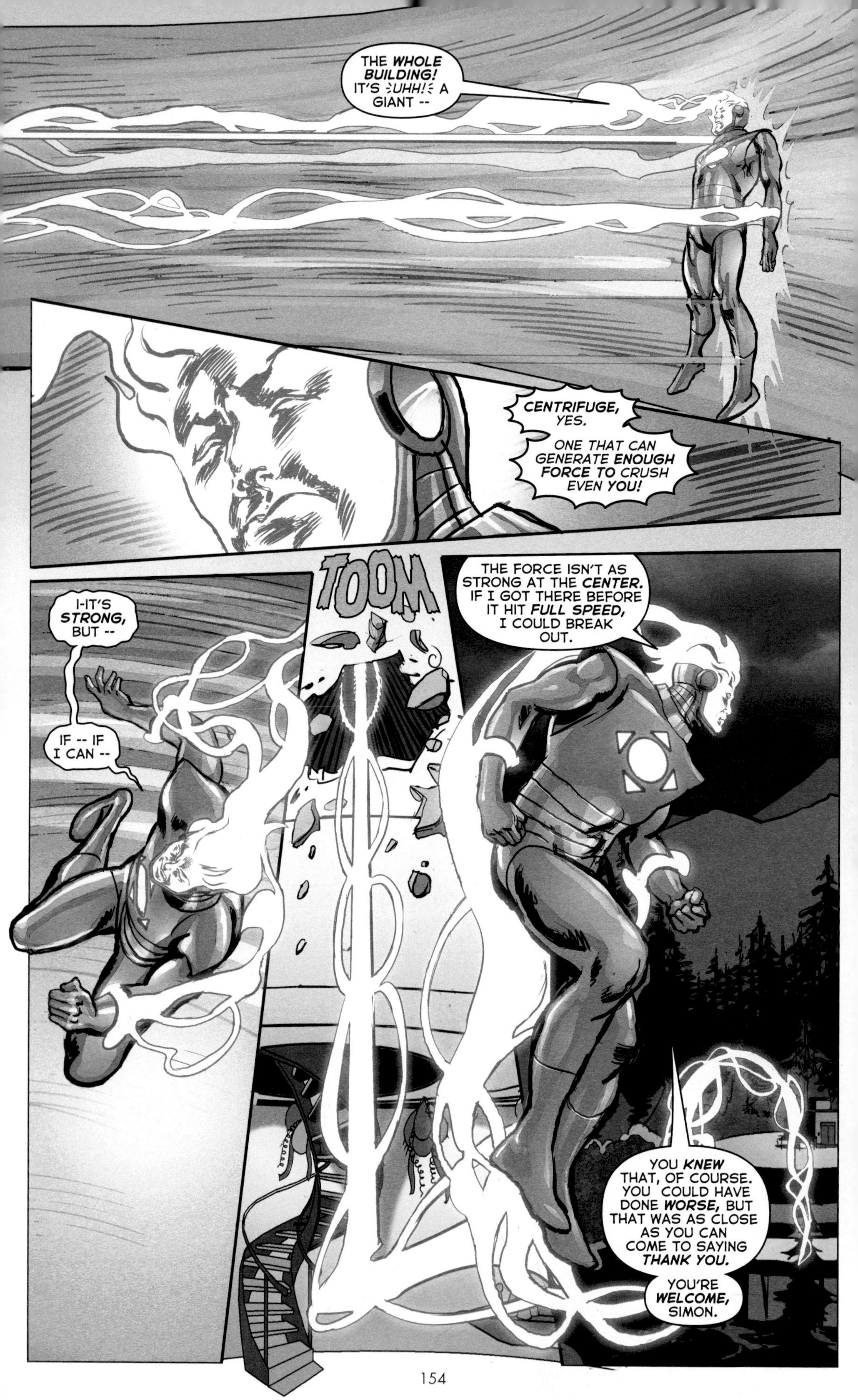
THE WHOLE BUILDING! IT'S UHH! A GIANT --
CENTRIFUGE, YES.
ONE THAT CAN GENERATE ENOUGH FORCE TO CRUSH EVEN YOU!
I-IT'S STRONG, BUT --
IF -- IF I CAN --
TOOM
THE FORCE ISN'T AS STRONG AT THE CENTER. IF I GOT THERE BEFORE IT HIT FULL SPEED, I COULD BREAK OUT.
YOU KNEW THAT, OF COURSE. YOU COULD HAVE DONE WORSE, BUT THAT WAS AS CLOSE AS YOU CAN COME TO SAYING THANK YOU.
YOU'RE WELCOME, SIMON.

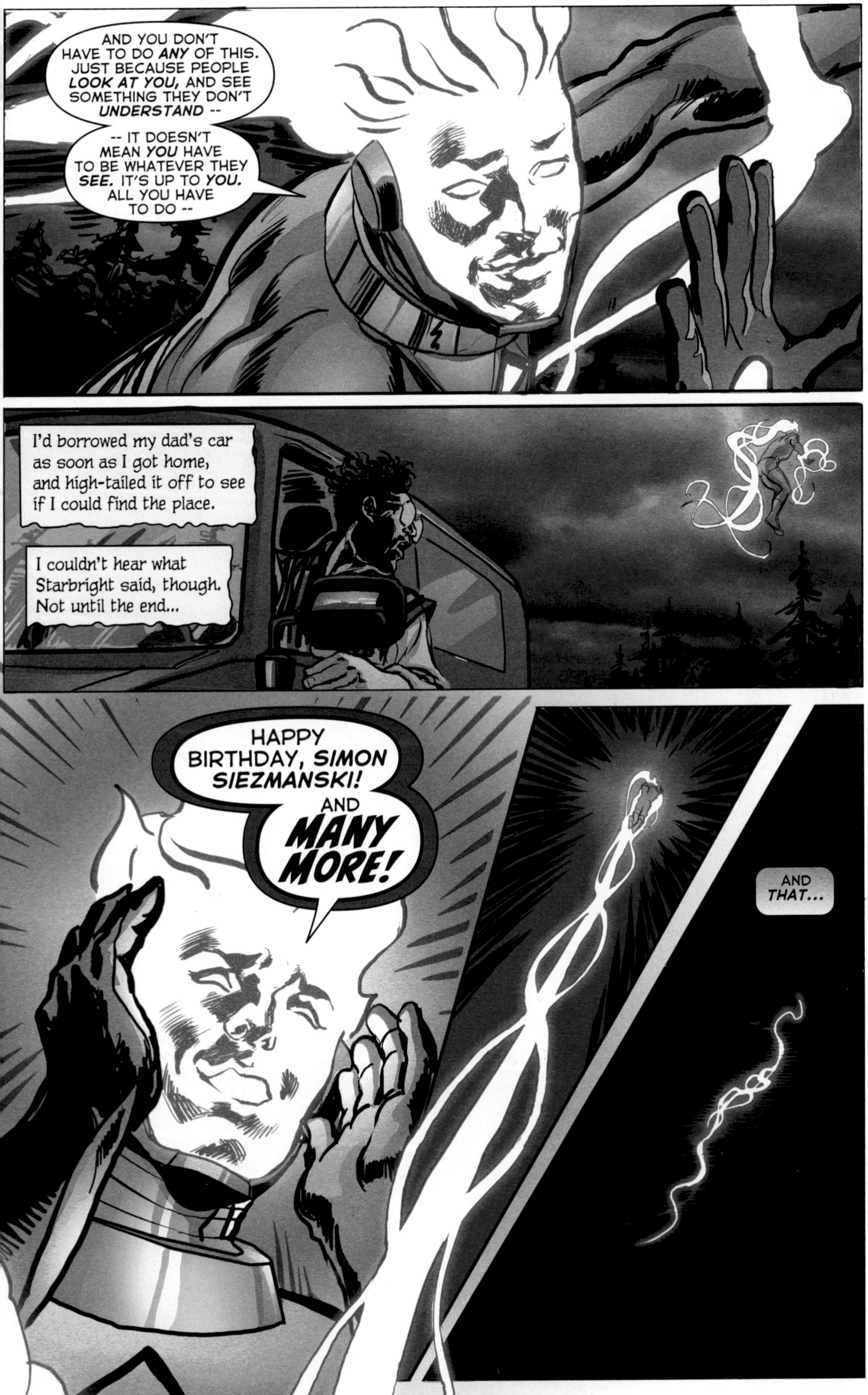
AND YOU DON'T HAVE TO DO ANY OF THIS. JUST BECAUSE PEOPLE LOOK AT YOU, AND SEE SOMETHING THEY DON'T UNDERSTAND --
-- IT DOESN'T MEAN YOU HAVE TO BE WHATEVER THEY SEE. IT'S UP TO YOU. ALL YOU HAVE TO DO --
I'd borrowed my dad's car as soon as I got home, and high-tailed it off to see if I could find the place.
I couldn't hear what Starbright said, though. Not until the end...
HAPPY BIRTHDAY, SIMON SIEZMANSKI!
AND MANY MORE!
AND THAT...

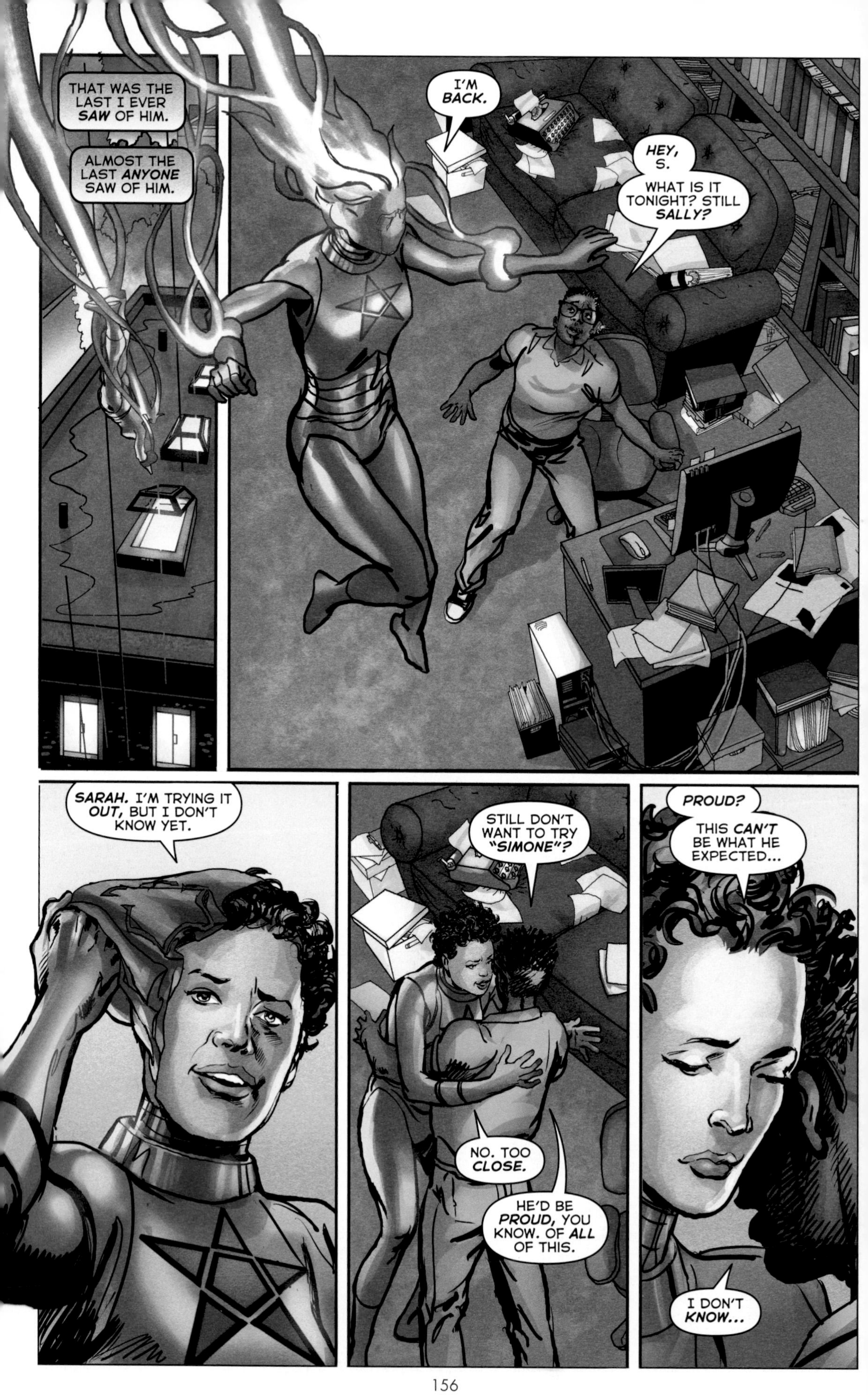
THAT WAS THE LAST I EVER SAW OF HIM.
ALMOST THE LAST ANYONE SAW OF HIM.
I'M BACK.
HEY, S.
WHAT IS IT TONIGHT? STILL SALLY?
SARAH. I'M TRYING IT OUT, BUT I DON'T KNOW YET.
STILL DON'T WANT TO TRY "SIMONE"?
NO. TOO CLOSE.
HE'D BE PROUD, YOU KNOW. OF ALL OF THIS.
PROUD?
THIS CAN'T BE WHAT HE EXPECTED...
I DON'T KNOW...

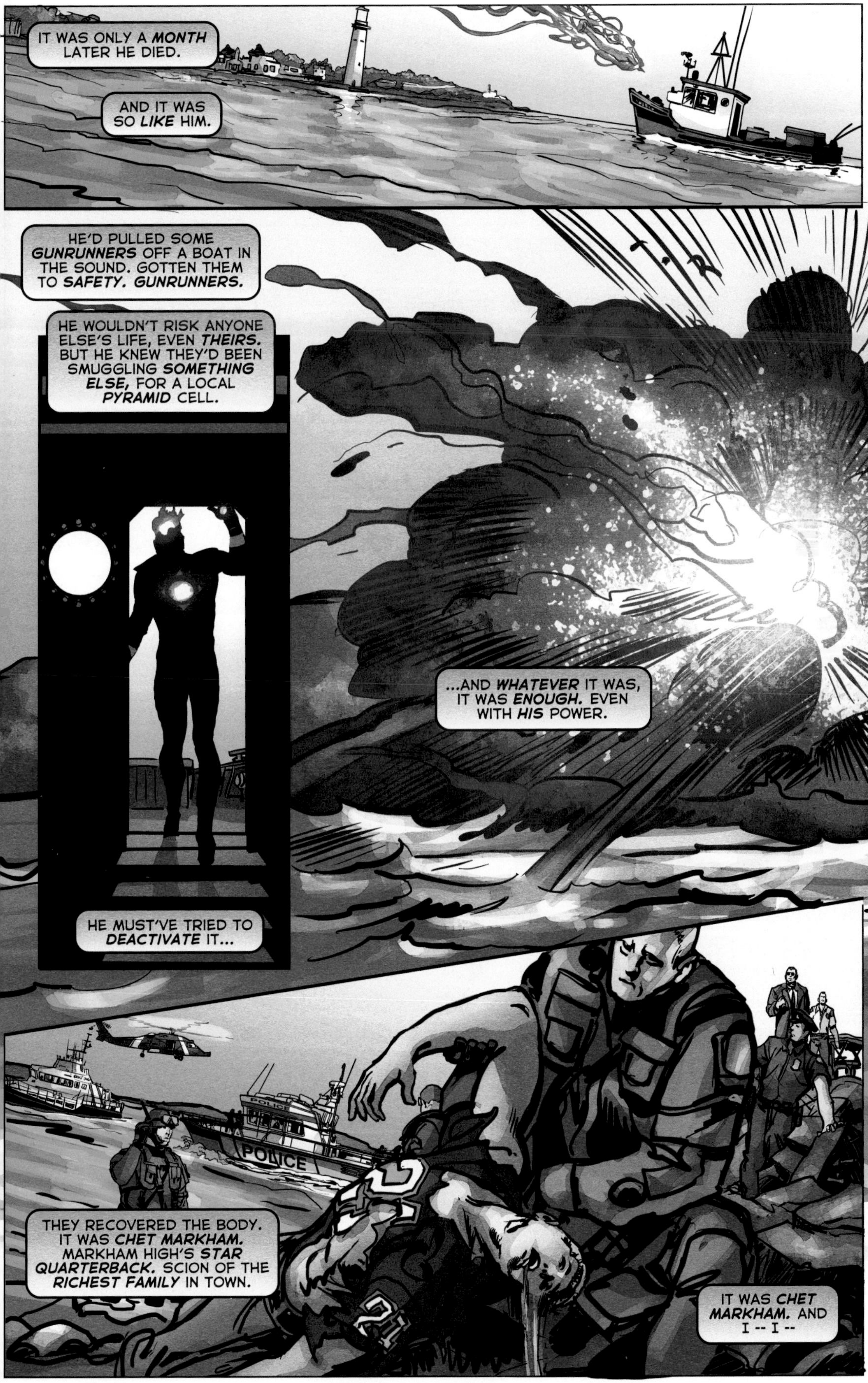
IT WAS ONLY A MONTH LATER HE DIED.
AND IT WAS SO LIKE HIM.
HE'D PULLED SOME GUNRUNNERS OFF A BOAT IN THE SOUND. GOTTEN THEM TO SAFETY. GUNRUNNERS.
HE WOULDN'T RISK ANYONE ELSE'S LIFE, EVEN THEIRS. BUT HE KNEW THEY'D BEEN SMUGGLING SOMETHING ELSE, FOR A LOCAL PYRAMID CELL.
HE MUST'VE TRIED TO DEACTIVATE IT...
...AND WHATEVER IT WAS, IT WAS ENOUGH. EVEN WITH HIS POWER.
POLICE
THEY RECOVERED THE BODY. IT WAS CHET MARKHAM. MARKHAM HIGH'S STAR QUARTERBACK. SCION OF THE RICHEST FAMILY IN TOWN.
IT WAS CHET MARKHAM. AND I -- I --

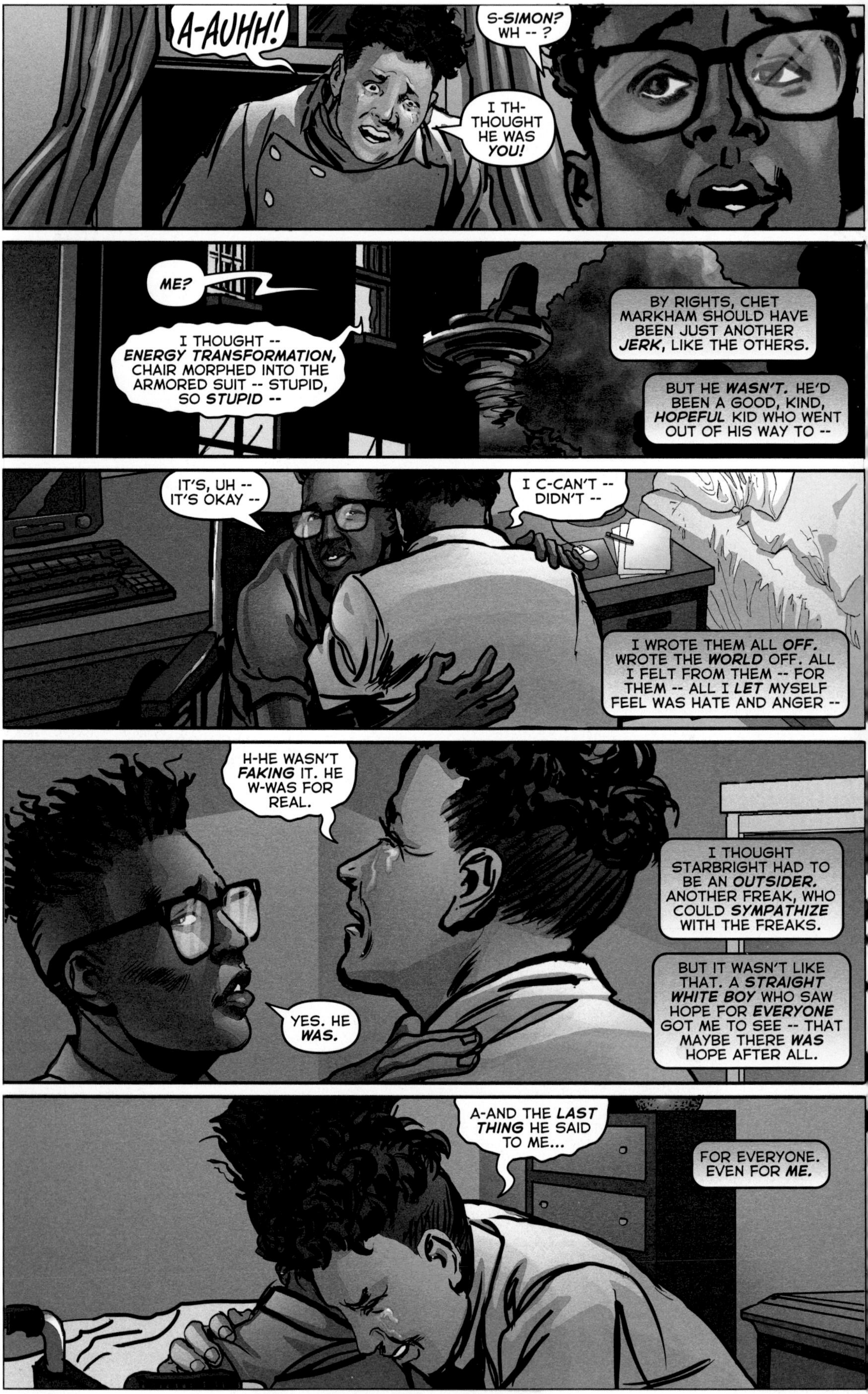
A-AUHH!
S-SIMON? WH -- ?
I TH- THOUGHT HE WAS YOU!
ME?
I THOUGHT -- ENERGY TRANSFORMATION, CHAIR MORPHED INTO THE ARMORED SUIT -- STUPID, SO STUPID --
BY RIGHTS, CHET MARKHAM SHOULD HAVE BEEN JUST ANOTHER JERK, LIKE THE OTHERS.
BUT HE WASN'T. HE'D BEEN A GOOD, KIND, HOPEFUL KID WHO WENT OUT OF HIS WAY TO --
IT'S, UH -- IT'S OKAY --
I C-CAN'T -- DIDN'T --
I WROTE THEM ALL OFF. WROTE THE WORLD OFF. ALL I FELT FROM THEM -- FOR THEM -- ALL I LET MYSELF FEEL WAS HATE AND ANGER --
H-HE WASN'T FAKING IT. HE W-WAS FOR REAL.
YES. HE WAS.
I THOUGHT STARBRIGHT HAD TO BE AN OUTSIDER. ANOTHER FREAK, WHO COULD SYMPATHIZE WITH THE FREAKS.
BUT IT WASN'T LIKE THAT. A STRAIGHT WHITE BOY WHO SAW HOPE FOR EVERYONE GOT ME TO SEE -- THAT MAYBE THERE WAS HOPE AFTER ALL.
A-AND THE LAST THING HE SAID TO ME...
FOR EVERYONE. EVEN FOR ME.

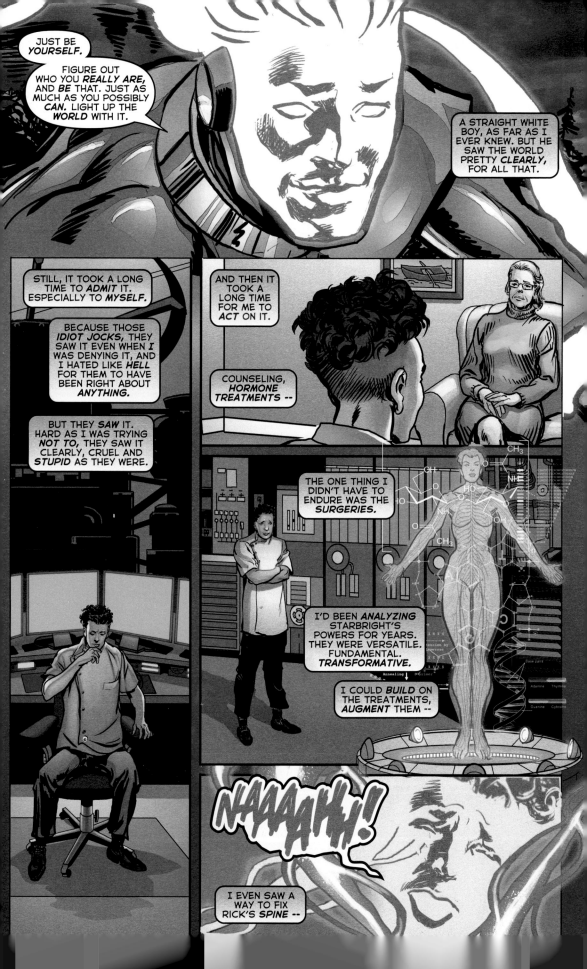

JUST BE *YOURSELF.*

FIGURE OUT WHO YOU *REALLY ARE,* AND *BE* THAT. JUST AS MUCH AS YOU POSSIBLY *CAN.* LIGHT UP THE *WORLD* WITH IT.

A STRAIGHT WHITE BOY, AS FAR AS I EVER KNEW. BUT HE SAW THE WORLD PRETTY *CLEARLY,* FOR ALL THAT.

STILL, IT TOOK A LONG TIME TO *ADMIT* IT. ESPECIALLY TO *MYSELF.*

BECAUSE THOSE *IDIOT JOCKS,* THEY SAW IT EVEN WHEN *I* WAS DENYING IT, AND I HATED LIKE *HELL* FOR THEM TO HAVE BEEN RIGHT ABOUT *ANYTHING.*

BUT THEY *SAW* IT. HARD AS I WAS TRYING *NOT TO,* THEY SAW IT CLEARLY, CRUEL AND *STUPID* AS THEY WERE.

AND THEN IT TOOK A LONG TIME FOR ME TO *ACT* ON IT.

COUNSELING, *HORMONE TREATMENTS* --

THE ONE THING I DIDN'T HAVE TO ENDURE WAS THE *SURGERIES.*

I'D BEEN *ANALYZING* STARBRIGHT'S POWERS FOR YEARS. THEY WERE VERSATILE. FUNDAMENTAL. *TRANSFORMATIVE.*

I COULD *BUILD* ON THE TREATMENTS, *AUGMENT* THEM --

NAAAAHH!

I EVEN SAW A WAY TO FIX RICK'S *SPINE* --

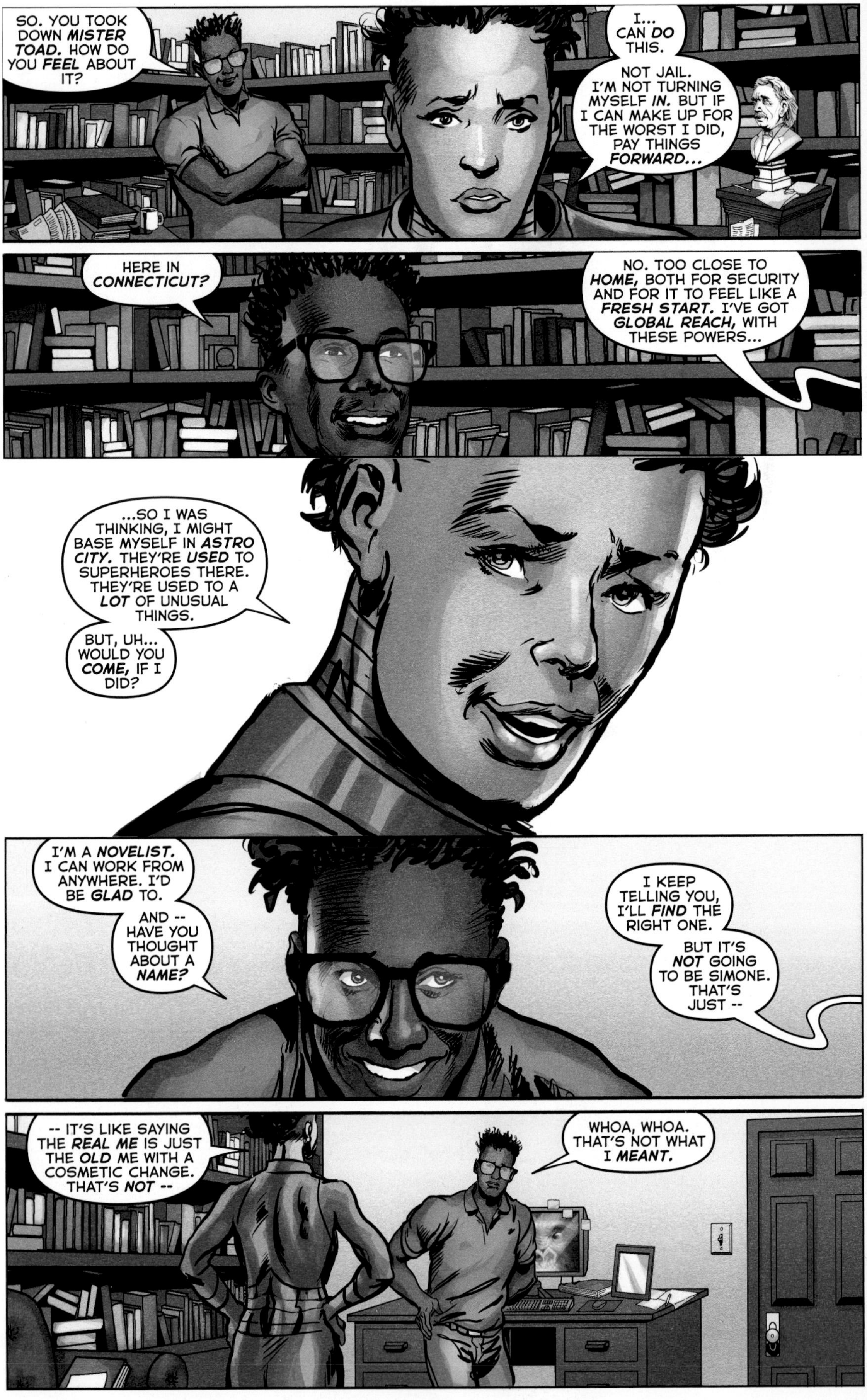
SO. YOU TOOK DOWN MISTER TOAD. HOW DO YOU FEEL ABOUT IT?
I... CAN DO THIS.
NOT JAIL. I'M NOT TURNING MYSELF IN. BUT IF I CAN MAKE UP FOR THE WORST I DID, PAY THINGS FORWARD...
HERE IN CONNECTICUT?
NO. TOO CLOSE TO HOME, BOTH FOR SECURITY AND FOR IT TO FEEL LIKE A FRESH START. I'VE GOT GLOBAL REACH, WITH THESE POWERS...
...SO I WAS THINKING, I MIGHT BASE MYSELF IN ASTRO CITY. THEY'RE USED TO SUPERHEROES THERE. THEY'RE USED TO A LOT OF UNUSUAL THINGS.
BUT, UH... WOULD YOU COME, IF I DID?
I'M A NOVELIST. I CAN WORK FROM ANYWHERE. I'D BE GLAD TO.
AND -- HAVE YOU THOUGHT ABOUT A NAME?
I KEEP TELLING YOU, I'LL FIND THE RIGHT ONE.
BUT IT'S NOT GOING TO BE SIMONE. THAT'S JUST --
-- IT'S LIKE SAYING THE REAL ME IS JUST THE OLD ME WITH A COSMETIC CHANGE. THAT'S NOT --
WHOA, WHOA. THAT'S NOT WHAT I MEANT.

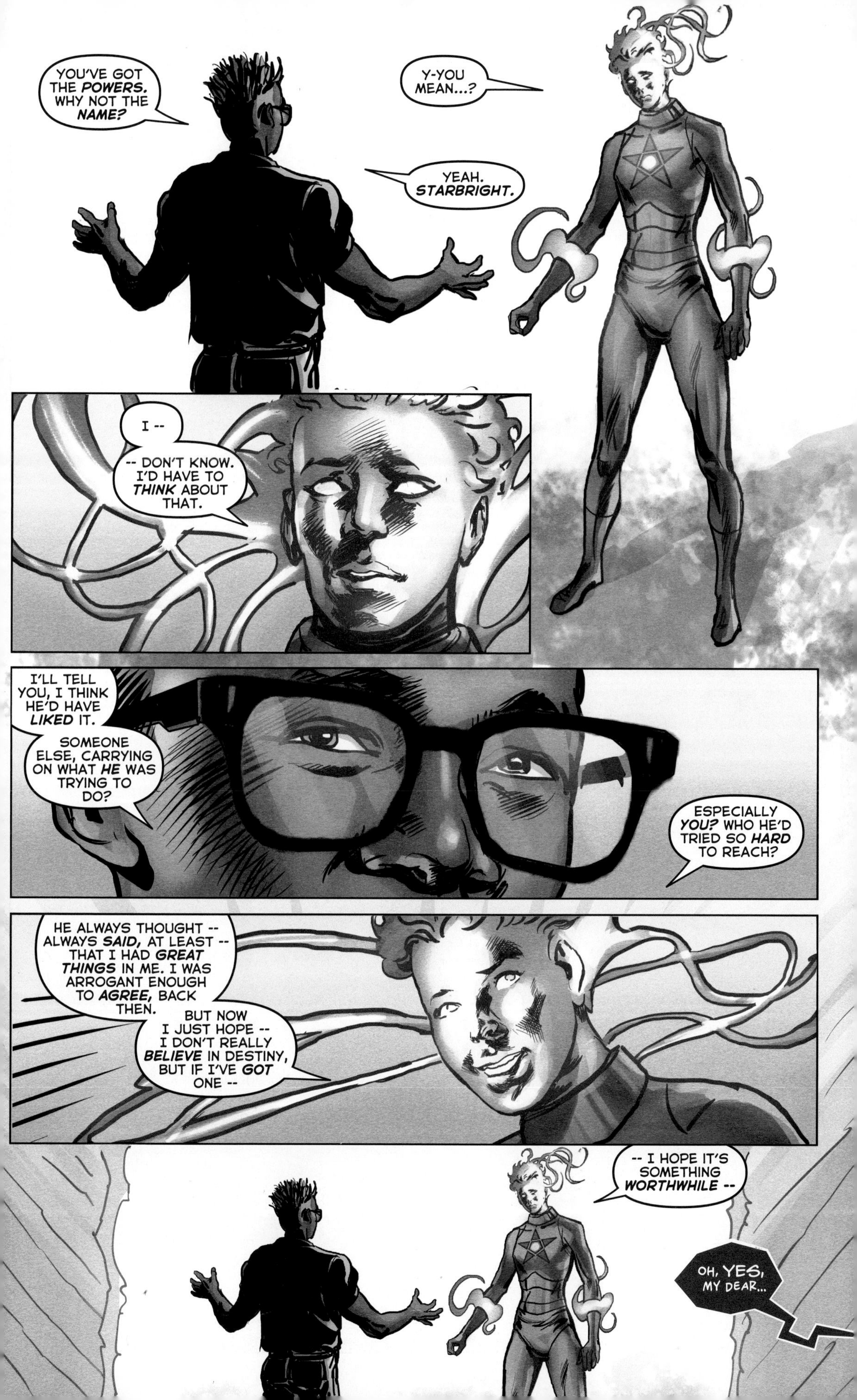
YOU'VE GOT THE POWERS. WHY NOT THE NAME?
Y-YOU MEAN...?
YEAH. STARBRIGHT.
I --
-- DON'T KNOW. I'D HAVE TO THINK ABOUT THAT.
I'LL TELL YOU, I THINK HE'D HAVE LIKED IT.
SOMEONE ELSE, CARRYING ON WHAT HE WAS TRYING TO DO?
ESPECIALLY YOU? WHO HE'D TRIED SO HARD TO REACH?
HE ALWAYS THOUGHT -- ALWAYS SAID, AT LEAST -- THAT I HAD GREAT THINGS IN ME. I WAS ARROGANT ENOUGH TO AGREE, BACK THEN.
BUT NOW I JUST HOPE -- I DON'T REALLY BELIEVE IN DESTINY, BUT IF I'VE GOT ONE --
-- I HOPE IT'S SOMETHING WORTHWHILE --
OH, YES, MY DEAR...

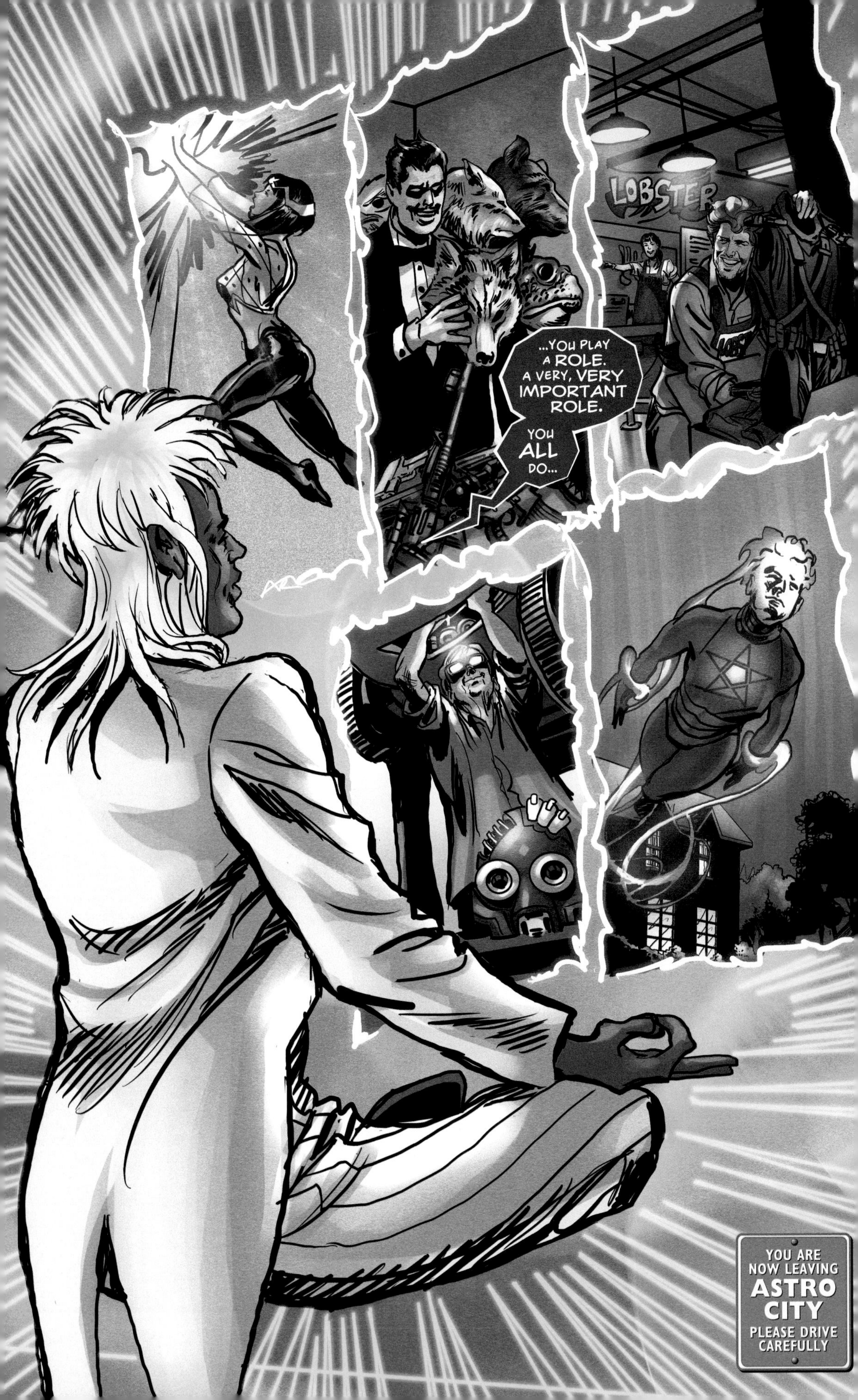
LOBSTER
...YOU PLAY A ROLE. A VERY, VERY IMPORTANT ROLE.
YOU ALL DO...
YOU ARE NOW LEAVING ASTRO CITY PLEASE DRIVE CAREFULLY

18 — returns
  — face
  — smile. Sally? Sarah.
      Not Simon...?
      No. Too close. Makes me feel fake.
          be proud

19 — two months
    saving dr.
    boom ---
    from water.

  — weeping. w
    thought he w
  me?
  he was golde
      He was
  he meant

            be
        time t
      uset ing.
      normore tr
    no surgery
      ever fixed

  how do you feel?
      I can do this. Turn self in, no. But make up -- pay forward --
  where? Connecticut?
  Astro City.

      I ---?
      don't know. Think o
  He'd be
 some
 rying. i ou --
  He always thought.
      I hope -- don't believe i- destiny
  destiny -- exists, something worth
          Oh, yes ...

4 Broken Man ... you ll play a role. Very important role.

— approach
— in ves. S. To
— face - sai
— Sally? Sarah
— Not what he exp
  I dunno

RAMID cell

Chet Markham. Overpowers
Family in town. By righ

      was one of them.
      But he never -- he

Thought
 was against me
              Only
  But --'if
  like him coi

 his powers -- transfor

silver adept

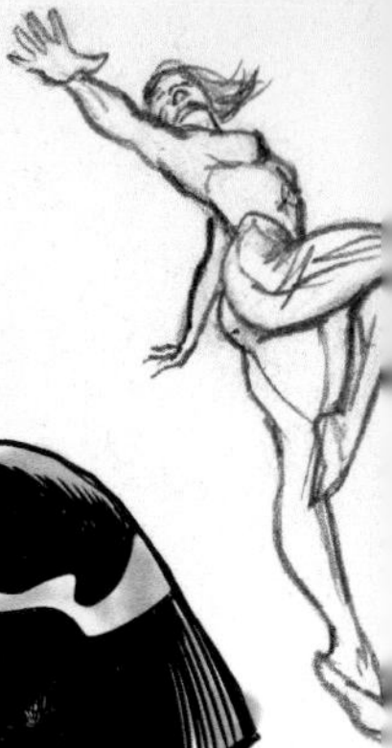

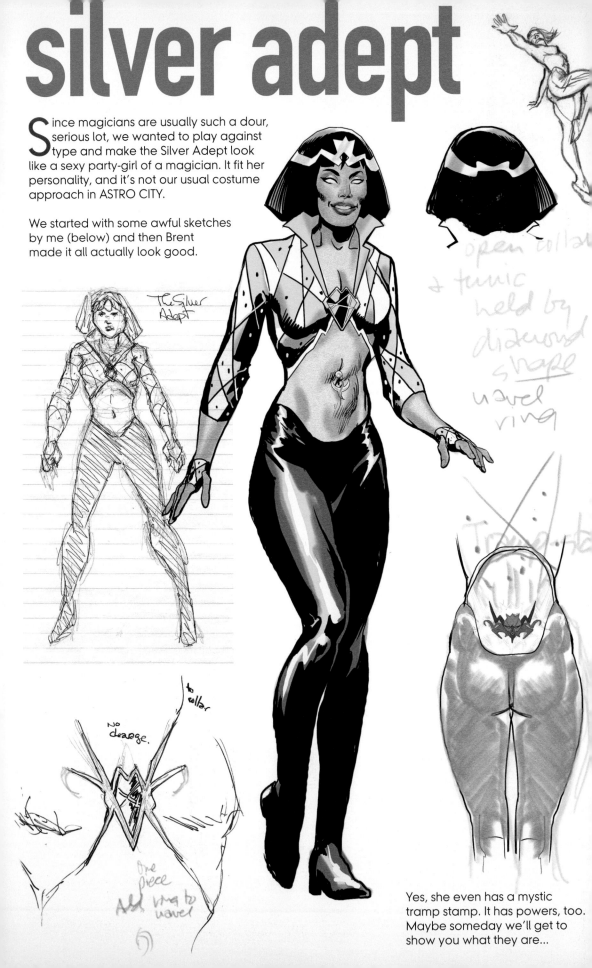

Since magicians are usually such a dour, serious lot, we wanted to play against type and make the Silver Adept look like a sexy party-girl of a magician. It fit her personality, and it's not our usual costume approach in ASTRO CITY.

We started with some awful sketches by me (below) and then Brent made it all actually look good.

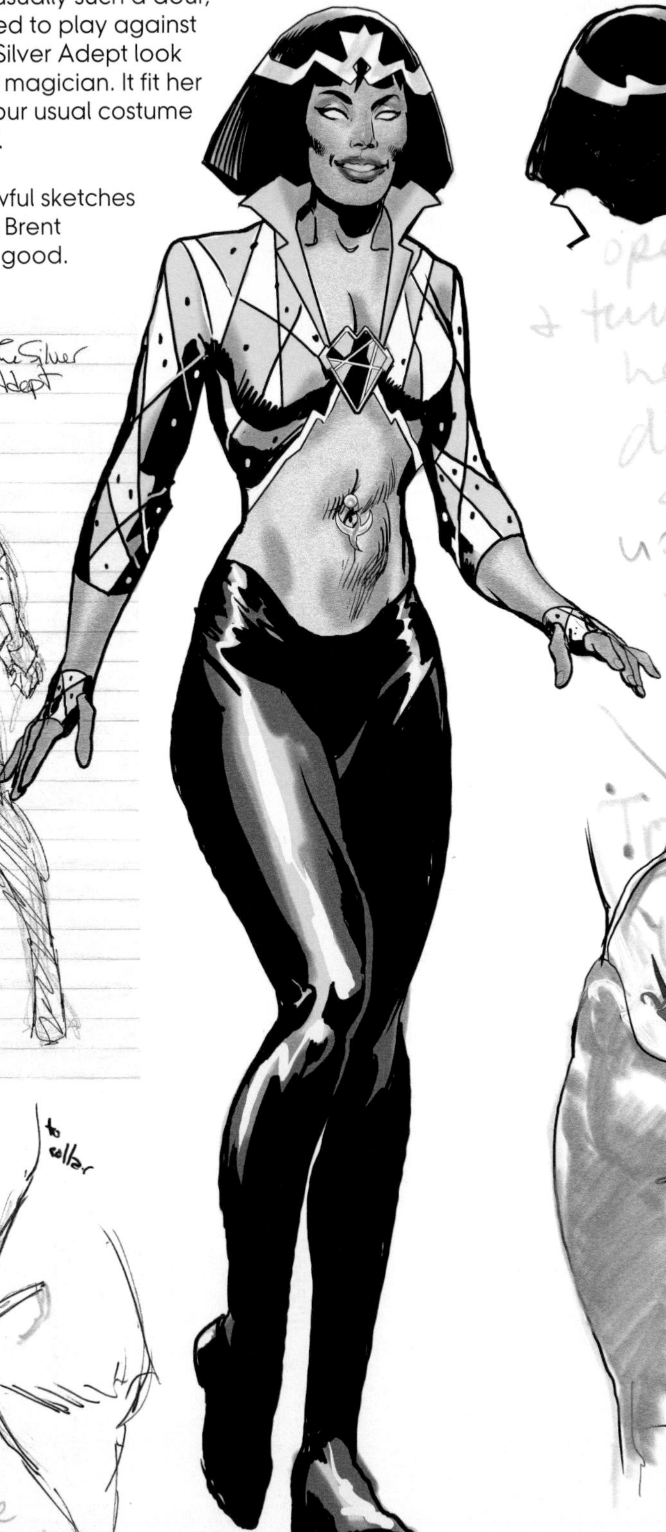

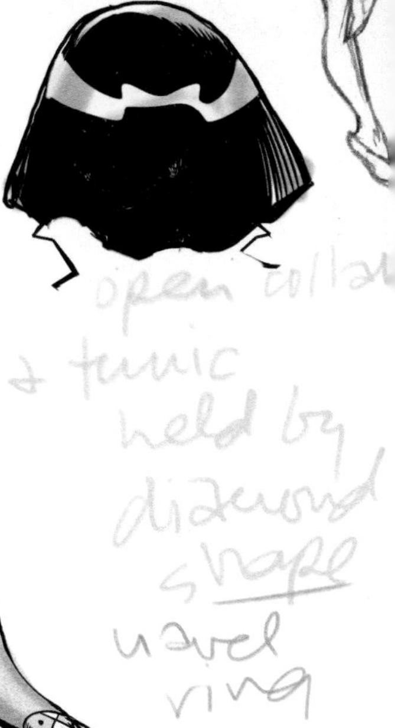
open collar
& tunic
held by
diamond
shape
navel
ring

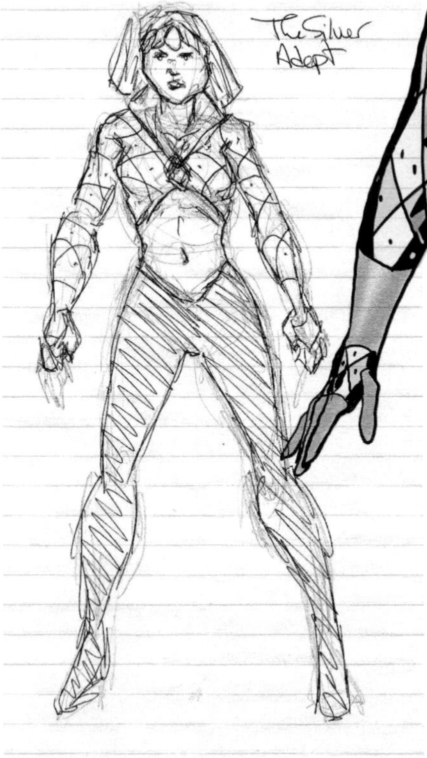
The Silver
Adept

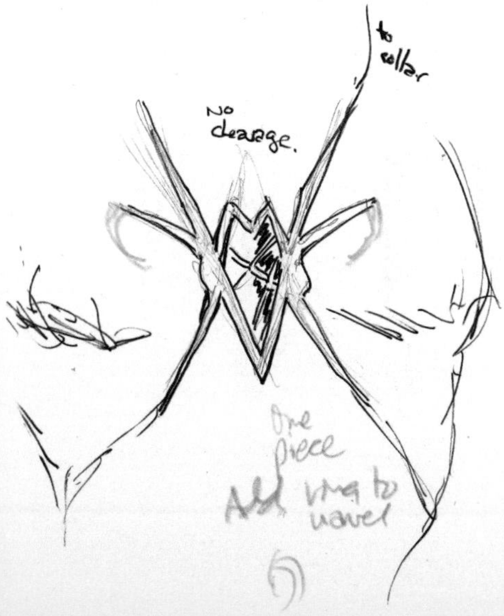
to
collar
No
cleavage.
One
piece
Add ring to
navel

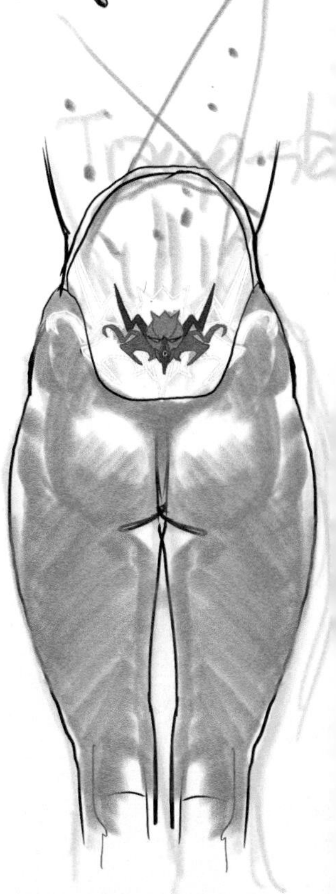

Yes, she even has a mystic tramp stamp. It has powers, too. Maybe someday we'll get to show you what they are...

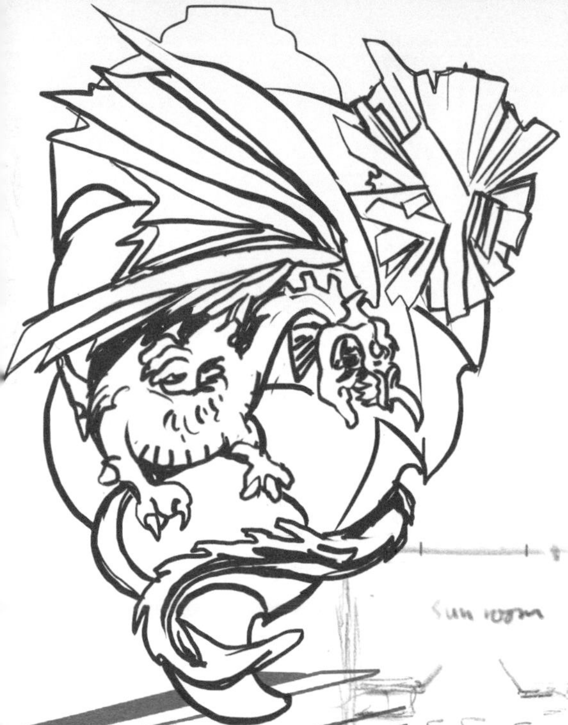

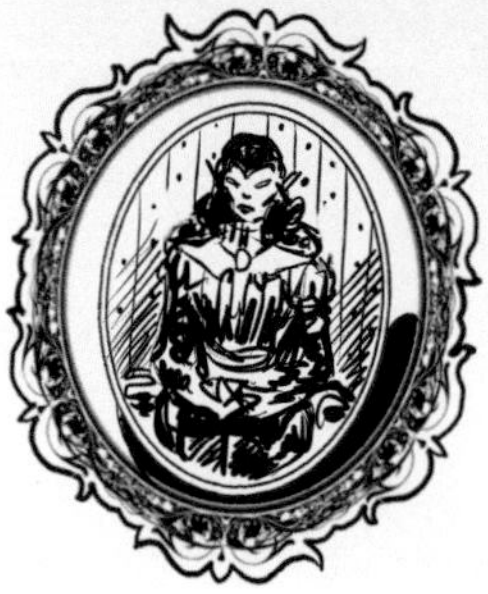

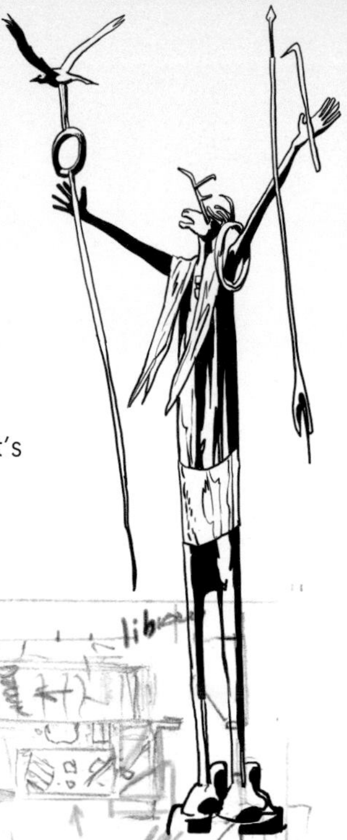

We also had to make the Adept's house look (a) mystic and (b) lived-in. Brent did a stunning job.

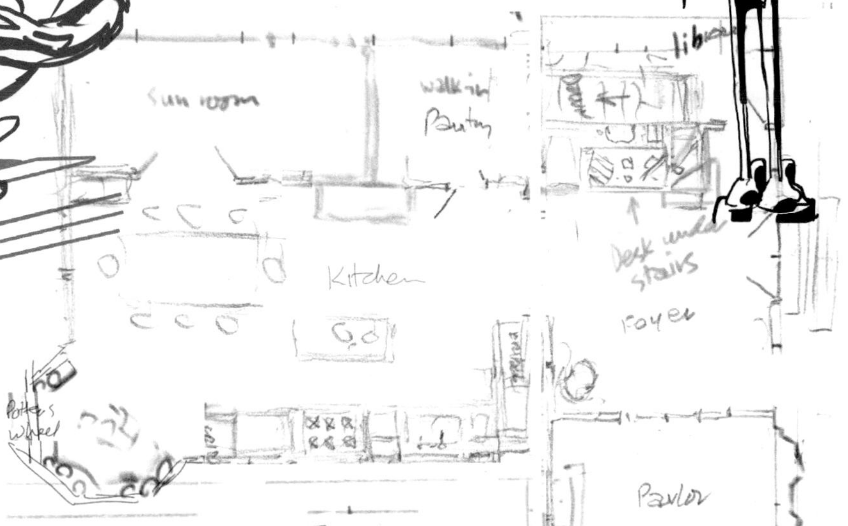
Sun room
walk in Pantry
Kitchen
Desk under stairs
Foyer
Potter's Wheel
Parlor

When you need reference on bookshelves and clutter, look no further than an artist's studio!

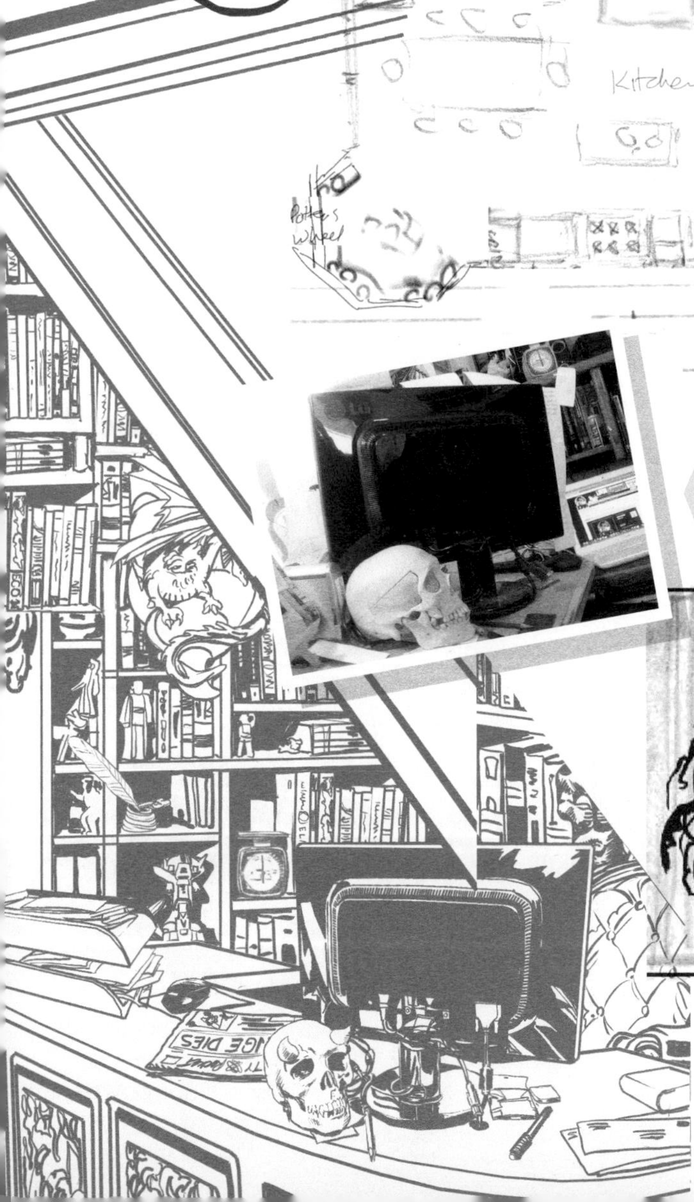

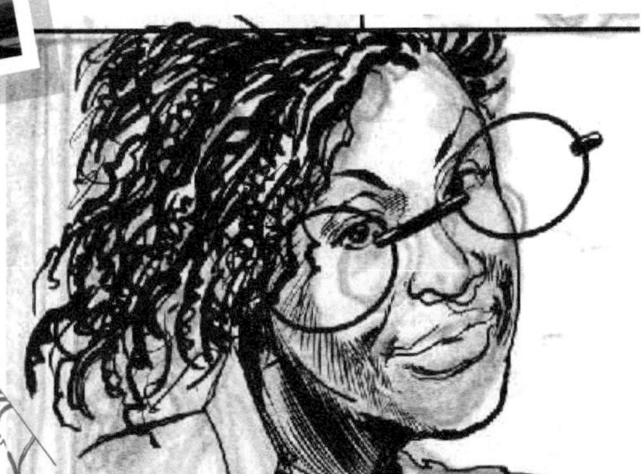

Raitha McCann started out younger and slimmer. But not everyone in a superhero comic should be in perfect shape. So she changed.

stone sea mages

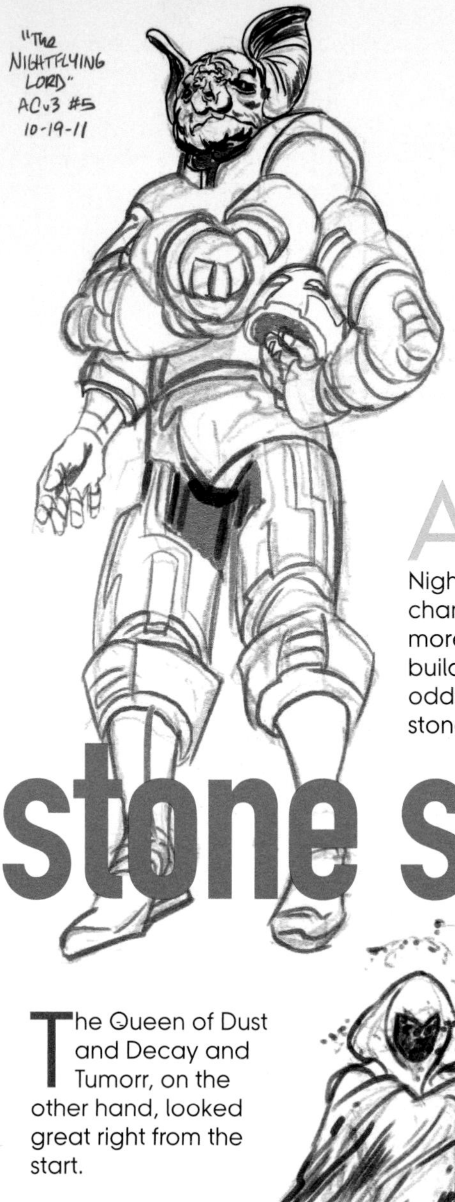

"The NIGHTFLYING LORD"
ACv3 #5
10-19-11

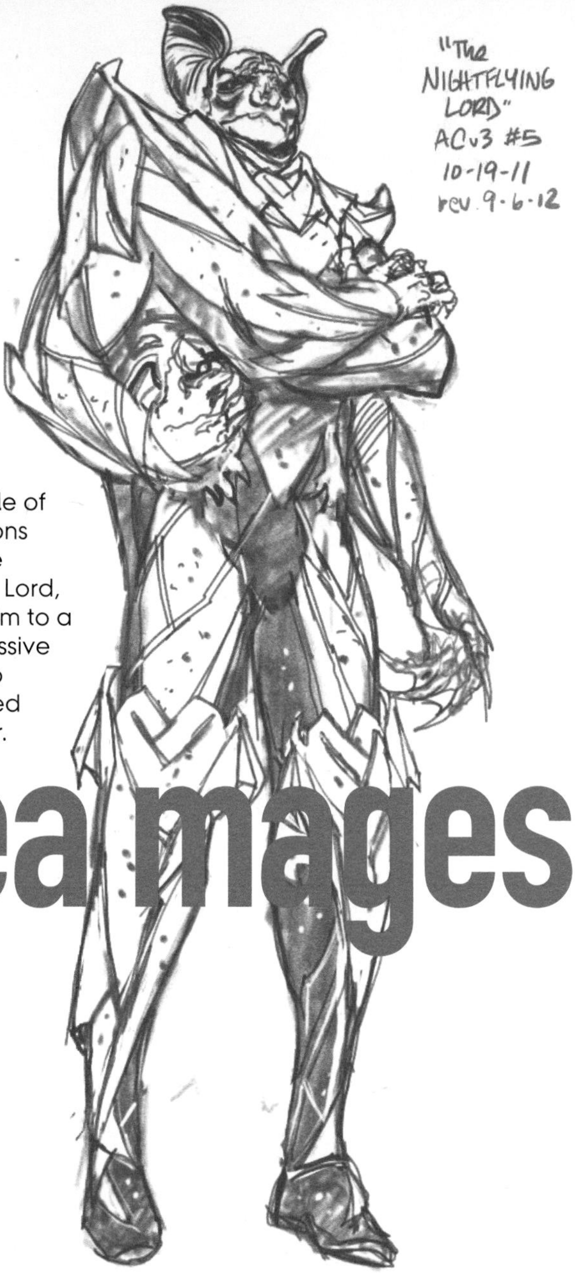

"The NIGHTFLYING LORD"
ACv3 #5
10-19-11
rev. 9-6-12

A couple of versions of the Night-Flying Lord, changing him to a more impressive build and to oddly-carved stone armor.

The Queen of Dust and Decay and Tumorr, on the other hand, looked great right from the start.

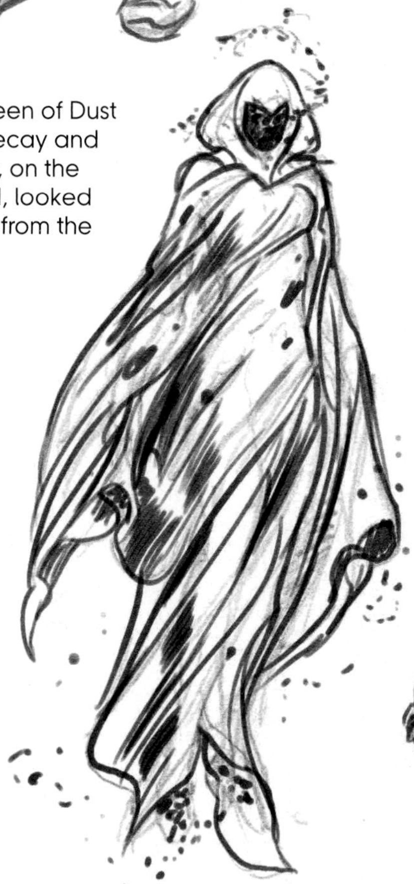

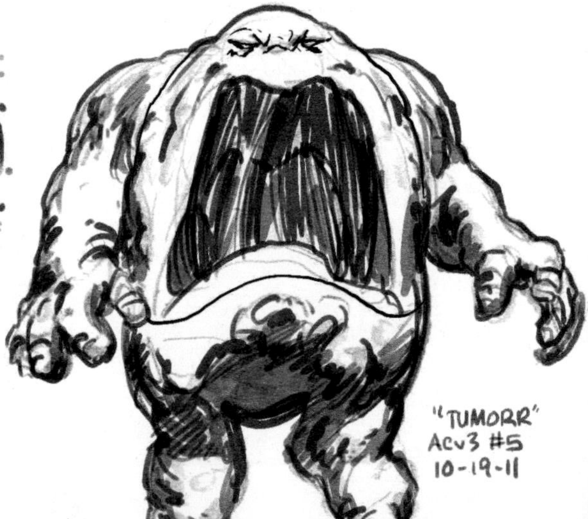

"TUMORR"
ACv3 #5
10-19-11

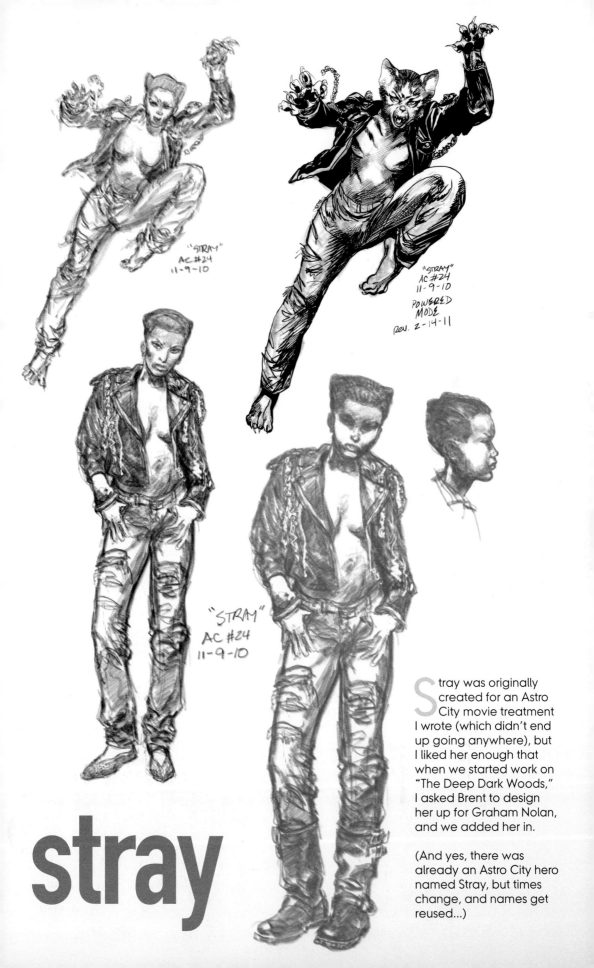

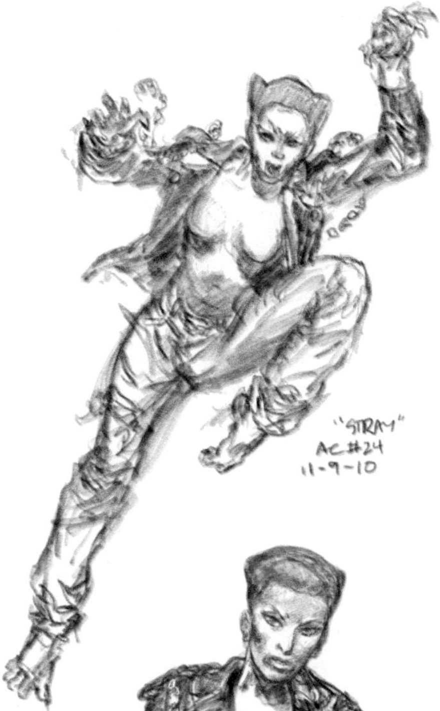
"STRAY"
AC #24
11-9-10

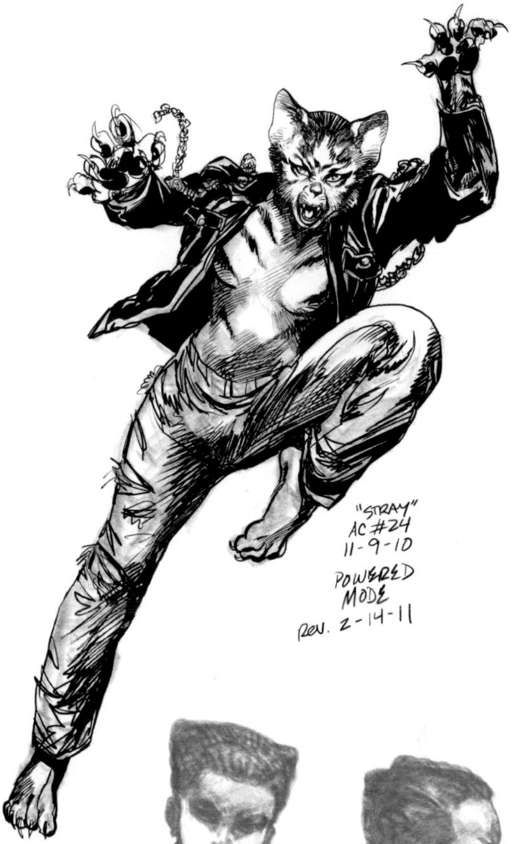
"STRAY"
AC #24
11-9-10
POWERED MODE
REV. 2-14-11

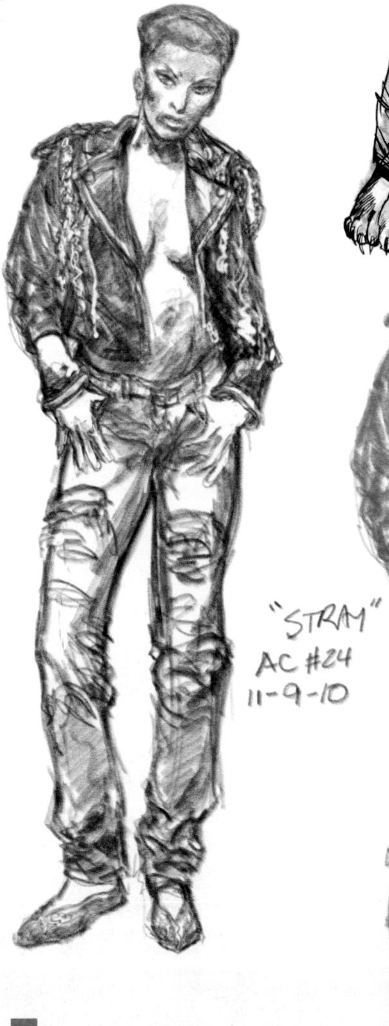
"STRAY"
AC #24
11-9-10

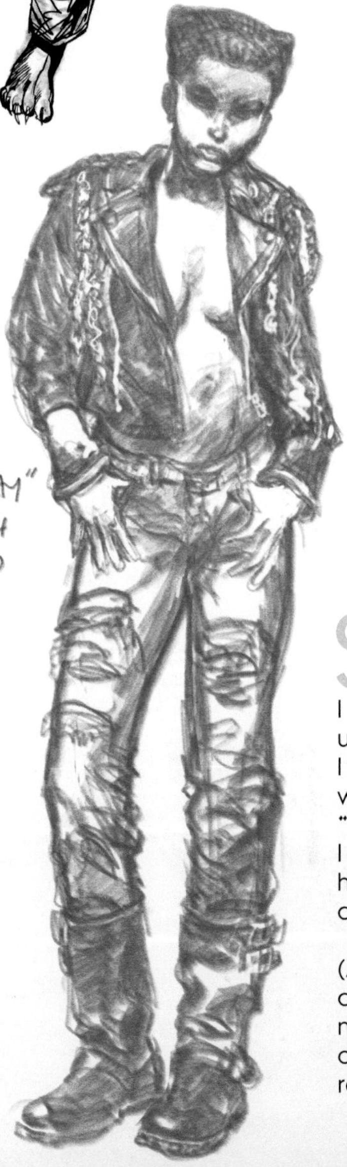

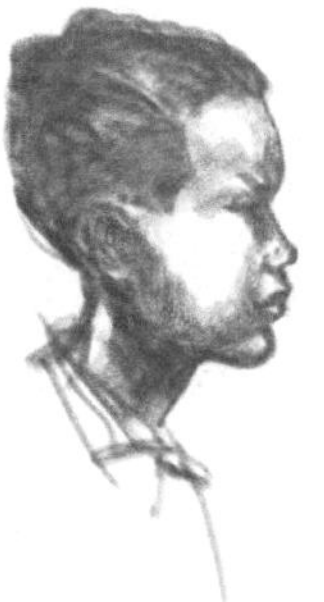

stray

Stray was originally created for an Astro City movie treatment I wrote (which didn't end up going anywhere), but I liked her enough that when we started work on "The Deep Dark Woods," I asked Brent to design her up for Graham Nolan, and we added her in.

(And yes, there was already an Astro City hero named Stray, but times change, and names get reused...)

gundog

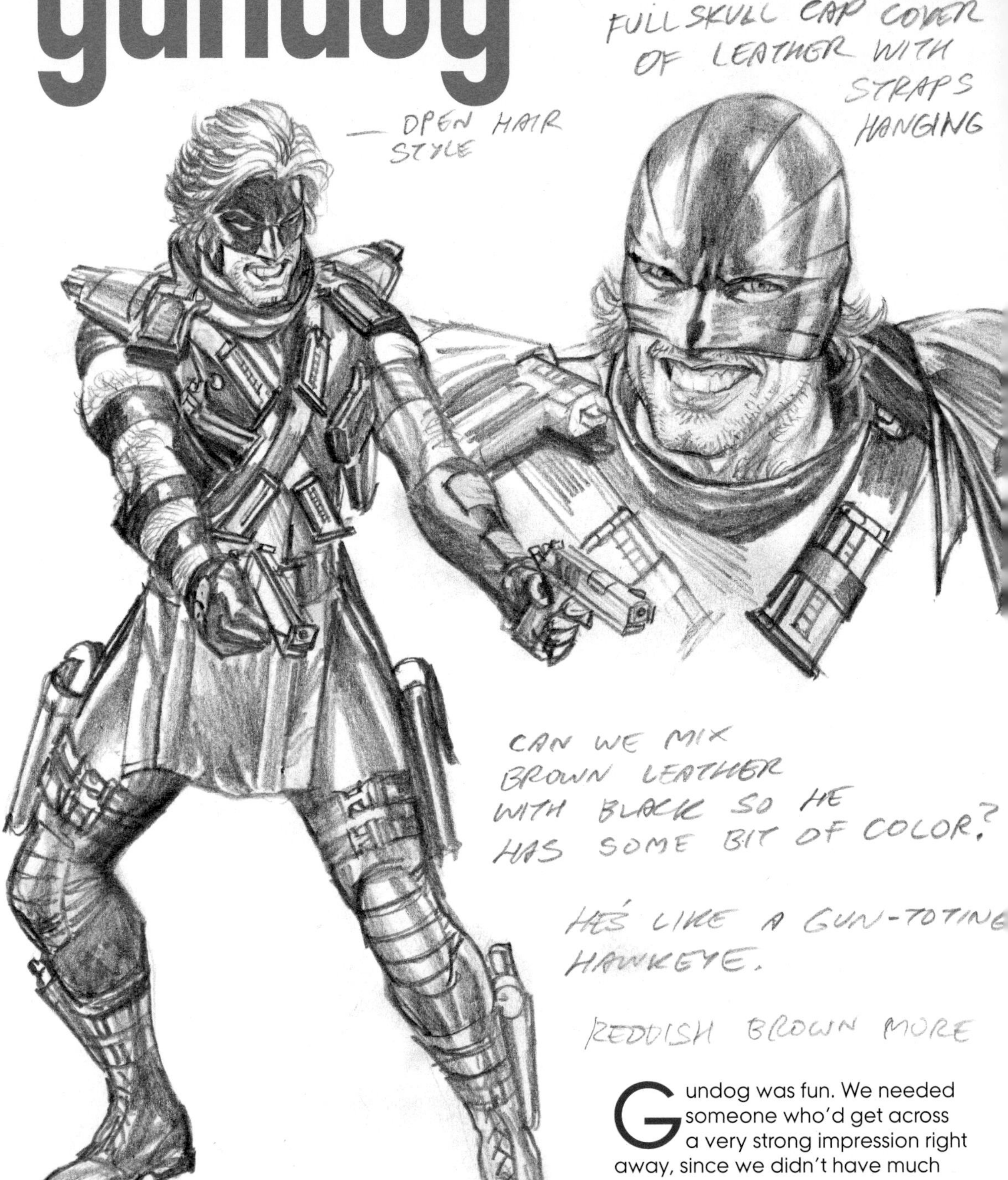
FULL SKULL CAP COVER OF LEATHER WITH STRAPS HANGING
— OPEN HAIR STYLE
CAN WE MIX BROWN LEATHER WITH BLACK SO HE HAS SOME BIT OF COLOR?
HE'S LIKE A GUN-TOTING HAWKEYE.
REDDISH BROWN MORE

Gundog was fun. We needed someone who'd get across a very strong impression right away, since we didn't have much room, so he needed to be simple, human and engaging. Alex's design for him sure was.

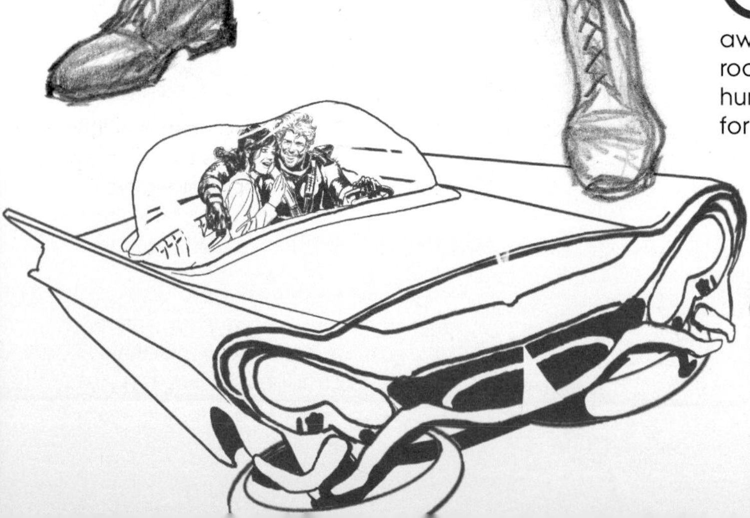

Gundog's car. Everything about him needs to say "hi-tech good ol' boy." I want to see this car again. Maybe in a chase scene.

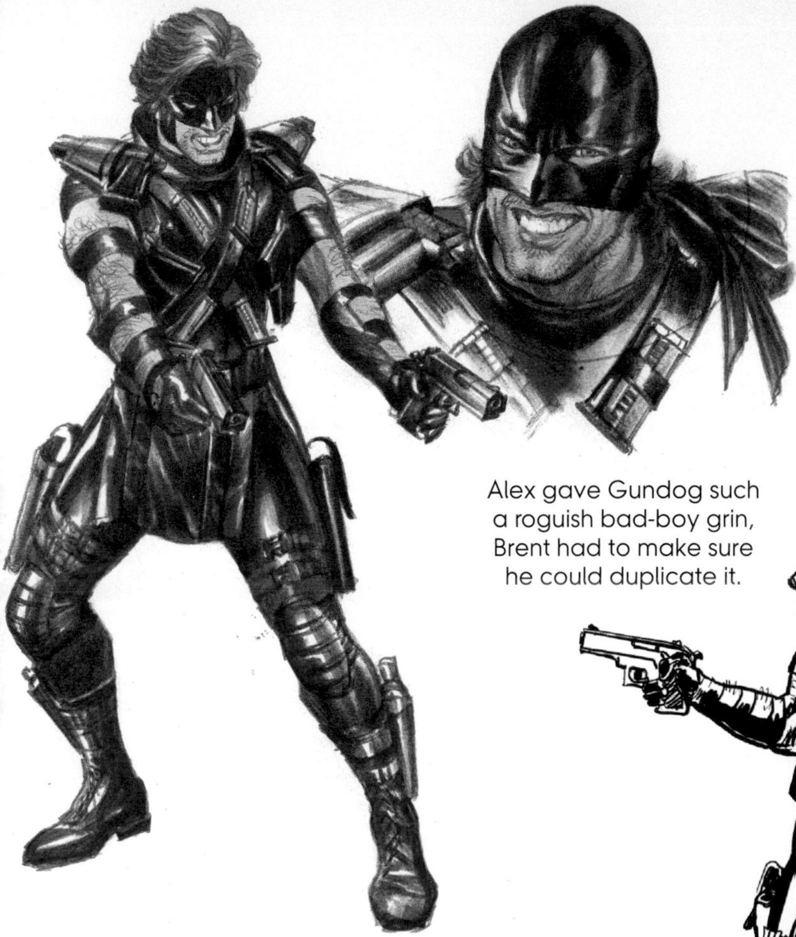

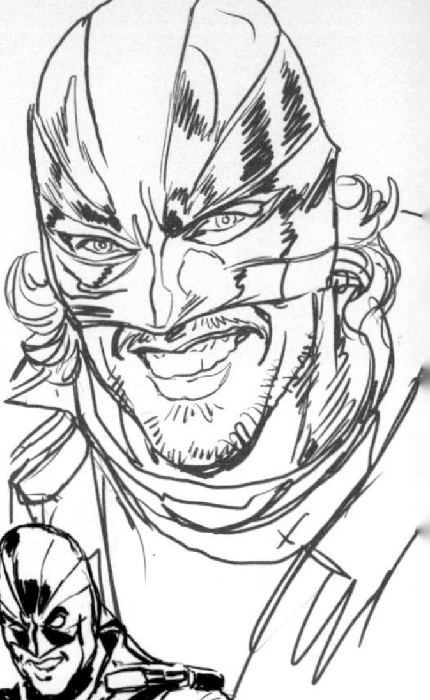

Alex gave Gundog such a roguish bad-boy grin, Brent had to make sure he could duplicate it.

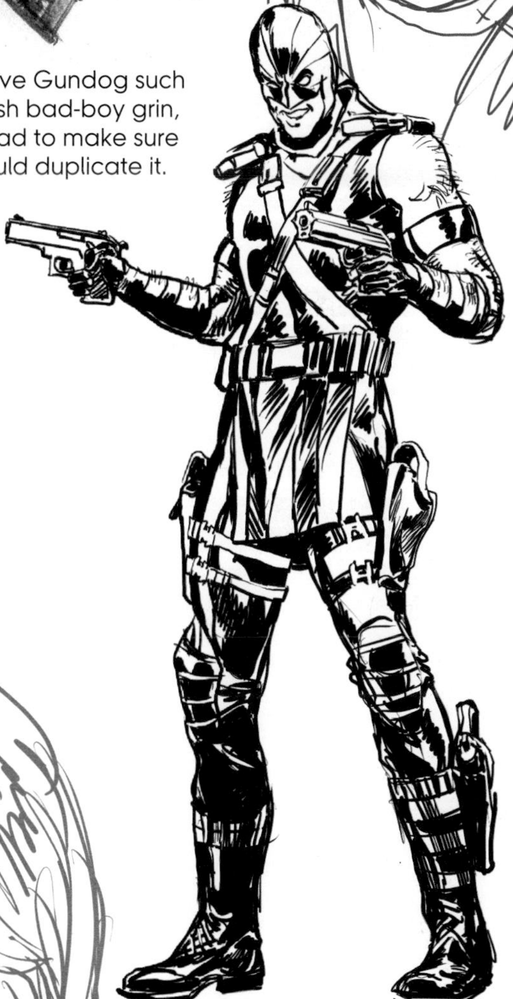

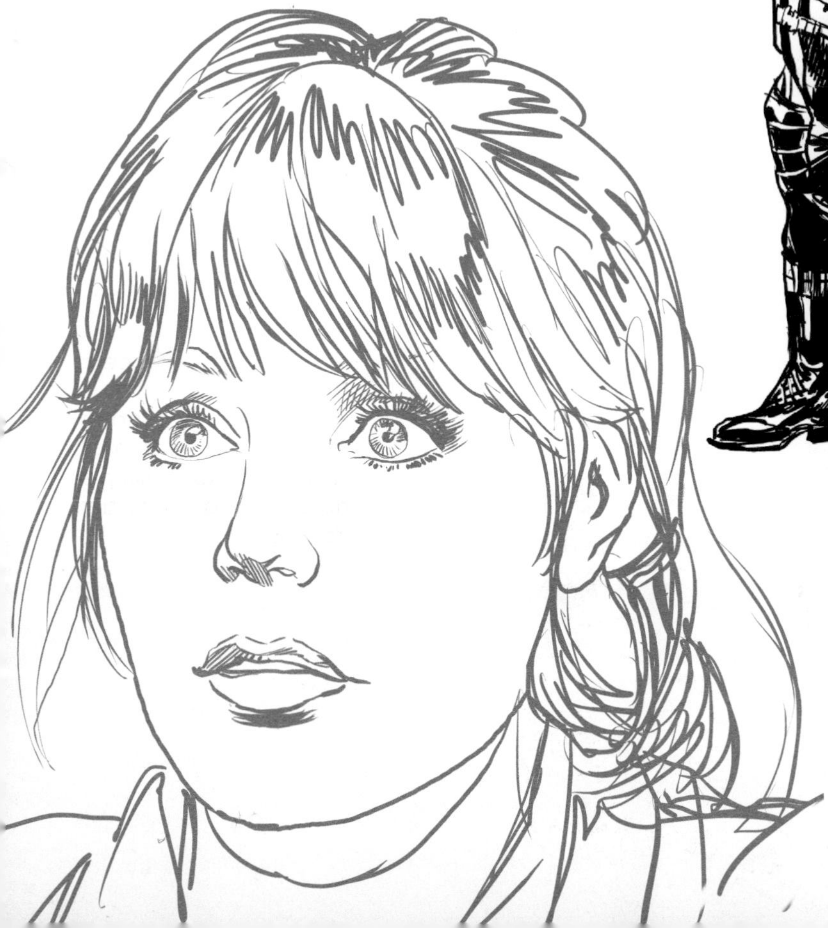

Laura had very little space to make an impression, too, and since we see her practically instantly (if temporarily) turn to crime — but we wanted readers to like her — she had to do it adorably. Brent took care of that.

When we started with the Dancing Master, we wanted something that felt old, formal, 19th-century at the latest. We tried that...

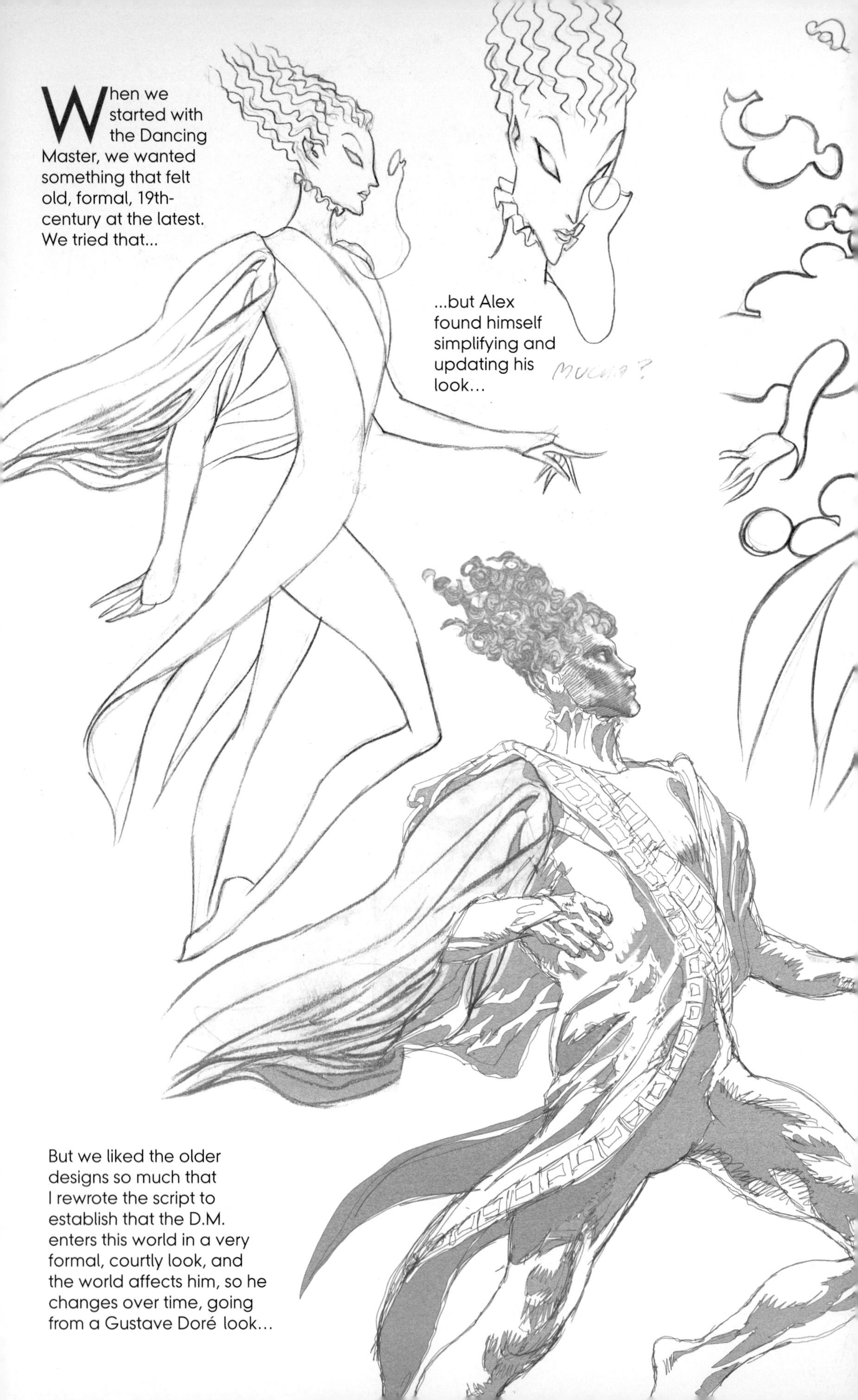
MUCHA?

...but Alex found himself simplifying and updating his look...

But we liked the older designs so much that I rewrote the script to establish that the D.M. enters this world in a very formal, courtly look, and the world affects him, so he changes over time, going from a Gustave Doré look...

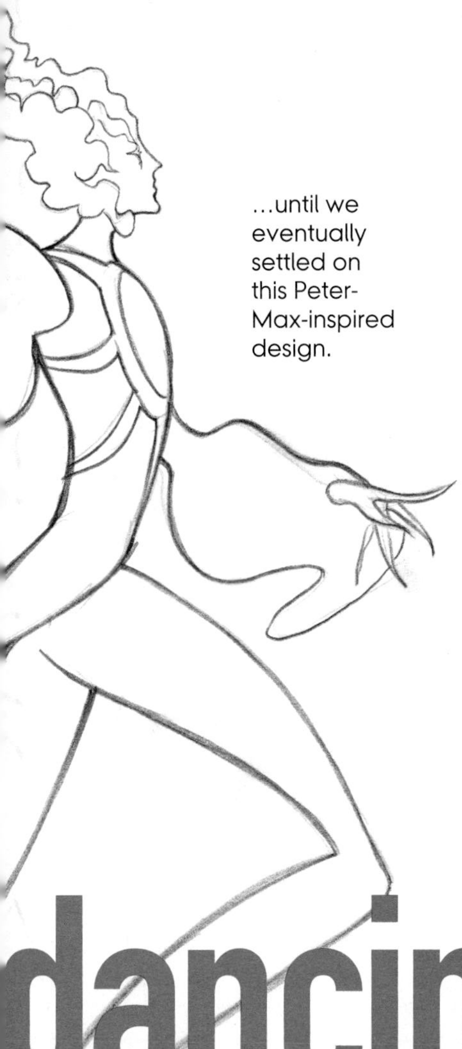

…until we eventually settled on this Peter-Max-inspired design.

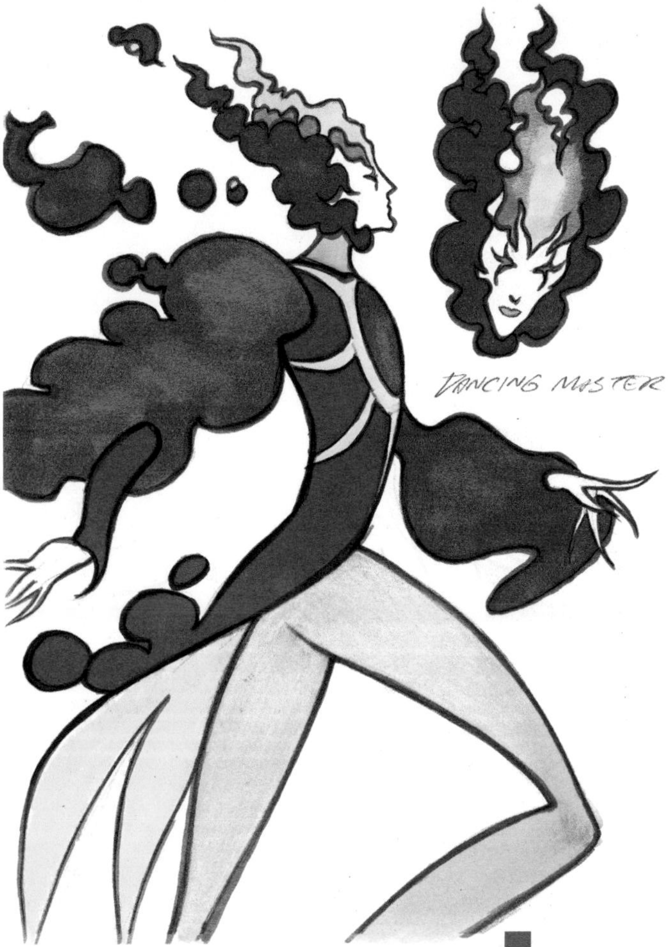
DANCING MASTER

dancing master

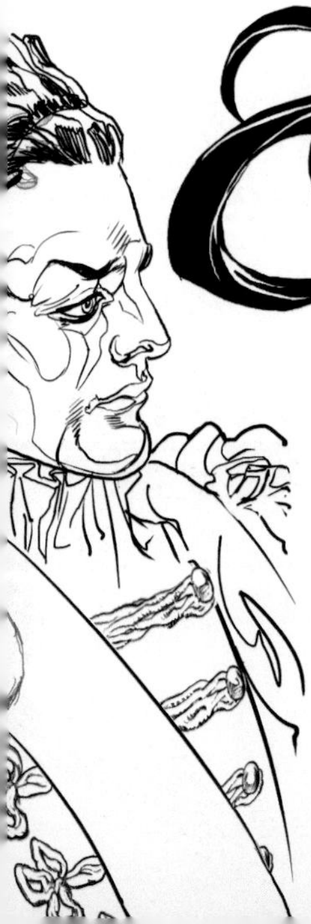

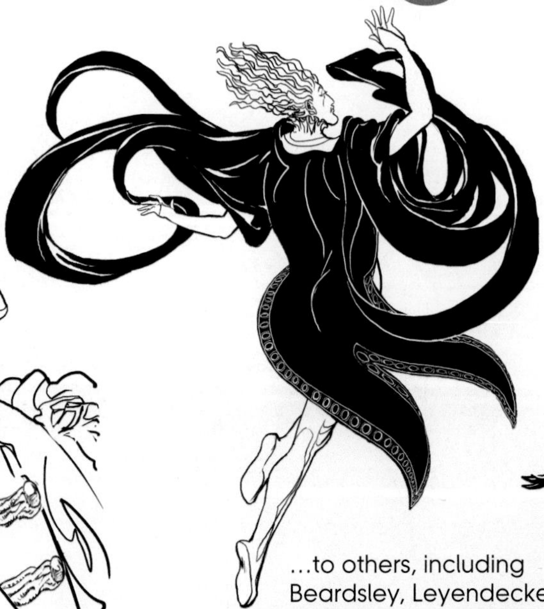

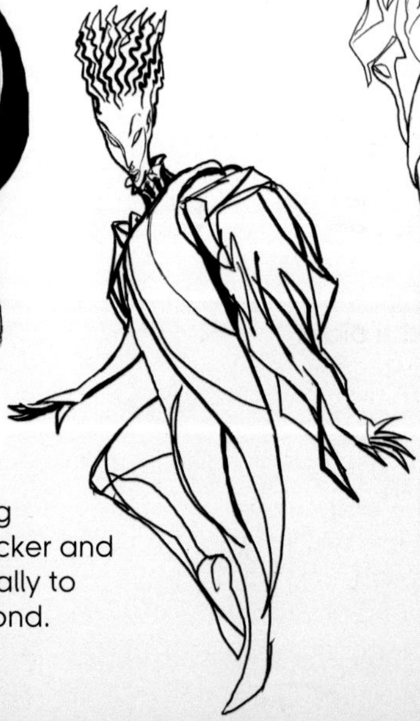

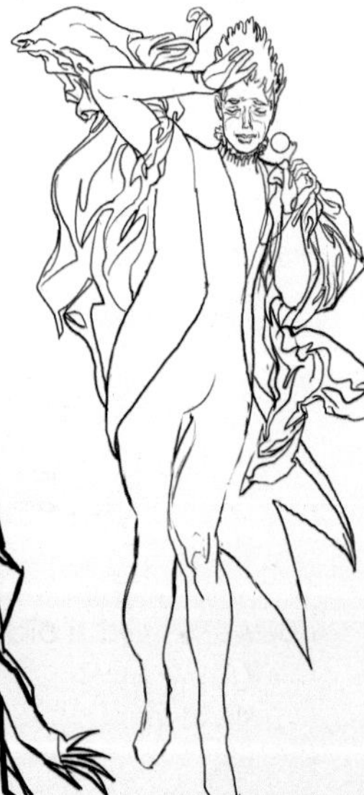

…to others, including Beardsley, Leyendecker and Mucha, and eventually to Peter Max and beyond.

robots

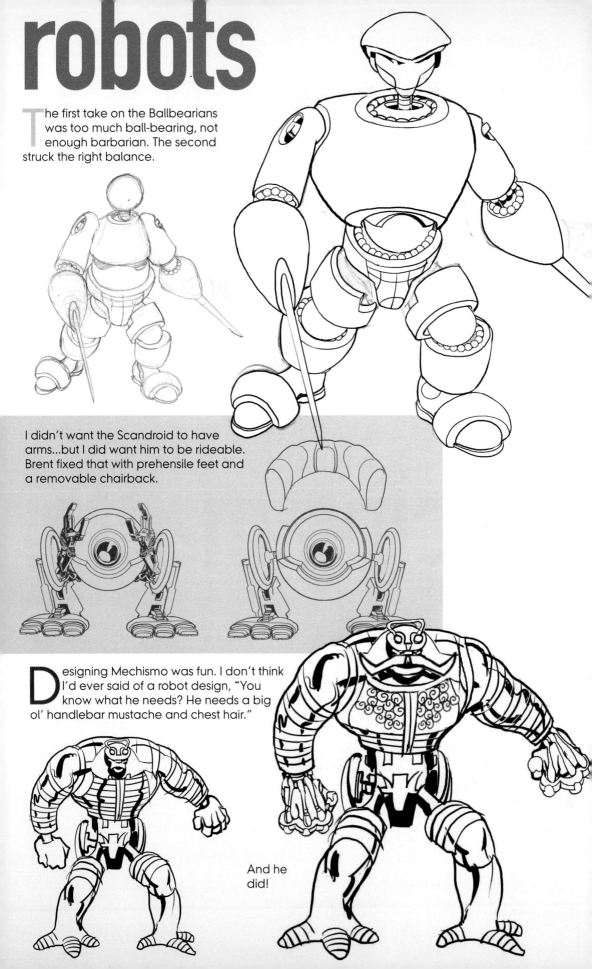

The first take on the Ballbearians was too much ball-bearing, not enough barbarian. The second struck the right balance.

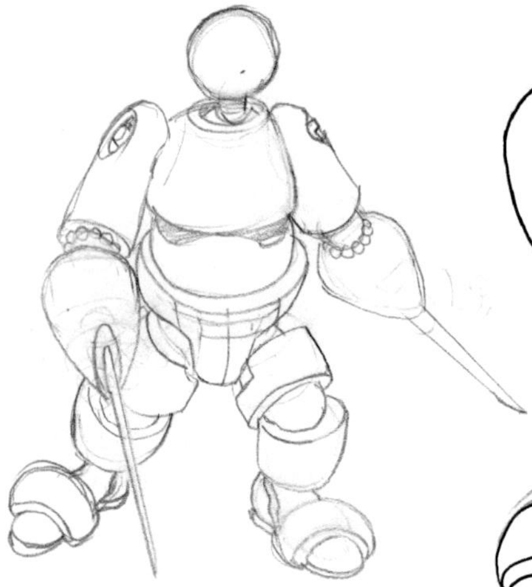

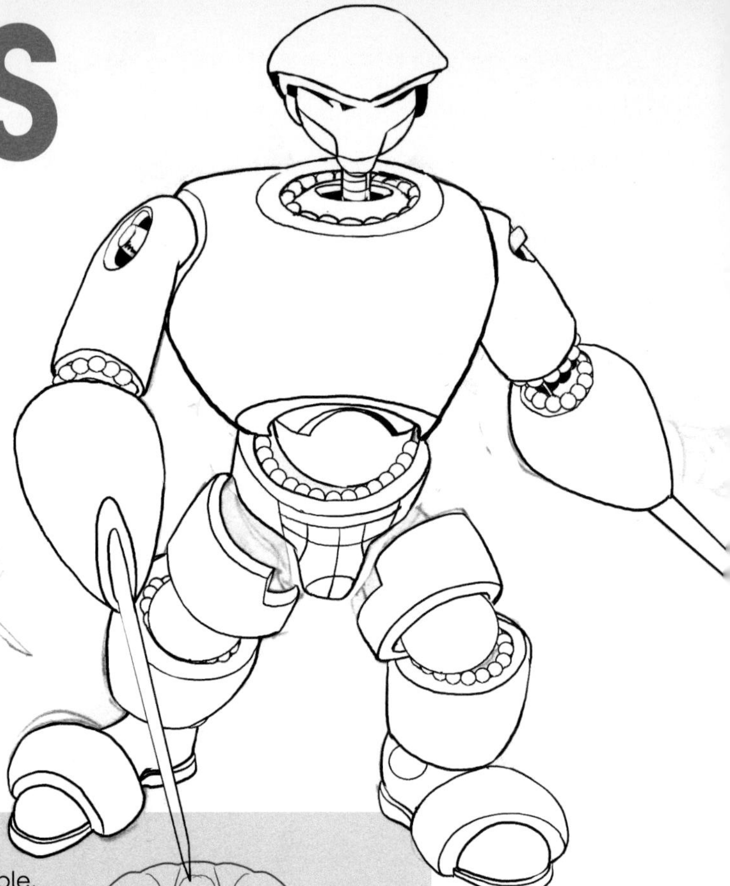

I didn't want the Scandroid to have arms...but I did want him to be rideable. Brent fixed that with prehensile feet and a removable chairback.

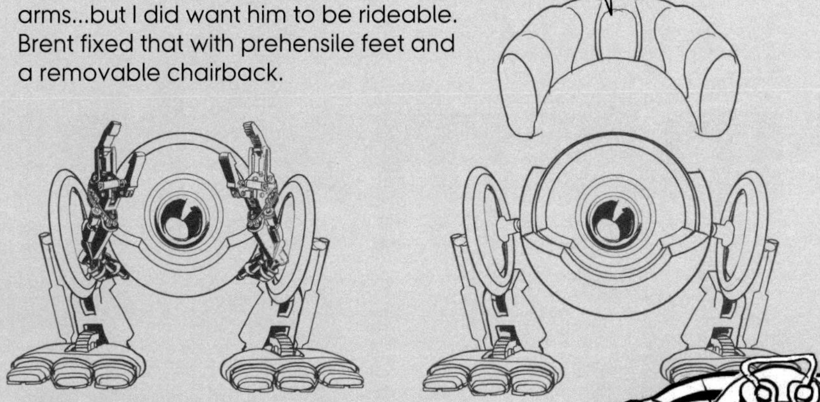

Designing Mechismo was fun. I don't think I'd ever said of a robot design, "You know what he needs? He needs a big ol' handlebar mustache and chest hair."

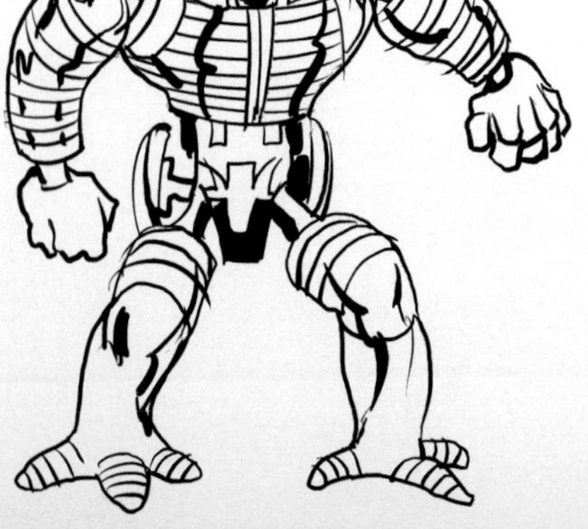

And he did!

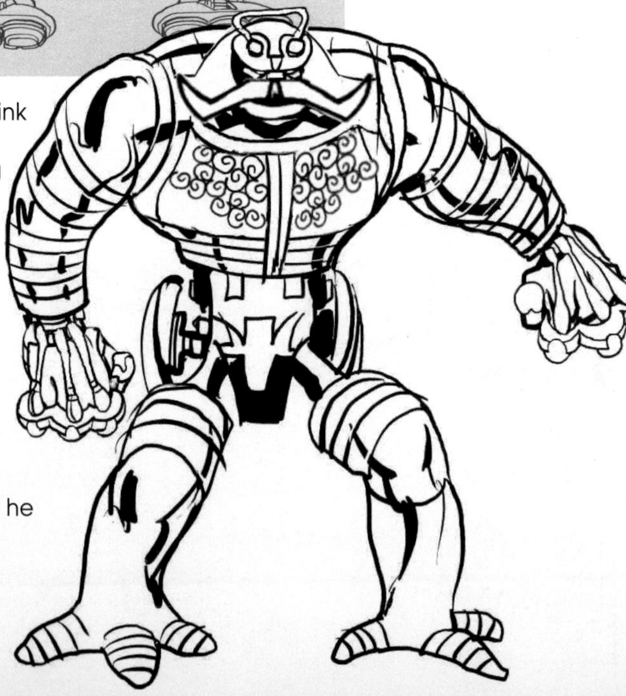

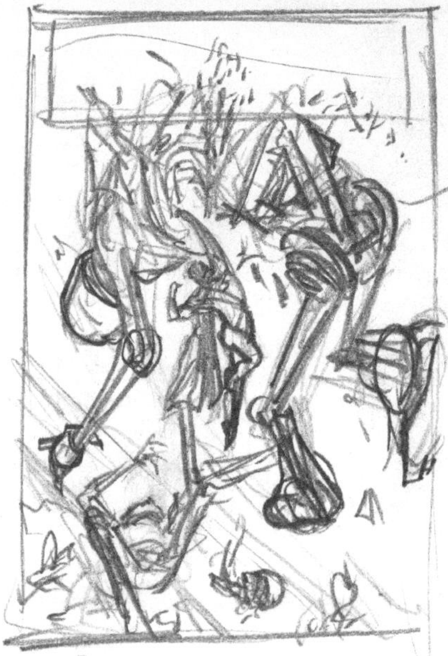

Alex's design and pencils for the cover to #14. We had a lot of robots in the story, but to make a powerful, iconic cover, it was best to focus on just one...

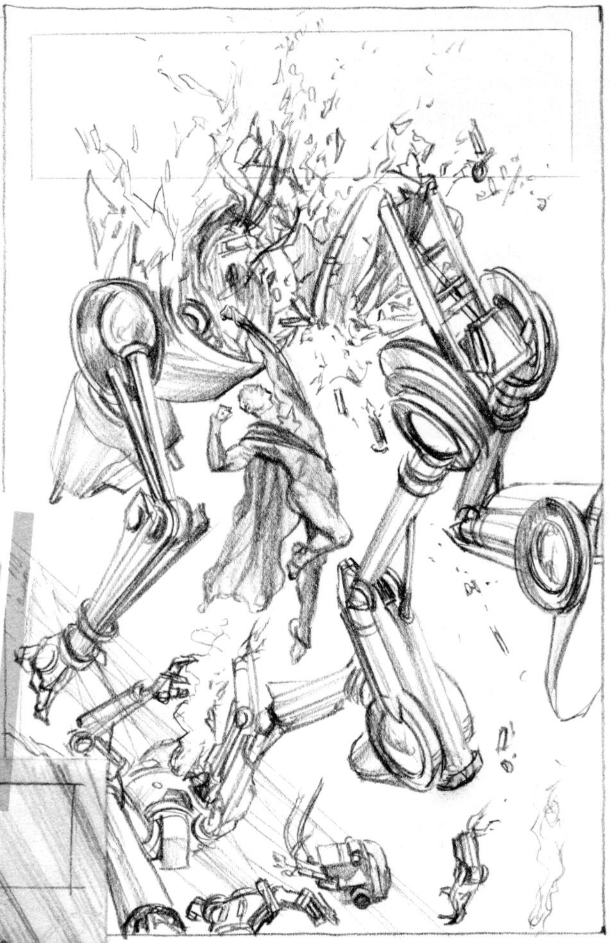

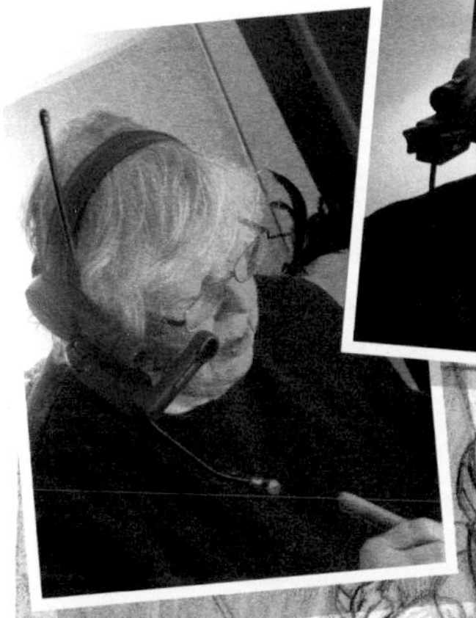

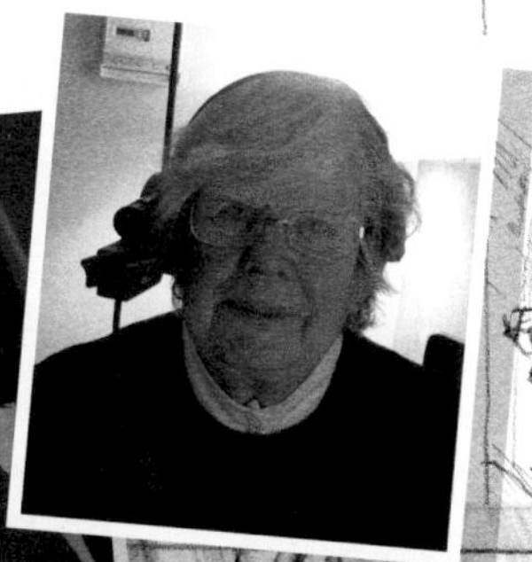

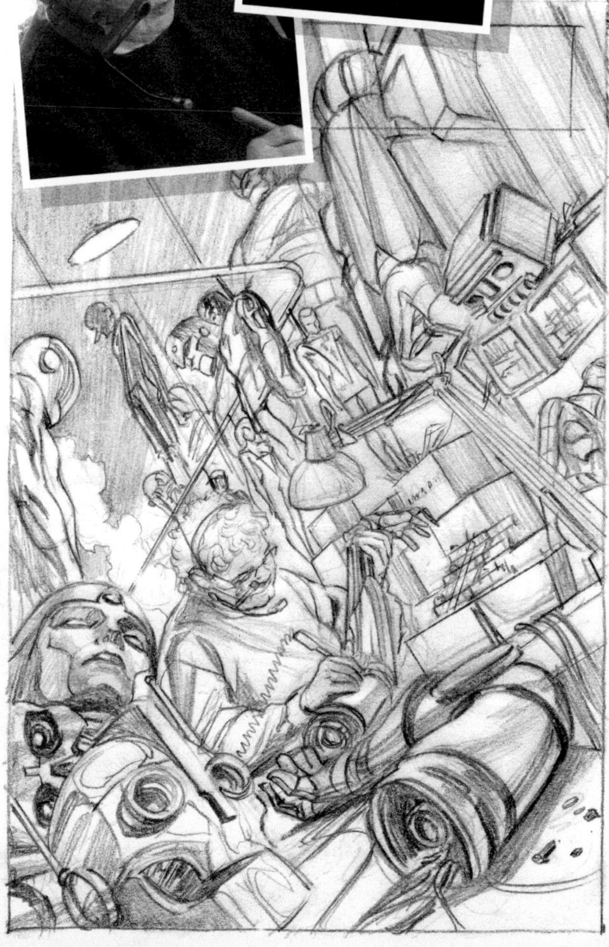

When I described the story of #14-15 to Alex, he said, "I've got the perfect cover model." And he did: A helpful relative of his named Dottie Thomas.

Oddly, she came out looking so much like my late mother-in-law, Phyllis Huntington, that we wound up sending Brent pictures of Phyllis at around college age to use in the flashback...

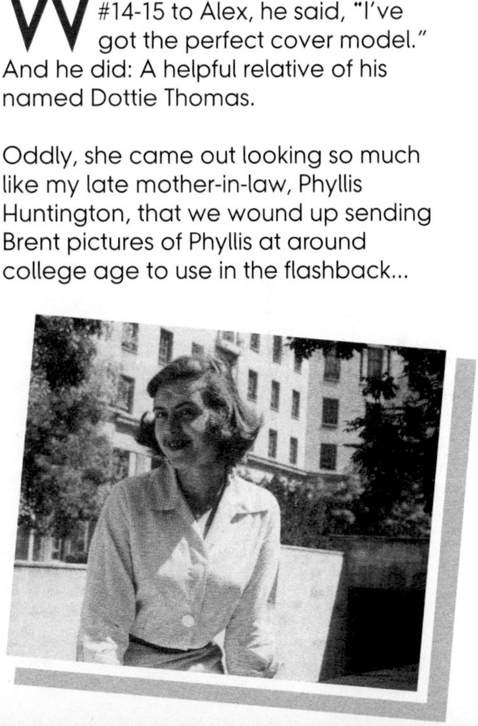

starbright

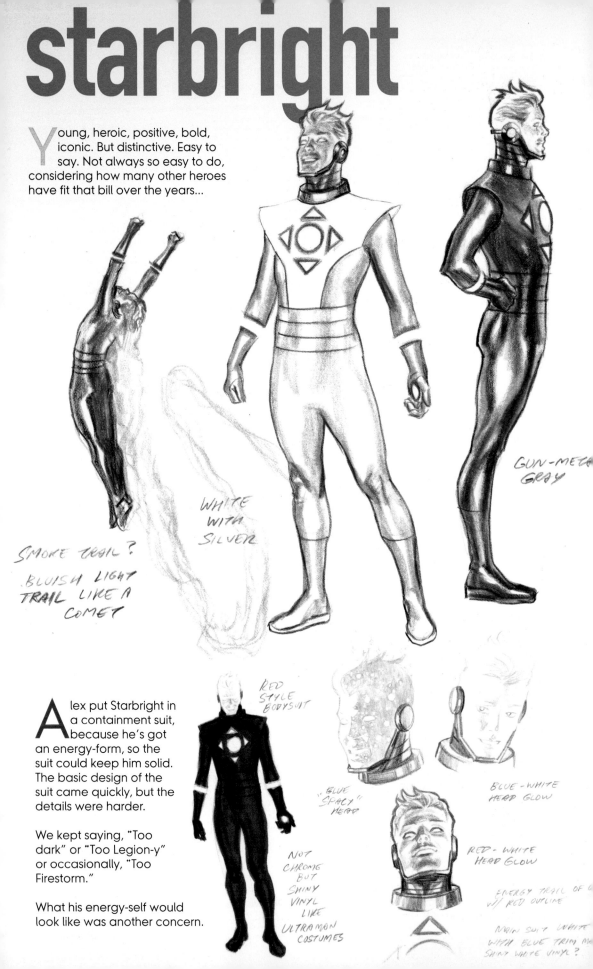

Young, heroic, positive, bold, iconic. But distinctive. Easy to say. Not always so easy to do, considering how many other heroes have fit that bill over the years...

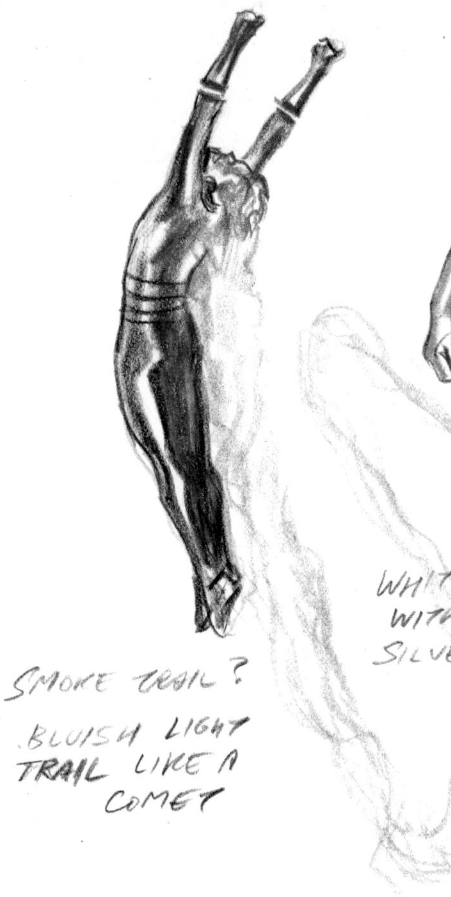
SMOKE TRAIL?
BLUISH LIGHT TRAIL LIKE A COMET

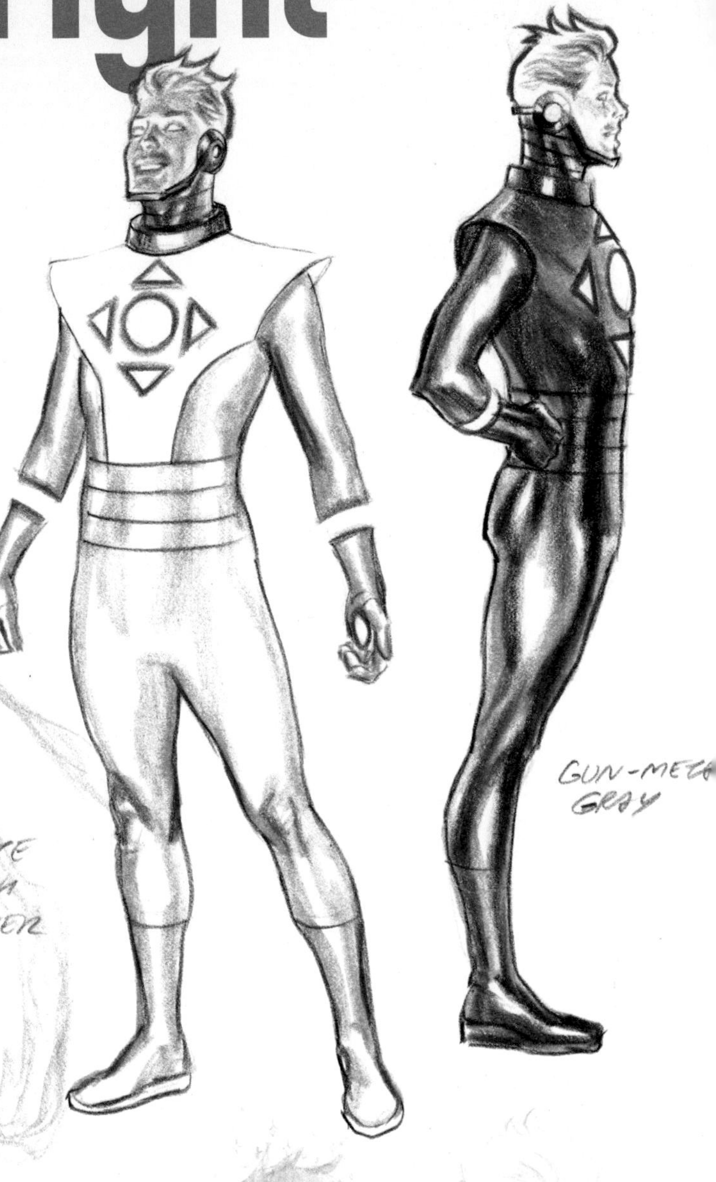
WHITE WITH SILVER
GUN-MET
GRAY

Alex put Starbright in a containment suit, because he's got an energy-form, so the suit could keep him solid. The basic design of the suit came quickly, but the details were harder.

We kept saying, "Too dark" or "Too Legion-y" or occasionally, "Too Firestorm."

What his energy-self would look like was another concern.

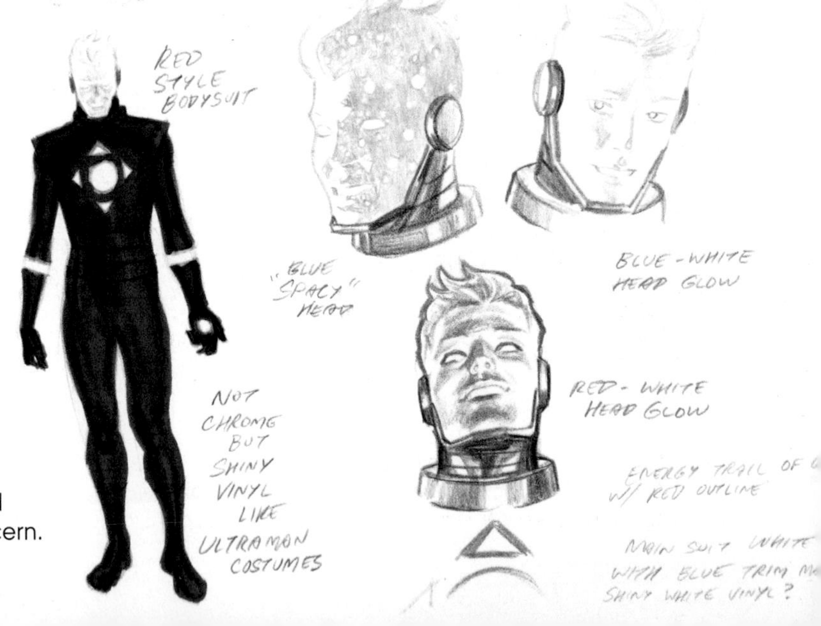
RED STYLE BODYSUIT
"BLUE "SPACY" HEAD
BLUE-WHITE HEAD GLOW
RED-WHITE HEAD GLOW
NOT CHROME BUT SHINY VINYL LIKE ULTRAMAN COSTUMES
ENERGY TRAIL OF
W/ RED OUTLINE
MAIN SUIT WHITE
WITH BLUE TRIM
SHINY WHITE VINYL?

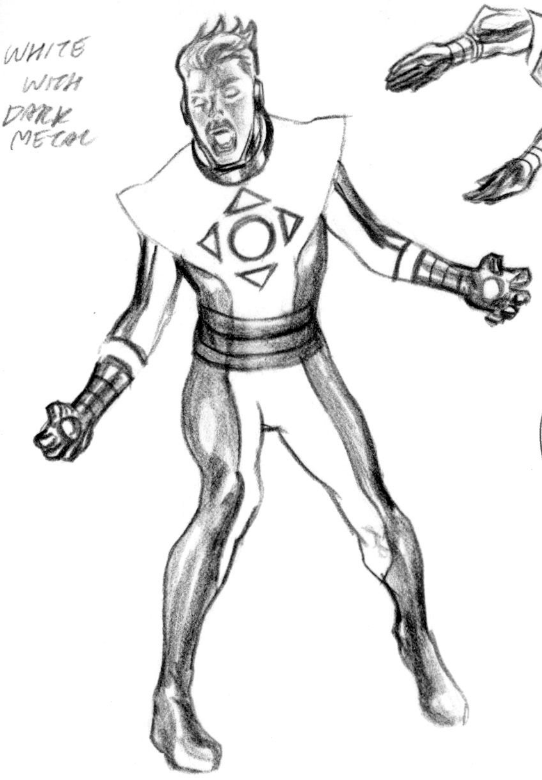
WHITE
WITH
DARK
METAL

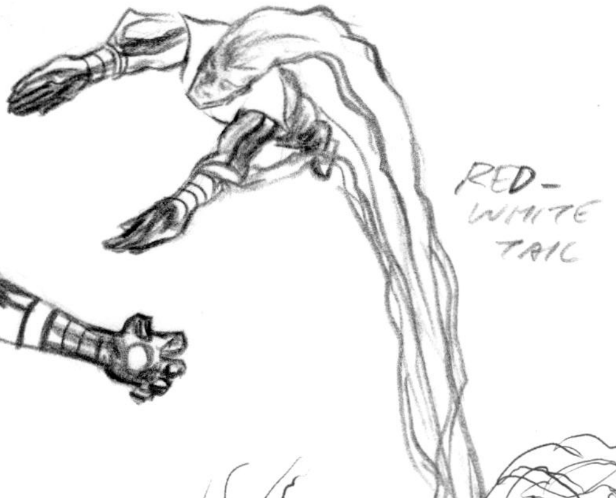
RED-
WHITE
TAIL

Another possible spin on him...

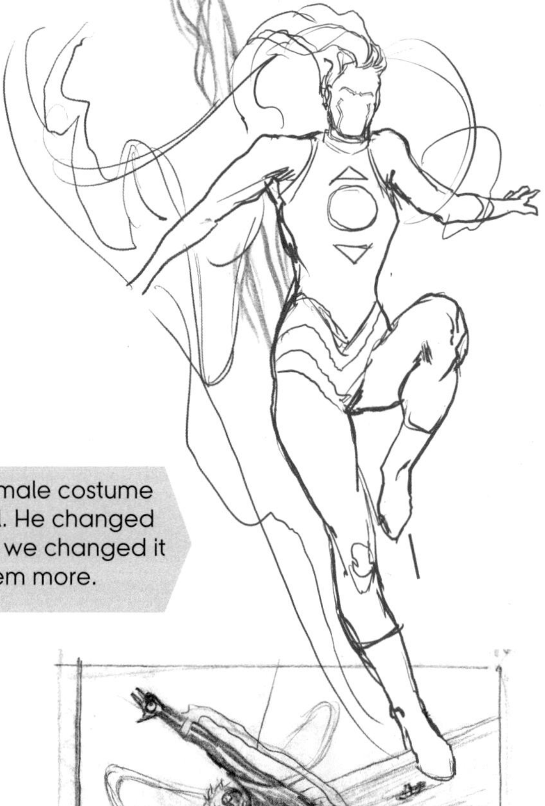

...and Brent's adaptation of Starbright's male costume to a female form, for the third-act reveal. He changed her emblem a bit, but in the actual story we changed it even further, just to differentiate them more.

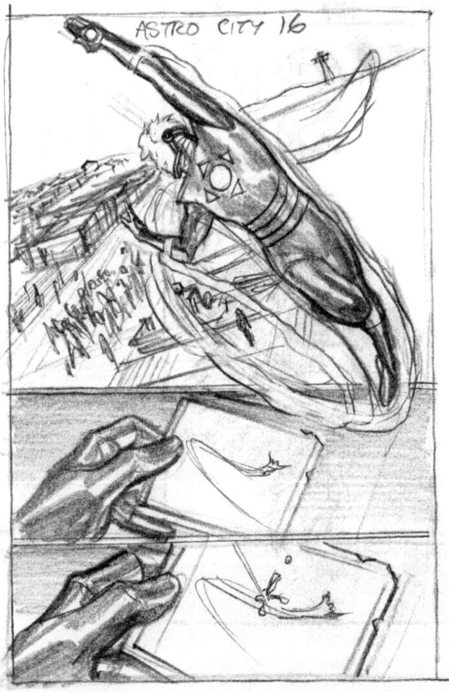
ASTRO CITY 16

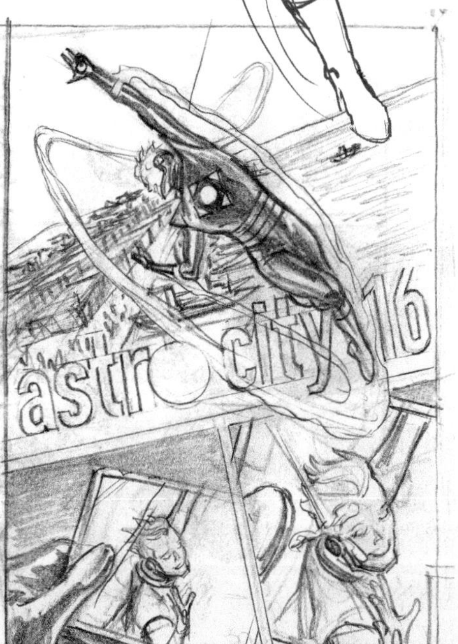
astro city 16

Alex's first design for the cover to #16, and his final design. We worked out the "plot" of this page (such as it is) over the phone, and then I wrote a script for him to draw from. Or maybe I wrote it after his final layout. Either way, it worked!

— Kurt Busiek

don't miss the rest of the astro city series:

astro city
life in the big city
KURT BUSIEK • BRENT ANDERSON • ALEX ROSS

KURT BUSIEK'S
Astro City
BUSIEK • ANDERSON • BLYBERG
SINCLAIR • ROSS • COMICRAFT
Confession
Introduction by NEIL GAIMAN

astro city
family album
KURT BUSIEK • BRENT ANDERSON • ALEX ROSS

KURT BUSIEK'S
Astro City
The TARNISHED ANGEL
COMPLETE AND UNABRIDGED
Introduction by FRANK MILLER

ASTRO CITY
LOCAL HEROES

ASTRO CITY
BROTHERS & OTHER STRANGERS
BUSIEK
ANDERSON
ROSS
SINCLAIR
COMICRAFT

ASTRO CITY
BROTHERS IN ARMS
BUSIEK
ANDERSON
ROSS
SINCLAIR
COMICRAFT

astro city
SHINING STARS
BUSIEK • ANDERSON • ROSS • SINCLAIR • COMICRAFT

astro city
through open doors

astro city
victory

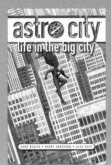

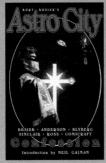

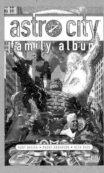

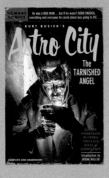

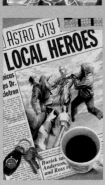

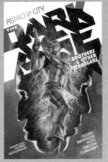

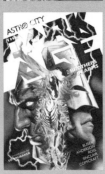

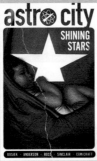

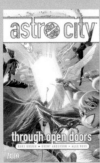

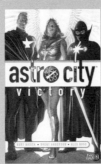

about the creators

KURT BUSIEK broke into comics after graduating college in 1982. Since then, he's been an editor, a literary agent, a sales manager and more, but is best known as the multiple-award-winning writer of *Astro City, Marvels, Superman, Conan, Arrowsmith, Superstar, Shockrockets* and many others. He lives in the Pacific Northwest.

BRENT ANDERSON began making his own comics in junior high school, and graduated to professional work less than a decade later. He's drawn such projects as *Ka-Zar the Savage, X-Men: God Loves Man Kills, Strikeforce: Morituri, Somerset Holmes, Rising Stars* and, of course, *Astro City,* for which he's won multiple Eisner and Harvey Awards. He makes his home in Northern California.

GRAHAM NOLAN has been writing and illustrating comics since 1984. He's worked on an array of characters from Superman to the X-Men, and was senior illustrator on *Detective Comics* for 6 years. An award winning artist, Nolan is also the co-creator of the iconic Batman villain Bane.

ALEX ROSS worked on *Terminator: The Burning Earth* and *Clive Barker's Hellraiser* before *Marvels* made him an overnight superstar. Since then, he's painted, plotted and/or written such series as *Kingdom Come, Superman: Peace on Earth, Justice, Earth X* and *Project Superpowers,* and won over two dozen industry awards.

ALEX SINCLAIR has colored virtually every character DC Comics has, and more besides. Best known for his work with Jim Lee and Scott Williams, he's worked on such books as *Batman: Hush, Superman: For Tomorrow, Blackest Night, Batman & Robin, Wonder Woman, Arrowsmith* and *Kingdom Come: Superman.*

WENDY BROOME was a longtime member of the coloring staff at Wildstorm Studios before going freelance in 2004. She's made a specialty of large-cast books, including *Wildcats 3.0, The Authority, Gen13, The End League, Thundercats* and *Top 10* as well as pitching in as needed on *Astro City.*

JOHN ROSHELL joined Comicraft in 1992, helping propel the lettering/design studio to its position in the industry. He's lettered thousands of comics pages, along with creating logos and fonts, designing book editions and more. He also writes the series *Charley Loves Robots,* which appears in *Elephantmen.*